NETWORKED BOLLYWOOD

Networked Bollywood provides the first interdisciplinary analysis of the role of stars in the transformation of Hindi cinema into a global entertainment industry. The first Indian film was made in 1913. However, filmmaking was recognized as an industry almost a hundred years later though Indian films have been circulating globally since their inception. This book unearths this oft-elided history of Bollywood's globalization through multilingual, transnational research and discursive cultural analysis. It illustrates how, over the decades, a handful of primarily male megastars, as the heads of the industry's most prominent productions and corporations, combined overwhelming charismatic affect with unparalleled business influence. Through their 'star switching power', theorized here as a deeply gendered phenomenon and manifesting broader social inequalities, India's most prominent stars instigated new flows of cinema and industrial collaborations, structured distinctive business models, and influenced state policy and diplomatic exchange, thereby defining the future of Bollywood's globalization.

Swapnil Rai is Assistant Professor of Film, Television, and Media at the University of Michigan, Ann Arbor. A scholar of global media industries, popular culture, and politics, Rai's research has appeared in various academic journals. Previously, she worked as a journalist in India and the United States.

NETWORKED BOLLYWOOD

How Star Power Globalized Hindi Cinema

SWAPNIL RAI

CAMBRIDGE
UNIVERSITY PRESS

CAMBRIDGE
UNIVERSITY PRESS

Shaftesbury Road, Cambridge CB2 8EA, United Kingdom

One Liberty Plaza, 20th Floor, New York, NY 10006, USA

477 Williamstown Road, Port Melbourne, VIC 3207, Australia

314–321, 3rd Floor, Plot 3, Splendor Forum, Jasola District Centre, New Delhi – 110025, India

103 Penang Road, #05–06/07, Visioncrest Commercial, Singapore 238467

Cambridge University Press is part of Cambridge University Press & Assessment, a department of the University of Cambridge.

We share the University's mission to contribute to society through the pursuit of education, learning and research at the highest international levels of excellence.

www.cambridge.org
Information on this title: www.cambridge.org/9781009400619

First published 2023

Printed in India by Avantika Printers Pvt. Ltd.

A catalogue record for this publication is available from the British Library

Library of Congress Cataloging-in-Publication Data

Names: Rai, Swapnil, author.
Title: Networked Bollywood : how star power globalized Hindi cinema / Swapnil Rai.
Description: Cambridge, United Kingdom ; New York, NY : Cambridge University Press, 2023. | Includes bibliographical references and index.
Identifiers: LCCN 2023045945 (print) | LCCN 2023045946 (ebook) | ISBN 9781009400619 (hardback) | ISBN 9781009400633 (paperback) | ISBN 9781009400602 (ebook)
Subjects: LCSH: Motion picture industry--India--History. | Motion pictures and globalization--India. | Motion picture actors and actresses--India. | Motion pictures, Hindi--History. | LCGFT: Film criticism.
Classification: LCC PN1993.5.I8 R276 2023 (print) | LCC PN1993.5.I8 (ebook) | DDC 791.43/0954--dc23/eng/20231002
LC record available at https://lccn.loc.gov/2023045945
LC ebook record available at https://lccn.loc.gov/2023045946

ISBN 978-1-009-40061-9 Hardback

For my loving family

CONTENTS

FIGURES

TABLES

ACKNOWLEDGEMENTS

Networked Bollywood has benefitted from many mentors, critics, research collectives, and institutions. The University of Michigan, Ann Arbor, and the College of Literature, Science, and the Arts (LSA) provided me with excellent institutional support and resources to pursue my scholarship. The Institute of Humanities at the University of Michigan supported the completion of this book with a year-long fellowship. I am incredibly grateful to Peggy McCracken and my cohort of fellows for their valuable feedback and support. The American Institute of Indian Studies's workshop was another unique opportunity for feedback from senior scholars and colleagues from which this book also benefitted. Many thanks to workshop mentors Jyoti Puri and Harleen Singh and my workshop cohort, Darshana Mini, Padma Chirumamilla, Ameera Nimjee, Jeff Roy, Sravanthi Kollu, Kritish Rajbhandari, and Sreyoshi Sarkar, for thinking with me and providing advice on an earlier draft of the book. The book also gained from summer-writing support awarded by the University of Michigan for two consecutive summers, the Provost's Faculty Research Support, and a publication subvention award from the College of LSA and the University of Michigan Office of Research. The Institute for Research on Women and Gender (IRWG) was yet another source of community and sustained intellectual engagement. IRWG provided valuable workshops, structured writing time, and feedback. I am particularly grateful to my IRWG colleagues, Rebecca Irvine, Allison Alexy, and Anna Kirkland.

Under the sponsorship of LSA, the complete manuscript was reviewed and workshopped by Nitin Govil, Ross Melnick, and my departmental colleagues. Their thoughtful and detailed comments were invaluable in refining my ideas and writing. My colleagues have been a source of intellectual stimulation and camaraderie: these include (in alphabetical order) Caryl Flinn, Chris McNamara, Colin Gunckel, Dan Herbert, David Marek, Giorgio Bertellini, Hollis Griffin, Jim Burnstein, John Valadez, Johannes Von Moltke, Mark Kligerman, Markus Nornes, Matthew Solomon, Melissa Phruksachart, Robert Rayher, Sarah Murray, Sheila Murphy, Umayyah Cable, Veerendra Prasad, Victor Fanucchi, Yeidy Rivero, and Yvette Granata. I am very grateful to Giorgio Bertellini for his continual support, careful reading of the manuscript, and thoughtful feedback. Johannes Von Moltke taught me how to think creatively about archival research while surviving a global pandemic. He helped me form networks and connections that enabled me to do archival work remotely in Germany and Russia. Thanks to Hollis Griffin for being a generous colleague and invaluable friend. Markus Nornes has been an excellent guide in orienting me to the university and alerting me to useful opportunities. Colin Gunckel, Matthew Solomon, Sarah Murray, Melissa Phruksachart, Yvette Granata, Umayyah Cable, and Ungsan Kim provided support and solidarity in times of need. Finally, special thanks are due to my department chair, Yeidy Rivero, and LSA dean, Anne Curzan, who have been exceptional leaders during the pandemic and a source of unstinting support and reassurance. I also appreciate the kindness of our outstanding departmental staff, Carrie Moore, Kevin O'Neill, Lana Naqshbandi, Lisa Rohde-Barbeau, Marga Schuhwerk-Hampel, and Mary Lou Chlipala. They have all been so thoughtful and meticulous in facilitating my research trips, research assistant payments, conference travels, and so on.

I was fortunate to find mentors and intellectual kinship at the University of Michigan beyond my departmental colleagues—Supriya Nair, June Howard, Allison Alexy, Ellen Muehlberger, Nilo Couret, Joyojeet Pal, Farina Mir, Matthew Hull, Krisztina Fehervary, Devon Powers, Lisa Nakamura, Will Glover, Leela Fernandes, and Mrinalini Sinha have been generous mentors and thoughtful and supportive colleagues.

This book began as a PhD dissertation completed in the Department of Radio, TV, and Film at the University of Texas at Austin, where I worked closely with my advisor, Shanti Kumar, and committee members Joe Straubhaar, Alisa Perren, and Thomas Garza. I owe a debt of gratitude to Shanti for his unstinting support, for constantly pushing me beyond my comfort zone and nudging me to pursue ambitious projects. Joe and Alisa have always been there whenever I needed them. A big thank you to Wenhong Chen, whose class on social capital and social networks sparked my thinking about organizations, individuals, and networked power. Thanks are due to Kathy Fuller-Sealey, Tom Schatz, and Suzanne Scott for reading the book proposal and reinforcing the merits of this project. It gave me the much-needed confidence to move to the next stage in the publishing process. Thanks to my graduate school colleagues—Alfred Martin, Caitlin McClune, Claire Lee, and Pete Kunze—for always lending a sympathetic ear.

Beyond the University of Michigan and the University of Texas at Austin, I was lucky to find support, collegiality, and mentorship at Wesleyan University, Brown University, and beyond. Lisa Dombrowski, William Pinch, Ashutosh Varshney, Lynne Joyrich, and Lina Fruzetti's engagement with my scholarship buoyed me at crucial moments. Matt Sienkiewicz, Aswin Punathambekar, Derek Kompare, Sean Griffin, Sundeep Muppidi, Prakash Younger, Ben Aslinger, Caetlin Benson-Alott, Dudley Andrew, Courtney Brannon Donoghue, and Suzanne Leonard have been a constant source of support and guidance. They indeed model kindness in academia. The invited talks I gave on this topic at Simmons College, Wesleyan University, and the Center for South Asia Studies at the University of Michigan were occasions to have valuable interlocutors point out emergent possibilities that helped shape the final manuscript. Thanks to Suzanne Leonard, Hirsh Sawhney, and Leela Fernandes for their kind invitations. In reading this book, my teachers from Miranda House College, the University of Delhi, and Jawaharlal Nehru University will find that their mentorship still shapes my scholarship so many years into my career. Thank you, Angela Koreth, Manju Kapur Dalmia, Sharmila Purkayastha, Masooma Ali, G. J. V. Prasad, and Harish Narang.

I am extremely thankful to my editors at Cambridge University Press, especially Anwesha Rana and Saniya Puri, who have collaborated with me, provided constructive suggestions, and extended necessary guidance to keep me on track with the publication timeline. I am indebted to the reviewers who gave so much of their valuable time to read the manuscript and provide rigorous feedback. Shanon Fitzpatrick and Robert Saute provided thorough and incisive comments that considerably improved the manuscript.

I started my career as a film journalist in the early 2000s when the Indian film and media industry was globalizing. This early experience has shaped some of the core questions I ask in this book. Answering those questions required a deeper exploration of the industry, which would have been hard to do without the help and magnanimity of my former colleagues—Madhu Soman, Arnab Banerjee, Saibal Chatterjee, Amit Banerjee, and Vijaya Sharma, all stellar journalists, who went above and beyond to get me industry contacts in Bollywood and shared their own insights with me. Thanks to Kabir Bedi, Shyam Benegal, Chikki

Pandey, Kunal Kapoor, Triveni Makhijiani, Suresh Iyer, Siddharth Bhatia, Sandeep Marwah, Avtar Panesar, Rafiq Gangjee, Amit Khanna, Taran Khan, Shahrbanoo Sadat, Vera Wessel, Karuna Badwal, Antoine Zeind, Amrit Gangar, and Purti Chaturvedi, who generously gave me their time and connected me to others in the industry. My brilliant research assistants, Ahmed Farahat, Lauren Beck, and Antonina Ovrutskaya, made it possible to conduct research despite the pandemic in Egypt, Germany, and Russia, respectively. I would also like to thank the helpful staff at the Nehru Memorial Museum and Library, Jawaharlal Nehru University, New Delhi, and the University of Michigan. Brendan J. Nieubuurt, Liangyu Fu, Evyn Kropf, Jeffery Martin, Justin Joque, Meredith Kahn, and Jefferey Pearson became my research lifeline as I navigated the complexities of finishing a multi-sited transnational project in Ann Arbor during a time of restricted international travel.

Writing during a pandemic was transformed into a joyous activity and a place for camaraderie and solace because of the people I wrote with—a special shout out to the writing wizards, especially Yasmin Moll, for bringing all of us together. Conversations and co-writing with Giulia Ricco, Melissa Borja, Rebecca Wollenberg, and Sangseraima Ujeed have kept me motivated during this unrelenting pandemic. I am also thankful to Emily Carman, Michael Reinhard, Silvia Viches, Lester Zhu, and Kate Fortmueller, my writing accountability partners. Weekly and monthly check-ins with them were critical in getting me to the finish line.

And now, to the people who make me feel warm and fuzzy during every successive Michigan polar vortex—my family. My daughter, Maitreyi, has been my biggest cheerleader. I started graduate school when she was an infant. She has since grown into a responsible sixth grader, always eager and willing to help. I would also like to thank my mom, who always came to my rescue whenever I needed it. To all those who helped care for Maitreyi while I was doing my fieldwork in India—my mom, dad, mother-in-law, sister-in-law, and Siddhu, I owe you all a debt of gratitude. A special mention is due to my brother, who drove me around for interviews, did his best to get industry contacts for me, and has always been a phone call away in times of need. My uncles (S. N. Rai, Alok Rai, and Vivek Rai), my cousin Prashray, and my dearest friends Chiranjita and Shreya were all incredibly supportive and helped me find valuable contacts in Bollywood. Last but not least, my husband, Mihir—thank you for always being there for me. I am unreasonably lucky to have your abundant love. You are my rock.

ABBREVIATIONS

ABCL	Amitabh Bachchan Corporation Limited
ANT	actor–network theory
BBC	British Broadcasting Corporation
BJP	Bharatiya Janata Party
CAA	Creative Artists Agency
CEO	chief executive officer
DDLJ	*Dilwale Dulhania Le Jayenge*
DVD	digital versatile disc
FFC	Film Finance Corporation
FICCI	Federation of Indian Chambers of Commerce and Industry
FTII	Film and Television Institute of India
ICCR	Indian Council of Cultural Relations
IIFA	International Indian Film Academy
IMPEC	Indian Motion Picture Export Corporation
IPL	Indian Premier League
IPTA	Indian People's Theatre Association
K3G	*Kabhi Khushi Kabhi Gham*
MOMA	Museum of Modern Art
MPAA	Motion Picture Association of America

NAM	Non-Aligned Movement
NFDC	National Film Development Corporation
NRI	non-resident Indian
OTT	over the top
POC	person of colour
PR	public relations
RSALA	Russian State Archive of Literature and Art
SRK	Shah Rukh Khan
UA	United Artists
UK	United Kingdom
US	United States
VCR	video cassette recorder
WME	William Morris Endeavor

INTRODUCTION

Star Switching Power in Networked Bollywood

It was a balmy April morning in Tampa Bay, Florida, as I sauntered along the promenade to attend the Federation of Indian Chambers of Commerce and Industry–International Indian Film Academy Awards (FICCI–IIFA) business forum hosted by the University of South Florida's Muma College of Business.[1] There was nervous energy and general anticipatory chaos in the conference room, where a panel on Bollywood's global collaborations was about to start. As we were waiting for things to commence, I cornered Santiago Corrada, president and chief executive officer (CEO) of Visit Tampa Bay and a host of this panel, for a conversation. He smiled at me and fidgeted with his hands as he produced brief responses to my questions about the event, which I pegged to a general American nonchalance towards Bollywood. It had been twenty minutes since the designated start time for the event, and the impatience was showing. People shuffled in their seats and paced in and out of the conference room. A sudden collective clamour in the room alerted me to the arrival of an important speaker. Bollywood star Anil Kapoor walked in with his usual swagger, and Corrada's nonchalance vanished. Swiftly angling through the chairs, he zealously shook Kapoor's hands. He was, it appeared, star-struck.

The panel comprised the who's who of corporate India, the Indian film and entertainment industry, and its US collaborators. The panellists included the director of the global consultancy firm EY, the executive director of the Tampa Hillsborough Film and Digital Media Commission, the president of the Confederation of Indian Industry, the CEO of the Film & Television Producers Guild of India Limited, film producers, and, of course, Anil

Kapoor. These business forums featured a range of topics from 'opportunities in Indo-US commerce' to 'healthcare and technology partnerships' anchored around the 2014 IIFA Awards, Bollywood's Oscar-style award show celebrating 100 years of Indian cinema. The IIFA forums were a spectacular and particularly generative space of global flows where all major stakeholders in India's industrial landscape and beyond were amply represented.[2] The attendees included Indian and American diplomats, key figures from the Indian-American diaspora, as well as individuals from the Indian and US film and entertainment businesses. But it was the presence of Kapoor that transformed what might have been a routine industrial business forum into, simultaneously, a *Bollywoodized* spectacle,[3] a spectacle where the interests of financial and political stakeholders combined with the enthusiasm of fans to promote a global Indian entertainment brand.

Significantly, Kapoor was present at the panel not as a mere actor but in his capacity as an entrepreneur and producer. His United Kingdom (UK)-based production company, Antila Ventures, had just been launched. Under its aegis, Kapoor hoped to produce content across multiple platforms, he told the *Indian Express*, proclaiming his company to be a 'gateway to international markets'.[4] Kapoor's global vision and organization had found backers in a Dubai-based investment-banking firm, MAS ClearSight, and Antila's first production venture was to be an Indian adaptation of the American drama series *24*. Having appeared in the original US version of *24*, Kapoor understood its nuances and how it could be adapted for a South Asian audience. During his company's official launch a week earlier, Kapoor noted in an interview with the *Hollywood Reporter* that he had 'long nurtured a dream of creating a global entertainment company. Given [his] vast experience in the Indian film industry and exposure in recent years in Hollywood, [he] felt the time was right to give shape and structure to this vision'. The Indian film industry is in 'dire need of good infrastructure', and Kapoor intended to 'plug the gap … by collaborating with studios of international repute to bring the best studio infrastructure to Bollywood', which could propel its further expansion at home and abroad.[5]

As a researcher of popular Indian cinema's globalization, I was brimming with questions about Bollywood's latest international collaborations. During the Q&A, however, my enthusiastic hand-raising proved futile, and the mic was handed to a sari-clad, middle-aged Indian lady. Visibly moved by the experience of seeing the star in person, she began with an anecdote that expressed how much she adored Kapoor and how many of his movies she had watched as a teenager. In an affective moment where she sought affirmation for both her fandom and youth, she asked Kapoor: 'We have all changed so much, but you still look the same. Still so handsome. How do you maintain such beautiful hair?' Warmed by the adulation, Kapoor regaled the audience with his haircare routine. Follow-up questions similarly complimented Kapoor's looks and fitness. A conversation ostensibly about industry transformations had quickly been transposed onto the star's body and affect—and hardly anyone but some panellists and I were still interested in Kapoor's production company or the global collaboration he was there to announce.

This FICCI–IIFA event in Tampa, held far from Bollywood's national home in Mumbai, illustrates Hindi cinema's globe-spanning networks. It also foregrounds the transnational mobility and significance of the star—in this case Kapoor, who prominently anchored the event—bringing together and bridging diverse stakeholders in Bollywood's global collaborations. In Bollywood, the star's power in enabling globalization, and shaping its directions, is paramount because, in the Indian cinema context, stars are more than stars; they are both the deal and the dealmaker. Whereas in Hollywood and other film industries, stars have predominantly been charismatic commodities constructed and sold by conglomerate industrial business networks, stars in the Indian Hindi film industry constitute the industry's business network in literal terms. As the heads and proprietors of some of Indian film and entertainment's most prominent corporations, Bollywood megastars combine overwhelming charismatic affect with unparalleled industrial power. Just as Kapoor positioned himself as Hindi cinema's 'gateway to the world' (and vice versa) at the FICCI–IIFA event, the star has long been the central catalyst for making international connections that have propelled the Bollywood behemoth's seemingly ever-expanding industrial trajectory.

Networked Bollywood delineates this trajectory, providing a new historical account of the expansion of Hindi cinema from its early twentieth-century roots to its current industry formation, theorizing the role of the star in Bollywood's globalization. Tracing the film industry's organizational and business structure, from small family-led film production clusters to a corporatized global entertainment network, this book argues that stars exerted a uniquely significant influence on Bollywood's business and globalization due to the historically fraught relationship between the Indian state and the mainstream film industry, which evolved without state support until

2001.[6] In this context, individual stars became the most invested catalysts of Hindi cinema's transnational dissemination, which they advanced primarily to further the expansionist goals of individual production companies and the broader industry rather than the priorities of the state. Through their affective personas, business practices, and personal relationships with other stakeholders, Bollywood stars served as the key architects of India's most profitable cultural sector and what is now the world's largest film and entertainment industry.[7]

While casting the star in the lead role in the story of Bollywood's globalization, this book departs from traditional approaches to cinema and star studies based on US or European film histories, which depict stars as commodities whose position and power depended on larger industrial and government structures. In the case of Hindi cinema, as we will see, an internationally interconnected agglomeration of differently positioned individual and institutional participants and stakeholders cohered around the star businessmen (and sparingly few businesswomen) who became the primary drivers that shaped the industry's business and its global expansion. The reasons why the star came to be so centrally situated and uniquely influential flow from Hindi cinema's industrial history, as this book will elaborate. A crucial factor that shaped this dynamic over the long term was the predominance of star-driven films, where star salaries made up most of a film's budget. The stars' sociocultural power in Indian society, which came not only from fans propelling them into demigods but their typically elite class and familial background, was another primal factor.[8] To capture the dynamics of star power, I consider stars as actors within sociocultural, industrial, and geopolitical networks. Foregrounding networks allows me to conceptualize the star's positionality, role, and power in broader systems while also analysing how stars used their power to influence these systems.[9] This relational sociological approach helps explicate how Hindi cinema stars acted (literally and figuratively) to catalyse growth into new economic, cultural, and geographic realms, propelling patterns of expansion that sustained them, their companies, and their ability to make new connections at home and abroad.[10] In this way, an industry that was already transnational from the start became more intensely and extensively globally networked, with key star nodes influencing this network's trajectories of globalization more powerfully than other stakeholders.

By emphasizing Hindi cinema's transnationally networked industrial formation and identifying stars as the primary catalysing nodes driving its expansion, this study offers an innovative conceptualization of star power, one that I argue is necessary to understand how Hindi cinema became Bollywood. *Star switching power*, it theorizes, is the ability of some stars to exceed the confines of the networks they belong to and act as 'switches' that illuminate new pathways and turn on connections with other networks that did not exist before.[11] Star switching power, and the abilities it confers to structurally transform the networks that produce it, emanates from a combination of affective and effective power—that is, it derives from a star's charisma on- and off-screen as well as the star's abilities, as a business owner, to directly effect industrial change.

Across the history of the Hindi film industry, effective and affective influence coalesced most potently in stars whose gender and social class positioned them at the centre of sociocultural, industrial, and political realms, thereby intensifying the impact certain male megastars exerted on Indian film and entertainment networks and their globalization. Theorizing star switching power, especially by analysing who possesses it and how they have used it to enact specific industry transformations, deepens our understanding of historical and contemporary relationships of power within globalized Bollywood while elucidating how and in what ways the Hindi cinema industry became so globally powerful. It also offers new ways to explore what Bollywood's global power means today and in the future for India and the world.

Networked Bollywood unfolds chronologically, with each chapter of the book focusing on a different era of Hindi cinema history through case studies of how prominent star figures and their specific business ventures contributed to the industry's globalization. As we will see, Hindi cinema's network has transformed across different historical eras. It evolved from a veritable studio system during British rule (a proto network) to a nascent global network formation dominated by family-led production clusters during the middle of the twentieth century (an emergent network) to the intensely interconnected global entertainment network whose corporatized structural coalescence in the 1990s led to the networked Bollywood behemoth of today (an agglomerated network).[12] Rather than seeking to impose a rigid periodization schema, I categorize these phases as proto, emergent, and agglomerated in order to mark important industry transformations, which always unfolded in relation to other historical changes—for instance, colonialism and independence, the Cold War, the liberalization of the Indian economy, or the rise of India as a world power. Each phase of Hindi cinema history I analyse contains certain residual characteristics from previous phases, and, in turn, each phase influences what will come to evolve because history, to borrow from Raymond Williams, is mixed and layered.[13]

Throughout all these periods, key stars created new business products, processes, and routines, cultivated national and transnational relationships, and developed novel industrial arrangements that helped the industry surmount border barriers and reach international markets that hitherto had been inaccessible. Star power varied in relation to different eras of globalization, yet overall, as the speed and intensity of globalization accelerated, star power also intensified. Just as importantly, however, this relational valence, as this book will reveal, throws into sharp relief an element of continuity: the power of star nodes and their consistent centrality in Hindi cinema's evolution. Across all these eras, it was stars and their switching power that most consistently and directly shaped these industrial, geographic, cultural, and political network transformations, intensifying over time the scale and speed of Bollywood's globalization.[14]

This book deploys history as method by integrating historical data and analysis to theorize structural and organizational change within Indian Hindi film and entertainment and situate stars as agentic actors within these processes of transformation.[15] It links institutional agency to specific historical conditions and foregrounds the relational embedded agency of stars as key actors within these processes. In doing so, it addresses the historical question of how stars, a group of centrally situated actors within Hindi film and entertainment institutions, gained the agency required to successfully define an industry's global trajectory. This book also foregrounds the relationality of this industrial context. Historical circumstances are outcomes of sociocultural processes; as such, they do not simply determine the constituent actors in the network at different moments in time; rather, history also plays the role of an agent. Using history as method thus helps me trace an epistemological and ontological correspondence between business history, organizational theory about structural changes, and sociocultural and geopolitical resonances that informed the Hindi film industry's expansion from small family-led production clusters to an expansive global industry.[16]

Thus, in telling this century-spanning story, this book offers critical insights into the significance of star power to the expansion of Bollywood from cinema to a global culture industry, a process that has been usefully described as 'Bollywoodization'.[17] Typical accounts of Bollywoodization periodize Hindi cinema's ubiquity as springing forth from the Indian state's legitimization of film-making as an industry equal to other industries and eligible for foreign direct investment at the turn of the twenty-first century. Immediately following this, the early 2000s were a moment when Bollywood became synonymous with India. Bollywood, hitherto a common sobriquet for the Indian Hindi film industry, swiftly evolved into a global moniker for all things Indian. Apart from capitalistic and materialistic circuits, the term also began circulating as an emblem of national cultural pride and a marker of diasporic Indian identity. Suddenly, the Bollywood industry itself acquired a ubiquitous and malleable quality, with Bollywood films being celebrated throughout India and the world.[18] With the arrival of Hindi films on the world stage, and as the industry revelled in its first Oscar-style IIFA Awards in London at the turn of the millennium, the term 'Bollywood' concretized as a signifier of the moment, marking the global arrival of the industry and culture.[19] This was also the moment when scholarship about global Bollywood took off. Tethered to the temporal arrival of Hindi cinema as a global industry which was also deeply connected to India's changing role in the world, much of this scholarship explained the industry's rise and interpreted its significance by centring industrial structures connected to twenty-first-century formations of state power and globalization.

In contrast, this book asserts that Bollywood's globality was not a singular moment of rupture in the 2000s but a historical continuum whose origins stretch back through many decades of Hindi cinema history. Offering an alternative narrative, this book defines Bollywood's globalization as the decades-long process through which multivalent global flows have made the Hindi entertainment industry's structure globally expansive and ubiquitous in terms of geography, industry, and influence. From the early Indo-German collaborations in the 1930s to the ubiquitous Bollywoodization of today, Hindi cinema's global flows and influence have been a continual factor in its development. It is in this vein that the term 'Bollywood' is deployed in this book, where I use it as a non-period-specific conceptual moniker that represents Indian Hindi cinema's industry's expansion, which, I argue, was driven primarily by the star. 'Bollywood', as a term, because of its transnational purchase, inherently epitomizes the push, pull, and squeeze of the global, which extends and intensifies in celerity and impact over time, thus capturing the Hindi film industry's encounters across a historical continuum.[20] While tracing how the proto, emergent, and agglomerated networks of Bollywood bleed into each other, coexist, overlap, leak, and residually accumulate new features, *Networked Bollywood* explains and historicizes this global percolation and cultural influence of the Hindi film industry along a continual spectrum on which its power increased incrementally as the extensiveness, speed, and impact of globalization intensified.[21] Moreover, in doing so, it illuminates, through its relational sociological approach and focus on the star and star switching power, different mechanisms and operations of structural power that, I argue, have long shaped Hindi cinema's globalizing industrial formation and remain central to Bollywood's global operations today.

It may at first seem counter-intuitive that it is through focusing on the star and star power that larger patterns and relationships of power come into view, which can help us more deeply explain Hindi cinema's globalization, conceptualize the relationships between its historical and contemporary structures, and theorize these structures as ones of power. However, as noted earlier, this book is not arguing for an individual-driven history but rather a relational one that helps theorize when and why certain individuals catalyse power and effect structural transformations. An individual's power in a network, as I discussed earlier, is not atomistical; it operates in relation to other nodes. Therefore, while this book focuses conceptually on the star, it emphasizes that star switching power does not operate in a vacuum. It operates within an industrial structure wherein star power, in turn, constitutes and is constituted by the industrial structure. Moreover, both star power and the industry are interconnected with global politics, culture, and state policy. This book, therefore, narrates a much larger story about star power in the Hindi film industry, told against the backdrop of contemporary economic globalization, cultural diplomacy, and post–World War II geopolitics. It illustrates how megastars buoyed by their switching power have been central to Bollywood's flows across lateral geographies and political blocs in regions as diverse as Egypt, the former Soviet Union, Germany, Afghanistan, and China. These diverse cultural contexts provide an understanding of Bollywood's cinematic exchange that was critical in galvanizing non-Anglocentric geo-cultural flows. *Networked Bollywood* thereby contributes to de-colonizing the history of cultural and cinematic influence by unravelling a lateral cultural and industrial history emanating from the Global South and its stars, predominantly across non-anglophone spaces.

This deep narrative engagement with the broad sociocultural and geopolitical structure of star power in a networked media industry necessitates an explication of industrial structure and the relational interdependence between star power and industry structure. It requires a new approach to understanding an industry's structural evolution and globalization in relation to stars as centrally situated nodal actors deeply and powerfully embedded within the industry and sociopolitical ecology. My interdisciplinary approach and framework of star switching power create a relational sociological lens that converges organizational, institutional, and sociopolitical networks to reveal a new way of looking at an industry's structural evolution and its globalization in relation to powerful individual actors—here, Bollywood's megastars.[22] This sociological lens also brings into focus the deeply gendered nature of this structural power that was consistently leveraged by male megastars.

To better understand this approach and its implications, in the remainder of this chapter, I will further explain why the Hindi film industry is best conceptualized as networked and elaborate on how the theory of star switching power explains key elements of networked Bollywood's structural evolution. Following a discussion of methodology, I end with an overview of the remaining chapters, whose case studies evidence the workings of star switching power in networked Bollywood.

NETWORKED BOLLYWOOD

Networks, in the simplest terms, are a set of interconnected nodes. They are an agglomeration of global and local institutional and individual nodes, adjustable in scale and connected to other networks. While scholars have used different metaphors to talk about Bollywood's global–local stakeholders, using terms like 'assemblages', 'corporatization', or 'convergence', the sociological and structural, and organizational framework of networks is most befitting to address the questions this book sets out to answer about Bollywood's globalization. Sociological networks deal with individuals or collective human actors that could be a range of things from firms and organizations to political parties or informal groups. Nodes and ties represent anything that has or builds some sort of connection. A node is the first basic element of a network and represents a primary unit of analysis. In our story, the megastar is the key node, and this book traces the industry's relationship with the critical and powerful star nodes and their contingent impact in shaping the industry's organizational structure, business practices, and access to global markets.[23]

Networks are deployed in this history of Bollywood's globalization using a dual perspective. They are articulated as sociological networks of power whereby some individuals, usually male megastars from elite backgrounds, attain and leverage their centrality in variegated sociocultural, political, and industrial structures towards specific goals, often at the expense of women and other liminal groups. I also conceptualize networks as an industrial formation that is structurally flexible and geo-temporally mutable and possesses a configurational multiplicity. In these instances, networks are deployed as business networks whose globalization impacts business products, practices, and processes.[24]

A network ontology is generative for this project because it presents multiplicities that are organized around the principle of perpetual inclusion and expansion.[25] Networks are reconfigurable, are constantly transforming, and they present an interconnected, multidimensional perspective that can bring together the political, the sociocultural, and the industrial in multiple valences of the local and the global. For instance, this book illustrates that as Bollywood's industrial network expanded and changed over time in relation to other nodes and networks, the industry was structurally altered in critical ways. It helps me narrativize how the industry transformed from small production clusters that dominated in the early decades after independence, later got mired in criminal economy networks in the 1980s, and were eventually corporatized a decade later as a transforming economy in the 1990s, which led to greater connections with cinema-adjacent industries and vertically integrated entertainment companies headquartered in India and abroad. A network framing helps me pose and answer multiple interconnected questions about Bollywood's evolving industrial structure, its globalization, and the working of star power within this structure.[26] Networks as a heuristic device are also central to this book because the temporal multiplicity and flexible transformation that characterize networks are instrumental to illustrating a three-part narrative about, first, how Bollywood's (primarily male) mega stars' social power and embeddedness in relations of power are connected to industrial structure and business; second, how businesses and organizations were changing; and, finally, in parallel, how all of these interconnected processes, in turn, were being impacted by politics and governmental policy.

Moreover, the flexible and transformative characteristic of networks can account for new technological connectivity in the informatics age and its impact on the various critical vectors in the story of Hindi cinema's globalization. This includes the impact of technologies like peer-to-peer file-sharing networks on film and media distribution or the influence of mediated digital fan networks on global star power and their consequent effect on politics, culture, or industry. In the larger structural ecology of Hindi cinema's global expansion, the network heuristic demonstrates the interconnected political economies of power that can operate through convergent and spreadable technology networks that came into play in the late 2000s.[27] A network framing device also lets me talk about fannish affect and its interconnections with other regimes of power that helped create the affective pathways for Hindi cinema's global flows. Such flows include the distribution of Amitabh Bachchan's films in Egypt because the president's wife was a fan or the undertaking of the global distribution of Raj Kapoor's films by India's prominent industrialists, the Hindujas, who were deeply moved by Kapoor's persona and on-screen performance.[28]

My conceptualization of Hindi cinema as a networked formation is fortified by Wendy Chun's theorization of the 'imagination of networks', which shows that networks are an epistemic tool that can dovetail with a social systemic study of the historical development of neoliberalism, global capitalism, and finance while also engaging with the salubrious modes of elaborating the aesthetic in relation to the social.[29] A multifaceted historical understanding of star power and how it was influenced by technology, fandoms, beauty pageants, and other vectors to create a new industrial formation across Hindi cinema and its variegated geo-temporal history can only be articulated through a network model. The network as a mode of sense making is best suited to map 'non-hierarchical, relational connections, interactions, processes and flows' across complex interconnected glocal systems.[30] Furthermore, this mode of sense-making articulates the 'fundamentally mobile, polycentric identities' of global film and media practices that simultaneously account for regional specificities while relationally connecting them to processes and methods that conceptually cut 'across time, spaces and geographies'.[31]

In summary, the framework of networks is generative in multiple ways. First, it explains the industry's organizational and structural formations on more significant business and globalization outcomes while accounting for the role of individual actors or nodes and the impact of their social and economic relationships, cultural influence, and embeddedness within the industry. Second, a networked framework considers 'both the structure and process of relationships that join individuals, groups, and organizations'.[32] Third, it simultaneously recognizes that individual actors or nodes do not function atomistically; instead, they exist within a system of individuals and institutions influenced by social, economic, and geopolitical factors. State and institutional policies, which are socially constructed, influence all of these.

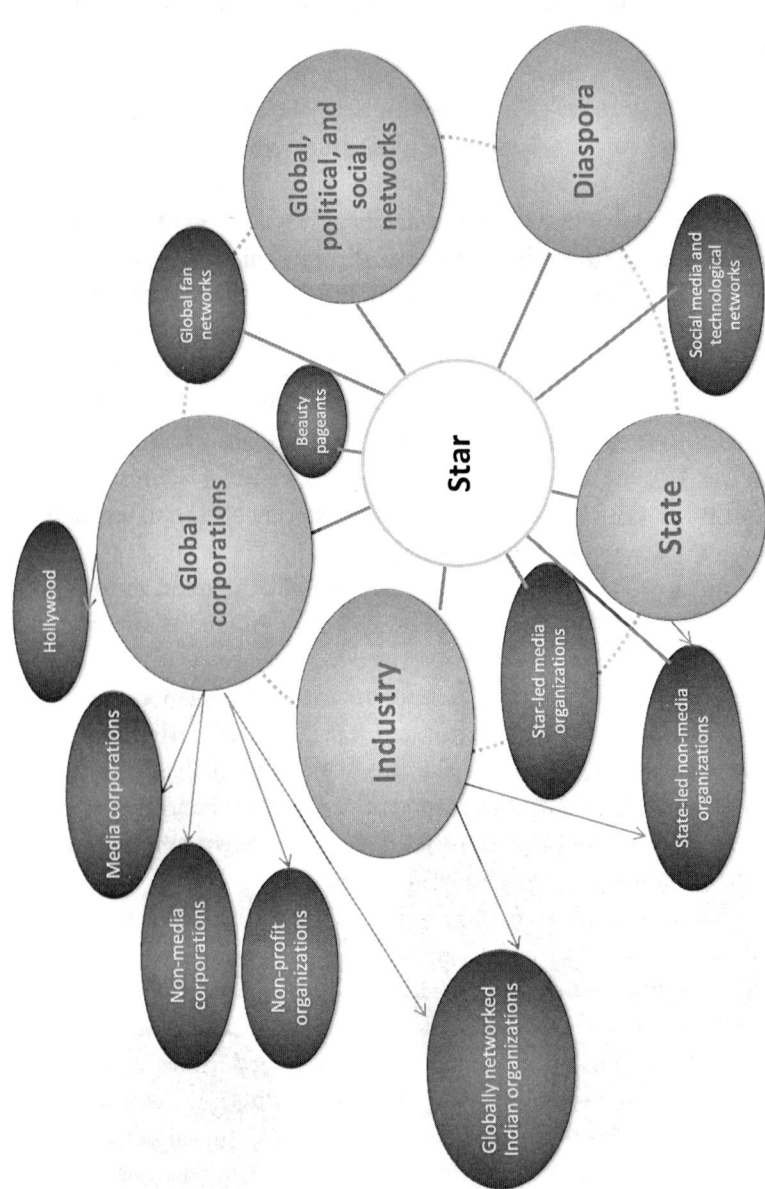

Figure I.1 The Bollywood network

Source: Prepared by the author.

Finally, the framework of networks recognizes that how individual actors exist and exert their influence and agency is socially inflected and dependent on their positionality, personal relations, and the networked nature of such relations.

STAR SWITCHING POWER

Conceptualizing the Hindi cinema industry and later the Bollywood entertainment behemoth in terms of a network draws our attention to specific network effects and their agents. 'Network effects' is a term derived from economics where the utility and success of a good or service, or a business model, create a phenomenon whereby that business practice or product is replicated and adapted quickly by the industry and users. While the adoption of certain business practices and innovative experiments with films by megastar businessmen created significant network effects in the industry's business practices, the idea of a network effect similarly applies to sociological and geopolitical networks the stars belonged to.

Significantly, the network ontology also draws our attention to what I theorize as network *affects*, which is the ability to mobilize the affective aura

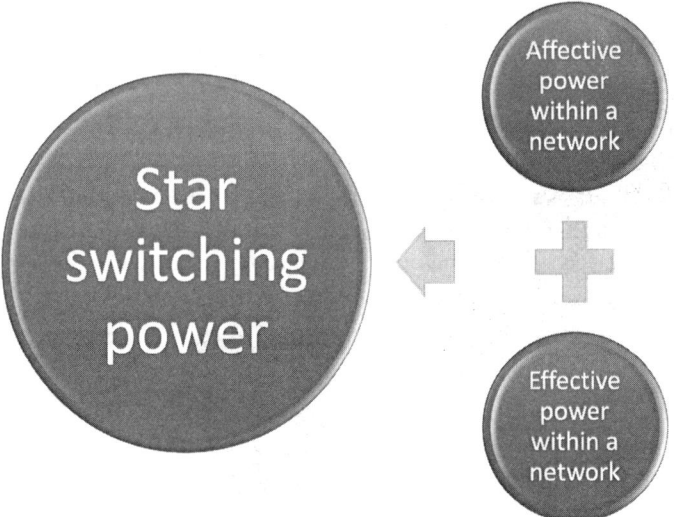

Figure I.2 The conceptual framework of 'star switching power'
Source: Prepared by the author.

and embodiment of star personas through multiple modes, from personal and social ties to technology-driven brandscapes. As I explained earlier, the effective component of switching power comprises of the star's direct power as a businessperson (often businessman) and sociopolitical influence, and the affective component is derived from the star's persona. The coalescence of the two components lent the megastar agentic primacy, or switching power, in the industry business to create network effects. Focusing on the embeddedness and centrality of stars as key nodes highlights the switching effects of star power in networked Bollywood and shows the extent to which the industry's historical transformations were shaped—or, in other words, effected *and* affected—by that nodal power.

My theoretical analytic of star switching power re-conceptualizes industry studies, global media, and star studies by viewing media globalization through the lens of stars as critical institutional vectors and change-makers within business and organizational networks. At the same time, I bring issues of affect into network studies and network analysis, which have heretofore been concerned predominantly with institutions and structures. Consequently, evaluating star switching power requires a multimethod approach that deploys network analysis to understand the relative effective and affective industry power of key actors. The effective aspect of star switching power, I theorize, is the star's ability to exercise direct control over other social actors in industrial or political networks, which, this book shows, happens via rules of inclusion based on elite sociocultural identity markers and, relatedly, coordination within networks. The affective component of star switching power, meanwhile, is derived from the stars' 'iconicity' and 'glamour' as constituted by their on- and off-screen personas. This star affect plays a role in accentuating the feeling around the star and, by extension, augments the likelihood of positive outcomes for the industrial or political goals the stars seek to accomplish. The power of star businessmen, as we have already seen through the example of Kapoor, lies in the embodied duality of their on-screen and off-screen charismatic affect that an industry node in another context—that is, someone like the media mogul Rupert Murdoch—does not and cannot possess. As Janet Staiger, Ann Cvetkovich, and Ann Reynolds have noted, '[P]erhaps we truly encounter the political only when we feel.'[33] This affective component of switching power, which is starkly different from power possessed by other actors in the network, allows megastars to bridge nodes and hubs[34] for previously unrelated networks and create connections where none existed before. Their effective power is what allows them to leverage these connections into the industry business and mobilize its global transformations.

Given the historically male-dominated structure of the Indian Hindi film industry, star switching power also elucidates how the normatively elitist and masculinist structures of Hindi film and entertainment have influenced who can possess switching power and the ways it is most likely to be used. As I will show, female stars' attempts at establishing themselves within the industry business often devolved into affective and direct labour without the ability to enact proportional industrial effects. In the post-independence nascent industry, when most popular male stars owned successful production studios, with the distinct exception of the immensely elite Devika Rani (whose grandfather was a Nobel laureate and father the surgeon general of India), similar efforts by female stars were either thwarted or remained unacknowledged by the industry.[35] Later, as India's economic policies altered the structure of the industry at the turn of the millennium, a window of opportunity emerged for some female stars with entrepreneurial ambitions to widen their gambit, following Cecilia Ridgeway's contention that when new kinds of work occur in environments that are in a state of flux, the combined novelty of the changes creates capacity and space for re-negotiating gendered expectations through industrial or organizational frameworks.[36] The agency of female stars remains limited, however, because the structures within which they operate are gendered, and in the networks in which they are embedded, power is more likely to be vested in institutional rather than individual actors or nodes.

My theoretical framework of star switching power integrates questions of gendered agency within industrial and business frameworks and elucidates its connections with affective and immaterial labour foisted on female stars. It argues that the construction of star affect works along hierarchies of social class, gender, age, and nationality. Star affect, which has come to be epitomized as a desired and aspirational ideal, is also permeated by a stratified structure that privileges certain types of identities.[37] The power in the embodied affect of stars also holds up hierarchical structural relations that are gendered, classed, and racialized. Embodied affect then becomes the circuit through which power is felt, mediated, negotiated, and contested.[38] Historically, stars who have come to possess switching power that exceeds the confines of their current networks in creating new industrial directions possess a high degree of sociocultural capital. However, women in similar positions have been unable to translate their position, capital, or affect into a direct industrial power like the male stars. This book's theorization of star switching power, by accounting for and explaining this overarching pattern, theorizes global networked Bollywood as a deeply gendered phenomenon.

Not unrelatedly, the rubric of star switching power also illuminates the foreign-relations dimensions of networked Bollywood, which were shaped by the individual star's varied impacts on cultural diplomacy. Throughout much of popular Hindi cinema's history, constant friction has existed between the interests of the mainstream film industry and the policies of the Indian state. As an alternative to the mainstream industry, the Indian state created a parallel cinematic network that was mobilized to create state-sanctioned 'good' cinema meant to project a favourable image of India to the world.[39] Unlike other industries that the state premeditatively and purposively involved in cultivating its cultural power, the mainstream Indian film industry existed tenuously, hoping to align with state agendas yet remaining glaringly outside of state-led discourses and an afterthought in state policy. In this context, the stars pursued their own global agendas, becoming bridging nodes between nations and transnational industries and producing new industrial structures that catalysed, often inadvertently, modalities of cultural diplomacy and soft power, some of which would later be utilized more intentionally by state actors.

With the early Hindi cinema network functioning through small-world ties with stars who acted as anchors and bridging nodes to global markets, stars leveraged their affective power over foreign audiences and fans to accomplish personal business and industry goals. This directed early expansion to non-aligned nations such as Egypt, neighbouring countries such as Afghanistan, and the socialist and communist circuit of the former Soviet Union and Eastern Europe that Nehruvian foreign policy had begun to favour. Through this process, some stars found a stake in transnational relations, becoming non-state interlocutors in projecting India's cultural image in a globalizing world. The mainstream Bollywood megastar's value to cultural diplomacy became a point of leverage that occasionally lowered barriers to the industry's ambitions for global expansion and recognition, thereby intensifying the international connections and paths of globalization that individual stars pursued using their switching power, which, in turn, broadened the star's cultural diplomacy reach. Unlike in the West, the Soviet Union, or China, it was not deliberate marketing-oriented thinking or an attempt to create state-driven propaganda or impact that primarily influenced

Hindi cinema's foreign relationships, but rather star switching power, whose impacts and reach expanded over time even while the industry became more supported and utilized by the state.

In other words, because of the networks the stars had already created or were creating, emanating from their sociocultural and political centrality in key networks of power, different forms of soft power and opportunities for cultural diplomacy resulted. A star's value within this diplomatic, cultural exchange was deeply tied to their affective power and direct personal ties to elite networks of power. For instance, in the case of Raj Kapoor, his father Prithviraj Kapoor's (also a Hindi film star) close personal ties with Jawaharlal Nehru created diplomatic opportunities for him. Hence, when Joseph Stalin expressed his admiration for Raj Kapoor's *Awāra*, Nehru invited Raj Kapoor and other Hindi cinema superstars to accompany him during his first official state visit to the Soviet Union in June 1955.[40] As the next chapter will elaborate, Raj Kapoor went on to mobilize the Soviet connection to further industry goals. Consistently, it was often through happenstance resulting from the star's affective power mobilized through fandoms, including those formed among foreign political elites, that stars found a stake in transnational relations and became non-state actors and interlocutors in projecting India's cultural image in a globalizing world. As the structure of the global network and its landscape changes and evolves, and access to information is democratized, international politics and diplomacy are redefined in this new space of information flows.[41] In this technologically mediated context of digital film circulation and online fandoms, individual non-state actors have more power to influence a nation's soft power and diplomacy discourse, particularly, as the book will reveal, in national contexts such as China, a nation with which India has historically had a fraught relationship. The Indian state, on occasion, has leveraged this accidental influence quite intentionally for diplomatic ends. As the industry changes and new technologies get incorporated, the nature of the star's affective power, reach, and influence becomes more expansive. Hence, as we move towards twenty-first-century networked Bollywood, fandoms mediated through technology become affective levers for mobilizing soft power, diplomatic ties, and industrial objectives.

The rubric of star switching power also helps us understand the various types of technologically mediated networks of formal and informal digital distribution, social media, and online fandoms that alter the nature of star switching power. Technological transformations created a space for networked affects that made the star brandscapes pervasive and ubiquitous, wherein technological assemblages mediated this power by generating multiple encounters with stars through websites, avatars, videos, apps, online forums, gifs, and other platforms, each allowing for a different experience or 'sensations of connectivity, interest, desire, and attachment'.[42] This kind of mediated, immersive *networked affect* of star brandscapes accords megastars like Shah Rukh Khan (SRK), arguably Bollywood's biggest star, an overwhelming, multimodal ubiquity.[43] Such networked affect simultaneously accounts for individual users, the collective bodies that emerge through those users, and the mediating effects of devices, platforms, interfaces, and companies.[44] The new technological affordances that occur via multiple platforms elicit feelings of closeness through their direct contact with users. The *affective economies* thus generated through the star's multitudinous circulation increase the star brand's affective value.[45]

This networked affect further manifests through digital fandoms. Important to note here is that with digital and social media technology, the nature of stars' affective power is visibly altered because of the changes in their relationship with fan networks. Whereas in the decades prior to the 2010s, star switching power's industrial goals were furthered through fannish relationships with elite networks of power, such as a powerful political figure being a fan of a star and therefore enabling exports or a co-production, technology-mediated fandoms work differently. The digital fandom ecology, to borrow Paul Booth's term, neatly dovetails with convergent industrial networks that cultivated a mediated and networked affective ecology for stars.[46] The effective power of contemporary stars like SRK and Aamir Khan is fuelled equally by the affective visual iconicity cultivated through their technologically mediated brandscapes. As Bollywood rapidly expanded from a film industry to an entertainment one, the nature of star switching power, disseminated through the mediated affective sensoriums of technology via fandoms and social media, was visibly transformed in part through their star texts and other pursuits. Apart from the direct effective relevance that their production organizations had to industry and commerce, the immensity of their networked affect gave contemporary stars such as SRK newfound global visibility and relevance in cultural diplomacy and bolstered their direct industrial power. Star switching power thus constitutively intersects with the industry's global dynamics, state policy, fandoms, and technology, intermingling to create a new spatial–cultural–industrial logic to mobilize star power towards the creation of a contemporary networked Bollywood that still bears the traces of earlier industrial formations, yet is also more closely associated with the Indian state.

METHODOLOGY AND CHAPTERS

Networked Bollywood revises normative approaches to the study of non-Western film and entertainment industries to offer a novel interdisciplinary methodology combining industry studies, star studies, global media studies, and network studies. The Indian film industry and its structural transformations provide a singular yet generative lens to think about stars as individual nodes with power that could capacitate and enable the 'Bollywoodization' and dissemination of Indian cinema as a global industry and brand the nation state as global. Bringing together industry, globalization, diplomacy, and networks through the lens of switching power to make this argument required a multimodal and multimethod entry point to understand the structure and the relational impact of the individual within the structure.

To foreground this centripetal logic that accounted for institutional practices, business transformations and innovations, state policy within and outside India, and their interconnections with networked power further inflected by an individual's sociocultural and economic centrality, I had to deploy a mixed-methods approach. To understand the historical trajectory of structural change in the industry in relation to the star businessmen (or, in a few cases, women) and their relative power, together with changes in state attitudes, policies, and the evolving economic and political ecology, I brought together archival analysis with semi-structured interviews with industry executives, veteran film journalists, and critics who understood the individual power dynamics of some stars vis-à-vis larger institutional structures. Additionally, I made ethnographic observations of Bollywoodized spaces like the IIFA, where the Indian Hindi film industry manifested itself within the larger global space of flows.[47] My previous career as a film journalist both in India and the United States (US) also informed my understanding of how the industry operates and manifests in global spaces.

My research methodology had to also reckon with the politics of the archive in the context of the Global South, where documents—if they have even been saved—lie buried under layers of dust and can be hard to access or find. As the director of the film facilitation office for India's National Film Development Corporation (NFDC) cautioned me, 'It will be hazardous for you to go through all that dusty paper. Just talk to the film people. I can give you some names.' Consistent with the state's historical indifference towards films, the current Indian government has gone a step further and decided to shut down four of its most reputed film archives. Journalistic coverage, therefore, became a primary means to understand this industrial history, and I relied upon the *Times of India* for factual information. The discursive positioning of the *Times of India* within the Indian mediascape as a popular chronicle of entertainment news was helpful. However, in the interest of writing a more cohesive multidimensional narrative, I looked at film magazines such as *Filmindia* and *Filmfare*, other newspaper and magazine archives, policy documents, letters from Indian politicians (Nehru, Indira Gandhi) to state officials and diplomats, and other material at the Nehru Memorial Museum and Library and the National Archives of India in New Delhi and its online database, Abhilekh Patal.[48]

Furthermore, since this book makes claims about industrial globalization and the global flows of Indian content, I wanted to understand and triangulate Indian claims about the global power of these exceptional stars through the international markets that the industry was claiming to impact. So I delved into international newspaper and magazine archives from those global regions: the *Kabul Times, Al Ahram, Al Dustur, Al-Riyad,* the *South China Morning Post, Der Spiegel, Die Zeit, Deutsche Welle, Ogoniok, Iskusstvo Kino,* and *Sovetskaia Kul'tura.* Through the help of research assistants, I also conducted research at the East–West Center Archives and at international archives such as the Russian State Archive of Literature and Art in Moscow.

This mixed-methods approach was productive in building in-depth case studies of stars and their organizations and explaining how they worked together to facilitate Bollywood's evolution as a globally recognizable industrial and national brand and cultural form. Constructing this narrative through multilingual and multi-sited archives helps me foreground a non-Anglocentric history of the dissemination of a central film culture from the Global South. Mapping Bollywood's exchange and flows across lateral geographies and political blocs across non-anglophone spaces such as Afghanistan, Egypt, Russia, China, and Germany, as this book does, shifts the conversation about geopolitical ties and the star's role in diplomatic contexts beyond the unremitting US- and UK-centric frameworks that dominate globalization and cinema studies. This book thereby contributes to de-colonizing the history of cultural and cinematic influence. These diverse cultural contexts provide a generative understanding of a new space of cinematic cultural power and industrial exchange that challenges imperialist anglophone notions of such encounters. What emerges, therefore, is a new historical and conceptual model of globalization that was once specific to India but that today is as ubiquitously apparent around the world as networked Bollywood itself.

This book is organized according to the type of network structure that was dominant in the Hindi film industry in specific time periods. The first phase articulated here as 'proto networks' delves into the 1940s, 1950s, 1960s, and early 1970s to describe the rudimentary yet global phase of family-led film production clusters that were spearheaded by stars. This phase is recounted predominantly in the introduction and the first chapter. The second phase, 'emergent corporate networks', covered in the second and third chapters, examines the decades of the 1970s, 1980s, 1990s, and the lead-up to the early 2000s, wherein the industry structure, hitherto mired in criminal economies, moved towards formal corporate networks. The third phase, 'agglomerated networks', explicated in the fourth and fifth chapters and parts of the third, begins in the early 2000s and investigates contemporary Bollywood's networked structure. In each of the three phases, star switching power manifests in distinctive ways. In each era, star agency is a relational power that is transformed based on the industry structure, state policy, and the relative clout that stars possess vis-à-vis other domestic and global nodes and institutions. The periodization is aimed at helping the reader visualize the global structural evolution of the industry as a historical continuum from a proto to an agglomerated and extensively networked industry while foregrounding star agency as a relational constant throughout the industrial transformations.

The term 'Bollywood', as invoked through the phases, conceptually signifies a set of spatial–temporal processes of change that connected the economic, the social, and the industrial, creating relationships that crystallized domestically and globally. The term 'proto-Bollywood' thus anticipates an industry that is desirous of becoming global, an industry marginalized by the nation state but hopeful of being embedded in processes that sustain the flows of capital, talent, and, predominantly, their film products. The post-independence proto-Bollywood acts as a locum for an aspirational global industry. Emergent Bollywood starting in the 1990s, coinciding with the liberalization of the Indian economy, represents a phase where those aspirations are enacted in a space that is structurally conducive for the global dissemination of the Indian Hindi film and the ensuing flows of capital, culture, geopolitical influence, and power. An agglomerated Bollywood network, in the post-Bollywoodization phase starting in the early 2000s, reflects the formation of various corporatized industrial clusters that get intensely interconnected as globalization processes accelerate.[49] This structural formation signifies the contours of what I call contemporary networked Bollywood. The three phases thus do not represent discrete entities but rather tendencies that evolved over time and influenced the industry; each had distinct attributes and particularities owing to changes in the Indian market ecology, cultural and economic policies, and the social and geopolitical climate.[50]

Each chapter in the book presents historical case studies of prominent star figures within a specific historical moment and examines their role in the Hindi film industry's globalizing transformations. The chapters delve into their specific business ventures and how each created or attempted to create cinema that would have transnational or even universal appeal. I also examine the industrial and diplomatic exchanges they enabled in the regions where they were most influential. By weaving together intersecting threads of star business biographies, industry structure, state policy, diplomatic exchange, and industry globalization, they tell the story of star power in networked Bollywood from the mid-twentieth century to today.

The first chapter, 'Of Vagabonds and Wayfarers', traces the early decades of Indian Hindi cinema, from the late 1940s to the 1980s, and views the industry as an early network where the primacy of stars led to the creation of star-led film production clusters. It historically situates why stars became such exceptional figures in the Hindi film industry and what factors influenced who could possess this exceptional power to create new business synergies and global connections. The chapter explicates the industry's family-led film-production clusters primarily undergirded by the star switching power of stars such as Dev Anand and Raj Kapoor, including their distinctive affective power—cosmopolitan and ideological—that enabled flows of Indian film and culture abroad. Set against the backdrop of Cold War geopolitics and political diplomacy, the chapter juxtaposes the influence of Raj Kapoor with Dev Anand and Shashi Kapoor (Raj Kapoor's brother) in oppositional political geographies—the US and the Soviet Union.

The second chapter, 'King of Kings', elucidates how star-led family-film-production clusters transformed themselves into corporations. It contextualizes the late 1970s and murky 1980s as a transitionary moment when state apathy for cinema exacerbated its illegitimate industry status, fomenting Hindi cinema's entanglements in mafia-financed criminal economies.[51] This chapter is primarily set in the 1990s and presents superstar Amitabh Bachchan as the main case study for star switching power, which drove transformative structural change in the wake of liberal economic reforms. I juxtapose Bachchan's protean power with similar attempts during the 1980s and 1990s by female megastars like Sridevi to foreground the masculinist and differential nature of star power in industrial contexts. The chapter simultaneously reveals that Bachchan's stardom affected diplomatic and industrial exchange with Afghanistan and Egypt. Anticipating the next chapter's discussion of star brands and network effects, it emphasizes how star branding as a norm was established for Amitabh Bachchan Corporation Limited and how this corporation generated a veritable network effect for other film and media companies. Finally, it elaborates on the synergistic collaboration between Indian national television and Hindi films and how television organically and somewhat opportunistically integrated with the Hindi film industry during this phase. This chapter marks the precipitation of a structural shift in the industry towards a corporate formation and a state-sanctioned trajectory for Hindi cinema's globalization and expansion from a film to an entertainment industry.

The third chapter, 'Global Dreamz', begins in the early 2000s and analyses two of Hindi cinema's contemporary stars, SRK and Aamir Khan. During a structurally transitionary phase at the turn of the millennium, when the film industry was struggling to keep up with the globalization of television and other entertainment industries, SRK and Aamir Khan, buoyed by their individual ambitions, set up their own production companies to create cinema that would appeal to a global audience. I illustrate how their consumable and conscientious affective power and its confluence with their direct power within the industry enabled the creation of successful organizations that served as conduits for Hindi cinema's expansion from Germany to China. In addition, the chapter explicates the changes in state policy, regulation, and diplomatic exchange with Germany and China, situating these stars as critical anchors for industry globalization and affective diplomacy in these spaces. It foregrounds their global vision, which worked in conjunction with the liberal economic climate to redefine the contours of the emerging networked Bollywood industry, leading to a re-conceptualization of entertainment writ large that can be seen most vividly in the connection between Bollywood and sports, especially cricket, with stars owning major sports franchises. The chapter also elaborates on this period as a phase that marks the beginning of agglomerated corporatized industry clusters. The growing multiplicity of global and local stakeholders in the Indian entertainment landscape led to the transformation of stars into celebrities—celebrities that can percolate globally across digitally networked affective spaces through social media, peer-to-peer file sharing, digital pirate spaces, and a multitude of advertising and marketing platforms. In the next decade, the 2010s, this incipient infrastructure of star-making begins to concretize, as the following chapter will reveal, through the rise of global and local talent agencies in intensely networked Bollywood. By the end of the first decade of the 2000s, although stars like SRK and Aamir Khan became exceptionally prominent business nodes within the industry, the nature of star switching power underwent a shift in response to the changing contours of the industry, providing new kinds of opportunities for female stars.

Thus, the next chapter, 'Global Beauty Queens', shifts the focus from the male stars' dominant switching power to Bollywood's contemporary female stars and their kind of switching power. It begins with an explication of the beauty pageant network that emerged in the early 1990s and created some of India's most globally recognized female stars such as Aishwarya Rai and Priyanka Chopra. The discussion exposes the gendered dimension of star switching power and argues that the power of female stars is diffuse and predominantly channelled as affective power, even though they can act as conduits for the industry's globalization. However, structural change within the industry creates a moment of flux where the gendered affective power is translatable to direct industrial power, as in the case of new-age Bollywood beauty queens like Chopra, who are especially effective in creating linkages to Hollywood and US industries.

The concluding chapter, 'Bards of Change', initiates a structural assessment of contemporary networked Bollywood that is being created by new nodes like transnational over-the-top (OTT) streaming platforms, international talent agencies, Hollywood studios, and Indian entertainment corporations such as Reliance Entertainment and Zee Entertainment Enterprises, all of which work in conjunction with star-led corporations like SRK's Red Chillies Entertainment and Aamir Khan Productions. Within this context, the chapter theorizes star switching power as a relational factor in the specific context and structure of the contemporary industry and the impossibility of the kind of authority and agency of contemporary megastars like SRK and Aamir Khan to be accessed by future stars, male or female. This concluding chapter reflects on power disjunctures and the stars' relationships with industry and diplomacy in contemporary, global, networked contexts.

Ultimately, it shows how gendered, diplomatic, and technological mediations of star switching power discussed throughout the book have created today's globally networked industrial Bollywood behemoth.

As the following chapters will unfold, this book offers an understanding of the Indian Hindi film industry's globalization through the stupendous power of Hindi cinema's megastars and their ability to mobilize, and even transform, the structures sustaining the Bollywoodization of the industry in the global arena. It explains why and how some megastars became critical drivers of change during different phases of the industry's evolution as catalysts in the manifestation of Bollywood as a global industry and as inadvertent adjuvants for soft power.

1

OF VAGABONDS AND WAYFARERS

Raj Kapoor, Dev Anand, and Hindi Cinema's Family-Led Film Clusters

Particularly during the Cold War years, you will find that the entire Eastern side was absolutely seduced by Indian cinema. I remember the one time we all went to the former Soviet Union as part of the Indian delegation for the Moscow Film Festival. We were travelling from Moscow to St. Petersburg by overnight train. There was a special coupe in which the Czars used to travel that was brought out and attached to the train; why? Because Raj Kapoor was travelling with us. And Raj Kapoor being Raj Kapoor, he invited many of us in that coupe where the Russians had provided him with an endless supply of champagne, cognac, and fruit. Their own leaders never got the kind of treatment that Raj Kapoor received.

—Shyam Benegal, veteran film director and producer[1]

Raj Kapoor, as the anecdote emphasizes, was a revered star in the Soviet Union when a newly independent India was trying to establish itself as a non-aligned nation in the context of the Cold War.[2] His film *Awāra* (The Vagabond, 1951) was an unexpected hit that endeared Soviet viewers to Indian cinema. Concurrently, the Soviets appreciated a few other major stars such as Dev Anand and Dilip Kumar, whose films *Rahi* (The Wayfarer, 1952, dir. Khwaja Ahmad Abbas) and *Naya Daur* (The New Era, 1957, dir. B. R. Chopra) also got Soviet releases. This chapter traces the history of Indian Hindi cinema's industrial exchange and globalization, from the 1950s to the 1980s, spanning the decades of the Cold War up to the beginnings of perestroika in the Union of Soviet Socialist Republics, commonly referred to as the Soviet Union. In recounting this history, it focuses on crucial star nodes and their nodal power within Indian Hindi cinema's formative industrial structure after independence. While recounting this history of star switching power, this chapter also situates how stars came to be Hindi cinema's global anchors with the most industrial power, when, during the late 1940s and early 1950s, the studio system that existed under British rule broke down. Indian Hindi cinema's post-independence industrial structure, we will see, was marked by significant transformations. The studios were replaced by a new structural formation wherein small independent film clusters dominated the production landscape. As the industry adapted to national and international developments after independence, a few megastars emerged as critical instigators of changes in the industry business and products that mobilized Hindi cinema to traverse global boundaries. These decades marked a proto phase in the industry's global formation and evolution where mutual connectivity with the wider global economic system was sparse, and the film industry could largely be characterized as an unorganized industrial sector. Perpetually hankering for legitimization by the state as a formal industry, film-making at this time was an aggregation of small-scale film-production clusters, dispersed distribution chains, non-contractual labour, handshake- and kinship-based deals, and reciprocal obligations, as this chapter will demonstrate.[3] Specifically, the chapter elucidates how Raj Kapoor and other stars such as Dev Anand and Shashi Kapoor, as megastar proprietors of some of Hindi cinema's prominent production companies, became the enablers of Hindi film's cinematic flows across adversarial geographies of the former Soviet Union and the United States (US).

In this chapter, I present a triadic narrative delineating the history of the globalization of Indian Hindi cinema in its proto phase and during the formative decades of Indian independence in the late 1940s and early 1950s through the 1980s, when Cold War geopolitics and the Indian state's insular economic policies begin to change. The narrative triad consists of (*a*) the industry's structural formation in this transitional period when Hindi cinema moved away from a studio system towards family-led production clusters, (*b*) the critical star nodes within this formative industry structure and network, and (*c*) their relative nodal power. The chapter explicates the industry structure during these early decades of Hindi cinema as a cluster of family-led production entities. This business structure was based on Indian social hierarchy, filial bonds, and a sensibility that privileges close-knit, small-world ties that primarily included the family unit and close friendships. After the breakdown of studios, since stars emerged as key industrial nodes with financial wherewithal, they could create their independent productions. Star-led production clusters thus became a central organizational and structural unit in Hindi cinema's nascent network. Many of these early family-led film-production clusters were also helmed by prominent directors and other pre-existing business nodes within the industry network. However, this structure was propelled forward by critical star nodes who could leverage their power and centrality within sociopolitical and industrial networks to accomplish key business and globalization goals for their production ventures and the industry at large.

Many of these stars endeavoured to create and distribute Indian cinema globally, albeit with varying degrees of success. These formative decades are significant both structurally and politically because the family-led film clusters created at this time remained structurally dominant (and still exist in a malleable form in contemporary Bollywood). Within this organizational structure, key family productions, often led by elite male megastars, prevailed at the exclusion of others. In the political context, this structure functioned within the geopolitical milieu of the Cold War, when both the Soviets and the Americans sought to influence the non-aligned Indian state. Again, the mega film star occupied prominence in this discourse of cultural bonhomie because of their exceptional affective pull in some cultural contexts, such as the Soviet Union, where some shared sociopolitical sensibilities between Indian cinema and Soviet culture magnified the appeal of Indian exports. The diplomatic relevance of film stars in the geopolitical discourse helped mollify the Indian state's derisive attitude towards popular cinema that leaders like Jawaharlal Nehru and Mohandas K. Gandhi thought of as debased, plebian entertainment. The newfound relevance of cinema and film stars in cultural diplomacy helped the megastars create some leverage with the Indian state. This ability to switch seamlessly between the political and the industrial realms thus helped stars like Kapoor and Anand to create business connections with the US and the former Soviet Union, respectively, thereby firmly entrenching the stars in the industrial history of Bollywood as prominent businessmen and catalysts of globalization. By reconstructing this era of Indian Hindi cinema's globalization, this chapter examines the praxis of this nodal star power, which only some stars get to possess, and illuminates how star switching power enabled Hindi cinema's particular temporal and geographic patterns of globalization during the formative decades after independence, from the late 1940s to the early 1980s.

THE GENESIS OF THE STAR'S NODAL POWER IN THE HINDI FILM INDUSTRY

The origin of the star's pre-eminent structural power in Indian Hindi cinema after independence lies in the demise of the studio system. A narrative of the star's structural power within the pre-existing nascent global industry and how the power changed after Indian independence in 1947 can be illustrated concurrently. The parallel narrative also helps illustrate how star power in the Hindi film industry operated differently at a structural level compared to that in Hollywood and other Western industries, where a conglomerate structure has been historically dominant.

Indian cinema's history is contemporaneous with Hollywood. The Lumière brothers introduced their Cinématographe at Watson's Hotel (present-day Esplanade Mansion) in Bombay (present-day Mumbai) in 1896.[4] The first film produced in India was *Raja Harishchandra* (King Harishchandra, dir. Dadasaheb Phalke), released in 1913.[5] During this early phase, under British rule, Hindi cinema's value chain was sufficiently global. The first Iranian sound film, *The Lor Girl* (1933, dir. Ardeshir Irani), was produced in India.[6] Some studios also engaged in collaborative partnerships with other European countries. Bombay Talkies, for instance, had a long-standing partnership with the German director Franz Osten and the film company Universum-Film Aktiengesellschaft (UFA). While the initial circulation of Indian films across the globe was limited, a 1932 British memorandum deemed films made in India suitable for distribution in the UK and Europe. After 1932, Indian films could, therefore, be distributed across these markets. The industry itself, in terms of collaborations and distribution, was sufficiently global. Indian films meant to be marketed across the empire easily circulated without restrictions and with relative ease between Australia, New Zealand, and Britain.[7] The Cinematograph Films Act (or Quota Act) of 1927, aimed at limiting the prevalence and influence of the American film industry, enabled the global circulation of Indian cinema. The quota initiative sought to inform 'colonial and dominion governments of the benefits of a porous, collaborative empire market'.[8] As a state-sanctioned industry during this colonial phase, Indian entities could avail themselves of similar legal and logistical opportunities as the British.

Following the Hollywood industry model, studios in India sought to cultivate stars and their alliance with the studios in similar ways.[9] The Hollywood star system, for instance, deployed economic practices that transformed the actor's labour into a commodity. The studios controlled star salaries and created an occupational hierarchy where stars with a personality and affinity for the camera received higher salaries than others, and the studios manufactured stars by carefully tailoring their image and marketing.[10] Modelling themselves on Western film industries, predominantly Hollywood, a studio system emerged in India with Indian studios wanting to integrate production, regularize their schedules, and build a marketing-friendly star system.[11] Although British imperial policy formally supported this industry structure, financing remained precarious. Most Indian industrial entities utilized their own resources, as there was dissent among the British about providing financial support to Indian producers.[12] The British resented supporting 'a luxury industry which without assistance [had] expanded rapidly and [was] earning good profits'.[13] This sentiment was fuelled partly by India's colonial status and the ongoing Indian independence movement. In addition, self-financing or financing outside of British imperial structures was seen by the Indian industry as a symbolic act of resistance against the empire.[14]

The early studios were set up as publicly listed companies and used market financing but usually were backed by independently wealthy businessmen. Bombay Talkies, for instance, was financially backed by Rajnarayan Dube, 'a young and dynamic businessman'.[15] The star as the studio owner was an anomaly during the pre-independence forties, with Bombay Talkies co-proprietor Devika Rani being a unique exception. Studios were prominent and dominated the industry, but by 1947 most studios had disintegrated. The breakdown of the studio system was predominately due to the arrival of independent producers in the early 1930s. J. Stenson, a supervisor for the Bombay Entertainment Duty Act, 1923, which provided for taxation of all entertainment and amusements, surmised from box-office receipts that Indian films, although fewer in number, were highly profitable, more so than imported films.[16] A glut of films created by independent producers led to several studios and production companies closing down.[17] Independent studios, new entrants in this nascent proto-network, hitched their market entry strategy to stars. These new entrants dismantled the studio system based on a 'shrewd calculation of the role of the star in the success of a film'.[18] The Indian domestic film market was now well established and difficult for foreign competitors to penetrate.[19]

Under the studio system, stars had reasonably moderate incomes, but star salaries emerged as the main point of contention as they were lured away from the studios by independent producers. This happened in conjunction with a nationalistic fervour that accompanied the moment of independence. In what was seen as a defiant, patriotic act against the British, the newcomer independents were backed by the 'surpluses of black marketeers', who hiked star salaries with unaccounted-for 'tax-free' money.[20] 'Black money' originated during wartime scarcity from the 'spoils of largescale profiteering [that] stayed outside the banks'.[21]

The newcomers claimed a spirit of independence from British structures as the reason formal studio systems should not exist. Many stars broke away from studios and now, with savings accumulated from their increased salaries, had the wherewithal to start their own independent productions. This created a formative industry structure based on post-colonial, antipodal logics, where the star became centrally situated in the industrial power dynamic that is dominant in Bollywood to this day. The other node that was similarly centrally situated in the reconfiguration of this nascent industry structure was, of course, the Indian state, but 'the Nehruvian state [was apathetic and] did not do for the film industry what it was committed to do for other industries'.[22] The most important aspect of the state's role in India's industrial dynamic was related to making financing and other policy support available, and the popular mainstream film industry was markedly left on the sidelines. Even as the state established a film-financing body, the Film Finance Corporation (FFC), almost a decade after independence, it generated a parallel state-sponsored art-house film-production network that benefitted only art-house film production. In this context of anticolonial struggle, increased star salaries, a growing audience, black market financing, and state indifference, the star emerged as an entrepreneur and prominent node in the Hindi film-production culture.

Star entrepreneurs existed as intermediaries between the state and the industry, where they marshalled their switching power in sociocultural and diplomatic contexts to create leverage with the state. We see the beginning of several star-led productions in this phase, including Raj Kapoor's R. K. Films, which went on to produce global hits like *Awāra*. The film not only marked the early global presence of Indian Hindi cinema but also created a unique diplomatic resonance that led Nehru to ask Kapoor to be a part of his cultural delegation to the Soviet Union during his first official visit. This post-independence phase also marks the shift in the nascent Bollywood network from a production-based industrial culture to an individual personality- or star-based film and industrial cluster. Furthermore, while the Indian state remained apathetic to the cause of Indian films, it continued to be a spectral influence on Indian cinema. What followed this historical inflection point was a mushrooming of independent, family-led film-production clusters, and some of the most globally prominent film-production entities that emerged were star-owned. The star businessperson has since dominated the industrial landscape of Hindi film and entertainment.

What was happening in India was distinctive and singular, although there have been a few comparable moments of stars asserting their industrial presence within early Hollywood. One parallel moment was Charlie Chaplin, Mary Pickford, and Douglas Fairbanks's founding of United Artists (UA) in 1919. The three stars joined forces with director D. W. Griffith and risked their own money to form a distribution company because they 'were constitutionally opposed to the studio system'.[23] Although UA found it difficult to sustain itself as an independent company amid other mighty corporate studios, this was an assertion of star agency in the business of films. Another moment when stars asserted their power as producers materialized when Hollywood majors were forced to divest following the Paramount decrees of 1948.[24] The decrees created a moment of flux for independent productions to emerge. Burt Lancaster, Kirk Douglas, and other stars, 'newly released from onerous studio contracts', asserted their power and creative control by starting their own production companies or demanding profit-sharing from studios.[25] The effort waned largely because the studio system was still dominant, and the new stars-turned-entrepreneurs were still dependent on the studios for financing and distribution. Eventually, the bureaucratic structure and 'aggressive deal-making' deterred the stars from continuing. Speaking of these entrepreneurial challenges and bureaucratic hurdles that quelled the creative entrepreneurial spirit, Billy Wilder remarked, '[W]e spend eighty percent of our time making deals and [only] twenty percent making pictures.'[26] Post-war Hollywood thus provided a moment of agency for stars like Lancaster and Wilder. Eventually, though, major studio agendas dominated, and the star's agency culminated into a 'dependent independence' in which financing and distribution were controlled predominantly by the studios.[27] There exists only a limited space for an assertion of industrial power in contemporary conglomerate

Hollywood, as Paul McDonald argues, where stars like Will Smith possess a similar dependent independence that is proportional to the capitalization of their star brand.[28] Thus, despite his global brand and star vehicle potential, Will Smith still needed Sony Pictures for his production venture Overbrook Entertainment to be successful.[29]

In contrast, post-colonial, political, and sociocultural logics that led to a vastly different industry configuration abruptly changed the narrative of star agency and power within the Hindi-film-industry business and its globalization. The stars operated relationally as intermediaries within Hindi cinema's industrial structure, and some—predominantly male—megastars possessed the centrality and power within this network to act as 'switches' that illuminated new pathways for the globalization of the Indian Hindi film and entertainment industry. No figure better illustrates this power than Raj Kapoor, whose intertwined personal biography, a cinematic oeuvre infused with socialist values, and charismatic star text in conjunction with his remarkable production company, R. K. Films, played an outsized role in determining key structural and geopolitical dimensions of Hindi cinema that were concretized following Indian independence and remain visible to this day.

NEHRU, RAJ KAPOOR, AND THE CURIOUS CASE OF POPULAR INDIAN FILMS IN THE SOVIET UNION

No one can deny the fascination of this strange Eurasian country of the hammer and sickle, where workers and peasants sit on the thrones of the mighty and upset the best-laid schemes of mice and men. For us, in India the fascination is even greater, and even our self-interest compels us to understand the vast forces which have upset the old order of things and brought a new world into existence.

—Jawaharlal Nehru[30]

Nehru, the first prime minister of independent India, very openly expressed his infatuation with the Soviets. Although India sought to maintain a neutral position and be non-aligned during the Cold War, Nehru's ideological fascination with socialism and the Soviet Union created a pull between the two countries, creating more significant avenues and possibilities for cultural flows. During an early exchange with Nehru, the US ambassador to India, Loy W. Henderson, concluded that Nehru was a 'non-communist rather than an anti-communist'.[31] For Americans, whose insistence on ideological binarism drove their Cold War foreign policy, India's fascination with the Soviet Union, in conjunction with US insistence on fostering close ties with Pakistan, would lead to suspicion and tension in Indo-US ties.

When cinema was becoming increasingly prominent in its diplomacy, the US invited an Indian film delegation to visit Hollywood in a gesture of cultural bonhomie. In 1952, the US State Department and major Hollywood film companies hosted the Indian motion picture industry leaders for a ten-day visit. The delegation included stars Raj Kapoor and Nargis,[32] among other producers, actors, technicians, and the chairman of the Indian Motion Picture Producers Association.[33] A highlight of the visit was a special preview of *Aan* (Pride, 1952, dir. Mehboob Khan), India's first Technicolor feature film. According to the news and trade press, which reported on the discussions, the visit was deemed a success. The American director Frank Capra, who hosted the delegation, said the visit 'will go a long way in cementing lasting goodwill between the two nations'.[34] This visit, Nitin Govil notes, was an attempt to 'stabilize the political indeterminacy of Indo-US strategic relations, [an instance of] American political science turned to culture'.[35] The Indian film trade magazines, like *Filmindia*, mocked this performative visit. Baburao Patel, the editor of *Filmindia*, remarked,

> [F]or sheer obtuseness of intelligence, it is difficult to beat the American mind. Because the Russians induced a group of half-a-dozen useless film people to go to Russia on a goodwill picnic some time ago, the obtuse Americans also took a crowd of a dozen and odd equally useless colts, crones, dugouts, gaffers, and greybeards on a honeymoon. But … why pull in the fair name of India … [which] as a nation has nothing to do with the odd assortment of funny-looking film people [see Figure 1.1].[36]

Patel's statement (with an obvious racist undertone) verbalizes the schism between the state and the film industry, highlighting the industry actors' eagerness to make these global connections, the nonchalance of the Indian state, and the covert political (not industrial but competitive) and ideological motives of the US in inviting the Indian delegation. Explicably, such state-initiated industrial encounters did not become common. The

credit in the film industry. He is a man who has bluffed his way through life without studying seriously any of our industrial problems or without being overfond of the art of motion picture production. Twenty years ago he opened a sausage factory called the Ranjit Movietone and produced cheap sausages merely for making money. And even the money he made once is not with him today. He has only Miss Gohar, his life-long partner in murdering motion picture art, left with him now. And she has also accompanied him to America and no one knows whether she is there as a stowaway, or as an onlooker or as a distinguished guest or as the woman who came to dinner. We know that on a previous occasion when Miss Gohar had flown from the Santa Cruz airport, she had gone as Chandulal's secretary to some conference in Geneva. Because we like Miss Gohar, let us hope that she at least has not accepted the shameful charity of the Americans like her tall-talking partner.

Chandulal Shah's free trip to the States is a disgrace to the Indian film industry. Rightly or wrongly, Chandulal is the President of the Indian Motion Picture Producers' Association and also the President of the Film Federation of India. As such his status, once again rightly or wrongly, is the same as that of his opposite number in America, Eric Johnston, the President of the Motion Picture Producers' Association of America.

Would Eric Johnston have accepted the charity and travelled as a free guest in India of the Indian Government? Even Frank Capra, one of the numerous Hollywood directors, when he recently visited India at the special invitation of the Government of India, himself paid for all his expenses including his taxi fare in New Delhi. He did not expect charity and India did not insult him by offering him charity.

But here is America with her flush of wealth and green culture selecting a crowd of mendicants and sending them on a free trip and in doing so insulting an ancient nation. And of all people, the President of the Indian film producers forgets his status and self-respect and accepts this charity. If that is not a disgrace to the whole industry, what else is?

Though we have nothing to do with this "phoney delegation" officially, we are almost sure that this odd group of half-educated actors, actresses, technicians and producers is going to provide a bad advertisement to our country. The very leader of this "delegation" does not know enough English to meet the Americans and speak to them on terms of intellectual equality. Economic airs are completely out of the question as these "delegates" are all travelling on the charity dole and Americans never forget this aspect of their hospitality when entertaining their hired "guests". They expect every "dole-boy" to play ball" and even Chandulal Shah—with his crazy, wandering mind—won't be allowed to talk nonsense even in his own "Inglis".

Though there was no earthly necessity of establishing any goodwill between the film industry of India and that of America—as there has never been any bad will between them—this phoney goodwill "delegation"—an offshoot of political rivalry between Russia and America

5

Figure 1.1 Caricature of the Indian film delegation that accompanied Baburao Patel's article in *Filmindia*

Source: Baburao Patel, 'A Burlesque Delegation', *Filmindia*, October 1952, 3 (digital archive of *Filmindia* at Jawaharlal Nehru University, New Delhi).

next state-initiated cinematic exchange, mentioned in the *Variety* archive, happened only in the 1980s when a film *utsav* (festival) was organized in the US in conjunction with the Festival of India in 1985. The *utsav* was part of a cultural programme initiated by Indian prime minister (and Nehru's daughter) Indira Gandhi and Ronald Reagan. The cinema retrospective featured several films by actor and director Raj Kapoor, Guru Dutt, and the Bengali art filmmaker Ritwik Ghatak, amongst others. This renewed interest in India amongst Americans, according to Victor Danilov (president of the Museum of Science and Industry, Chicago), was fuelled by several media-related and political factors, namely the popularity of the film *Gandhi* (1982, dir. Richard Attenborough), the television series *The Jewel in the Crown* (1984) alongside the Bhopal chemical disaster and the assassination of Indira Gandhi (in 1984).[37] The *utsav* reflected the Indian state's heavy investment in promoting state-supported parallel cinema, exemplified in films like *Gandhi*, that was co-created by the state-led National Film Development Corporation (NFDC). Interestingly, despite the state's pre-eminence and centrality in the festival dynamic, Raj Kapoor and his popular mainstream Hindi films remained the cynosure of the film *utsav*.

The festival opened at the Museum of Modern Art (MOMA) in New York with R. K. Films's global hits *Aag* (Fire, 1948, dir. Raj Kapoor) and *Awāra*. Raj Kapoor was invited to the event to introduce his films, which was followed by a retrospective tribute to his cinema. All notable films of his directorial career, from *Awāra* to *Mera Naam Joker* (My Name Is Joker, 1970) and *Satyam Shivam Sundaram* (Truth, Godliness, Beauty, 1978), were screened. Kapoor was the only mainstream director included in the festival (all the others were from state-sponsored parallel cinema networks). The prepotency of his presence and popularity was abundantly emphasized in MOMA's public relations (PR) document for the event:

> RK's singular and gargantuan talent subsumes a variety of influences and affinities—Chaplin, Frank Capra, Orson Welles—with even a touch of Russ Meyer apparent in the later work. At times, his oeuvre recalls the work of a 19th century European literary giant whose sympathy for the underdog, protean activity, inexhaustible energy, and penchant for excess earned him fame and a national reputation as early in life as Kapoor. Yes, Raj Kapoor is—to a degree—the Victor Hugo of Indian cinema.[38]

The piece further noted Kapoor's popularity in other parts of the world, especially in the Soviet Union. This PR accompaniment to a retrospective, set decades after the film's original 1951 release, reveals the industrial and political schism between Indo-US political and industrial ties and the reception of popular Indian film culture that reflected and refracted a complex Nehruvian socialist macrocosm. Moreover, for this very reason, it throws into sharp relief the quality and quantity of Kapoor's star switching power, which simultaneously bridged oppositional superpowers, state and non-state arenas of culture, and three decades of Cold War–era development. To better understand this switching power, it is imperative to first understand the underlying Hindi film industry out of which Kapoor emerged; this includes understanding its structural dimensions as well as its social and ideological ones, which oriented its globalizing trajectory first toward the Soviet Union.

THE INDUSTRY STRUCTURE: DEFINING FAMILY-LED FILM CLUSTERS

Family film clusters led by prominent stars or directors emerged in this post-independence moment. As mentioned earlier, the breakdown of the studio system because of hikes in star salaries instigated by newcomer independent producers situated the stars as critical players in the Hindi film industry's business dynamic. Family-led film clusters characterized this early network structure of the Bollywood industry. Several major stars and directors dominated these clusters by bringing together their team of collaborators, often family members, friends, or past acquaintances who worked on their films. Most leading male actors (plus some female actors) ventured into film production soon after the demise of the studio system. The three stars part of the Russian bonhomie—Raj Kapoor, Dev Anand, and Dilip Kumar—were proprietors of their independent film-production entities. Anand started Navketan Films in 1949, Kumar launched Citizens Films in 1956, and Kapoor founded R. K. Films in 1948.

The first film produced by Raj Kapoor's R. K. Films was *Aag*. The film's release in August 1948 was timed to coincide with the anniversary of Indian independence. As noted in the Introduction, the formation of these film-production clusters helmed by stars-turned-producers was in consonance with the spirit of independence touted by the newcomer independent producers—the instigators for the breakdown of the studio system. Expectedly, the pre-release announcement for Kapoor's first home-grown production symbolically proclaimed and affirmed the spirit of independence. The film's classified advertisement in the *Times of India* noted that as the 'nation celebrates the anniversary of its freedom, the [film] artist desires freedom from convention that only free India can provide'.[39]

This message was reflected in the films themselves. Raj Kapoor's *Aag* was a stylized black-and-white feature that narrated the tale of an upper-class young man who breaks away from his traditional family to thrive as an artist and build a career in theatre. The hero's quest blended the trio of romance, beauty, and truth. The parable symbolically presented the 'story of youth' that paralleled the young Indian nation. Kapoor's narrative envisaged this as the story of every youth wherein the protagonist asserts that 'creating your own destiny isn't easy', exhorting young India—both the newfound nation and its youth—to sit up and take notice. Even though *Aag* was only moderately successful, it established a few aspects of Kapoor's family film-production cluster that exemplified and helped create a new kind of dominant industry structure and Kapoor's oeuvre in general.

Social ties and personal networks were paramount in forming this early network structure after the demolition of the studio system. Important to underscore here is that Raj Kapoor's father, Prithviraj Kapoor, was a crucial node within the nascent Hindi film industry. Prithviraj played the lead in *Alam Ara* (Ornament of the World, 1929, dir. Ardeshir Irani), the first Indian movie with sound. He worked for the Imperial Film Company during the studio era and formed his own theatre, Prithvi, a few years before independence, where Raj Kapoor honed his acting skills to become a part of the industry business. Bunny Reuben, a career publicist for leading production houses in the Indian Hindi film industry, in his biography of Raj Kapoor, narrates Kapoor's early career as follows: Kapoor exhorted his father, Prithviraj, that he wanted to be an actor, director, and producer, and Prithviraj reacted favourably to his son's request: 'The following morning, Prithviraj took his eldest son to Sardar Chandulal Shah. "My son wants to learn direction …". It was all fixed up, and Raj Kapoor joined Ranjit Studios [also known as Ranjit Movietone] as the third assistant to Kidar Sharma.[40]

Beyond Rani's Bombay Talkies, Ranjit Movietone was another well-distinguished studio where Raj Kapoor received his training. Both opportunities, according to Reuben, were created because of close personal ties. Kapoor's training and early career is a narrative about close social and personal ties that existed for Kapoor because of his father. As an industry insider, he could apprentice and learn at the top studios. He also benefitted from his father's theatre, Prithvi, which provided an avenue for honing Kapoor's performance, creating and deepening other industry connections. Reuben's book, alongside another biography of Kapoor written by his daughter Ritu Nanda, are key revelators in discerning Kapoor's social world and his entrepreneurship that becomes emblematic of the emerging network structure of these post-independence family-led film-production clusters.

Starting with his first film, *Aag*, Raj Kapoor built a team of collaborators and actors from within the industry based on close personal and familial ties. For example, his close friend, Khwaja Ahmad Abbas, an Indian People's Theatre Association (IPTA) member with Marxist leanings, wrote the screenplay for most of his films, including *Awāra*. In addition, his then girlfriend, Nargis, starred opposite Kapoor in most of R. K. Films productions, and all other vital roles were played by family members (see Figure 1.2).

In a diary entry, Raj Kapoor recognizes the small-world nature of these close collaborations and why they led to positive outcomes in realizing a collective creative vision: 'Among those nearest to me may be counted my co-workers Nargis and Khwaja Ahmad Abbas. Both, in their own way, have taught me to speak with the voice of all rather than with my own voice.'[41] *Awāra* epitomized a typical family-led film cluster wherein film production was defined through close personal ties. Kapoor's father played his on-screen

Raj Kapoor's then girlfriend, Nargis, played the role of his love interest.

Raj Kapoor's friend, Khwaja Ahmad Abbas, wrote the screenplay for the film.

Raj Kapoor's father, Prithviraj Kapoor, played the role of his on-screen father.

Raj Kapoor's younger brother, Shashi Kapoor, played the role of his younger self.

Raj Kapoor himself directed, produced, and played the main lead in the 1951 global hit *Awāra*. The film was created under the banner of Kapoor's production studio, R. K. Films, founded in 1948.

Figure 1.2 R. K. Films: a family-led film-production cluster

Source: Prepared by the author.

father, his brother enacted Kapoor's younger self, and his romantic partner, Nargis, played his love interest in the film. The screenplay was written by Abbas, the music was composed by his friends Shankar and Jaikishen, and the film was picturized by Radhu Karmakar, Kapoor's permanent collaborator. He remained the cinematographer on all of Kapoor's projects for over four decades.

It is essential to reflect on what this kind of family- and close-ties-driven structure, which flourished for so long and exists in an abridged form even in the contemporary context, helped accomplish from a business and creative perspective. Varied literature on close ties from a sociological and business perspective has noted the value of such small-world networks because they are built around group cohesion and trust. This type of business structure also helps with motivation, reduces conflicts, and enhances the possibility of thriving in the business environment.[42] The 1980s MOMA retrospective on Kapoor notes these aspects in his oeuvre as a filmmaker, director, and producer:

> RK chose his collaborators wisely. His studio became a quality talent pool, a stock company that worked with him on film after film: cinematographer Radhu Karmakar; Mukesh, Kapoor's playback singing voice for most of the films; art director M.R. Achrekar; composers Shankar and Jaikishen; the left-wing poet Shailendra, lyricist of *Awāra*'s songs. The stunning Nargis was RK's principal leading lady for nearly a decade—on and off screen. They co-starred in 17 movies and became the Garbo-Gilbert couple of Indian 50s cinema.[43]

As R. K. Films got further established in the industry, Raj Kapoor, in order to diversify production, encouraged his assistants to become full-fledged directors under his banner. Several of his co-collaborators came from his close circle because his family, through his father, Prithviraj Kapoor, had been central to the film industry since its inception. Prithviraj was a prominent theatre personality when Indian cinema emerged from the established theatrical business and traditions. Kapoor's effective switching power, which lent him the ability to exceed the established industry networks and create new connections, was primarily derived from his direct power as a member of the industry's first family, a notion that the success of Kapoor's R. K. Films helped solidify. This kind of deeply interconnected small-world network led to the clustering and dominance of this structural form. Consequently, family-led film-production clusters helmed by prominent stars and directors remained dominant within the industry for several decades. Using *Awāra* again as an anchoring case study, let us look at Kapoor's film oeuvre to define the affective aspect of his switching power that, in conjunction with his direct effective power, helped establish him as a global star.

AWĀRA: THE TOUCHSTONE FOR KAPOOR'S IDEOLOGICAL SWITCHING POWER

Awāra came at a time when films were of a totally different nature. We still had remnants of British imperial dominance, and we wanted a new social order. I tried to create a balance between entertainment and what I had to say to the people. *Awāra* had everything. It had the theme of class distinction. It had the greatest juvenile romantic story wrapped in poverty that the post-independence era had inherited…. Could this ever happen to a young man in such circumstances? With a song on his lips and a flower he went through all the ordeals that socio-economic disruptions could bring about. The change that the people wanted, they saw in the spirit of the young man who was the vagabond, the *Awāra*.

—Raj Kapoor[44]

As Raj Kapoor notes in this reflection, the film *Awāra* carried ideological heft, which not only became a primary reason for its popularity within and outside of India, but also lent credence to the popular Hindi film industry to present its demands to a nonchalant state. Additionally, it helped establish R. K. Films's centrality in the post-independence industry structure and concretize Kapoor's affective ideological switching power that stemmed from the ideological tenor of his film narratives.

Awāra tells the story of a mother and child abandoned by a self-righteous father. Thus, despite being born into a privileged family, the son is raised in the slums and is tempted into the world of petty crime. Raj Kapoor's character grows to be a vagabond and petty thief mired in the illicit world of the city and eventually gets accused of attempted murder. The film evokes the nature-versus-nurture debate and foregrounds how social institutions fail individuals. Kapoor's character of the vagabond stages a fictive heroism and expresses a nihilistic optimism in life itself as he skips along singing, 'Awaara hoon, ya gardish main hoon aasmaan ka taara hoon [I am a vagabond, I am going through adversity, but I am a star from the sky].' The hero is naïve, but the city teaches him harsh lessons. The hierarchical, callous society is equally implicated in the vagabond's loss of innocence. Wearing too-short trousers, an ill-fitting jacket, and a goofy hat, Kapoor tried to embody a global Chaplinesque street urchin. The persona of the uprooted and declassed criminal came to define Kapoor's affective pull. This vagabond character helped him build his oeuvre through future directorial projects, *Shri 420* (1955) and *Chhaliya* (Cheater, 1960), amongst others, wherein his cinema interrogated social hierarchies and boundaries of birth and legitimacy. Kapoor's vagabond persona is tied to the architecture of his film narratives that follow, his affective star appeal, and the resultant switching power.

There was a socialist zeitgeist embedded in *Awāra* that resonated in the Indian domestic context, with Nehru envisioning India as a socialist, democratic republic. It also found concurrent resonance in communist- and socialist-leaning geographies outside of India as well as in other regions in the Global South. Dina Iordanova's historiography of this cinematic exchange between India and the non-anglophone world points to the enthusiastic reception of *Awāra* from the bazaars of the Arab world and Africa to the remote towns and cities of the Soviet Union and Eastern Europe.[45] The circulation of *Awāra* was most prominent in and around the Soviet Union and other socialist and communist national contexts. For instance, the film's warm reception among the Soviets prompted the Indian state to send the film along during Vijaya Lakshmi Pandit's (Indian diplomat and Nehru's sister) goodwill mission to China, where it also acquired an iconic status.[46] There are similar trajectories of the cinematic flow of *Awāra* to Eastern Europe that were filtered through the warm Russian reception. Besides, the Soviet Union turned out to be the market where Raj Kapoor's cinema and, to some extent, Hindi cinema at large had a sustained formal engagement that lasted well into the 1990s.

As mentioned earlier, the socialist narrative of *Awāra* lent Raj Kapoor's star persona ideological weight. Despite the general negligence towards popular Hindi cinema, Kapoor and his films were considered differently by the Indian state. His affective *ideological* star persona was cemented over time, wherein Kapoor's image of the marginalized everyman got lionized. His ideological switching power stemmed from the on-screen embodiment of the vagabond that society and its institutions should care about, given the socialist thrust of the newly independent Nehruvian state, yet the vagabond is forsaken and ostracized. By recreating the character in several subsequent films—*Shri 420, Chhaliya,* and his last pièce de resistance, *Mera Naam Joker*— the trope of the vagrant and the incisive societal commentary encapsulated within that trope came to define his affective star persona and ideological switching power. In his analysis of the sociological imagination of the Indian public, Ravi Vasudevan notes that the complex intersection of Kapoor's on-screen characters that flout the law but are loveable reveal fissures in the emerging nation state. This sociological imagination lent Kapoor's affective persona a peculiar redemptive quality and a sociological transcendence.[47] This transcendence, Vasudevan notes, impacts memory, mobilizes popular discourse, and widely impacts the political realm. These arguments help circumstantiate and solidify my claim that a star's switching power, a coalescence of their affective and effective position in sociocultural, political, and industrial networks, helps them exceed those networks. It is precisely this ability to transcend the limitations of their immediate networks that stars like Kapoor possessed that enabled them to create new globalization pathways and connections for their individual business and production ventures and, consequently, for the industry at large. This star switching power functioned both within and outside the realm of the nation state and for the domestic and the global public.

The ability to switch and create new connections, as Raj Kapoor did for the Soviet Union, is understandably not simply created by the affective transcendence of on-screen personas. It is created by the culmination of the affective switching power with a direct sociocultural power, which is a Bourdieuan cultural power determined by one's class, caste, gender, and politics, amongst other aspects that add to such power. As mentioned earlier, Kapoor possessed a distinct primacy and centrality in industry networks because his father, Prithviraj Kapoor, was a pioneering figure in the Hindi film and entertainment industry. As the industry materialized via Indian theatre, which formed its backbone, Prithviraj, a thespian, was a part of this early change.[48] He thus became a pioneering figure in the discourse of Indian cinema and, due to his political activism, in Hindi cinema's interconnections with Indian politics as well. Prithviraj was a strong supporter of Nehru and the Indian National Congress and was the first star-turned-politician appointed by Nehru in 1955 to the Rajya Sabha, the upper house of the Indian parliament. Prithviraj famously submitted a proposal in the parliament to abolish capital punishment, citing that a newly independent India, 'with her traditions and ideals, was eminently suited to give a lead to the world' and should set an example.[49] In another instance, while debating the Hindu succession bill, he argued that illegitimate children should not be made to suffer for the 'crimes' of their parents but deserve the 'deepest sympathy'.[50] His stance in the parliament resonates with the ideological values embedded in his son's film *Awāra*, an enterprise wherein Prithviraj played the role of the vagabond's elite father who abandons his family. It is critical to point to this sociocultural–political absorption and intermeshing of on-screen and off-screen ideologies and personas that curiously bleed into each other, lending stars like Raj Kapoor their switching power. In a similar curious blending of the affective and effective, Nehru, having heard of *Awāra*'s success in the Soviet Union from Russian prime minister Nikolai Bulganin, mentioned it to Prithviraj, which led to a Bollywood delegation accompanying Nehru on his formal visit to the Soviet Union.

The ideological power wielded by Raj Kapoor, therefore, is twofold. One facet of it is Bourdieuan in that Kapoor was part of an elite artistic class and family that had a direct and close connection to the country's highest political leadership.[51] The second aspect that lent Kapoor's power more structural and ideological weight in the temporal space of a newly independent India was R. K. Films's close connection to the IPTA. The IPTA was a travelling troupe engaged in raising people's morale in the context of Gandhi's Quit India Movement, the Second World War, and the ensuing Bengal famine. This theatre movement had a Marxist communist leaning, and Prithviraj Kapoor, Raj Kapoor, and the latter's close friend and collaborator, Abbas, were all part of this movement. The ideological weight of this organization and the way Kapoor's early films mirrored the social concerns of a newly independent India foregrounded by the IPTA situated him differently. Thus, although he was part of the popular cinema that Nehru and Gandhi derided, Raj Kapoor's films and his film company could be an exception. It is also essential to foreground that a chasm between the mainstream film industry and the state still existed. Devika Rani, the proprietor of the Bombay Talkies studio, an exceptional female star with switching power, was on the verge of retirement and wanted the existing mainstream film production to function with due state support. She used her social and political clout to help organize a film seminar on 27 February 1955 to voice the industry's concerns and grievances that the state could address.[52] Rani was the executive director of this event, and Kapoor's father, Prithviraj, was appointed the director. Nehru's daughter and future prime minister, Indira Gandhi, was part of the social and organization committee. Moreover, curiously enough, the event also included a Chinese observer delegation. An article in the *Times of India* about the seminar rhetorically noted that

> after forty years of existence and for a long time claiming to rank second only to Hollywood in output, why has the Indian film industry failed to make its mark on the international screen. Japan, which lagged far behind in the thirties, has today not only ousted India from its second place but is producing pictures that rival the best from America, Britain, or Italy. This should provide food for thought not only for those engaged in the film industry but to the state, whose concern it should be to promote and foster an industry so vital to the progress and cultural advancement of the nation.[53]

The six-day seminar focused on a broad range of industry concerns, from censorship and heavy state taxation to developing more cinemas across the country. According to Rani, this was the first time that people 'who have grown up with the industry and been through its ups and downs will get this fine opportunity to meet on a neutral platform to discuss their problems'.[54] Despite the effort and fanfare surrounding the event, few tangible solutions emerged for the mainstream industry's problems. The state, however, realized the critical import of films (albeit of the right kind) and their possible impact on education and cultural diplomacy. This event set things in motion for Nehru's FFC, instituted in 1960. The setting up of the FFC created a parallel network of state-sponsored cinema that towed the state line about cinema being a tool for art and education. The mainstream Hindi film industry was visibly absent from this network, with a few exceptions like Raj Kapoor. Indeed, it is Kapoor's exceptionality in this respect that illustrates the mechanisms of star switching power and its transformative impact.

ROMANCING THE SOVIET UNION

Raj Kapoor's obituary in the *New York Times* proclaimed that the Russians had 'three Indian Heroes: Jawaharlal Nehru, Indira Gandhi and Raj Kapoor … probably in the reverse order'.[55] Kapoor's *Awāra* was first released in the Soviet Union on 23 September 1954. In the context of the cultural thaw initiated by Nikita Khrushchev during the Cold War, wherein the Soviets were trying to influence newly independent nations like India, Sovexportfilm, the state body representing the Soviet audiovisual content industry, opened its offices in India. In July 1953, N. P. Koulebiakin took charge of the Mumbai office and selected ten films, including Kapoor's *Awāra* and *Rahi* (starring Dev Anand and produced by Abbas), to be screened in the Soviet Union.[56] *Awāra* met with unprecedented success and sold 63.7 million tickets.[57] Hearing about Kapoor's growing fame, Nehru invited him on his first diplomatic visit to the Soviet Union. Concurrently, *Rahi* also impressed the Soviets. Nehru's delegation to Moscow included three Bollywood actors—Raj Kapoor, Dev Anand, and Dilip Kumar—whose movies had been screened in the Soviet Union during the Sovexportfilm-initiated exchange.

The tenor of the Soviet visit was entirely different compared to the visit to the US a year later. People were already familiar with these Hindi film stars, and the response to the repeat screenings of their films was euphoric. Herein, Raj Kapoor struck a special chord with the Soviet audiences. According to the journalist Oxana Naralenkova,

> [Raj Kapoor] left the Soviet people literally besotted. Kapoor's shiny ZIS (the grand-style Soviet automobile meant to ferry the actor back to his hotel), which was parked outside the Udarnik movie theatre, never left the curb. The crowd simply picked the car up (with Kapoor in it) and carried it off.[58]

The ebullient reception of Kapoor and his films advantageously supplemented Nehru's fascination with the Soviets and influenced the future tenor for India's non-alignment in the Cold War. The inclusion of stars was an aberration from the Indian government's typical diplomatic cultural exchange. The Indian Council of Cultural Relations (ICCR), set up by the state in 1950 and housed in the Ministry of Education, primarily preferred the idiom of classical dance and music as 'high culture'. Cultural cooperation was the leitmotif of Nehru's non-alignment, and the ICCR was critical to that vision. However, the ICCR, to this day, tends to emphasize only performing artists, dancers, and musicians.[59] The inclusion of the three film actors, Kapoor, Anand, and Kumar, was primarily due to the unexpected popularity of Kapoor's *Awāra*. *Awāra* and Kapoor, therefore, possess an epistemic centrality in understanding the Hindi film industry's exchange with the Soviet Union and other secondary markets in Eastern Europe and Turkey. Moreover, *Awāra*, and R. K. Films itself, also exemplify the typical family-led film-production cluster helmed by popular stars or directors that characterized the industry at this time and would continue to dominate in the decades to come.

PARALLEL NETWORKS OF EXCHANGE IN THE SOVIET UNION

Post-independence India was one of the critical backdrops against which the 'cultural cold war' was fought primarily because of Nehru's commitment to non-alignment. However, the cultural and political investment of the Soviet Union was more visible and of greater strategic significance to India. The literary–cultural exchange focused on varied aspects of Soviet life, including Soviet literature (*Sovetskaia literatura*) and magazines such as the *Sovetskaia Zhenshchina* (Soviet Woman) that appeared (from 1957) in Hindi and twelve other Indian languages. Gautam Chakrabarti points to the centrality of the left-leaning Marxist IPTA movement—of which Kapoor, his father Prithviraj, and close friend Abbas were all a part—in initiating an early film exchange with Moscow. Chakrabarti points out that these early individual figures operated independently and organized a local chapter of the Friends of the Soviet Union in 1948, where they discussed how 'the USSR valued and supported cultural workers'.[60]

The Soviets' concerted effort in the 1950s to initiate a cinematic cultural exchange with India was primarily aimed at acquiring popular mainstream films; the Nehruvian state, however, held a cautious, sceptical view about the moral and political value of this kind of media. Mosfilm, a mammoth studio that dominated Soviet film-making before perestroika in 1991, led the industrial charge in this exchange. Mosfilm's *Kamennyĭ Tsvetok* (The Stone Flower, 1946, dir. Alexander Ptushko) was the first Soviet full-length colour feature film screened for an Indian audience in 1948, although the acting in the film, a *Times of India* critic noted, was 'perhaps a little stiff by our standards'.[61] To make the Soviet cultural presence known and acceptable, Koulebiakin, the representative of Sovexportfilm in India, wrote an open letter to the *Times of India* explaining his organization's purpose. The object of Sovexportfilm, Koulebiakin noted, was to acquire 'outstanding feature films produced in India ... to strengthen the bond of friendship between the two great countries' so that the Russian people 'may correctly assess the glory of the culture and philosophy of India'. He also insisted that whether the state requires it or not, 'it is our desire that the Indian Government should finally guide us and help us in the selection of films to be exported to the Soviet Union'.[62] Paul McGarr points to the underlying tension between Sovexportfilm and the Indian state over the selection of films.[63] His findings about mainstream popular cinema, primarily *Rahi*, point to a simmering tension. The Nehruvian state, invested in modernizing India, wanted to control the narrative of mainstream cinema, which was not necessarily driven by the same values propounded by the state. Although the mainstream film industry was seemingly invested in nation-building, the mainstream films imported to communist countries, according to the state officials, were conveying '[the] most degrading and undesirable impression of the country and its people'.[64] This impression of the mainstream Hindi film industry by the Indian state was detrimental to the global dissemination of popular Indian cinema and the growth of the industry at large. The Soviet Union, with its open offer for cinematic exchange, became an interesting case that, on the one hand, established the state's apathetic attitude towards the film industry and, on the other hand, also foregrounded how individuals with switching power could navigate these power structures to accomplish goals for their individual organizations.

As noted earlier, the Kapoor family had a close relationship with Devika Rani, a studio owner, part of the crème de la crème of Indian society, and perhaps the only female star in this era with switching power. As a result, the film fraternity, predominantly through Rani's efforts, was able to organize the 1955 film seminar. The *Times of India* noted the novelty of such an event wherein film personalities from all over the country were provided with a 'cultural platform' to discuss '"on an academic level" their art, their ideals, and the problems of the film industry and its future'.[65] The organization of the seminar was entrusted to Devika Rani and Prithviraj Kapoor. The event was inaugurated by Nehru, with most of the film industry, including leading producers, directors, technicians, actors, writers, distributors, and exhibitors, in attendance. While these stakeholders hoped to make the state realize the needs of the industry and recognize it as such, the term 'academic' became the operative keyword of this interaction. Sure, the state realized that films were essential and set up a parallel film-finance corporation to promote the kind of cinematic narratives the Nehruvian state wanted to invest in. However, none of the financial or policy benefits trickled down to the mainstream popular film industry. Creating an international distribution stream for films created by Bollywood's family film clusters fell on individual networks and stars with switching power. Thus, the Kapoor family, specifically Raj Kapoor and R. K. Films, remained among the few standalone examples whose films were consistently exported to the Soviet Union. Raj Kapoor's close friend and screenwriting collaborator, Abbas, a staunch Marxist, also remained a crucial figure in this dynamic, and his ideological understanding of the Soviets helped Kapoor.

The film *Pardesi* (Foreigner, 1957, dir. Khwaja Ahmad Abbas and Vasili Pronin; Russian: *Khozhdenie za tri moria*, or Journey beyond the Three Seas), the first Indo-Soviet collaborative production, was initiated through the mainstream Hindi film networks. Based on the life of Afanasy Nikitin, a Russian trader who visited India in the fifteenth century, the film starred Nargis, Raj Kapoor's co-star in *Awāra*, as the main lead, and Prithviraj Kapoor played the grand vizier Mahmud Gawan. Again, interconnected small-world, independent family- or friend-led production clusters were at play, and this film was co-produced by Mosfilm in collaboration with Abbas's Naya Sansar Productions. Abbas, a successful director, and screenwriter, possessed direct industrial and political power and thus led the first collaboration. What was distinctive about Raj Kapoor's star switching power then, if Abbas, too, could initiate a co-production? Kapoor's switching power was different because of its affective dimension that could exceed networks and continue collaborative co-production even in the wake of waning state interest. As Abbas himself recounts in *Sovetskaia Kul'tura* (Soviet Culture), a weekly Soviet newspaper,

> In Autumn 1954, Soviet viewers became acquainted with the young Indian—a tramp, a person, a funny character, who sang 'Awāra hun' (I am a tramp). Since then, numerous friends and fans of the artist's talent who played the role of this tramp lovingly called him 'Ivan Kapoor.' 'Ivan Kapoor' immediately became popular here. He was known in Moscow and Vladivostok, in the Arctic ices, where pilots drop iron boxes with the film about the tramp on the drifting polar stations, in the ancient Bukhara, where Uzbek boys sang the songs from 'Бродяга' (*Awāra*) in Hindi.... I remember how one time, during one of his trips to Georgia, a crowd of people besieged a hotel. People wanted to see their favorite 'tramp.' Soviet people became in love with the artist from the heart, and Raj Kapoor, from his side, responded to these feelings with full reciprocity. One time he told me: 'A strange thing happened to me: I fell in love with the entire nation.'[66]

Abbas understood Raj Kapoor's unique affective pull for the Soviet audience and, through his journalistic writing in India and the Soviet Union, helped further cement Kapoor's ability to exceed the constraints of the mainstream industry. An archival search into the Indo-Soviet cinematic exchange at the Russian State Archive of Literature and Art (RSALA) in Moscow reveals that after the successful production of *Pardesi*, several mainstream independent filmmakers from India were keen on collaborating with the Soviets and assumed it to be an easy exchange. The reality, however, was quite different. The Soviet responses to the outreach efforts for collaborative productions were tied to a precise idea of value to the Soviets—for instance, one response letter from I. Rachuk, the deputy head of administration for film productions in the Soviet Ministry of Culture, noted, '[W]hile making films within cooperative productions, we follow the principle that a script should depict life and connections of both nations or sides. In your scenario, which is actually built on one Indian actor, we do not see a need for the Soviet side's participation'.[67] Another proposal by Utpal Dutt, a filmmaker supported by the Indian state's parallel cinema network, was met with a similar response. The Soviet rejection letter agreed that their proposed film would be 'amusing for the Indian youth, but the participation of Russian children [in the project] seems to us to be very fanciful and conditional'.[68] While these are a few representative examples, the RSALA in Moscow has archived multiple similarly worded rejection letters. Given this context, Kapoor and his collaborative venture with Mosfilm, *Mera Naam Joker*, was a notable exception. It was Kapoor's labour of love and was many years in the making.

It is crucial to note that switching power cannot be possessed by just any node in the network, and the star switching power of megastars like Raj Kapoor manifests only when the effective and the affective coalesce meaningfully. So, despite Abbas's talent and ideological affiliations, he lacked the affective pull and charisma that a node like Kapoor had. Similarly, Nargis's treatment and positioning within this network reveal how deeply gendered star switching power is.

Nargis was the star of the first Indo-Soviet co-production, *Pardesi*. She was also Raj Kapoor's girlfriend and an unacknowledged creative collaborator and investor in R. K. Films; she harboured similar ambitions as Kapoor. However, in contrast to Kapoor, she was treated very differently by the Soviets. An internal letter written by the Ministry of Culture to V. T. Stepanov reveals that, during her visit to the Soviet Union in the context of *Pardesi*, Indian guests were neglected by Mosfilm and Galvka. The letter regretfully stated,

> Being in Moscow, [the] famous Indian actress Nargis let us know about her wish to meet the head of Soviet cinematography. The film director, Comrade Harlamov, informed Comrade Surin and Fedorov about her wish; however, Nargis was not hosted by anyone, and she returned to her motherland. Moreover, her colleague from film production, Strizhenov, did not even walk her to the airport because her plane departure was too early.[69]

This instance also reflects a more significant gendered bias that prevented female stars, despite their affective appeal, from possessing similar switching power to that of stars like Kapoor. This masculinist gendered habitus defined what Indian cinema's female stars could accomplish for the industry both within and outside the country.

For instance, the nascent industry in this early networked phase, which began in the 1940s, was dominated by structural and social imbalances created by class, caste, and religious differences that were deeply exacerbated by gender. With the unique exception of Rani, who was exceptionally elite—being the granddaughter of Nobel laureate Rabindranath Tagore, the daughter of the surgeon general of India, educated in London, and the proprietor of a studio—other women stars during this phase, such as Durga Khote (a high-class Brahmin) and Nargis (a Muslim from the film fraternity), who made similar attempts to produce films, got starkly different outcomes. A comparative look at Rani's, Khote's, and Nargis's careers reveals how religion, caste, and class also starkly shaped this gendered habitus. Rani and Khote were both upper-class Brahmin women. In contrast, Nargis hailed from a chequered background, and Khote, too, fell into financial difficulties in later life that impacted her class status. The parallel story of these three female stars helps situate how gender inflected by multiple sociocultural and economic vectors led to the female stars' inability to be a 'switch' and move outside of the network's parameters to create new directions despite their affective pull and other similarities with male stars.

Like Rani, Khote belonged to an upper-class family. Her family was not exceptionally elite, but Khote's parents were wealthy and highly educated. Her father was an attorney. Similarly, her mother was educated at an elite English-medium school and committed to the Indian freedom movement.

Khote herself attended Mumbai's prestigious St Cathedral School. However, unlike Rani, Khote's privilege quickly dwindled as the Khote family lost their fortune in the stock market. Her husband's early demise, followed by her father, made Khote's acting career the primary means of sustenance for her sons and maternal family. Her sister's acquaintance got Khote her first cameo in a Bollywood film, *Farebi Jaal* (1931, dir. Mohan Dayaram Bhavnani). In her autobiography, Khote describes the chicanery and unscrupulousness she experienced:

> Nobody in my family knew what film acting meant.... Farebi Jaal means 'Web of Deceit.' When the film was released, I found myself trapped in the web.... Mr. Bhavnani, shrewd businessman that he was, took full advantage of my name: that is the name of both my families. Newspapers carried huge advertisements headlined, 'Introducing the daughter of the famous solicitor Mr. Laud and the daughter-in-law of the famous Khote family.' ... the film turned out to be the very dregs.[70]

Khote's account makes some critical aspects of her work apparent. First, as a high-caste woman from a renowned family, her foray into filmdom was entrenched in immaterial labour—'the cultural content of the commodity'— that helped redefine public opinion about women's respectability in films.[71] Second, as a widowed mother, she undertook enormous 'affective labor' in moving beyond acting to producing films, documentaries, and television programmes. Michael Hardt elucidates affective labour as caring labour immersed in the corporeal and somatic but with an immaterial affect.[72] This affective labour produces social networks and forms of community. Yet Khote constantly struggled to balance her precarious position as a high-caste and upper-class woman working in cinema and as an entrepreneurial producer by constantly performing the emotional labour of keeping her familial and high-caste social relations under control and continuing in her chosen profession. Khote, too, made a career in films more accessible and acceptable to upper- and middle-class women and was a pioneer in the film industry. Nevertheless, her reasons for joining films were not based on her ability to exceed the limits of her network and do something novel. Khote was driven to the film industry because of her family's deteriorating financial circumstances. Her experience, therefore, was not about power but need. Being a star relegated to supporting character roles in mainstream Hindi cinema, Khote lacked the significant affective component and aesthetic capital or star switching power that a star like Rani possessed in abundance. Khote, hailing from an upper-class, high-caste background, possessed social capital. However, films (the structured context within which she had to operate) were constituted by deep-seated gendered hierarchies, and her family's dwindling fortune diminished her social capital. The core of her experience within the industry allowed her to make some choices, such as starting her own production company, Fact Films. It was, however, constrained predominantly by gendered perceptions and social and familial hierarchies. Her social and industrial macrocosm remained mired in affective and immaterial labour.

Khote's narrative thus veers between effective network power and material affective labour. To overcome a network's limits and create new directions for the industry, a star must possess switching power whose effective and affective dimensions work in tandem. Nargis, too, was similarly burdened with providing for her maternal family. Unlike Rani and Khote, Nargis had a chequered family history. She belonged to a Muslim family and was the daughter of a courtesan, Jaddan Bai, who had the unique distinction of being Hindi cinema's first female music director. Nargis started her acting career at age five, and unlike Khote, she possessed superlative beauty and was an industry insider. Her switching power, albeit to a lesser degree, was derived from her affective, value-driven star persona created through films like the Oscar-nominated *Mother India* (1957, dir. Mehboob Khan). Nargis's circumstances interacted with her habitus in ways that prevented her from moving outside the constraints of her network. She did not possess class-, caste-, or religion-based centrality, which constrained her ability to engage in her production work because of rigid patriarchal structures within and outside the home. Doing something new within a rigid habitus, Pierre Bourdieu points out, is a 'habitus divided against itself', a constant negotiation with itself and its ambivalences'.[73] Despite being a famous star, Nargis's invisible production efforts speak to a similar dynamic of duality where she is subject to ambivalence and negotiation. She never overtly assumed an assertive role in her production efforts because both her attempts were dominated by the male figures in her life, her brother Akhtar Hussain and her lover Raj Kapoor. The experience of these female stars in the early post-independence Bollywood network shows the varied intersections between women's material labour and affective labour that 'involves the production and manipulation of affects'.[74] This affective labour is needed to create and maintain relationships that result in emotional responses: '[A] feeling of ease, well-being, satisfaction, excitement or passion.'[75] Nargis's role in her own production company, her partnership with R. K. Films, and her entire habitus can be explicated through the paradigm of affective labour and its intersections with tangible material labour.

Although Nargis, more prominently than Khote, possessed affective power because of her 'stardom' and was able to 'represent India's screen industry' in various instances, such as her visit to the US as part of India's official delegation, her starring in the first Indo-Russian co-production, or her film getting nominated for an Academy Award, when it came to female stars in the early Indian cinema network, their power remained limited to the affective realm. Only exceptionally privileged stars like Rani could possess both effective and affective dimensions of star switching power. In contrast, for male stars like Raj Kapoor, their affective pull was situated differently and further facilitated by other actors in the industry network. For instance, Abbas rightly understood the impact of Kapoor in the Soviet Union and, through his journalistic and other writing, helped facilitate and propel Kapoor's films to become the notable exceptions that helped define and, in many ways, sustain the global presence of Indian cinema in the Soviet Union because, despite the projected bonhomie, there was a coldness towards the mainstream Indian film industry in the Soviet Union, as evidenced in the treatment of the industry at large. However, Kapoor was treated differently. Additionally, as mentioned earlier, his collaborators like Abbas capacitated that power and Kapoor could thus emerge as a critical bridging node in Indo-Soviet cultural diplomacy.

When the first Indian film festival was held in Moscow in September 1954, the Soviet minister of culture, Georgy Alesksandrov, announced that this festival marked a new step in Indo-Soviet relations and that the exchange would play an important role in strengthening cultural ties between the two countries.[76] The announcement was followed by the visit of a fifteen-member Indian film delegation led by Abbas, which included Kapoor, Anand, and Nargis, amongst others. As noted earlier, this first film festival and *Awāra*'s unprecedented popularity established Raj Kapoor as a critical industry node with a cultural influence that the state could leverage. On the mainstream industry front, specifically for Kapoor and R. K. Films, the film festival became a key hub for the presentation and circulation of their films. Consistently, journalistic coverage of the Indian film festival underscored the warm welcome extended to Kapoor because of his immense popularity and the special attention paid to his films' screening.[77] In succeeding years, Kapoor

Table 1.1 Screenings at the Soviet-wide Indian Film Festival (23–29 September 1954)

Location	Screening information	Income (Soviet rubles)	Films
Almaty, Kazakh SSR	64 screenings 42,500 viewers	Not available	*Two Acres of Land* *Hurricane* *Awāra* (Part 1)
Leningrad, Russian SFSR	Screenings: not available 33 theatres > 1 million viewers	Not available	*Two Acres of Land* *Hurricane* *Awāra* (Part 1)
Riga, Latvian SSR	125 screenings 1 theatre, 1 club 83,243 viewers	Not available	*Two Acres of Land* *Hurricane* *Awāra* (both parts)
Frunze, Kyrgyz SSR	Screenings: not available 62,000 viewers	237,000 p.	*Two Acres of Land* *Hurricane* *Awāra* (both parts)
Vilnius, Latvian SSR	2 theatres 130,000 viewers	Not available	*Two Acres of Land* *Hurricane* *Awāra* (both parts)
Kishinev, Moldavian SSR	137 screenings 147,000 viewers	208,000 p.	*Two Acres of Land* *Hurricane* *Awāra* (both parts)
Stalinabad, Tajik SSR	*Two Acres of Land*: 8 screenings 3,923 viewers *Hurricane*: 14 screenings 10,292 viewers *Awāra* (Part 1): 11 screenings 6,729 viewers Total: 33 screenings 20,944 viewers	Not available	*Two Acres of Land* *Hurricane* *Awāra* (Part 1)

Source: Collated from thirty-three different official reports about these screenings circulated within the Soviet Ministry of Culture that are archived at the Russian State Archive of Literature and Art (RSALA) in Moscow.

was appointed as jury chairman for the Indian International Film Festival, which predominantly featured Soviet films.[78] Further, Kapoor's films were regularly screened at the Soviet Festival of India held in the Soviet Union and found distribution through Soviet government-facilitated channels. Correspondingly, the Soviet state conducted additional screenings of these films in remote parts of the country. Table 1.1, collated from documents in the 1950s and 1960s folder of the RSALA in Moscow, reveals the breadth of this distribution network.

All the festival screenings exceeded expectations. For instance, the festival in Kishinev generated 197 per cent of the planned income from the film. The screenings were accompanied by a special orchestral programme dedicated to the quest for peace for all nations. In addition, Soviet and Indian flags were placed in the cinema hall, and there was a radio broadcast on the political meaning of the festival as a tool for improving cultural connections and cooperation between India and the Soviet Union in their *fight* for world peace.[79] The Soviet state thus played an essential role in the circulation of popular Hindi cinema. Raj Kapoor and his film-production company, R. K. Films, emerged as central industry nodes within this dynamic of exchange and collaboration with the Soviets, and Kapoor leveraged his personal ties with the Soviet political networks to put in place a grand collaborative production with Mosfilm that was almost six years in the making. Based on a screenplay by Abbas, *Mera Naam Joker* was conceptualized as a collaborative project with the Soviets—a collaboration Kapoor could enable because of his networked power within the Soviet political and cultural landscape. He had close ties with Russian government officials and was in direct conversation with the Ministry of Culture of the Soviet Union about the collaborative production and casting of Russian actors, including a young Russian ballerina and an entire circus troupe.[80] Thematically, the film was a continuation of the vagabond trope, an on-screen persona that was already captivating for the Russians. Speaking of the film, Kapoor noted the resonances with his oeuvre and described the Joker as an integral culmination of his on-screen personas and affective appeal:

> The character of the Joker is the character of 'the little man'—as embodied by me in films such as *Awāra*, *Shree 420*, and *Jis Desh Mein Ganga Behti Hai* (The Land Where the Ganges Flows, 1960)—but rounded out and complete with a spiritual dimension. For years I have had images of all of mankind's gods and spiritual leaders on the walls

of my cottage, and to them, I bow my head in prayer every night.... The Joker embodies all that is spiritual and selfless ... it embodies all the teachings of the world's great spiritual leaders who led lives of suffering themselves in order to make mankind happy.[81]

While the Soviet collaboration was prominent, Kapoor envisioned *Mera Naam Joker* as a global film and dedicated eight years of his career to bringing this project to fruition. The film was a lengthy magnum opus with a runtime exceeding four hours. Due to its extraordinary runtime, the film was screened in three parts for Soviet viewers. Different theatres in a city would occasionally screen one or multiple parts, either on the same day or on a three-day cycle; this afforded audiences a degree of flexibility when choosing how they consumed the film.

The relationship between the Indian state and the mainstream industry was still fraught when *Mera Naam Joker* came along. The industry believed that the state's interest was limited to exercising draconian control through censorship and taxation while offering no support in terms of policy, financing, or legislative protection. At the 1955 film seminar with Nehru, the industry representatives raised this issue, making a plea for the abolition of the entertainment tax. Nehru, however, responded with a nonchalant dismissal stating that 'he did not see why entertainment should not be taxed'.[82] Simultaneously lamenting the common public's taste, Nehru expressed his disappointment that there was a 'pitiably small' Indian public that reads compared to the sizeable number that watches films.[83] The film seminar was an exercise in futility. It did not lead to any tangible outcomes for the mainstream film industry, and until *Mera Naam Joker* came along, the tenor of the industry–state relationship stayed constant. The industry complaints asserted that the state income tax in a film's capital budget was an 'open loot' met with constant indifference.[84] In the meantime, having realized the global popularity of some of these films, the state set up an export body in 1964, the Indian Motion Picture Export Corporation (IMPEC), a subsidiary of the State Trading Corporation, to help support the export of films. The state, faced with a foreign exchange crisis, wanted export earnings to go up. Their directive also included goals such as exploring collaborations with the Americans, identifying films suitable for foreign audiences, gaining entry into non-traditional markets, and simplifying the procedure for foreign collaborations. However, again, mainstream films and key production nodes like R. K. Films had to contend with one more governing body that would hamper rather than facilitate their organization's goals to distribute its film products globally.

Raj Kapoor blamed the inefficient IMPEC for the failure of his globally ambitious *Mera Naam Joker*. The only market where the film was immensely successful was the Soviet Union. Kapoor openly critiqued the IMPEC for the failure of his global vision for his film, stating that the government allocated very little money for the organization to function effectively. The organization, he remarked, 'lacked the know-how and initiative to function effectively in a highly speculative [film] trade'. Kapoor further asserted that the IMPEC did not create global outlets, had no influence, and ended up helping the private international distributors from whom Indian film producers wanted relief in the first place. As a result, *Mera Naam Joker* failed to recuperate Kapoor's costs and was labelled a 'colossal flop' except in the Soviet Union. The Soviets paid their highest price for the acquisition of Kapoor's film. Kapoor ruefully lamented that if not for the Soviet Union, 'I would have been completely ruined. This is no credit to the IMPEC either, for the [Soviet] deal was negotiated and concluded by me, IMPEC merely acting as a broker.'[85] Kapoor charged the IMPEC for underselling his film in other regions and making no effort to utilize the funds earned by an Indian film in certain countries like Burma (present-day Myanmar), Egypt, Ceylon (present-day Sri Lanka), and Indonesia, where foreign exchange regulations barred the repatriation of funds. Moreover, the IMPEC did not set up any barter agreements or offices in these countries.

NETWORK EFFECTS: OTHER STAR-LED GLOBALLY AMBITIOUS PRODUCTIONS

Evidently, the state mechanisms were flawed and were working to hinder rather than facilitate a global exchange for the Indian Hindi film industry. In this context, it was through the network-making switching power of stars like Raj Kapoor that accomplished key globalization goals for their organizations and the industry. By now, the centrality of the stars in this early industry network was firmly entrenched, and the global popularity of Kapoor's films set off a network effect. Others, like actors Dilip Kumar and Nargis, attempted to venture into production and create global projects but were met with limited success. Kumar ventured into film production with his film *Gunga Jumna* (1961, dir. Nitin Bose). He tried the film festival circuit and entered his film at the Karlovy Vary International Film Festival in former Czechoslovakia, a festival where Kapoor had the honour of being the first Indian to win the Grand Prix Award. Kumar's earlier success in the US with his film *Aan*, India's first Technicolor film, which was picked up for international distribution by Film Locations and represented by Mike Frankovich (Film Locations's sales head), prompted him to try the American market.[86] *Aan* was distributed in America following the first Indian film delegation's visit to the country in 1955. It quickly elevated to one of the most profitable, globally successful Indian Hindi films of the time. According to the film's director and producer, Mehboob Khan, 'it was brought in at $750,000, and its production cost had already been retrieved in the Indian market'.[87]

Dilip Kumar thus identified the US as a target global market for his home production *Gunga Jumna*. He visited the US and, replicating the Indian state's preferred method for cultural exchange, tried to organize an Indian film festival there to screen his films. Kumar's brother, Aslan Khan, was tasked with showing the films from coast to coast.[88] As with other features during this phase, the effort aligned with state ideology. Speaking of his endeavours, Kumar asserted that 'it is not only an economic project. If I were only interested in money, I would have stayed in India, but with me, it is a cultural cause as well, to let the Western world see what India is capable of'.[89] In 1964, *Gunga Jumna* was screened by the Indian delegation visiting the US. The delegation included Kumar and was spearheaded by A. S. Naik, the chairman of the IMPEC.[90] The delegation also explored the possibility of using Hollywood's blocked funds—money that could not be repatriated because of currency conversion restrictions in India— for Indo-US co-productions. These attempts illustrate the network effect put in motion by Raj Kapoor's global success. However, none of these efforts could sufficiently replicate the success of Kapoor in the Soviet and East European markets. The US market seemed open to dialogue but not enthusiastic about the Indian film product. Thus, several global attempts like Kumar's met with limited success (see Table 1.2). This international distribution strategy was prominently motivated by the individual efforts and ambitions of these stars, producers, and businessmen, which is evident in their concerted effort to enable a global distribution network for Hindi cinema. However, their efforts were motivated by various connected industrial factors exacerbated by the Indian state's indifference to popular mainstream film-making.

Table 1.2 Box-office grosses for Dilip Kumar's *Gunga Jumna* (1961, dir. Nitin Bose) in Mexico

	Mexico City box-office grosses (October 1966)				
Release date	Theater and capacity	Film	Release co.	Length run	Gross in US dollars
29 September	Alameda (1,974)	*Blood in Rio Bravo* (Mex.)	Pel. Nac.	2 weeks	12,385.92
13 October	Alameda (1,974)	*Juan Pistolas* (Mex.)	Pel. Nac.	2 weeks	11,590.08
15 September	Americas (3,200)	*Darling* (Br.)	Pel. Nac.	4 weeks	42,941.12
13 October	Americas (3,200)	*Masquerade*	U.A.	1 week	6,481.28
Oct 20	Americas (3,200)	*Hold On!*	M.G.M.	1 week	7,364.16
25 August	**Arcadia (1,301)**	***Gunga Jumna* (India)**	**Pel. Nac.**	**6 weeks**	**27,502.88**
29 September	Ariel (2,154)	*Sons of Katie Elder*	Para.	1 week	6,220.80
29 September	Internacional (4,147)	*Sons of Katie Elder*	Para.	3 weeks	30,700.88
29 September	Continental (2,348)	*Girls on the Beach*	Para.	1 week	4,341.44
20 October	Continental (2,348)	*Bus Riley's Back in Town*	Universal	1 week	4,583.04
21 July	Diana (2,046)	*Scheherzade*	Cent. F.	11 weeks	119,976.32
22 September	Latino (2,547)	*The Singing Nun*	MGM	4 weeks	36, 871.36
6 October	Metropolitan (2,583)	*Blood and Black Lace*	Cent. F.	3 weeks	26, 527.68
29 September	Mexico (3,500)	*Arabesque*	Universal	4 weeks	54,505.28
11 August	Orfeon (2,800)	*Juventud sin Ley*	Sotomayer	9 weeks	67,935.36
6 October	Palacio Chino (3,741)	*Forbidden Cargo* (Mex.)	Pel. Nac.	1 week	3,697.60

(*Contd*)

Table 1.2 (*Contd*)

			Mexico City box-office grosses (October 1966)			
Release date	Theater and capacity	Film	Release co.	Length run	Gross in US dollars
29 September	Polanco (2,600)	*Arabesque*	Universal	2 weeks	19,910.72
13 October	Polanco (2,600)	*Woman of Straw*	U.A.	1 week	9,136.64
15 September	Roble (2,565)	*Cast Your Cares to the Wind* (Mex.)	Pel. Nac.	4 weeks	37,816.96
6 October	Vriedades (2,762)	*Father Goose*	Universal	2 weeks	17,015.04

Source: *Variety* magazine archive.

Dilip Kumar, who was also the president of the Film Producers Guild of India, during his 1964 US visit revealed some of the issues the industry was facing and why there was a dire need to expand globally.[91] He was in the US to establish a connection for the newly instituted state body, the IMPEC (mentioned earlier), to facilitate the North American distribution of Indian films. However, Kumar did not mince words in identifying the Indian state and its heavy taxation structure for entertainment as one of the industry's chief obstacles. 'The scale of taxation which sees approximately 50% of all box office receipts beings skimmed off the top into the government's pocket,' he asserted, was a significant hindrance to the industry's development and killed the producer's incentive.[92] He also elaborated on the lack of foreign exchange reserves in India that directly impacted film production because the Indian film industry had to import all its raw stock, camera, and lenses. Hence, despite its domestic mass market, it was important for the Indian film industry to create a foothold in global markets.

Thus, owing to their ability to create distribution networks, the megastar-producer becomes the primary loci of power in this context. For star switching power to truly manifest in the way that it did for Raj Kapoor, the star's centrality in sociopolitical networks is also crucial, as is the connection with the global market they are hoping to cultivate. The US turned out to be a tough market for Indian star productions, although it was not due to a lack of aspiration or effort. Raj Kapoor, Dilip Kumar, and Dev Anand were the three top stars of the golden age who, having accompanied Nehru on the trip to the Soviet Union, looked for comparable possibilities of collaboration with the Americans. Anand's and Kumar's films *Rahi* and *Naya Daur*, respectively, met with a warm reception from the Soviets, if not the overwhelming response that *Awāra* did. Kumar, as noted earlier, tried to replicate a similar model with the Americans and create a deeper industry connection. However, his efforts were met with limited enthusiasm by the American state and industry.[93] Following Kumar's 1964 visit, an article in *Variety* reiterated the reasons why Indian films would never work in the US. With a competitive rather than supportive tenor, the article noted,

> [T]he Indian industry has much to do before it can hope to make a dent in the western film world.... Indian films, with their emphasis on music and spectacle, have little appeal for foreign tastes, while domestic Indian audiences, also growing restive, have not been developed to the point where they will accept fare too far removed from their escapist formula.[94]

Dev Anand—another megastar with industry centrality, who was Raj Kapoor and Dilip Kumar's contemporary and proprietor of his family production venture, Navketan Films—tried to understand and bridge the foreign taste divide in his collaboration with US production company Stratton Films. Several of his strategic choices in the collaboration process reflect deliberate thinking in his attempt to create a film product with distinctive elements that would work for American tastes. The success of *Rahi* in the Soviet Union and the controversies with the Indian state and Sovexportfilm concerning the film pulled Anand in the direction of the Americans. Throughout his career, he tried to create global cinema focused primarily on the US market. His first attempt, *The Guide* (1965, dir. Tad Danielewski), also the first Indo-US film collaboration, was the first step in that direction. The film, as conceptualized for the American market, addressed the many shortcomings of mainstream Hindi cinema mentioned in the *Variety* review earlier. *The Guide* was based on a realist novel by R. K. Narayan. Two separate versions of the film were shot, and the American version was in English, produced by Stratton Films and directed by Tad Danielewski, whereas the Hindi version was directed by Anand's brother, Vijay Anand. The American version had no songs, very deliberately de-emphasizing the music and spectacle

Figure 1.3 Dev Anand with Nobel laureate Pearl S. Buck, screenwriter of *Guide* (1965)

Source: Embassy of the United States of America, New Delhi.

of mainstream Bollywood. Comparing both versions of the film, the *Times Recorder* from Ohio noted, '[T]he Indian version of the film has about seven songs. The American version has sexy love scenes.'[95] The screenplay for the film was written by Nobel Prize–winning author Pearl S. Buck, whom Anand knew personally and who was an essential network connection in enabling this collaboration. The co-produced venture, however, according to *Variety*, was Stratton Films and Danielewski's 'Made in India Indie'.[96]

Anand's connection with Buck was crucial in enabling this collaborative venture, wherein Anand took the lead in foregrounding these industrial ties with the US to the Indian state. During one of Buck and Danielewski's early visits to India, Anand arranged for a reception for them to meet with the governor of the state of Maharashtra, Vijaya Lakshmi Pandit, Nehru's sister and a prominent figure in Indian cultural diplomacy. However, the rift with the state and the state's derision of popular cinema remained. Befittingly, Anand's character in the American version of *Guide*, which could escape the state's heavy-handed censorship, overtly decries the country's shortage of foreign exchange reserves and its dire implications for the country. Introducing a maharaja's palace to his tourists, the titular Guide notes:

> This miracle of ingenuity ... has survived more than 200 years of battles, monsoons and great men and women of all races ... only to succumb at last to the shortage of foreign exchange. Therefore, the Maharaja is converting the palace to a hotel, to attract the foreigners and pound sterlings and thus giving India the capability of purchasing transistor sets, radios, and machine guns.

In a tongue-in-cheek fashion, Anand's Guide pronounces the central issue facing the industry couched in satire that still underscores why foreign collaborations like *The Guide* were needed. The reception of the American version, however, was cold. Danielewski and Buck claimed that they had already earned back their investment in the picture 'via surefire receipts from the Indian version' with songs and dances that turned out to be a super-hit film.[97] The American version, whose coverage was still Orientalized despite the careful attention to 'Americanizing' the film, turned out to be a colossal flop. In the film's review, an American trade magazine critic claimed that '[*The Guide*] is an outstanding example of what can be accomplished when a western film director and a western writer choose to make an otherwise completely Oriental film. The potential market for *The Guide* is still the art theater.'[98] The *New York Times* had an opposite, albeit more damning, take:

> [W]hereas the backdrop is authentic, the romance of a provincial Indian tourist guide with the dancing-girl-wife of an older merchant seems partly artificial and contrived, much more in the Hollywood spirit than in that of, let us say, Bombay. And the development of the narrative continuity is so erratic and frequently slurred—so clumsy and artless, to be plain-spoken—that both story and emotion are vague.[99]

The English version was an early experiment that was neither here nor there. Although the Hindi version was a massive hit, for his part, Anand and Navketan Films made very little money on the project, with the bulk of the profits going to financiers who charged him a very high rate of interest.[100] The Hindi version, directed by Anand's brother, Vijay Anand, became a massive hit in India and is still considered a cult classic.

The box-office failure of *The Guide* in the US did not deter Anand; he remained invested in the globalization process through collaborations with the West. After *Guide*, he acted in *The Evil Within* (1970, dir. Lamberto V. Avellana), produced and distributed by Twentieth Century Fox. In Anand's own words, *The Evil Within* was 'a story about smuggling that was much too confused. [The film] was a failure.'[101] For his feature *Lootmaar* (Plunderage, 1980, dir. Dev Anand), Anand went to London looking for stunt performers and crew.[102] In his next film after *Lootmaar*, *Swami Dada* (1982, dir. Dev Anand), Anand recasts himself as a swami, recalling his role in *Guide*, and cast American model Christine O'Neil to play his disciple. He also had his film dubbed in English. By this time, Anand, with his ventures and connections in the Western film industry, was a notable celebrity visible to the Western trade press. So this time around, Anand's visit and his upcoming film were mentioned in Peter Noble's column in *Screen International*.[103] As a star node, he created publicity and networks that enabled the global distribution of *Swami Dada*. The film was screened at the Cannes Film Festival and was bought by foreign distributors.[104] From the 1950s to the 1980s, Anand was a vital node that enabled Indian Hindi cinema's global flows. His celebrity status was well established in the West after *The Guide*, and he could configure networks that ensured global distribution for some of his films. His initial forays into the American market were backed by the Motion Picture Association of America (MPAA), which hosted a press conference for his film *Hum Dono* (Both of Us, 1961, dir. Amar Jeet), and he possessed the ability to enable a co-production like *The Guide*.[105] Anand stands out as an important bridging node with switching power, enabling global flows for Indian cinema in the early decades after independence. Anand's Navketan Films remains another prime example of a family-led industry cluster that continued to thrive. The Anand brothers—Dev, Chetan, and Vijay Anand—produced multiple hits for the mainstream Bollywood industry.

For these film-production clusters or any industry, structural formation with close, small-world ties, certain core competencies, innovations, and ambitions carry through. In addition, such clusters provide close industry connections and means for knowledge transfer, create paths for innovation, and provide the flexibility to compete.[106] This was evidenced in Raj Kapoor's creation of R. K. Films, built on the existing industrial connection and knowledge of Prithviraj Kapoor's industrial clout and theatre venture, Prithvi. Expectedly, the next production company to have global ambitions and venture into film collaborations and partnerships not simply with the Soviets but also with the Americans and the British came from the Kapoor family industry cluster with Shashi Kapoor, Raj Kapoor's brother who played the latter's younger self in the film *Awāra*. His case points to the broader dissemination and ambition of the Indian family film clusters, the intricacies of star switching power, and the affective and effective permutations that enable it to exist.

A FOOT IN MULTIPLE GLOBAL MARKETS: SHASHI KAPOOR'S WAYFARING INROADS INTO GLOBAL CINEMA

Why I get very angry is because if their *Gone with the Wind*, *Sound of Music* and *Hatari* can be shown in our smallest towns, why can't our films? After all, cinema everywhere talks about the same things—about mothers, fathers, sons, wives, fornication, and death.

—Shashi Kapoor, 1983[107]

Shashi Kapoor is another critical figure in the global flow of Indian cinema who was central to many of India's global co-productions, through which he hoped to expand the reach of Hindi cinema to the West, specifically the US and the UK. However, unlike Raj Kapoor, Shashi Kapoor fell into the realm of a 'good actor', and his production attempts carefully straddle the line between popular mainstream cinema and festival-oriented 'good cinema' favoured by the Indian state. This favourable position helped Shashi Kapoor to stand out even within his illustrious family network as the Bollywood actor with the most international profile, with dozens of Hollywood co-productions under his belt. His unique positionality within the industry and political networks, combined with his vision and ability to incorporate the Indian state's cinematic objectives, helped him enable Indian cinema's global flows, despite a lack of overwhelming affective power like that of his brother—except in the UK, where he was immensely popular.

Shashi Kapoor's film career started in the 1960s and spanned several decades. When his career began, Nehru started to take some interest in cinema, having experienced the influence of films and film stars. As a result, a state body, the Film and Television Institute of India (FTII), was set up in 1960 to encourage parallel art-house cinema. At this time, Shashi Kapoor became a central figure in propagating parallel art-house cinema and attempted to leverage it to enable Hindi cinema's global flows. In May 2015, when Shashi Kapoor was conferred India's highest cinematic excellence award—the Dadasaheb Phalke Award—India's minister for information and broadcasting, Arun Jaitley, credited him as the star who 'brought Hindi cinema and Hollywood closer'.[108]

How did Shashi Kapoor finally bring Hindi cinema and Hollywood closer together? To understand this, it is essential to examine his role as an important node in the evolving industry network of the 1960s and 1970s. Merchant Ivory Productions, a partnership between Ismail Merchant and James Ivory that enabled some of Bollywood's first global collaborations involving Shashi Kapoor, represents an excellent example of the interrelationships between personal and industry networks. It also reveals the organic structure of the Indian film industry, which operated through family or personal networks, showing just how closely intertwined personal and industry networks were. Networks operate through the interaction of social actors. Compared to his brother, Shashi Kapoor, being a part of the same family production cluster, possessed an equal degree of embeddedness in industry networks and similar structural equivalence.[109] In sum, he possessed the same kinds of connections and social relations within the industry's larger structure as Raj Kapoor. His affective power, however, was not similar to the latter's. Nevertheless, he arguably had a wider personal global network and greater clout because of his British wife, Jennifer Kendal. He also strategically leveraged the newfound state to work alongside other emergent diasporic nodes like Ismail Merchant and Merchant Ivory Productions to achieve his expansion goals. Merchant's interest in Indo-US co-production is also an instance of a diaspora node getting added to the Bollywood network to support its globalization. The network, by definition, expands and structurally evolves as a new node gets added to it.

When Merchant first met Shashi Kapoor, the latter was already in the limelight with his first Bollywood feature, where he played the lead. Merchant recalls his first meeting with Kapoor, which occurred when the former gatecrashed a party for journalists organized to promote the latter's film *Char Diwari* (Four Walls, 1961, dir. Krishan Chopra): 'We gatecrashed and were offered *nimboo pani* [lemonade]. I said I am making a film. How would you like to be in it?'[110] Thus, the Merchant Ivory film *The Householder* (1963, dir. James Ivory) came about. Merchant Ivory films are essential to the context of Hindi films' globalization because they consistently enabled the industry's collaborations with Hollywood. Moreover, the films they produced were often set in India and employed Indian talent (cast and crew).[111] The earnings of American film companies, which could not be repatriated because of Indian legal regulations, were spent on Merchant Ivory films that were set in India but created with a global audience in mind: 'This practice became the financial base of [the Merchant Ivory] operation there in the 1960s, and Ismail exploited the situation very ingeniously.'[112] Hollywood's blocked funds in India thus influenced this history of exchange between the Indian and American film industries.[113]

Although within the Western discourse about Merchant Ivory films, the producer–director duo takes centre stage as the primary node, Shashi Kapoor was an undeniably key bridging figure behind this successful collaboration. At the same time, the presence of Merchant points to the diaspora network that has been critical to the global dissemination of Indian cinema, a desire closely tied to identity. Before state interest in the diaspora became pronounced in the 1990s (as the next two chapters will elaborate), diasporic actors like Merchant, the Hindujas (a business family), and Dharam Das (a businessman) became critical nodes in enabling individual star production clusters' ambitions beyond the literally non-existent efforts of the Indian state. For instance, the Hindujas, who ran one of India's earliest global businesses with interests primarily in Iran, became the global distributors for Raj Kapoor's films. Personal friendship and a fannish affect for the star led the Hinduja family to buy the overseas rights to his film *Sangam* (Confluence, 1964, dir. Raj Kapoor) for GBP 100,000, the highest amount paid for any Hindi film at the time.[114] The film was released in Iran and ran continuously in movie theatres for a year and a half, all because the Hindujas had a close relationship with Kapoor, who happened to show them a preview of his film at R. K. studio.[115] Merchant, on the other hand, apart from the economic motivations related to blocked funds, wanted to make globally oriented Indian films and his ambitions aligned with those of Shashi Kapoor. In his interviews, Shashi Kapoor talked about his close collaborations with Merchant Ivory which started in 1962 with *The Householder* and lasted throughout his career. Kapoor focused on building individual relationships and friendships, which influenced both his production ventures and the India-centric British Raj films that Merchant Ivory went on to make.[116]

Shashi Kapoor, in the 1960s, 1970s, and 1980s, thus emerged as a critical node around whom the interests of multiple stakeholders converged, including the industry, the state, and diasporic production networks. He is one of the rare actors to earn the distinction of acting in international co-production ventures, mainstream Bollywood, Indian parallel art-house cinema, and theatre. Later in his career, he also produced and directed films. What are the factors that made Shashi Kapoor a unique node with the power to constitute new network configurations? This power is different from an 'old boys network'—it is complex, subtle, and negotiated.[117] However, connectivity with important nodes and networks is central to configuring new networks—in this case, global networks that enable the flow of Indian cinema. Although the dynamic of networks is negotiated, personal networks play a crucial role in rendering power or connectivity to a node. Shashi Kapoor was born into the illustrious Kapoor film family, often referred to as the first family of Bollywood. His father, Prithviraj Kapoor, and older brothers, Raj and Shammi, were renowned figures in the industry. Since Bollywood was an organically structured film cluster, such personal ties ensured Shashi Kapoor's access to a variety of networks. However, even within his illustrious family, Shashi Kapoor is notable for his international resume, including numerous co-productions in Hollywood.

A recent article in the *Hollywood Reporter* attributes Shashi Kapoor's international sensibilities to his marriage.[118] It suggests that his presence in international films was somehow rendered 'more acceptable' because of his association with his British wife and in-laws. The relationship lent him an embodied, symbolic, institutional, and cultural capital in both the post-colonial Indian and Western industrial contexts (British and American). Kapoor married Jennifer Kendal in 1958, just before the start of his career as an actor in mainstream Bollywood. Before that, Kapoor was a part of his father's theatre troupe and later joined Geoffrey Kendal's Shakespearana, a travelling theatre company that performed Shakespeare's plays all over India. Kapoor's romance with Geoffrey's daughter blossomed while he worked for Shakespeareana, and they married a few years later.[119] The story of Kendal's theatre troupe inspired the Merchant Ivory film *Shakespeare Wallah* (1965, dir. James Ivory). The narrative about a British troupe peddling Shakespeare in post-colonial India while their very existence is threatened by the popularity of the upcoming Bollywood industry was inspired by the Kendal family's experience. The inspiration for the screenplay came from a diary that Kendal kept, and all of Shashi Kapoor's British family were cast in the film to play themselves.[120] Thus, after *The Householder*, Kapoor enabled the production of feature films through his personal networks. With the profits from *The Householder*, *Shakespeare Wallah* was made in English with a global audience in mind. Kapoor, therefore, could help create a global project involving his family and other Bollywood talents—a project that received accolades worldwide. At this time, Merchant was in a cash crunch, and Kapoor decided to help him out in exchange for the Indian distribution rights for *Bombay Talkie* (1970, dir. James Ivory).[121] He remained the constant figure in future Merchant Ivory projects set in India. He also starred in other non–Merchant Ivory Hollywood and global productions like *A Matter of Innocence* (1967, dir. Guy Green), *Siddhartha* (1972, dir. Conrad Rocks), *Sammie and Rosie Get Laid* (1987, dir. Stephen Frears), *Jinnah* (1998, dir. Jamil Dehlavi), and the television miniseries *Gulliver's Travels* (1996, dir. Charles Sturridge). The sign value of his globality enhanced Kapoor's capital in a Western brandscape-driven value ecosystem. It presented him with several possibilities that enabled him to strategically bring the Indian state's and Western industry's interests together with those of his family's film-production cluster. He attempted to replicate the Merchant Ivory model of international co-production and distribution and the strategic utilization of film festivals as a critical node for the global circulation of cinema. In a clear instantiation of what Michael Keane calls cultural technology transfer, Kapoor, inspired by Merchant, set up a production company called Vidushak Arts (renamed later as Film-Valas) that initially focused on creating global Indian festival films like *Junoon* (The Obsession, 1978, dir. Shyam Benegal), *36 Chowringhee Lane* (1981, dir. Aparna Sen), *Kalyug* (1981, dir. Shyam Benegal), *Vijeta* (The Victor, 1982, dir. Govind Nihlani), and *Utsav* (Festival, 1984, dir. Girish Karnad).[122] Kapoor tried to bring together state and industry agendas through these films. He and his wife wanted to create '[an] accessible art house cinema', with a concerted global vision circling through the international film festival circuit.[123]

Junoon, *36 Chowringhee Lane*, and *Utsav* were films that fit the parallel art-house cinema mould encouraged by Nehru. Most of the talent and crew for these features came from the FTII, the institute created and patronized by Nehru. For ideas for new films, Shashi Kapoor obtained prints from the FTII to review.[124] He attempted to create meaningful cinema that brought together Nehru's elevated vision for the medium with the mainstream industry to create films that could circulate globally. Many of these films did rounds at international film festivals and won awards. For instance, *Junoon*, a story about a stranded British family in the wake of the first Indian rebellion against the British in 1857, played at the Montreal World Film Festival, the Cairo International Film Festival, the Sydney Film Festival, the Melbourne International Film Festival, and the Moscow International Film Festival. It was also the inaugural film at the International Film Festival held in New Delhi.[125] Similarly, his other production ventures, such as *36 Chowringhee Lane* and *Utsav*, played at various film festivals. Kapoor's wife, Jennifer Kendal, who played the lead in *36 Chowringhee Lane*, won a British Academy of Film and Television Arts (BAFTA) nomination for her performance. In addition, *36 Chowringhee Lane* was selected as the best film at the Manila Film Festival. The film was distributed in the UK and did reasonably well there.[126] *36 Chowringhee Lane* dealt with the topic of mixed racial identity and the cultural insider–outsider binary by depicting the life of an Anglo-Indian English teacher in post-colonial India. In 1982, the film received state appreciation through the National Award for Best Direction. However, the subject matter and language of the film were directed towards a foreign audience. The film was in English, with a little Hindi and Bengali sprinkled in. *36 Chowringhee Lane* was selected as India's official entry for the Oscars in the Foreign Language Film category. Following Merchant Ivory's example, Kapoor was trying to create films about India that would appeal to a larger global audience.

Shashi Kapoor's next venture, *Utsav*, premiered at the Oxford Film Festival and was screened at Filmex in Los Angeles.[127] Filmex was an international film exposition that started in 1971 and later became AFI Fest, the American Film Institute's film festival.[128] Kapoor attended the exposition with the intent of finding distributors for *Utsav* in the US. In an interview with *Variety*, he noted that he could recover only half of his budget for *Utsav* from the Indian market and was looking to distribute the film internationally.[129] *Utsav* was a historical drama set in India in 400 CE, likely the Gupta period in Indian history, and drew from two Sanskrit plays: *Charudatta* (300 CE) by Bhāsa and *Mrcchakatika* (400 CE) by Śūdraka. The film shows a courtesan's house in a state of disarray in a city where there is an underground political movement plotting to overthrow the tyrannical ruler. The film uses tropes from Sanskrit drama and is narrated by a *sutradhar* (one who holds all the threads in a narrative) who happens to be Vātsyāyana, the author of the *Kamasutra*. Vātsyāyana is an observer at the courtesan's house and uses these observations for writing his famous work; intertwined within this turmoil are two love stories. The narrative of the film attempts to bring together the exoticism and eroticism associated with India in the West while at the same time evoking a glorious national heritage, a past when India was more liberal. *Utsav* was directed by Girish Karnad, a director from the FTII, and the Sangeet Natak Akademi, two institutes set up by Nehru in the 1960s. This project represented another attempt to create cinema aligned with the state and to present an authentic version of ancient India. The film was a complex experiment in that it sought to create a product for the domestic and global market while aligning with state-sponsored media institutions and objectives. The film was made in two languages, Hindi and English, and a teaser for the film was released at the Cannes Film Festival to create a buzz in the international market. Kapoor acted in it to leverage his international celebrity status:

> It is my ambition to break into the international market. I know it is difficult, especially with our stars being practically unknown in the West. From this lot, I am the only one they know, really, thanks to Ivory-Merchant films, *Pretty Polly* and *Siddhartha*. The trouble is that the American distributors think that there is now a world outside the US. Even for *Gandhi* [referring to the 1982 film directed by Richard Attenborough] nearly five million dollars had to be spent on publicity to attract the audiences.[130]

While understanding the enormity of his task and the scarcity of resources to do things the Hollywood way, Shashi Kapoor was still buoyed by the Merchant Ivory model of creating films about India for an international audience. He conceptualized *Utsav* as just such a crossover film; however, Kapoor did not want to leave out the Indian market either. He wanted to include the state's vision of 'good cinema'—or, at the very least, curry favour with the state institutes that patronized and promoted the government's vision of 'good cinema'. With all this in mind, Kapoor produced *Utsav* in Hindi and English, and it was written and directed by Karnad, the Oxford- and FTII-educated director. The experiment was unsuccessful; the film was panned by Indian critics as 'bawdy', 'jittery and self-conscious' erotica.[131] Although it was screened at multiple film festivals, the film could not find an international distributor. Kapoor lamented that his international edit without songs was 'na ghar ka na ghat ka [neither here nor there]'.[132] Kapoor's son Kunal Kapoor expressed a similar disappointment with *Utsav*:

[N]obody in the international market was interested in that period in India. The movie was neither art-house nor commercial. I imagined it to be a Douglas Fairbanks kind of adventure. I think Girish [Karnad] should have made the film more glamorous and sexy. Dad was financially wiped out by *Utsav*.[133]

Utsav was a disastrous failure, probably due to a lack of clarity about what kind of entertainment would work for a Western market. Shashi Kapoor was inspired by the Merchant Ivory model, but the latter's films about India had focused solely on international audiences, paying little to no attention to the Indian market. Kapoor's venture was created to appease all the crucial nodes in the Indian Hindi film network and, at the same time, create a global product. He could not ignore the Indian market because he was a celebrated star in the mainstream Hindi film industry.

On the other hand, the subject of the film was chosen to conform to the state ideals of creating art films, and *Utsav* was all about the sexually permissive society of India in the fifth century. Despite being a failed experiment, *Utsav* is a good case study of the Hindi film industry network's key star nodes. Shashi Kapoor attempted to create a product that would work with the mainstream industry and state agendas as well as possess the ability to travel globally (or at least to the Western markets—the US, the UK, and Europe). This lack of focus and multiplicity of stakeholders partially contributed to the film's failure. Nonetheless, *Utsav* was a notable attempt by a star node to globalize Indian cinema. After the financial debacle of features like *Utsav* and *36 Chowringhee Lane*, Kapoor set his sights on a more 'culturally proximate' and receptive market: the Soviet Union.

Again, the idea of Bollywood's family-led film cluster and its operation through small-world network ties comes to the fore. Just before the time of perestroika, a Kapoor family scion could leverage the existing affective and effective ties with the state and the industry, created through his brother's association with the Soviets, to enable a joint Indo-Soviet co-production, *Ajooba* (Wonder, 1991). The film was co-produced by Russia's Gorky Film Studio, Shashi Kapoor's Film-Valas, and another Indian production company, Aasia Films. It was directed jointly by Shashi Kapoor and Russian director Gennadiy Vasilev. The film was an Oriental fantasy set in the kingdom of Baharistan, and it starred megastar Amitabh Bachchan who, fittingly, is the subject of the next chapter as the megastar of the 1990s. The film derived its fantastical elements from multiple cultural registers ranging from *The Thief of Baghdad* (1940, dir. Michael Powell, Ludwig Berger, and Tim Whelan) to classical Indian fantasies like *Chitralekha* (1964, dir. Kidar Sharma) to the Arthurian legend of Excalibur. *Ajooba* was replete with action, magic, and romance, adhering to popular Hindi cinema's 'masala', a confluence of genres similar to a blend of spices used in Indian culinary tradition to enhance taste and flavour.[134] Influences from fantasy tales across the world made the film an eclectic mix. Apart from featuring Bachchan as the lead, the film also featured other actors from the Kapoor clan, such as Shammi Kapoor and Rishi Kapoor, Raj Kapoor's brother and son, respectively. The film's primary cast was Indian, with a few Soviet actors in supporting roles. The film was shot in the Soviet Union, and many of the crew were Soviet. Two versions of the film were made. The Russian version was titled *Chernyĭ prints Adzhuba* (Black Prince Ajooba). *Ajooba*, with its lavish costumes and sets, cost USD 6 million to produce.[135] The production time for the film was pretty long—over three years—and put an added strain on the film's budget. Unfortunately, the film was not successful at the box office. However, Bachchan acquired the distribution rights for the film for the Delhi–Uttar Pradesh territory in India, and the film turned out to be a huge success there.[136] Shashi Kapoor, on the other hand, lost a lot of money on this venture, and *Ajooba* was the last of his global forays.

Despite these financial failures, Shashi Kapoor remained one of the most notable global star nodes in the Bombay cinema network for several decades. Throughout his career, from the early 1960s to the late 1990s, his position as a star node was unique in the extent to which he tried to bring together state and industry objectives while striving for a global audience. Even though he did not experience much financial success with his ventures targeted at Western markets, Shashi Kapoor's mainstream Bollywood films, such as *Jab Jab Phool Khile* (Whenever the Flowers Bloomed, 1965, dir. Suraj Prakash), had widespread appeal in North Africa, particularly in Morocco and Algeria, where movie theatres played this release for two years.[137] Some of Kapoor's ventures were profitable, while others incurred financial losses, but for him, the pursuit of global Indian cinema was constant. He stands out as an important node with global recognition, celebrity appeal, and the switching power to enable global co-productions for Bollywood cinema.

First, what does this mean in terms of power? Second, which stars in this early formative network get to possess this switching power? Lastly, why does this power vary from star to star? This chapter reveals that one of the primary components for star switching power to manifest is the coalescence of direct network power merging with a unique affective appeal. Shashi Kapoor and Raj Kapoor were part of the same family film cluster and possessed similar direct power, yet their ability to switch and create new networks was somewhat varied. Speaking about his brother, Shashi Kapoor identified the great affective pull that allows some stars, like his brother, to accomplish more: 'Raj Kapoor was a born showman. He was able to capture attention whether, on stage or screen, he was able to mesmerize his listener', a quality so intense that 'he could get away with murder'.[138] An affective pull or mesmerizing charisma is an unquantifiable variable in this assessment of switching power. However, all other factors being constant, a star's exceptional affect lends them the power to create new paths for their individual ventures within this temporal industry network. Another critical aspect of star switching power and its role in industry globalization illuminated by this chapter is network effects when other stars who are also centrally situated in the industry network make similar production efforts with varying degrees of success. Most Hindi cinema stars, because of their inherent industrial centrality due to historical factors, did possess the ability to bridge nodes. However, all bridging nodes do not possess the switching power to configure networks and define network goals. Businessmen like Rupert Murdoch or Elon Musk— despite their effective business clout, similar to that of Hindi cinema's stars in the Indian context—do not possess the affective excess that someone like Raj Kapoor did to mobilize political, diplomatic, and industrial networks to accomplish goals for R. K. Films.[139] Similarly, someone like Shashi Kapoor, despite the effective network centrality, did not possess the affective excess to create new markets.

This chapter has also explained the evolution of the post-independence film industry as a cluster of family-led productions that uniquely defined Hindi cinema's organizational configuration for over four decades. The megastar in the next chapter, Amitabh Bachchan, came to prominence in the following decades of the 1970s and 1980s. Like Raj Kapoor, Bachchan was also distinctively situated at the centre of political, economic, and industrial networks and buoyed by his immense affective appeal. As the Indian economy was globalizing, the industry mired in criminal economy networks in the 1980s rapidly transformed when the Indian state instituted economic reforms to welcome global foreign investment. The next chapter unveils how Bachchan led the charge in this transitioning industry structure as it transformed from small production clusters towards ambitious corporate organizations. Explicating the globalization of Indian cinema through Bachchan's popularity in other non-aligned geographies like Egypt and politically fraught ones like Afghanistan, Chapter 2 presents the tenets of an emerging Bollywood network, built on the structures elucidated in this chapter, with Bachchan situated in the apotheosis of these inchoate changes.

2

KING OF KINGS

Amitabh Bachchan and the Emergence of Bollywood's Corporate Networks

I remember Amitabh Bachchan was going to come to Kabul in the 1980s. Unfortunately, that time war was going on, and a girl walked up to the President and requested him to ask the warring parties to stop [fighting] for a day for the sake of Amitabh Bachchan.

—Shaida Mohammad Abdali, Afghanistan's
ambassador to India (2012–2018)[1]

In war-torn Afghanistan, 'one thing that all Mujahideen[2] groups agreed on was Amitabh Bachchan'.[3] President Mohammad Najibullah's (1987–1992) repeated insistence that Bachchan make a film in Afghanistan attests to the actor's prodigious fandom.[4] Consequently, Bachchan's *Khuda Gawah* (God Is My Witness, 1992, dir. Mukul S. Anand), in which he played an irreproachable Pathan, part of the dominant ethnic group in Afghanistan, was shot there. His popularity spanned other parts of the world as well: Egypt, parts of the Middle East, Nigeria, and West Asia.[5] Omar Sharif, the Egyptian actor known for his Hollywood roles, noted, '[T]his Amitabh Bachchan seems to be more popular than me in Egypt.'[6] Not surprisingly, Bachchan was chosen as the star of the millennium in a 1999 British Broadcasting Corporation (BBC) poll, beating Lawrence Olivier, Charlie Chaplin, Cary Grant, Robert De Niro, and Marilyn Monroe, among others.[7] Not only was his stardom global, but he also had political and economic clout in equal measure. His near-fatal accident on the set of the film *Coolie* (1983, dir. Manmohan Desai) summoned prime minister Indira Gandhi and her son, Rajiv, to his bedside and sent the nation into mourning.[8] Two years hence, Bachchan ran for a seat in parliament on Gandhi's Congress party ticket, winning by a landslide. In the 1970s, 1980s, and early 1990s, the Indian cinemascape abounded with Bachchan, earning him the moniker of Hindi cinema's *shahenshah* (king of kings).

This chapter spans the mid-1970s to the early 2000s when Bachchan dominated Hindi cinema's landscape locally and globally, explicating his *protean* star switching power in the sociocultural, political, and economic realms that enabled him to be a significant change-maker for the film and entertainment industry. The chapter presents a triptych that illustrates (*a*) the emergent Bollywood network, (*b*) the key nodes that get added to it in this incipient phase of globalization, and (*c*) the switching power Bachchan—the king of kings—has within it.

Specifically, the first part of the triptych explicates the Indian Hindi film industry's transition as it developed parallel to state-endorsed art cinema networks and became deeply mired in a mafia-led criminal economy. It further elucidates mainstream Hindi cinema's move from the shadow economies of criminal networks to a formalized early corporate network structure, in which Bachchan played a key role. It delineates the scalar growth of Hindi cinema's industrial network as it shifts from a proto to an emergent phase owing to critical interlocutions with external economies, actors, and policy changes that significantly alter the broader consumer and media market, creating opportunities and ambitions as well as constraints for the Indian Hindi film industry.[9] It also traces allied market power through the cosmetic industry and the Miss World pageant, which integrates with the Indian market that helps the transformation of Hindi film into a global entertainment industry.

The second part of the triptych foregrounds the processes of global flows of cinema and cinematic soft power to the Greater Middle East (specifically, Egypt and Afghanistan) and changes within the Hindi film industry's macro environment during this phase of structural transition, illuminating the leveraging of political networks in furthering industry goals via stars like Bachchan and their prodigious fandom. And lastly, it highlights prominent structural changes such as 'corporatization'—that is, the move towards an industry structure where corporations rather than private individuals or the state became direct beneficiaries of the liberalization of the Indian economy. In this context, it explains the conceptualization of a 'star as a brand' initiated by Bachchan's media entertainment company, Amitabh Bachchan Corporation Limited (ABCL), and elucidates how ABCL—both its successes and failures—transformed business practices into Bollywood's inchoate globalizing and corporatizing industry network in which film converged with other media forms and related consumer industries.[10]

Bachchan's ability to mobilize affects and catalyse important structural and business transformations emerged, this chapter argues, from his star switching power's dynamic protean quality, which developed over numerous decades. Whereas traditional perspectives of star studies posit that star images are constructed in and through media texts, this is not the main story here.[11] Bachchan's iconicity endured through the decades as he inhabited a range of different star personas that fit the tenor of different eras and areas of India and the world, developing a star text that was polysemic due to the evolving nature of his on-screen characters. Bachchan's star persona and affect changed with each phase of his stardom. In the 1970s and 1980s, following the emergency period wherein the Indian government suspended the civil liberties of the Indian people, Bachchan transformed from the erudite, urbane bourgeois hero of Hrishikesh Mukherjee's films to an agent of social change and the angry young man of *Zanjeer* (The Chain, 1973, dir. Prakash Mehra), *Deewar* (The Wall, 1975, dir. Yash Chopra), and *Sholay* (Embers, 1975, dir. Ramesh Sippy). The late 1990s and early 2000s saw a further transformation in his star image when he reinvented himself as the benevolent patriarch of the post-liberalization era in films such as *Kabhi Khushi Kabhi Gham* (Sometimes There Is Joy, Sometimes There Is Sorrow, 2001, dir. Karan Johar) (*K3G*) and *Mohabattein* (Love Stories, 2000, dir. Aditya Chopra). The polysemy of his online screen persona and its resultant affective power worked in tandem with his effective power within shifting political and industry networks in which he would also play starring roles; Bachchan's star switching power is, therefore, protean in that it proved to be politically fluid as he performed a sagacious 'doubling' of identities and, in doing so, often mediated key areas of political, economic, and social tension.[12]

Furthermore, Bachchan's symbolic power, derived originally from his affective star persona as the angry young man railing against an unjust system, irreproachably coexisted with his effective network power derived from his close ties with the state via the Nehru–Gandhi family. The significant economic reforms that the Indian government embarked upon after three decades of socialism led to the evolution of a novel Bachchan persona. The late 1980s and 1990s saw far-reaching changes in economic policy that broke public sector monopolies, abolished licensing controls, lowered customs duties, and opened up the economy for foreign investment.[13]

The coolie working the docks in 1975's *Deewar* transformed himself into the industrialist and patriarch of *Sooryavansham* (Lineage of the Sun God, 1999, dir. E. V. V. Satyanarayana), *Mohabattein*, and *K3G*, commendably laborious in upholding social order. In his transfigured filmic avatar, Bachchan is the locus of authority, a signifier of modernity conjured within the larger framework of elite bourgeois liberalization.[14] His affective power was mediated through these transitioning star personas as his roles seamlessly progressed and mirrored the key structural transformations of the Hindi film industry. Meanwhile, the emergent corporatizing network channelled through Bachchan's switching power over the years, which was explicitly gendered as masculine, made formal inroads abroad, especially into Egypt and Afghanistan.

Together, Bachchan's affective star persona and his effective power situated him as a critical bridging node as the Hindi film industry transitioned to a liberalized economic environment marked by accelerated globalization. A bridging node potentially connects peripheral networks to powerful cliques and diverse networks.[15] The prestige, centrality, and social capital of Bachchan and his switching power's protean nature increasingly allowed him to connect the emergent Hindi film industry's network to the interconnected influx and efflux of global economic, technological, and sociocultural flows. Peeking behind the criminal economies of mafia networks that had shadowed mainstream Bollywood was a somewhat 'formalized', 'corporatized' vision and structure steered by Bachchan's switching power as he then tried to position himself as a 'one-man corporation' in a tenor similar to his 'one-man army' star image. The duality of this power allowed him to reconfigure his star persona through other networks, such as beauty pageants and television as well, while simultaneously embodying a benevolent celluloid patriarch. On the one hand, Bachchan's power derived from relations of sociability that could mediate activities in the context of globalization and induce people to switch networks and become part of new and different contexts.[16] On the other hand, this power was enriched by star power and affect that, for Bachchan, was easily transformed and transfigured, giving him much individual agency within Bollywood's early liberalizing network's social structure at a critical moment of globalization. His switching power was gendered and masculinist in nature, much more able to affect industrial change than female stars like Sri Devi—known as *the female Bachchan* because of her ability to pull crowds to the box office—or his wife, Jaya Bachchan, whose brand value was also simultaneously monetized by ABCL. Thus, the king of kings fostered the further popularization of Hindi cinema and the emergence of Bollywood's corporate networks in singular ways.

MAPPING THE INDUSTRIAL CONTEXT: FROM CRIMINAL ECONOMIES TO THE EMERGENCE OF A PROTO-CORPORATIZED NETWORK

There is a much-fabled narrative that Bachchan's career in Bombay cinema got its start because of prime minister Indira Gandhi. Bollywood star and producer Sunil Dutt signed Bachchan to role-play a mute in his film *Reshma Aur Shera* (Reshma and Shera, 1971) because of a letter of introduction from Gandhi to the celebrated actress Nargis Dutt, Sunil Dutt's wife. Gandhi also introduced him to filmmaker Khwaja Ahmed Abbas.[17] Gandhi, the daughter of Jawaharlal Nehru (India's first prime minister), held office from 1966 to 1977 and again from 1980 until her assassination in 1984. She was part of the early efforts mobilized by Devika Rani to recognize cinema as a legitimate industry that could partake in the same benefits offered by the Indian state for other industrial sectors.

Like her father, Gandhi understood the critical import of cinema. In letters to Dorothy Norman,[18] she wrote about *Gandhi* (1982, dir. Richard Attenborough), co-produced by the Indian state-run NFDC and Britain's Goldcrest Films, and lamented that 'no Indian filmmaker ha[d] been inspired by the greatness and the drama of that magnificent mass movement or [its] remarkable men and women'.[19] Gandhi and her father, Nehru, before her, while cognizant of the needs and import of the mainstream film industry, were consistently caught between the need for promoting 'good cinema' and supporting the existing film industry. In the process of promoting a 'moral', 'socially responsible' cinema, a directive pushed on the industry since the first Film Enquiry Committee report in 1951, Nehru and Gandhi created a parallel state-led network of quality art films.

There was an inherent elitism to the approach, a marker of social and cultural capital in an institutionalized, post-independence state.[20] Filmmaker and historian Chidananda Das Gupta notes that despite the festivals, awards, institutes, and film finance corporations,

> the English-educated middle class has only created a plaything for itself—a minority cinema for the initiated few.... [I]n spite of fond

hopes cherished by some, [it] will never replace the mass cinema or
even modify its spirit. The traders of the commercial cinema may at
the most offer ritualistic homage to a *Sanskar* [Good Actions] or *Uski
Roti* [His Bread] while keeping the course of their juggernaut absolutely
unchanged. [It is] not only a failure of Indian cinema; it is a part of the
failure of leadership in the entire area of culture since Independence—
as far as the masses are concerned.[21]

Within this state-driven discourse of 'good cinema' and its culmination in
a parallel network for film production were imbued legitimating differences
between a state-sanctioned industry network and a baser, mass-oriented
mainstream cinema. Bollywood thus existed tenuously, outside of state
discourse, devoid of state funding.

Out of the reports of the first Film Enquiry Committee in 1951, which
reported on the unregulated industry spoils from wartime profiteering,[22]
came a film finance corporation in March 1960 to 'help finance films and
promote the interests of the industry'.[23] The state's facilitation of film financing
sought to promote 'good cinema' that would foreground national culture and
education, reflect the rich heritage of the country, and 'raise public taste and
set new evolutionary trends so that the climate be created for the making
of better pictures'.[24] Having received an education in Switzerland, England,
and Nobel laureate Tagore's educational complex Shantiniketan, Gandhi's
taste was hardly plebian, and she lamented the 'violence', 'crudity', and
'dimness of mind' represented by mainstream cinema.[25] Gandhi identified
the 'cultural pervasiveness' and mass appeal of cinema and exhorted the
medium to 'educate', 'elevate', and enlarge the sympathy of the audience.[26]
Her marker of taste cultivated a social hierarchy wherein a 'taste' for 'good'
cinema became a marker of class.[27] Bollywood was left to fend for itself, while
formal state financing went to art and social-issue-oriented cinema in Hindi
and other regional languages. Mainstream Hindi cinema, with its mass
appeal, remained, however, a point of contention. In the 1970s (arguably a
time of more rigorous policing and censorship), she appointed a board whose
taste she could vouch for, including her friend Teji Bachchan (Bachchan's
mother) and Hrishikesh Mukherjee (the director that created the urbane,
elite star persona for Bachchan).[28] Teji Bachchan was a well-known social
worker who established the Hindu Shakespeare Manch theatre group, and
Mukherjee was the director of award-winning films.[29] Their credentials

spoke to the eminence of their 'taste'—a familiarity with Western classics and high culture. Gandhi's letters to her American friend Norman are replete with references to Western high culture, including filmmakers Franco Zeffirelli, Alain Resnais, and Stanley Kubrick.[30] Arguably, the industry was built around defining and enforcing distinctions in the Bourdieuan sense.

Although the FFC was established in 1969 through the Gandhi government's interventionist policies and elite vision, it eventually created a parallel network for film production that competed with popular or, as some saw it, plebian mainstream Hindi cinema. In his address to the Filmfare awards, I. K. Gujral, the information and broadcasting minister in Gandhi's cabinet, noted that 'the bond of the people' unites politicians and artists. Yet, at the same time, he decried the regressive tendencies of mainstream cinema. He acknowledged creating a parallel film-production network by the Indian state and offered to 'share power' with the industry if they abandoned their 'laissez faire' approach and shared social responsibility for promoting good values among the masses.[31] In the years that followed, state support for mainstream cinema remained notional and increasingly focused on taxation. A parliamentary debate (1985) on aspects of the black market economy in India identified high taxation as the primary cause for the persistence of an illegal shadow economy that intensified in the 1980s.[32]

Despite starting his film career in the parallel state-driven film network playing the narrator in *Bhuvan Shome* (1969, dir. Mrinal Sen), one of the first films funded by the newly instituted NFDC, Bachchan quickly gravitated towards mainstream Bollywood. His first major success in the Hindi film industry came with *Zanjeer* in 1973. It marked the inception of his image as an angry young man, an image deeply mired in Bollywood's criminal economy networks. But Bachchan's persona evolved. In *Zanjeer*, at the urging of criminals and miscreants, the well-meaning upholder of law deviated from his path. In later films like *Deewar*, *Sholay*, and *Don* (1978, dir. Chandra Barot), he embraced the mafia and his outlaw status.

In *Zanjeer*, Bachchan plays Vijay, the common man, brimming with rectitude to fight the villain Teja, who, in the melodramatic tradition of Bollywood villains, is evil personified. The impulse to avenge society, morality, and justice takes on a personal meaning as Vijay recognizes Teja as the murderer of his parents via a horse-shaped pendant around Teja's wrist, a visual evocation of the trauma embedded in Vijay's childhood subconscious. The dramatic moment of revelation is filled with sonic reverberations of brass and drums, fast intercutting between Vijay's recurrent traumatic nightmare about a white horse and his current confrontation with Teja, and close-ups of Vijay's bloodshot eyes amid a staccato chime of bells. The aesthetic and the narrative present the story's logic, intercutting shots with visual and aural motifs that evoke an unambiguous interpretation of 'virtuous anger' among the 1970s audience.[33] The film marked the genesis of a new angry-young-man genre driven by affect encapsulated within Bachchan's raw anger at sociopolitical injustices. The semiotics and somatic enactment of Bachchan's anger and the resultant affect were central to the genre. Noted critic R. Mazumdar credited Bachchan with a 'vulnerable anger ... symptomatic of its time' and capable of using body language to transmit the modern and traditional, the Eastern and Western. 'What was unique about Bachchan ... was a novel use of space, an economy of words in his dialogue, a restraint in his anger and an immense and total control on [sic] his body.'[34]

Bachchan's individual heroism, a virtuous anger against a corrupt and ineffectual system that consistently failed the 'common man', proceeded film after film. In a cultural and political moment when the populace was weary of a heavy-handed state, Bachchan's persona was the 'blurred mirroring of the sociopolitical issues'.[35] His films became the fecund space wherein collective proletarian political and cultural anxieties played out.[36] They provided a cathartic restoration against the institutional failure, social disorder, and discontent that had come to typify Gandhi's emergency years. Javed Akhtar, the screenwriter for most of Bachchan's angry-young-man films, describes the character as a vigilante who had lost trust in the state and social institutions.[37] However, despite Bachchan's representation of a socialist working-class hero who is circumspect about and derisive of the system, his films escaped the state's heavy-handed censorship. The director and screenwriters of Bachchan's *Sholay* were surprised when the film was cleared for release with relatively minor censor-board cuts. They had anticipated government 'resistance on the grounds that the film risked triggering civil unrest',[38] because, in Bachchan's crime dramas, the gangster morphed into a hero. His character in *Deewar* is said to be loosely based on Bombay gangster (and film financier) Haji Mastan. This character emerged in a time of political turmoil when, in the words of popular filmmaker J. P. Dutta, 'the constitution of India was suspended in mid-air' and the 'Mumbai mafia was in high gear'.[39] Bachchan's hero transforms into the outlaw on-screen, humanizing the outlaw's (Mastan's) story. The narrative of *Deewar* is strewn with dissent and political unrest wherein Bachchan's character, Vijay, refuses to be trampled upon by an unjust system. Hence, he chooses crime and becomes a leading underworld mafioso. His brother, Ravi, whom Vijay and his mother could afford to educate, in contrast, joins the police. The film's denouement presents a defeated, fatally injured Vijay, shot at by his own brother with blood splayed over his signature white coat as he stumbles over the steps of a Shiv temple. His struggle intensifies through the sonic discord of temple bells as he holds them to make his way to his mother's lap asking for her forgiveness and blessings. The scene creates empathy for Vijay's interiority and struggle. Yet it is, in a Gramscian sense, a return of the errant outlaw to the ideological fold of religion, state authority, and morality. Priya Joshi notes the multiple parallels between Gandhi and Vijay's mother, Maa, in *Deewar*. Gandhi's 1971 election campaign slogan, 'India is Indira, Indira is India', formulated national imagery wherein she was both the mother and the nation, and her family psychodrama reverberated closely in *Deewar*.[40] The film solidified Bachchan's screen persona as the angry young man by depicting the tension between an authoritarian state and brewing, rebellious discontent among the masses. Yet, while glorifying the mafia's fight against the system, the film reinforces hierarchy. The state reigns supreme, and Vijay's anarchy is tamed in his sorrowful demise. Widespread rebelliousness is tamed in its on-screen extension as public anger against Gandhi and her authoritarian suspension of civil liberties is channelled into Bachchan's cathartic release. Yet he simultaneously imbibed a performative 'doubling' where in films like *Don*, his embodiment of the suave mafia boss and village bumpkin creates equal affect. Bachchan's ability to project 'mutually opposite traits' through a single face, a performative doubling, is mirrored in his interrelationships and network power across political, industrial, and socio-economic realms and thus renders him with switching power across all these contexts.[41]

The 1980s saw a different kind of on-screen persona for Bachchan. In films like *Muqaddar Ka Sikander* (Conqueror of Destiny, 1978, dir. Prakash Mehra), *Laawaris* (The Orphan, 1981, dir. Prakash Mehra), and *Namak Halaal* (Loyal Servant, 1982, dir. Prakash Mehra), the anger is dissipated and Bachchan's hero 'absorbs the world's paradoxes in such a way that he appears to know life as exhaustively as possible and then moves beyond it'.[42] Bachchan was a star with mass appeal at this time, but given the quality of mainstream Hindi cinema, his audience profile changed. Critics accused his films of being 'loud', 'gaudy', 'brash', and sometimes 'overtly obscene', and his audience was, in the larger hierarchy of taste, lowbrow.

In this moment of transition, a shift in technology and politics introduced the video cassette recorder (VCR). This widely adapted middle-class entertainment technology brought the cinematic experience to their living rooms. The 'frontbenchers' in movie theatres moved to balcony seats and became the primary audience that Bollywood catered to. Mainstream Hindi cinema satiated 'uncouth' and 'vulgar' sensibilities and 'not-terribly tacit theories of politics and society', and it thrived on 'shock[ing] the haute bourgeoisie with the directness, vigour and crudity of these theories'.[43] With the rise of the hitherto suppressed lower classes and rapid urbanization, this was a time for populist politics within the political realm as non-Congress parties were making their presence felt.

The affective constituent of Bachchan's protean switching power existed within his easily malleable, shifting star personas and his individual, real-life narrative as a member of the sociocultural and political elite. As the early 1980s were a significant moment of transition, marking a shift in his audience profile, he was now a mass entertainer whom proletarian audiences idolized as a 'kindred soul', more of a 'doer than a thinker'.[44] Bachchan's star image and populist appeal, alongside his sociality with the political elite, lent him immense 'network power' to mobilize change. His star image and persona worked in conjunction with the 'value-laden associations derived from his personal history'. While he manifested a proletarian-friendly screen persona, the Bachchan affect was construed and mobilized with an understanding of his illustrious background: his poet father, socially elite mother, and family's close ties with the Nehru–Gandhi family.[45]

Vijay Mishra, Madhava Prasad, and Susmita Das Gupta have remarked on Bachchan's star persona and how it could diverge to create parallel texts that went beyond his individual 'personal charisma' and easily seep into 'political, aesthetic and institutional values'.[46] This ability to exceed the networks to which he belongs, be it the industry, the political elite, or his individual star persona, lends Bachchan his exceptional protean switching power. Charisma anchored his switching between networks. In an era where the industry lacked any state support or structure, it lent him the ability to mobilize new structural changes within the industry's business practices. He was a bridge between political, sociocultural, and industrial realms, and at each moment of inflection, his star persona shifted in relation to the tenor of the flux among industrial, political, and social values. During the final years of Gandhi's tenure in office in the early 1980s, Bachchan's angry young man had morphed into a vigilante—he was no more the revolutionary but an upholder of law and order on the fringes of society. As the nation had settled into Gandhi's authoritarian leadership, Bachchan's cathartic, raw anger was no longer needed. He had morphed into an entertainer, and his films did not need complex arguments or a high ideological stance. He could be a hero of easy virtue, and with shifts in the audience profile, they saw in him 'a kindred soul, not some high and mighty judge'.[47] Bachchan, as the entertainer, was all-encompassing, leaving no space for other characters; his heroines were an appendage in the larger scheme of his films. As his wife and Bollywood actor, Jaya Bachchan, once remarked, '[A]t the time that I married Amitabh, a new kind of cinema and a new breed of filmmakers were emerging on the scene. [In their films] Amitabh Bachchan was the hero, comedian, and villain all rolled into one. Where was the role for the heroine?[48] This universalism, as many gender and film theorists have noted, reflects broader ideas about men being the normative choice.

Bachchan thus dominated the industry narrative through the power of his populist and explicitly masculine on-screen persona and its resultant affect, all of which coexisted with the parallel delineation of his 'quiet, cultured, public schoolboy' image. His contrary personal and public personas accentuated his allure and charisma—a study of contrasts that could affect the plebeian and the genteel alike. Moreover, he remained recalcitrant about the schism between the personal and on-screen personas. He stopped giving interviews to journalists—a tortured sub-group—given the strict state surveillance of ideas and thoughts during Gandhi's regime. Film magazines that he condemned for spreading rumours about him blamed Bachchan for the state's curbing of film gossip during the emergency era.[49] Evidently, being in-between varied spheres of industrial, political, and social influence enabled him to bridge those spheres and mobilize new affective and effective networks of power.

The year 1984 was monumental for Bachchan and Indian politics. Gandhi was assassinated by her personal bodyguard on 31 October 1984, and her son Rajiv (Bachchan's schoolmate and best friend) was hurriedly sworn in as the new prime minister. In December, the general elections had Bachchan contesting against leading opposition leader Hemwati Nandan Bahuguna from Allahabad—the hometown of the Bachchans and the Gandhis. A *Times of India* article from 1984 described the fervour for Bachchan

> [whom] everyone knows ... as the 'chhora Ganga Kinarewala' [the lad from along the banks of the Ganga, a refrain from Bachchan's popular song in *Don*]. The spontaneous applause he receives from the village elders and boys and girls signifies that the message has gone home. After all, dialogue delivery is no problem for this screen idol, especially when he himself has prepared the lines.

The *Times of India* identified the 'Bachchan wave' and asserted that 'shopkeepers, cycle-rickshaw pullers, panwalas, teachers and students talk appreciatively of Amitabh and expect development to be speedier if he wins'.[50] Their support was spectacular and remarkable because Bachchan's rival, Bahuguna's Dalit Mazdoor Kisan Party (Lower-Caste or Downtrodden Labourers' Farmers' Party), was formed on the premise of support for these downtrodden groups. The press dubbed the election the battle of the '*neta* and *abhineta* [the politician and the actor]' and 'guile and glamor'. Bachchan was battling the purportedly 'wiliest' incumbent, who was 'invincible in the polls'.[51] He registered a spectacular win, trouncing Bahuguna by a margin of 187,975 votes.[52] Thirty-six years hence, no politician has come close to Bachchan's margin.[53]

Bachchan's political affect pulled multiple levers. His on-screen persona as the 'lad from along the banks of the Ganga' evoked a star aura and association with the place. It claimed that he was a rightful denizen of this sleepy town on the bank of the Ganges. A rootedness, as in the sense of place and belonging, fostered membership in a collective identity, and in the case of Bachchan, his on-screen and personal narrative converged to generate affect. He was one of 'the people', and therein lies the quality of his switching power. He was the downtrodden on-screen playing the pariah and concurrently a member of the political and social elite with a diction that was both perfect and popular. His political affect was accentuated by his family pedigree and ties to the town of Allahabad. In the coalescence of cinema and politics, the extra-cinematic sphere included places and spaces where the visual iconicity of the star was constructed and became germane. A fan from Allahabad illustrates the semiotic iconicity of Bachchan. She reiterates the vectors of his polysemic image that results in a deep cultural absorption of his persona and stardom:

If you're in Allahabad, Amitabh Bachchan is your serious business. His face would look down upon you benignly from the boards of barbershops, the backs of hand-drawn rickshaws.... Amitabh Bachchan's name would lace all conversations you heard, as a stand in for a varied range of adjectives. To a friend with a case of the braggadocio, it was perfectly acceptable to say, 'Bade Amitabh Bachchan ho gaye ho [Yes, you're a proper Amitabh Bachchan now!]' ... even the nuns at the convent school that I went to, one he attended, too, would flick a stick on our open palms ... and say e-n-u-n-c-i-a-t-e like Ami-tabh. The 'h' of his name always fell on your ears with a gravity of its own, a weight and reminder of the history and legacy that we were a part of because of him.[54]

For this blogger fan, Allahabad's experience is contrived through the imbrications of affect, habit, and the practice of Bachchan's charisma, persona, and stardom. She describes an affective sensorium wherein Bachchan is enmeshed in the very experience of the place. The affective atmospheres and the sensation of the diverse social material discourses all point to the omnipresent Bachchan. Whether it is billboards and cut-outs that visually overpower the local market or the cultural memory of Bachchan, his affect is a vector in constructing the emotional geography of the place. The cumulative affective sensorium drowns us until we no longer begrudge his more troublesome aspects, which include his morally ambiguous stances on the Kathua rape or his thinly veiled conservative nationalism. Bachchan's diametrically opposite on-screen representations of the righteous and incorruptible render boundaries between politics and the real persona fallible and obfuscating: 'There is a realization that while [Bachchan] outgrew us, most of us back home never outgrew him. In fact, no other actor, no other public figure, no other brand outgrew him ... he is the light that never goes out.'[55] Bachchan has seeped into the city's affective atmosphere. Emotional and almost divine resonance attests to his protean power, which allows him to exceed the confines of his immediate networks and become central to the processes of identity-making for the audience and places alike (see Figure 2.1).[56] And as the next section shows, his 'affective sensibility' through which fans construct meanings in the cultural world, with which to determine where to invest time, money, and self, exceed beyond the local to global places and spaces spanning the Pashto and Dari communities of remote Afghanistan to the provincial and urban centres of Egypt.[57]

Figure 2.1 Fans of Amitabh Bachchan, whom they consider an incarnation of God, chanting hymns while performing a traditional Hindu religious ceremony before a portrait of the actor in the eastern Indian city of Kolkata

Source: Reuters/Sucheta Das.

MATTERING MAPS: AUDIENCE, INDUSTRY, TECHNOLOGY, AND BACHCHAN'S RESONANCE IN GLOBAL SPACES

Shahrbanoo Sadat's *Parwareshgah* (2019, The Orphanage) sculpts with exactitude the 'mattering maps' of Bachchan for the Afghan audience that help elucidate his resonance in global spaces.[58] Sadat's film begins in 1989 with an opening shot of Kabul's Cinema Shahr, where Bachchan's film posters monopolize the screen (see Figure 2.2). The next shot introduces us to our protagonist, Qodratollah, an orphan who makes a living reselling Bollywood tickets.

As 15-year-old Qodrat navigates a complex sociopolitical nexus that involves the Soviet Union, Afghanistan, and mujahideen fighters battling for national control, his interiority is reflected through Bollywood. As geopolitics plays on in the backdrop, Qodrat's emotional responses to life's

Figure 2.2 A still from *Parwareshgah* (The Orphanage, 2019, dir. Shahrbanoo Sadat): Cinema Shahr theatre, in Kabul, playing Bachchan's *Shahenshah* (King of Kings, 1988, dir. Tinnu Anand)

Source: Shahrbanoo Sadat/Luxbox.

trials and opportunities are mirrored through his fandom for Bachchan. His first teenage crush and blossoming love is mediated through a Bachchan song sequence: 'Jaane kaise kab kahan iqrar ho gaya' (I don't know how, when, or where I said yes to love) (*Shakti*, [Strength, 1982, dir. Ramesh Sippy]), where he imagines himself as Bachchan. Qodrat copes with the harrowing feeling of a friend's accidental death by a hand grenade they stole from an abandoned Russian tank by reminiscing about Bachchan's ode to 'eternal' friendship: 'Yeh dosti hum nahi chodenge' (We will not let go of this friendship) (*Sholay*). The final moments of the film, when the mujahideen seize Qodrat's orphanage as Soviet troops withdraw, are sonically fuelled by Bachchan's vigilante refrain from *Shahenshah* (King of Kings, 1988, dir. Tinnu Anand), where the teenager emotively embodies Bachchan and single-handedly attacks dozens of mujahideen. The audience and our protagonist are left hopeful as the lyrics from *Shahenshah* assert, '[I]n dark nights, on dark streets, every persecution brings out a messiah, whom people call the Shahenshah [king of kings].' As the credits roll in, Qodrat's affective faith in Bachchan and his screen persona enable the audience to skirt the harrowing feeling of things that might follow.

    Parwareshgah was screened at the Cannes Film Festival's Directors' Fortnight and is the second part of a pentalogy based on the diary of Anwar

Hashimi, Sadat's friend who lived through the tumultuous 1980s in an orphanage. Sadat constructs the 'mattering maps' of Hashimi's Bachchan and Bollywood fandom as a fragment that can be mustered to understand the affective economy of Bachchan in Afghanistan. 'It wasn't Anwar alone who loved Bollywood to distraction,' asserts Sadat.

> All of Afghanistan is in thrall of Bollywood. They regularly watch Indian movies, and that is why most Afghans can speak Urdu. The people of Afghanistan know Bollywood songs from the 1960s to the 1990s by heart. When you walk around in Kabul or eat in a restaurant or ride a taxi, it is impossible not to hear Bollywood songs.[59]

Her protagonist, Qodrat, with his room plastered with Bachchan posters, constantly measuring his life set to the tracks of Bachchan's songs, reflects the enormity of Bachchan and Bollywood fandom.

Fandom is an affective network, and fans are mobilizers of affective economies that intersect with geopolitical and industry configurations and help to shape how these configurations are networked. The configurations of Bachchan's (and Bollywood's) popularity in Afghanistan stem from a complex intersection of cultural, political, and social ties and networks between the two neighbouring countries. Mapping the flow and exchange of resources and cultural goods, we note Afghanistan's great political import for India. In the context of the Cold War, Nehru had initiated the Non-Aligned Movement (NAM) in a bid to de-colonize the newly independent countries. The first-ever summit for non-aligned nations, held in Belgrade, included Afghanistan.[60] The primary objective of NAM was to assert self-determination and independence and resist the power-block influences of rivalries triggered by the Cold War.[61] During Gandhi's reign in the 1970s, India promulgated cultural treaties and exchanges, offering Afghan residents 30 scholarships to acquire expertise in cinematography, music, and archives, among other fields. During the exchanges, the *Kabul Times* noted that the Afghan deputy minister for information and culture, Mohammad Khaled Roashan, insisted on a 'joint programme for production of films' with India.[62] The affinity for mainstream Bollywood films and stars that pre-existed in Afghan culture led to Hindi cinema being centrally situated in this geopolitical network of cultural exchange, influence, and public policy. In the 1970s and 1980s, most films that played in Afghan theatres were from India.[63] The higher purpose of cinema, however, lies beyond 'just a means

Figure 2.3 Afghan children looking at posters of Indian movies being screened at a cinema in Kabul

Source: Associated Press/Rafiq Maqbool.

of recreation.… It should also provide a good source of education for the people.'[64] Although the Indian state preferred high culture and 'good cinema', and, therefore, generally neglected mainstream Hindi films, the cultural flow of Bollywood percolated through the various industry networks, with stardom as its most important vector (see Figure 2.3).

Physically close to Afghanistan, the Indian film industry already had actors, directors, and producers like Feroze Khan, who claimed an Afghan lineage. Khan's *Dharmatma* (Righteous Soul, 1975) was the first Hindi film to be shot in Afghanistan. The director was invited to film in the country by the king and prince.[65] The industry network, therefore, was connected to central cultural and political networks and nodes in both countries. Additionally, the star affect was construed in cultural terms, in that the audience euphorically engaged with Khan, who already claimed an Afghan Pathan lineage and construed Bachchan in similar terms. Fans claimed he could be nothing but a Pathan because 'otherwise, how come he is so tall'.[66] Within Bollywood's output and manifestation, the Afghan Pathan recurred often; he was brave, loyal, and righteous, and Bachchan's characters imbibed these virtues culminating in his last 1990s superhit, *Khuda Gawah*, wherein he embodies this honorary Afghan identity. *Khuda Gawah* featured opulent Afghan locales and repurposed a war-torn Afghanistan into a mythic, exhilarating locale inhabited by muscular, swashbuckling equestrian Pathans. The figure of the Pathan and its sociopolitical and cultural resonance within the Indo-Afghan context made *Khuda Gawah* a meta-movie, one that simultaneously referenced Bachchan's star image, Bollywood narrative, and aesthetic conventions about Pathans and the sociocultural and political ties between the two countries. At a time of great political turmoil in Afghanistan, *Khuda Gawah* evoked the country's glorious, traditionalist past through Bachchan, a Pathan wronged by society and neighbouring India. In other words, the film circulates a sympathetic perspective on Indo-Afghan ties.

The melodramatic mode of delivery that draws polarities between ideas and values associated with truth and justice versus the evil conundrum of injustice and wrongdoing accentuated the image of Bachchan as a righteous Pathan. This film, produced at the behest of Afghan president Najibullah, who insisted that a Bachchan movie be filmed in Afghanistan, helps us unpack the interconnections between the media industry and geopolitical networks and how they were influenced by star power. It brings together politics, personal experiences, and public life within the realm of stardom-creating affective and effective economies. *Khuda Gawah* is a meta-narrative because it maps the sociocultural and geopolitical imaginaries of Afghanistan, wherein the convergence of political and Bollywood industry networks culminates in a film that is imbued with political function.[67] The geopolitical uncertainty of Afghanistan in the temporal moment is resolved through building a moral geography and trust in the Pathan epitomized in Bachchan's character, Khudabaksh. The film enables us to map the political geography of Indo-Afghan networks and ties at the level of state and industry through Bachchan's protean switching power and ability to bridge these domains. Najibullah's government was drawn into the throes of civil war again in 1992, the same year as the film's release. The Soviets withdrew, and the US-backed mujahideen that morphed into the Taliban assumed control over the country. Through the ebb and flow of political unrest and disruption, Bollywood films and culture continued circulating in Afghanistan, despite cinema being banned by the Taliban, through formal and informal shadow economies enabled by technologies like the VCR and digital versatile disc (DVD). Nevertheless, Bollywood and Bachchan remained a source of respite, as one journalistic account of the US–Taliban war recounts:

[We were on the frontlines] with three Alliance fighters hiding behind sandbag trenches [letting loose] a volley of gunfire ... with Taliban infantry sitting atop another house just 200 metres away return[ing] the fire ... [but] [e]ven as bullets whizzed around, [our guide] Sabghatullah was more interested in talking about Amitabh Bachchan. For him, like most Afghanis, war is just another day in his life.[68]

Bachchan and Bollywood, however, were anchors that veered Afghans away from their dreary reality. Taran N. Khan, author of *Shadow City: A Woman Walks Kabul*, narrates the cultural absorption of Bollywood beyond Bachchan as an affect and idea seeped into the culture:

In Kabul, Bollywood is many things. At times, it is an omen, a portent of things to come. A filmmaker friend told me that during the years of civil war, he would listen to the radio nervously with his group of soldiers each morning. 'If the first song of the day was by Rafi [Bollywood singer], our company would advance, and the enemy would have to retreat. If it was Mukesh, the other side would move ahead.' At other times, cinema is celebration and ritual—there are few weddings that would be complete without a rendition of *Parde mein rehne do*, to which revelers dance with veils drawn over their faces. It can be a declaration of machismo, as in the boast of shop-owners who sell pirated VCDs [video compact discs] of films within a day of their release in Mumbai. It is irony, it is politics and history. In [Bollywood's] complicated embrace, Kabul creates the entire satisfying canvas of life.[69]

Although towering personas like Bachchan accentuate the appeal and embody a predominant charisma, the affect is not entirely star-driven. The charisma, however, is embedded within the larger superseding cultural form of Bollywood replete with masala—music, song, dance, melodrama, and, of course, Bachchan—elements that have, through cultural osmosis over the course of decades, found a way into the fabric of Afghan society. Hence Qodrat, Sadat's protagonist in Kabul of the 1980s, possesses no one but Bachchan and Bollywood to express his liminal triumphs, anguish, and bravado. As the mujahideen attack his orphanage, the tenuous ties of Soviet and American political stakes are fraying. Qodrat finds momentary agency as he envisages himself as Bachchan's *Shahenshah*, a vigilante who exudes masculinity and power and successfully asserts authority despite his liminal status. In moments of calamity, he conjures up momentary power through Bachchan and Bollywood. Like the liminality of Qodrat and his fandom in the larger context of Afghanistan, the Indian film industry similarly existed and circulated through liminal routes in Afghanistan, Dubai, and other parts of the Middle East of its own accord through the affective labour of fandom and informal economies rather than state-supported export of cinema.

In this context, Egypt emerged as a country where atypically formal, state-led networks initiated the cinematic exchange. Gamal Abdel Nasser, the second president of Egypt, and Yugoslavian president Josip Broz Tito were Nehru's main allies in his call for 'positive neutralism' and non-alignment during the Cold War. The political bonhomie culminated in cultural flows, and cinema was at the forefront of this exchange. An article published in the Egyptian magazine *Al-Kawakib* stresses the importance of Indo-Egyptian political ties and their centrality in the context of cinema when it called for strengthening 'the ties between ourselves and the great Indian people who have stood with us through the darkest times' and praised 'Egyptians who believe that nationalism require[s] that they act as unofficial ambassadors by developing commercial and spiritual ties … through [the] cultural exchange [of] Indian films'.[70]

The article further mentioned an Indian–Egyptian film distribution agency (al-Wikala al-Misriyya al-Hindiyya li-Tauzi'al-Aflam) that had undertaken the distribution of Indian films in Egypt.[71] Cinema and other forms of mediated cultural power became central to the NAM alliance. NAM, however, as Gabica Bockaj notes, was never more than a mediatic apparatus composed of conferences, speeches, gifts, and diplomacy through cinema, stars, and icons.[72] Cultural and environmental similarities, music, and the manifold attractions of Bollywood masala made Hindi cinema valuable for this rapprochement between the two cultures. The socialist-leaning ideology of Hindi cinema also aligned with Nasser's Arab socialism. Within this instance in which political networks initiated the global flow of Indian cinema, the star, peaking with Bachchan, continued to be the real draw.

The Egyptian reception of Indian cinema and the ramifications of high and low culture made for a complex exchange. Walter Armbrust, studying the perception of India in Egyptian films and magazines from the 1930s to the 1950s, points to a 'contemptuous othering' for Indian film and culture. Egyptian films and magazines engaged with Indian cinema but accompanied their engagement with the Egyptian elite's disparaging views; yet India and Indian cinema claimed a 'ubiquitous non-presence, an over-familiarity that bred contempt'.[73] Yet this image shifted in the 1950s and 1960s with the political elites' alignment in a somewhat 'rhetorical linking' of both societies to the non-aligned movement.[74]

The post-Nasser Egyptian state expressed an aversion to Indian cinema, projecting it as detrimental to the local film industry and Islamic morality. Following Nasser's death in 1970 and an increased inward focus by the Sadat regime, state support for the local film industry waned, and in 1971, a mandatory exhibition law required cinemas to reserve screens for exclusive showings of Egyptian films. The ministerial decree first limited the showings of Indian films, later to be banned entirely, as 'a box-office threat given their ubiquity and general appeal to audiences'.[75] Egypt thus instantiated another exemplary instance wherein Bachchan exceeded his network's constraints in garnering unprecedented popularity in an era when state network mediation and support were non-existent. He again found proletarian allies and cultivated fandoms that operated across gender and class divides.

In a rare video documenting his visit to Egypt in 1991 to attend the Cairo International Film Festival, Bachchan's teenage female fans wrote his name in blood. The event's organizer noted that more than 3,000 people were at the airport to greet him, shouting his name and crying at the sight of their revered star.[76] Famous Egyptian stars, including president Anwar el-Sadat's wife, Jehan el-Sadat, welcomed him during his 1991 visit.[77] The restrictions on Indian films after Sadat's assassination became even more stringent.[78] Antoine Ziend, the founder and chairman of United Motion Pictures (an Egyptian film distributor), blames the Hosni Mubarak regime (1981–2011) for the disappearance of Hindi films from Egyptian theatres.[79] In a 1988 interview with the Egyptian daily *Al Ahram*, local film distributor Badi Shobi claimed that

> since *Sangam* (1964) was shown in Egypt, I [have been the] one who imported Indian films … about fifteen films in ten years. Egyptian films only show local criticism; Indian films compensate for this, as they have proven to suit all tastes, including Egyptian. I am surprised that we restrict its import and give freedom to other films.[80]

Bachchan was central to this Egyptian circuit of Bollywood fandom. His film *Mard* (Man, 1985, dir. Manmohan Desai) received permission to be screened at cinemas in Cairo and sold more than a million tickets during its run.[81] Commenting on the film's success, the local newspaper *Al Ahrar* quipped that while his film gets a million *mushaahid* (views), Egyptian cinema stars are like a million *shahiid* (martyrs).[82] The article further noted that 'the popularity of Indian cinema has reached a point that one of the theatres in the Shubra neighbourhood causes daily traffic due to the incessant congestion at the doors'.[83] The author decries the Ministry of Culture for chasing and expelling Indian films from Egyptian theatres and applying these laws especially harshly to Indian films to protect an Egyptian film industry that misuses these laws.[84] Evidently, within Egypt, Bachchan and his fandom epitomized a star cult that found its way to the devoted fans, sometimes through cinema but often through the circuitous networks of new technology and pirate shadow economies.[85]

Even though the Egyptian government perceived Indian cinema as a threat to its local industry and the Indian state remained indifferent to the fate of Bollywood, Bachchan's star image and appeal kept mainstream Hindi cinema relevant on a global scale—especially in places like Egypt. Star switching power, however, does not operate in a vacuum. It derives its power from its contemporary industry, political, sociocultural, and technological networks, which it reconfigures. Hence, Bachchan's presence in the Middle East was further augmented and sustained by the introduction of new technologies, such as the VCR, which created informal shadow economies for the circulation of Hindi films through pirate networks. With its 'inherent portability' and 'ability to circumvent national and legal boundaries', it proved a technological catalyst for the percolation of Bollywood across the Middle East, Africa, and Asia, triggering a critical node in the proto-network structure:

> The VCR enabled Indian films to circumvent government censors, duty collectors and canal agencies (through which all film imports/exports had to pass), and to establish a reliable supply network worldwide without first acquiring the 'critical mass' upon which Hollywood's global operations have relied historically (that is, vertically integrated major studios organized in the MPAA cartel). In contrast to the block-booking and mass monopoly practices through which the US industry established itself during the photochemical era, the pattern of distribution achieved by Indian films through playback media over the last 25 years can instead be seen as exemplary of the effective targeting of a dispersed, (mostly) niche audience through demand-driven film distribution undertaken along a chain of relatively small entrepreneurs.[86]

Bollywood financing mired in the pre-existing criminal economy networks accentuated the ability to skirt legal circumscriptions and create a parallel shadow economy for the circulation of Hindi films. This globality was thus created at the cost of lost economic capital that further weakened Bollywood film clusters, including their demands and claims made of the Indian state. Taran Khan, in her account of Kabul, notes that during the Taliban regime, 'truckloads of Hindi movies arrived via Pakistan'.[87] Prior to this, even during the civil war years, Hindi films did brisk business in major theatres in cities like Kabul and Mazar-e-Sharif.[88] Although garnering transnational fame for stars such as Bachchan, the emergence of this technology-led network severely depleted the revenues of struggling Bollywood film-production clusters. Bachchan himself noted in a BBC interview in 1983 that Bollywood films on video had begun to obliterate the overseas market for Indian films because people stopped going to the theatres to watch films. This technological shift thus hurt the existing industry nodes financially despite enabling the global popularity of Indian films and stars like Bachchan. Bootlegging and piracy took a digital turn as the next wave of technological change came to the fore with the DVD. As Bollywood networks moved towards a more formalized networked structure in the 1990s, this informal economy waned, giving way to a newer structure. Bachchan's protean power matured and morphed again as he established himself as a change-maker and bridge as large-scale transformations reconfigured the Indian economy and the place of the film industry within it.

STAR BRANDS, ABCL, AND THE NASCENT PROTO-BOLLYWOOD NETWORK: THE 'MAGIC POTION' OF LIBERALIZATION (1980S–2000S)

I do not minimize the difficulties that lie ahead on the long and arduous journey on which we have embarked. But as Victor Hugo once said, '[N]o power on earth can stop an idea whose time has come.' I suggest to this august House that the emergence of India as a major economic power in the world happens to be one such idea. Let the whole world hear it loud and clear. India is now wide awake. We shall prevail. We shall overcome.

—Manmohan Singh, former finance minister of India[89]

Economic reforms in India started gradually in the 1980s with 'liberalization' and subsequently 'globalization', steadily creating a movement toward 'a new externally oriented, consumption-led path to national prosperity'.[90] Liberalization in the 1990s was a pivotal moment when post-haste government divestitures and foreign corporate investments came packaged with the rosy allure of global products, brands, and media.[91] The 'magic potion' of liberalization had won quite a few converts.[92] While the Indian film industry was not yet an official industry, the government welcomed foreign investment in the television sector.[93]

At this critical moment of inflection, Bachchan was the first to envision a global corporatized film industry and set up an Indian entertainment conglomerate, Amitabh Bachchan Corporation Limited. In the early decades after independence, Bollywood's attempts at globalization led by individual stars like Raj Kapoor, Shashi Kapoor, and Dev Anand were often motivated by personal ambition. However, in the new liberal economic climate of the 1990s, global forays and 'corporatization', rather than unorganized family-led industrial clusters, were the norm for other industries. At this significant juncture, Bachchan emerges as a pivotal switching node to configure and programme networks to enable the Indian Hindi film industry's globalization.

The emergent Bollywood network and the new nodes that materialized in the 1990s revealed that although nodes with switching power were at the helm of networks, power was not exclusively vested in individual nodes such as Bachchan but existed diffusely in their relationships and ecosystem that star nodes like Bachchan could create with other nodes or networks. Thus, we see vital shifts within the Indian entertainment industry as it acquired the semblance of a network, and its critical nodes emerged. Those nodes included: (*a*) global institutions (ranging from the World Bank to the Miss World organization) that now had a newfound interest in India as a growing market economy; (*b*) a nascent global Indian television sector that was thriving due to deregulation and foreign investment; (*c*) domestic non-media conglomerates that showed interest in the media sector; (*d*) transnational media corporations seeking to invest in India; and (*e*) the Indian diaspora, a focus for the government and the economy in the wake of liberalization. These novel nodes and networks were central to the global flows of Hindi cinema. A star with relational agency and network-making power, such as Bachchan, could configure global networks in this media landscape. The 1990s were the first time that the language of brands, branding, and stars-as-brands took centre stage in India's film industry.

This part of the triptych elaborates Bachchan's relational agency within and between political, economic, social, and industrial networks and his ability to configure and operationalize new networks that created the groundwork for the globalization of Indian cinema.

As noted earlier, star nodes with switching power were central in this emerging network; however, that power was diffuse. It was relationally dependent on the evolving industrial ecosystem and the relationships star nodes such as Bachchan could create within it. However, Bachchan's centrality in these processes is undeniable, and, in this phase, one notable reason why he could mobilize a 'brandscape' built around his stardom.

A brandscape is an environment where brands are invested with meaning, and consumption is tied to varied global flows as consumers partake in the creation of meaning. In a branded world, consumption becomes an expressive activity wherein the sign value of consumed goods takes precedence over their functional value. The expressive element is tied to a brand's immaterial value, the aesthetic and emotional merit embedded with the product's aura and image. The trust and affect vested in the brands generate value and capital and are treated as equity.[94] The mobilization of a brandscape around his star aura signalled a moment of metamorphosis not simply for Bachchan. Instead, it instigated a moment of catalytic change. In leveraging his brand equity as India's leading superstar, Bachchan opportunistically invoked the political, ideological, industrial, and social discourse embodied by his on-screen and off-screen persona. In interviews, he noted that he was the first to conceptualize the imminent changes as the industry landscape was shifting due to liberalization. He emerged as the local star brand with global equity and clout to actuate a structurally transformative vision:

I will sort of blow my own trumpet a little bit here. In 1995, when I started ABCL … the idea was to formalise or corporatise this very potent entertainment industry. It came about from discussions with people in the West who saw India as a new frontier. My lawyers would say, 'You should get your house in order because the Americans are coming.' In my initial talks with executives, I had said that within five years, all big corporations are going to land here and buy us out. Hollywood … moved into United Kingdom and eventually destroyed the industry. Then they moved into Europe and its cinema vanished.… And they are moving absolutely in the same direction in India as well. I think we can share each other's expertise and build our own systems and standards. We must check piracy and strengthen our laws. Earlier, it was an individual pursuit, but I am happy that something I started in 1995 is being followed.[95]

Through mobilizing his brand, Bachchan positioned himself at the core of the emerging configuration in the film industry's nascent network-like structure as he morphed again, Proteus-like, to embody the adage that French producer Alain Chamas coined for him: 'This man is not just a star. Amitabh Bachchan is an industry.'[96]

This is not a narrative about aggrandizing the role of Bachchan, but it seeks to foreground the network-making power and primacy of switching nodes that can connect a varied set of networks to achieve specific goals. A star with switching power, Bachchan configured global networks due to the relational agency and network-making power he possessed in the neoliberal media landscape, which was channelled by and manifested in ABCL. Although Bachchan envisioned ABCL as a Walt Disney-style vertically integrated, convergent media conglomerate, Bachchan's brand and celebrity formed the core of his entertainment and media corporation. With 'brand power' and brand equity, he was anointed as India's first 'star brand', and with his brand functioning as his relational agency, ABCL accomplished many goals for Indian Hindi films. First, ABCL's corporate network laid the groundwork for the formal recognition and future 'corporatization' of Indian films. Second, it emphatically established the celebrity star as a switching node within the emerging Bollywood network and that it took star-led attempts to take global flows of Indian cinema to the next level. The power of the star in post-liberalization India was a far cry from the 'dependent independence' their Hollywood contemporaries experienced in a post-studio system.[97] Third, ABCL, the 'first-ever experiment of its kind',[98] set an example for the industry to emulate. Lastly, ABCL set an example for the industry to emulate and set off a network effect wherein other stars and domestic corporations began experimenting with corporatization. Seeking a kind of Weberian rationalization, the domestic film corporations wanted to partake in the neoliberal logics of the economy and claim their share in the liberalizing media market.

Why was this switching or metamorphosis from an iconic star to a brand easy for Bachchan? As the country embraced neoliberalism, Bachchan's iconicity shifted. He could easily morph into the capitalist mould of corporate power enabled by a shift in his affective power that created a new brand identity. The segue from an iconic star to an iconic brand seems perspicuous if we delve into the elements that create an iconic brand. Douglas Holt notes that a brand becomes iconic when it performs identity myths that create simple fictions that drive away cultural anxieties by creating imaginary, aspirational mythical worlds.[99] Bachchan's fiction and affect had always been aspirational, yet the manifestation of that affect was widely different in the 1990s. His on-screen persona was no longer rebelliously cathartic. While it continued to be aspirational, his persona was now also conformist and imbued with structural power. It was a power that Bachchan always possessed in real life as a cultural, political, and social elite, but the 1990s saw the persona projected on-screen as he resolved to leverage his brand equity through ABCL. The strategy, the embodiment of the Bachchan brand, was imbued with cultural, ideological, and sociological objects, strategies, values, and meanings constructed by his films and persona. The primary way to construct these objects and imbue them with meaning was through cinematic embodiment. Thus, the harrowed, non-conformist police inspector from *Zanjeer* was now the patriarch of *Suryavansham*, *Mohabattein*, and *K3G*, belabouring the need for order. In *Mohabattein*, Bachchan plays the imposing principal (Narayan Shankar) of an elite residential school, Gurukul. With his rigid posture and 'gimlet-like eyes', he can stifle every transgressive thought among Gurukul students. His school purports to value 'tradition, excellence, and discipline' wherein Shankar embodies the emergent nationalistic neoliberal values being embraced by the Indian state. Bachchan's power morphs into a neoliberal avatar in the 1990s as the state and economic networks undergo change. His 'performative doubling' presents us with a pro-establishment Bachchan. The social milieu and realism of his on-screen personae are antipodean. No more the inspector or coolie that endures the humiliation of an ineffectual and unjust system, Bachchan's on-screen persona is now an upholder of the traditional systemic values. Although his character is presented in opposition to the new consumable hero of liberalizing India, embodied by Shah Rukh Khan, Bachchan's character personifies the institutional, sociocultural power he possessed and mobilizes off-screen, and it was markedly upper-class, upper-caste, and pro-establishment. The films that followed concretized Bachchan's transformation into the Hindu majoritarian, pro-establishment, elite consumerist persona. The films that followed—*Armaan* (Desire, 2003, dir. Honey Irani), *Baghban* (Gardener, 2003, dir. Ravi Chopra), *Kabhi Alvida Naa Kehna* (Never Say Goodbye, 2006, dir. Karan Johar), and *Baabul* (Affectionate Father, 2006, dir. Ravi Chopra)—had Bachchan morphing into a contemporary 'benevolent patriarch', the 'quintessential cool, hip dad', embodying the duality of liberalizing India where modernity purports to coexist unproblematically beside tradition.[100]

The transformative change in Bachchan's on-screen persona to a bourgeois, liberal modern figure was seductive, and his newly created affective sensorium claimed power and authority. The affective economies existed 'in-between' the brandscape constructed and deployed by ABCL as the brandscape unfolded through protean articulations with 'varying social formations and political, symbolic, and moral economies ... to impose a homogeneous "globalized" code of conduct in the marketplace'.[101] ABCL was Bachchan's vehicle, which helped in the culmination of star switching power for the globalizing marketplace by synthesizing his brandscape and starscape. As he performed the identity myths of liberalizing India, which allayed the cultural anxieties of globalization by presenting a transformative model, his organization incorporated global flows of capital and media into an all-encompassing brandscape that brought together characters, places, and production entities, leading to a change in the structure of the Bollywood film industry.

ABCL represented the initial move toward the formalization of the industry. It marked a move away from the informal *hundi* system of financing that was prevalent in Bollywood. *Hundi* was an unofficial system; lacking in legal accountability, it was often connected to 'illegal money laundering networks' and served as a system of tax evasion.[102] Being a formal corporate industrial entity at this juncture entailed—at the very least—a legal source of financing and registration under the state-mandated Companies Act.[103] Corporate governance requirements also warranted standard accounting practices, business plans, targets, time schedules, and insurance mandated by financial institutions and banks.[104] Thus far, Bollywood's family-led film-production clusters had existed outside of these formal structures that were being put in place by the government. Bachchan was the first in the film industry to set up a corporate entity funded through bank loans and equity investment.[105]

Bachchan's corporatized organization sought vertical integration by starting in-house production, distribution, and marketing. He searched for and nurtured up-and-coming talent in-house like the old Hollywood studios. The company also set up a nationwide talent agency that would conduct searches throughout the country for the most talented actors and musicians. Additionally, ABCL ventured into the management of entertainment events and publishing. The company quickly multiplied its operations from 1996–1997, hoping to reach a lofty market capitalization of INR 1,000 crore (equivalent to USD 13.8 million) within five years.[106] Kotak Mahindra, a private bank, set the ambitious—by domestic standards—market capitalization figure for ABCL, although the bank's spokesperson qualified its statement, admitting 'it was the first time that the bank was [attempting] to calculate the brand value of individual personalities' (see Table 2.1).[107]

Significantly, the ABCL brand included Amitabh Bachchan and his wife, Jaya Bachchan, also a Bollywood actor. Jaya Bachchan received her training at the state-sponsored FTII and was arguably more of an actor than a star. The bank's assessment pegged Jaya Bachchan's brand value to be only one-fifth of her husband's and rated Amitabh Bachchan as a 'megastar' brand with more influence and celebrity charisma. The bank's assessment of brand value points to critical issues of sexism and gender bias in the mainstream Hindi film industry, a fact that obliterates the appeal, agency, and potential switching power for female stars in a male-dominated industry landscape, where women's power was often contingent on being tied to male movers and shakers (a topic that is explored further in Chapter 5).

In this ambitious endeavour, the entire corporation was tied to a single 'brand', a lone star persona. Sceptics saw Bachchan's corporate vision as hyperbole ABCL, they said, was 'too high, too far, too soon'.[108] The corporation was also set up on the premise of a circular, iterative logic—to

Table 2.1 Amitabh Bachchan Corporation Limited's (ABCL) projected earnings, 1995–1998 (INR million)

	1995–1996	1996–1997	1997–1998
Commercial sales	95	210	485
Television/Video	185	291	453
Event management	80	260	450
Film production	81	57	122
Celebrity management	40	75	100
Film distribution	35	75	90
Audio	53	63	83
Publishing	5	7	10
Total	574	1038	1793

Source: Kotak Mahindra Finance Limited; Robin Abreu, 'ABCL Already Gaining from Amitabh Bachchan Magic', *India Today*, 30 November 1995, 1.

use the Bachchan brand widely and iteratively to develop other brands. The other brands could be new stars that ABCL created and popularized.[109] The language of brands and branding was paramount during this phase of national economic liberalization. According to Celia Lury, brands mediate the demand for products and services within the global economy and organize the global flows of people, products, events, and images.[110] Within the marketing lexicon, a brand is anthropomorphized, whereas the strategy of branding stars reverses that process; a person is actualized as a brand: 'With a brand, symbolic and economic value are conjoined in the marking of difference.'[111] To have 'value', brands must deliver economic value. Bachchan, the biggest star of the 1970s and 1980s, could conceive of the economic value of his stardom, and—in an era replete with new private and global investments—the economic value of his stardom was assessed as strong, even infallible.

Soon after incorporating the Amitabh Bachchan brand, the actor attempted to extend his brand commercially. Brand or business extension occurs when a brand name is leveraged in a different category to create a competitive advantage.[112] The Bachchan brand endorsed BPL, an Indian consumer electronics company that had recently started manufacturing television sets. Bachchan agreed to endorse BPL products for an annual endorsement fee. BPL, in turn, would sponsor and invest in television and television software events, audio releases, and foreign and domestic films promoted by ABCL. The brand-extension announcement, recognizing further opportunities, stated: 'Mr. Bachchan can endorse shampoos, soaps, as long as BPL does not make them.'[113] Bachchan took the idea of brand extension a step further with a 'Star Trek' talent hunt that would create stars, and Bachchan's endorsement would recursively create other star brands. Thus, ABCL was metaphorically and literally the incorporation of the logics and practices of global economic, organizational structure and business within the Indian Hindi film and entertainment industry.

The 1990s were a time when investment capital was flowing into India because of its liberal economic policies in all industrial sectors *except* films. In this newly configured economic marketplace, the star figure acted as a critical bridge able to synchronize a global network for the film industry. Bachchan declared himself uncomfortable 'being a brand', but he noted Hollywood's export-earning power and countered that Indian stars are better known than Hollywood's: 'I don't see why this should not be a major export earner.'[114]

Liberal economic policies and their imagined impact were palpable in his statement, and so was his appeal beyond Indian shores. Furthermore, Bachchan made a case for a global Bollywood. The distribution arm of ABCL, however, started its operations by bringing key Hollywood films to Indian audiences, acquiring Indian distribution rights for Quentin Tarantino's 1994 classic *Pulp Fiction*, and alongside Modi Films International (a non-celebrity-led distribution company), it was one of the early entrants to take advantage of the import-liberalization process.[115] Changes in the government's import policies were advantageous for Hollywood because companies like ABCL and Modi Films ensured a quicker release of American films in India.[116] ABCL also acquired the Indian distribution rights for Shekhar Kapur's controversial film *Bandit Queen* (1994), based on an Indian female bandit Phoolan Devi's life. Co-produced by Britain's Channel 4 and the Indian production company Kaleidoscope Entertainment, the story of a lower-caste woman turning into a bandit because of repeated assaults by upper-class men proved controversial. Indian censorship of the film was unacceptable to the director, and the real-life Phoolan Devi threatened to sue the film company because of the uproar. It was, however, internationally acclaimed, and even though (or perhaps especially because) its distribution in India was embroiled in controversy, it generated box-office revenue.[117] The distribution arm of ABCL attempted to bring foreign films to the Indian market and participated in global co-productions like *Bandit Queen*. This first phase for the industry was, therefore, more about incorporating the global within the local. At this point, all the global flows enabled by ABCL were unidirectional, and the organization did not attempt to create global Indian films.

On the film-production front, an early film co-produced by ABCL was *Bombay* (1995, dir. Mani Ratnam), another venture mired in controversy. *Bombay* was a love story between a Hindu man and a Muslim woman set against the backdrop of the 1992 Bombay (Mumbai) communal riots. The censor board delayed the film's release for fear of inciting further violence. An Indian court eventually cleared the Hindi version of *Bombay* for release a few months after its Tamil version, reasoning from the Tamil experience that turned out to be orderly and uneventful. The film was well received at the box office and, like *Bandit Queen*, turned out to be successful for ABCL.[118] The global distribution prospects for the film, however, appeared bleak. It was screened at the Edinburgh Film Festival and won a political film society award in the US; however, the film could not find an international distributor. Thus, during the first year of its incorporation, ABCL produced and distributed

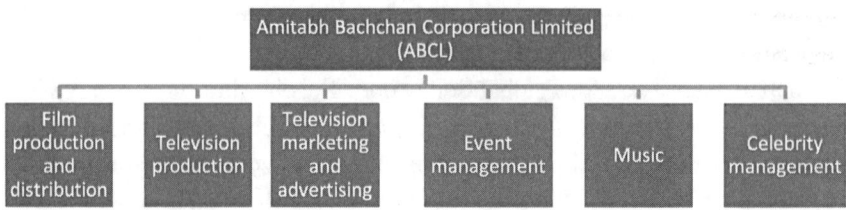

Figure 2.4 Amitabh Bachchan Corporation Limited's (ABCL) subsidiaries
Source: Prepared by the author.

two controversial films but registered a profit of INR 18 crores (roughly USD 2.25 million).[119] In the first year, then, ABCL acted mainly as a conduit for bringing global media and entertainment to India rather than exploring the global potential of Indian films and stars, as Bachchan had envisioned.

Since the corporation was conceived as a Disney-like conglomerate, ABCL expanded its operations to other aspects of the film value chain, including music, talent management, and event management, to leverage its talent brand equity and other related areas such as television production and marketing (see Figure 2.4).

ABCL became part of an emerging narrative of a megastar-led organization. At the same time, it was also mired in controversy and financial troubles. The incorporation of the Bachchan brandscape within the more prominent logics of neoliberal capitalism was a protean move that failed Bachchan because of its schismatizing relationship with the star brand and image that he had embodied thus far. His iconicity as the 'anti-establishment' star failed him in part because he transformed himself into the avaricious industrialist he had spent decades fighting on-screen. This dilemma was gradually resolved in the 2000s. However, it reiterates the argument about Bachchan's network power as he mobilized and precipitated global commerce for Bollywood's liberalizing network. One of ABCL's most significant contributions in this regard was the incorporation of other global nodes and networks within Bollywood. The three distinctive networks that ABCL mobilized and helped incorporate within Bollywood's global logics were global beauty pageant and cosmetic industry networks, diaspora networks in anglophone countries like the US and the UK (directly aligned with state policy), and television industry networks that had hitherto been solely favoured by the Indian state, which deliberately excluded the film industry from benefitting from newly instituted liberal economic policies. These networks enabled trans-regional cooperation and aligned with the Indian state's neoliberal economic policy objectives.

ABCL's decision to host the Miss World pageant in India was purposeful in its symbolic value. The contest was a vehicle for India's public policy and global perception as a developing, liberalizing economy. At the same time, it was a spectacle to promote conspicuous consumption and capitalism that was welcomed by state-implemented liberalization.[120] The networks instigated by the event created routes for global flows of content and talent for the film and entertainment industry. They anchored political visions and policy objectives and created neo-networks of exchange and cooperation. In many ways, Bachchan and ABCL were 'sophisticated mediators' in the ways they could envision India's aspirational place in the global world order after liberalization. Acknowledging the critical intervention of Bachchan's ABCL in the Miss World context, the chief editor of *Femina*, India's leading women's fashion magazine, noted that organizing the contest was a way to make India progress: '[The Miss World contest] can tell people that we are no less than any other country. Today we have liberalization but no real action because Indian politicians lack imagination and sophisticated thinking.'[121] Herein, Bachchan and his organization manifested as a key bridging node and mediator that could exceed the government's restrictive 'traditional' imagination and bring global media, culture, and, more importantly, foreign investment to the country.

The 1996 Miss World pageant, however, also introduced controversy that speaks to the limits of this strategy. The controversy related to the context clouded ABCL and possibly led to the organization's early demise. Bachchan's switching power was critical in enabling the coveted contest to be held in Bangalore. The pageant was hailed as an economic milestone for the Indian entertainment, advertisement, and tourism industries. The Indian press lauded the Miss World contest and the Michael Jackson concert that preceded Miss World as the biggest entertainment event ever hosted by India.[122] The pageant transformed the industry by appealing to global institutions and their interests in India and precipitated the formation of a proto-global Indian film and entertainment network. As Bachchan was gradually undergoing an on-screen transformation aligned with the off-screen mobilization of the nascent industry network, his iconicity shifted and acquired new meanings. At this moment, his star identity and the myths that the star brand was built upon were drastically reconfiguring themselves in tandem with the audience's cultural anxieties about globalization.

Concurrently, from an industry standpoint, the organization of the Miss World contest in India represented the incorporation of the multi-billion-dollar global beauty industry into the Indian economy and its film and entertainment sector. Contrary to the neoliberal globalization argument, the pageant presented that the world was flattening and creating opportunities for India to stake its claim as a rising economy—the Miss World contest also epitomized the crisis of Indian cultural globalization that played out against Bachchan's populist brandscape. The cultural crisis presented Miss World as a 'depredation of multinational capital',[123] like McDonald's or Coca-Cola. In the guise of culture and beauty, the contest peddled the multi-billion-dollar global beauty industry to a new liberalizing market. When the contest was staged in Bangalore, India's global capital flow and its influence on a liberalizing India were starkly evident. The Miss World would attract an audience of over two billion people across 115 countries, revealing 'the new India on show: liberal, expensive, Westernized and full of imported goods ... [while] [m]any of the poor wait with open palms outside Bangalore's air-conditioned shopping malls and warehouse-sized department stores, neither of which existed anywhere in India five years ago'. Cultural change was afoot. Five years earlier, restricted access to foreign goods meant Indian women had but one cosmetics purveyor, Lakmé. With import and investment rules changing, L'Oréal, Yardley, Avon, and Revlon entered India's market with billion-dollar investments.[124]

Cultural theories of globalization have often emphasized the homogenization of global culture, best epitomized in the phrase 'McDonaldization',[125] but the 'Miss Worldization' of Indian culture created a curious camaraderie among Muslims, right-wing Hindu groups like the Rashtriya Swayamsevak Sangh (RSS) and Shiv Sena, radical feminists, and other women's groups, farmers, and political parties. Even real-life 'bandit queen' Phoolan Devi commented on the futility and cultural corrosiveness of the event: 'Parading half-naked women will not enhance the image of Bangalore or India.... [Bachchan] should have put his energy in some worthy cause instead of organizing a beauty pageant.'[126] All the anxieties about globalization on the social and economic fronts in these first few years of liberalization were manifest on the cultural front. Critics claimed that the Miss World contest was an affront to Indian culture. Bachchan was at the centre of the controversy, positioned as the lone figure with the power to bring about these outrageous cultural transformations. Bachchan's on-screen angry young man, which relentlessly opposed the system, stood in stark opposition to Bachchan, the purveyor and organizer of global beauty contests and 'Miss Worldization'. Unemployed young men, feminist women, and farmers mounted protests: a self-immolation by a protestor in Tamil Nadu, a barrage of threats, an attack on the ABCL office in Bangalore, and massive rallies and marches. The result was a clampdown by the state that deployed the army to convert the venue—M. Chinnaswamy Stadium—into a fortress for the smooth running of the pageant. The discontent with globalization, its inequitable distribution of wealth, and a visible neoliberal shift in erstwhile socialist state policies generated mass panic and apprehension. It played out as fear of cultural imperialism through global and colonial institutions, interestingly picking up on some of the organizers' own language.

For instance, in 1996, a few days prior to the Miss World contest in India, Julia Morley, the organization's managing director, noted that the event was an opportunity for 'many people to know about Indian women ... it's good that people have been able to get to know the Indian woman without visiting'.[127] Highlighting the contest's post-colonial framework and how 'exotic India' and Indian women were packaged by an organization run by Britons and offered up for global consumption as tourism, critics argued that the organization was repurposing women's historical oppression as women's empowerment and promoting a 'mass leisure culture'.[128] The protests in India, in turn, emphasized a range of issues relating to postcolonialism, global leisure culture, commoditization, and women's oppression veiled as women's empowerment.

Additionally, the protests tied into the definition of a new liberalized India. Rupal Oza brings attention to the pageant's spectacle and how protests against the spectacle evoked nationalism and the nation's global context.[129] According to Oza, the debate and resistance to the contest 'reinforced the idea that spaces such as the nation or the global are discreet and fixed "places" rather than persistently dynamic and mutable "ideas"'.[130] Nevertheless, Oza dissents, asserting that 'the ideas of geography, globalization, and their intersection are ever-mutable'. Space, therefore, is always a historical conjecture and a social form that derives its meaning from the social processes that are expressed through it.[131] The contest itself set in motion new spatial nodes, creating a space for economic, cultural, and technological flows for the Indian entertainment sector through its choice of venue. The geographic mutability to Bangalore instigated by Bachchan's corporate endeavours was again representative of an industrial shift—it marked a shift in the industry's focus—from regionalism to internationalism. The dialectic of Bachchan's modernization and ties to tradition again get played out here in his presence in Bangalore; the lad from along the banks of the Ganga was now the Miss World entrepreneur.

The idea of Bangalore as a global, cosmopolitan city hosting a world-class entertainment event made a case for Bangalore not just as a 'global city' but also as an emerging media and entertainment capital.[132] The discourse surrounding the event exemplified the centrality of place within the network. As Doreen Massey argues, 'the spatial' is dynamic and extends across different scales, from the global to the political to the national, down to social relations within the city. Space or place, therefore, is not exclusive or fixed; it is formed 'out of social interrelations at all scales',[133] necessary to 'study the production of spatial forms on the basis of the underlying social structure'.[134] In the protest within the city, we witnessed social interrelations as farmers, women's rights activists, left-wing parties, religious right-wing parties, and unemployed youth all registered their dissent at different scales. Then, too, we had other vital nodes, like the state government of Karnataka, the Miss World organization, and Bachchan and his ABCL—all-powerful agents working at different scales. Bachchan yet again claims centrality within these global spatial flows, as these discourses of space and place are largely filtered through the populist iconicity of his stardom. While Julia Morley may have envisioned the Bangalore backdrop as bringing exotic Indian women to the world, the real face of the contest for the Indian people was Bachchan, the megastar steering these new global flows.

With ABCL offices being attacked and Bachchan's nude effigy on fire, he degenerated from the idealist angry young man of the 1980s to a materialist corporate businessman of the 1990s. In Indian media coverage, Morley, at best, remained a sidekick to Bachchan's superstar persona, which garnered all the negative media attention. Whereas coverage from the international press centred on the pageant and the protestors, with only a brief mention of ABCL, Indian newspapers ran headlines exclusively about Bachchan and ABCL: 'Six "angry young men" ransack ABCL's Bangalore office', 'Women's organization promises to fight to the finish: ABCL to deploy defence forces for protecting Miss World participants, venue', 'Amitabh Bachchan offers to hold talks with anti-pageant activists', 'Pageant protesters display nude Amitabh cut-out',[135] and so on. Within the Indian context, Bachchan was the central node for this emergent global context; however, since this global context was so locally so contentious, he gradually lost his affective agency as the economy of hate pulverized his domestic brandscape and ABCL alike. Additionally, financial mismanagement led to heavy debts, and Bachchan's conflicts with his frontline staff brought about the demise of ABCL in 1998 when the company ended its operations amidst 50 legal litigations filed against them to settle debts.[136]

Bachchan, who primarily focused on bringing the global to India, also first tried to export Indian content to the world. As the state's concerted focus remained on the television sector, Bachchan had early on, prior to Miss World, aligned his organization's goals with state interests and focused on exporting Indian content to diasporic markets through satellite television. In 1994, along with his brother, Ajitabh Bachchan, he acquired joint stakes in TV Asia, a US television channel targeted at the diasporic Indian population. Within two years, TV Asia had 12,000 subscribers.[137] Following the success of Vision of Asia, the first television programme, and ITV, the first and only television network that catered to the diasporic South Asian population, New Jersey-based TV Asia upped the ante by adding the allure of a Bollywood megastar as their financier. It provided coast-to-coast service through cable and satellite.[138] Bachchan's television operations in the US turned out to be a successful venture, although he had to temporarily acquire NRI (non-resident Indian) status and spend considerable time in the US to make the investment successful.[139] Diaspora (or NRI, in the state nomenclature) emerged as an essential and strategic node within the emergent Bollywood network at this time—as they materialized as a coveted audience for the Indian media industry that could bring in higher revenues. Bachchan's rescue from financial bankruptcy happened through television and international investment as an NRI. The upswing in his fortunes and nationwide popularity occurred in 2000 when Bachchan started hosting *Kaun Banega Crorepati*, the Indian adaptation of *Who Wants to Be a Millionaire?* The show initially aired on News Corp-owned Star TV and later moved to Sony Television. With this role, Bachchan revived his fortunes, rebranded his waning stardom, and resurrected ABCL, in 2001, as AB Corporation. Under its new name, Bachchan's entertainment organization focused on its core competency: film production.

His prior attempt through ABCL, however, created a veritable network effect. Several Bollywood personalities followed ABCL's lead in leveraging the content-creation opportunity offered by television. They reinvented or created formally incorporated companies with the vision of going public. Subhash Ghai, another prominent filmmaker, set up a television production company,

Drishti India Limited, which produced another Bollywood song-clip programme called *Chitrahaar*. Ghai made his offering unique by interspersing songs with comments by film personalities.[140] Similar to Bachchan in his TV Asia endeavour, Ghai sought to market these Indian shows internationally. Ghai set up his venture in association with film distributor B. L. Agarwal and television journalist Anuradha Prasad, producing content for individual television channels, including Doordarshan, Zee, Star, and the BBC, and bringing Hindi feature films to television audiences.[141] Shanti Kumar, Purnima Mankekar, and others have pointed to television's centrality within the Indian nationalist identity and imagination. The 1990s were a time when transnational and trans-local networks simultaneously emerged, leading to and defined by hybrid electronic vernaculars with global, national, and regional aspirations and affiliations.[142] Film, which was not yet an industry, had to align with television, the central media industry, to stay relevant and become part of lucrative economic and global flows. With the steady rise in television channels and the associated need for programming, the industry partook in the benefits of an open economy.

It was no coincidence that Bachchan was the first figure in the industry to enter the television sector. He had a grand-scale vision and, based on branding his stardom, encouraged other nodes to recognize the possibilities. Ghai and others that followed fit Manuel Castells's theorization of 'programmers', nodes that possess the ability to programme networks based on larger network goals. Star switching agents like Bachchan, on the other hand, could create new networks where none existed and ensure the strategic corporation of nodes to meet the networks' goals. Stars with switching power can exceed the network to create new directions, business models, and network goals. They also possess the ability to programme networks. Programming, however, is a different level of power that depends on the node's position in the social structure. As in the case of filmmakers such as Ghai, Mukul Anand, and others also identified 'TV software' (a curious term used for television content at that time, most likely meant to evoke parallels with the fast-rising IT industry) as a lucrative business venture for film-production houses. From mainstream directors such as Ghai and Anand to independent film directors like Shyam Benegal and Govind Nihalani, filmmakers recognized television as the next big opportunity. If filmmakers moved to television, it was for the prospect and possibilities. The process of making off-beat, small-budget films without stars and seeing them through until they are sold is long and sometimes heartbreaking. For some, it became impossible to start another film while an unsold one lay in the cans.[143] Like Benegal, Nihalani also pointed to the crass, commercially driven film distributors whose whims dictated the fate of independent Hindi cinema. Television offered an attractive alternative to such filmmakers.[144]

So far, all the early nodes invested in film–television synergy were male. Closing in on the gender gap, Sridevi, a famous female star at the time (who was often paired with Bachchan and played opposite him in *Khuda Gawah*), also invested in a production company, Sridevi Securities Limited, with plans of going public. The company later morphed into Sridevi Productions, partnered with Sridevi's husband, the filmmaker and producer Boney Kapoor, and created films and television shows. The venture was successful and, by 2005, had an expected annual turnover of INR 1,000 crore (10,000 million).[145] Recently, following Sridevi's unexpected demise in 2018, her husband, Boney Kapoor, announced his maiden Tamil production with an acknowledgement that 'I have managed to fulfill my wife's dream' of producing a Tamil film. The tweet not only points to a hierarchical understanding of vernacular film production in India (Sridevi got her start in the Tamil film industry) but also reveals a hierarchical perception of the ways in which women's achievements are framed through a gendered schema that foregrounds the men in their lives, which, as we have already seen, was also the case for Jaya Bachchan.[146]

Reverting from gendered hierarchies to state policy and industry hierarchies it instigated—at this moment in the 1990s the film industry and production hubs desperately hoped that the state would focus its attention on film-making and legitimize it as an industry. Gulshan Rai, a producer and distributor of Hindi films, including Bachchan blockbusters like *Deewaar* and *Trishul* (Trident, 1978, dir. Yash Chopra), hoped that sooner or later the government would be 'bound to make new policies, grant reliefs … we've been under pressure too long. Black days have to give way to white'—a reference to the underground and criminal economy networks in which Bollywood had been embroiled.[147]

While the television industry thrived under economic reforms and a new broadcasting bill, the film industry—still struggling for legitimacy—was left far behind. Bachchan presented an alternate business model to leverage the new flows of global capital in television and other industries and profit from it. He created and helped programme alternate networks of filmmakers and other celebrities who had learned what not to do from the failure of Bachchan's expansive corporate vision yet saw the inherent potential in it. Thus, parallel production networks surfaced in the film industry, a phenomenon theorized as a 'network effect'. Figures at the helm of parallel networks saw ABCL's global, Hollywood-like vision as a point of reference in creating a corporate organization. Dinesh Gandhi, a Bollywood financer and film producer who worked on popular films like *Tezaab* (Acid, 1988, dir. N. Chandra), attested to Bachchan's 'excellent business sense' and noted, 'He's all set to use his charisma and popularity.'[148] Shyam Shroff, another noted financer and distributor, expressed his scepticism but hoped that ABCL's new business model worked out so that other film companies could generate revenue.[149]

Networks with their multiple nodes and smaller independent actors were emerging as the relationship between film and media sectors was getting redefined. Bachchan possessed the network-making power to configure his own organization and set other parallel networks in motion. In this case, power still lay within network relationships; however, powerful nodes like Bachchan stood out as distinct from others. The Miss World contest organized by Bachchan was a key vehicle for international lifestyle and beauty commodities. The top global cosmetic brands, such as Revlon, Maybelline, Oriflame, Avon, and L'Oréal, were now vying for a share of the Indian market.[150] Oriflame, a Swedish cosmetics company, even set up its India operations in Mumbai. Consumers in post-liberalized India represented the third largest export market for these global cosmetic giants.[151] While Bachchan and ABCL may have orchestrated and programmed the big-picture goals that led to the Miss World contest being held in India, other nodes and stakeholders existed. These entities included the Indian state, global corporations, domestic corporations, the Miss World organization, and other smaller but important nodes such as Miss World's country-level counterpart, the Miss India organization, and its sponsor, *Femina* magazine. The Miss World event epitomized the relational power structures and interests at play within this network. Bachchan, because of his 'connectedness' with the nodes and their stakeholders, in addition to his overwhelming star affect, possessed the switching power to enable this network. Yet the network itself was changing, particularly with the addition of new global circuits and networks such as beauty pageants that neatly dovetailed with the international cosmetics industry that was looking towards the newly liberalized and populous Indian nation as a coveted market.

The next chapter delves into the switching power of two prominent stars of the new millennium, Shah Rukh Khan and Aamir Khan, who helped

Bollywood gain a prepotency and globality beyond the acknowledgement that Bachchan alone could accomplish. The two stars help solidify and further the idea of star brandscapes instigated in the 1990s via Bachchan, creating important business changes that converge the film industry with a broader entertainment ecology that includes everything from cricket to live events, thus leading Hindi cinema's foray into a convergent, mediated, and veritably diverse global network.

3

GLOBAL DREAMZ

Shah Rukh Khan and Aamir Khan Usher Global Bollywood into the New Millennium

I was intrigued by [*Kabhi Khushi Kabhi Gham* (2001, Shah Rukh Khan's film)], but I was even more intrigued by the effect it had on my mother. I cannot remember ever seeing my mother cry, not even at funerals. But there she was watching this film, and she had tears running down her face.

—Julia Wessel, editor of German Bollywood magazine *Ishq*[1]

Julia Wessel, a twenty-five-year-old German student, was so moved by the phenomenon and fandom around Shah Rukh Khan (hereafter, SRK) that she quit her cultural anthropology degree to edit a German Bollywood magazine.[2] SRK's popularity among his German fans spurred the creation of fanzines, industry infrastructure, and collaboration that opened up a new market for Bollywood in the early 2000s. Bollywood and SRK's enthusiastic reception was transposed to the realm of cultural diplomacy when Michael Steiner, the German ambassador to India (2012–2015), created a Bollywood-style video, 'Lebe Jetzt [Live Now]: Loving Bollywood Too Much'.[3] The video, a homage to SRK and Bollywood, featured the German envoy dressed as SRK. Along with his wife and the Indian foreign minister Salman Khurshid, they lip-synced the lyrics of SRK's song 'Kal Ho Naa Ho' (Tomorrow May Never Come, 2003).

In October 2019, ahead of a summit between the Chinese president, Xi Jinping, and the Indian prime minister, Narendra Modi, China's ambassador to India, Sun Weidong, invoked Bollywood megastar Aamir Khan (hereafter,

Khan) (beloved by the Chinese) to emphasize the cultural bonhomie between India and China.[4] At the height of the cross-border skirmish between India and China in 2017, Khan's *Dangal* (Wrestling Competition, 2016, dir. Nitesh Tiwari) became a means to de-escalate tensions, as the Chinese envoy repeatedly emphasized Xi's admiration for Khan and love for Bollywood, describing Xi as the 'biggest promoter of Bollywood in China'.[5] Khan's inroads into the Chinese market were catalysed by distribution through pirate economy networks. His film *3 Idiots* (2009, dir. Rajkumar Hirani) instigated a cult fandom that created these inroads for Bollywood into China.[6] *3 Idiots* has 1.4 million ratings on Douban, a film website in China similar to IMDb, on which it is ranked the twelfth highest-rated film of all time.[7] Chinese film and social media websites like Douban, MTime, and Weibo abound with fans centred on Khan, addressing him variously as 'Uncle Mi', 'Uncle Shu', and the 'conscience of India'.[8] Khan has more than a million fans on the Chinese microblogging site Weibo. Not surprisingly, as the two neighbouring countries aspire to minimize their multi-billion-dollar trade deficit and strengthen their tenuous relationship through film collaborations, the figure of Khan often appears as an intermediary in the Sino-Indian diplomatic exchange.[9]

SRK and Khan prominently made their mark in the Bollywood mediascape during the late 1990s and early 2000s, and this chapter shows how this mediascape was evolving both geographically and in terms of the kinds of power wielded by the Hindi film industry domestically and abroad in places as varied as Germany and China. The first decade of the new millennium (2000–2010) was a critical inflection point when the Indian film and entertainment sector was undergoing rapid structural and policy transformation. While Bachchan was recovering from the ABCL debacle, SRK and Khan emerged as significant star switching nodes with network power and global influence. This chapter illustrates the star switching power of mega-celebrities like SRK and Khan at the turn of the millennium and the mutable neoliberal context in which they created a novel 'space of flows'.[10] These two stars, it argues, served as mediators and bridges determining economic, political, and symbolic flows for the Indian entertainment industry. As Bollywood rapidly expanded from a film industry to an entertainment one, the nature of star switching power, disseminated through the mediated affective sensoriums of technology via fandoms and social media, was visibly transformed in part through their star texts and other pursuits. Apart from the direct effective relevance that their production organizations had to industry and commerce, their affective sensorium's immensity gave SRK and Khan newfound global visibility and significance in cultural diplomacy and cinematic soft power discourses. In this phase, the industry's global dynamics, state policy, fandoms, and technology intermingled to create a new spatial–cultural–industrial logic to mobilize star power toward the creation of a contemporary networked Bollywood.

During this period (2000s–2010s), the changing relationship between industry structure and state policy gave rise to a contemporary networked Bollywood where a diverse set of global, local, and institutional networks and individual nodes intersected. Film production was finally recognized as a legitimate industry by the Indian state. The early 2000s were a transformative phase because various 'environmental factors [that] influenced Bollywood's evolution' changed.[11] The media ecology during this rapidly liberalizing economic era was a dialogic process where 'the informal logics' of an unorganized industry fused with the logic of an organized market. Policy changes, especially in terms of film financing, now made it easier to access formal capital, and Bollywood's production clusters began to transform.[12] What emerged in this phase was an agglomerated network comprised of multiple interconnected clusters, including Bollywood's traditional family-led productions that were transforming themselves into vertically and horizontally integrated companies, Hollywood studios that were setting up Indian subsidiaries, and organized sector enterprises like Indian telecom giant Reliance that were investing in film and media. As a result, a variegated global and local linguistic and territorial media market emerged. The celerity and vibrancy of the Indian Hindi film industry had intensified and evolved into an agglomerated network enmeshed in the flows of global capital, technology, and influence. The industry, too, evolved from a single-product film industry to 'being systematized into the grid of a broader consumer and entertainment economy'.[13]

Megastars SRK and Khan emerged as change-makers and catalysts within a network that was in a state of flux and evolving into an agglomeration of global nodes ranging from major Hollywood studios to home-grown globally networked media corporations like Reliance (a telecom and petroleum company with newly acquired media interests) and Zee (part of a conglomerate with wide-ranging interests in infrastructure, packaging, and financial sectors), which illustrates Bollywood's ascendant role in the Indian industrial and corporate sector. These changes in industry structure, state policy, and the relationship between the two strengthened the interconnection of star brandscapes, fandoms, and new technology to star agency. The gendered nature of star switching power and the inability of female stars to access it in the same way as their male counterparts tenuously challenged the inequitable logic of the emerging networked structure and its ability to create equitable flows of capital, technology, organizational interactions, and images—flows that expressed 'the processes dominating our economic, political and symbolic life'.[14]

Within this emerging industrial structure, SRK and Khan existed as critical star nodes—key mediators and bridges in creating a global 'space of flows'—but differed from one another in important, and in some respects compatible, ways; SRK's star switching power was 'consumable' and Khan's 'conscientious'. By leveraging the economic, political, technological, and symbolic spaces through effective and affective switching power, the star duo mobilized captive markets for Bollywood in Germany and China, accomplishing key diplomatic and industrial goals as they ushered Bollywood into a new millennium. Through their production companies—Red Chillies Entertainment and Aamir Khan Productions, critical industrial nodes that worked in conjunction with their star personas—they mobilized their *consumable* and *conscientious* switching power to effectively marshal collaborations, projects, and alliances that disseminated Indian Hindi films beyond their traditional markets. As star switching power works through the mobilization of affective and effective economies, for Khan and SRK to manifest this agentic power that brought about a visible transformation in Bollywood's global presence, the structure within which they were operating had to be different as well.

The polyptych that this chapter presents first delineates the evolving structure of Bollywood from the 2000s to the 2010s when SRK and Khan emerged as crucial nodes. It reveals how that structure evolved relationally as state policies focused on diasporic investment helped create a specific genre of diaspora films and, thereby, a diaspora star archetype epitomized by SRK. It also analyses the expanding Bollywood network at this juncture as it organically dovetails with the globalizing television industry that came to be the early beneficiary of the state's newly instituted economic policies. Reflecting on the structural changes resulting from the addition of multiple stakeholders, from the diaspora and the television industry to Hollywood studios, the chapter explains how Bollywood has constitutively expanded from a film to an entertainment industry. Second, it elaborates on the nature of the stars' switching power as consumable (SRK) and conscientious (Khan) and its evolution and mobilization in relation to their brandscapes and technology. It illustrates the mobilization of switching power to create a global 'space of flows' for cultural diplomacy that is non-state-centric and is anchored by and predominantly a result of industrial exchange. It also reflects on the gendered dimensions of this kind of power, as well as on why it proved especially effective in certain global spaces because of broader patterns of domestic policy and international affairs.

INDUSTRY STRUCTURE: A NETWORK EMERGES

The 1990s through the early 2000s was a period of rapid transformation for the Indian media. As Chapter 2 discussed, Amitabh Bachchan and ABCL were critical nodes and change-makers in projecting a vision of a global, 'corporatized' film and entertainment industry. Following ABCL's failure, which many touted as an idea only a little before its time, other family-led film-production clusters like Yash Raj Films registered themselves as corporate entities. In a 1999 interview, Yash Chopra noted ABCL's innovative vision and the opportunity afforded by the transitional moment of the 1990s: '[Y]es, ABCL is [now] one big sad story. But it should not deter others from going corporate. Globally ... the entertainment industry is thriving, but we [still] cannot feel the effects in this country.'[15] The network effect, the idea that a product or service becomes more valuable as others start using it, precipitated by ABCL's vertically integrated corporate model, led to the creation of several key corporatized industry nodes in the Indian film and entertainment sector. Most notably, Yash Raj Films and Reliance Entertainment were strategic in defining SRK and Khan's effective global switching power. In a rapidly transforming industry topography, a formal and legal industry status for films finally, after many decades, created possibilities for legitimate financing and partnerships.[16] The early 2000s to 2010s afforded critical moments of inflection in creating a Bollywood network wherein Hollywood nodes and globally networked home-grown media corporations like Reliance Entertainment appeared in the Indian film and entertainment sector. By 2008, Disney, Viacom, Warner Bros., Sony Pictures, and Twentieth Century Fox had all made deals and collaborations with India.[17] All the studios had by now set up an India production arm and partnered with a prominent Indian production company to produce globally viable Hindi films.[18] The star switching power of SRK and Khan, as it manifested and mobilized in this mutable mediascape, was quite different from the protean star power of Bachchan.

Unlike the industry landscape of the preceding two decades, the late 1990s and 2000s were a moment of symbiosis where culture and celebrity glamour inextricably mixed with the neoliberal economic flows of capital and investment, organizational structure, and business practices that were shaping the Hindi film industry and India at large. Globally, stars were understood as emanations of a broader production system rooted in contemporary capitalism. In the context of Hindi films, stars emerged as central, dominant nodes driving the production machinery and participating in the processes, not simply essential glamourous presences emanating from the wider system but rather as direct mobilizers. The star switching power that materialized in this era was a malleable power wherein stars like SRK and Khan possessed direct agency and structural power as owners of leading production companies. Their power as it evolved in a changing industrial structure, however, was also discursive and relational. The possibility of enacting that power depended on other actors or nodes' presence in the networked structure.[19]

THE GENESIS OF A GLOBAL NETWORK

As noted earlier, the 'magic potion' of liberalization trickled down to television while the film industry watched in awe, wondering at the possibilities. A *New York Times* article captured the zeitgeist of globalization and neoliberal consumerism doled out through television's satellite revolution:

> Increasing numbers of Indians are basking in the rays of rock videos and uncensored television for the first time. For decades, Indians [had] been restricted to the fare served by state television, known as *Doordarshan*, a diet of tedious discussions by government bureaucrats, ancient Hindi movies ... and new programs often distinguished by their heavy censorship and age. This fall, new channels began appearing on Indian televisions—MTV rock videos, all day sports channels ... mix of news and entertainment. This rush of new technology has overwhelmed India's glacial bureaucracy and charged into uncharted and unregulated waters. And no one is waiting for the government to act.[20]

SRK's career launched at a time when the television and film-industry networks integrated new avenues for talent outside of Bollywood's traditional family-led industry film clusters. At this moment of television primacy, SRK was anointed to filmdom by a television audience.[21] His acting career started with a guest appearance on *Wagle Ki Duniya* (Wagle's World, 1988–1990), a comedy show on Doordarshan, India's public broadcaster. He later moved to headline roles in popular Doordarshan serials *Fauji* (Soldier, 1989) and *Circus* (1989–1990). He was cast in a string of television shows, such as *Dil Dariya* (Generous Heart, 1988–1989), *Doosra Keval* (The Other Keval, 1989–1990), *Ummeed* (Hope, 1989), and art-filmmaker Mani Kaul's four-part made-for-television movie *Ahmak* (The Fool, 1991). Filmmakers were now being lured to television, and film stars of previous eras were producing programmes for television: Durga Khote's DK Productions was producing *Wagle Ki Duniya*; Hema Malini, Bachchan's contemporary and popular superstar of the 1970s, was directing the television serial *Noopur* (Anklet) for Doordarshan and wanted to move into film production and direction. Impressed by SRK's role in *Fauji*, Malini offered him a role in her directorial debut film, *Dil Aashna Hai* (The Heart Knows the Truth, 1992). This moment of symbiosis between film and television briefly turned out to be a great equalizer in, according female stars, a moment of power and opportunity in direction and production. Following Malini, Kundan Shah, the director of SRK's television show *Circus*, cast him as the male lead in his film *Kabhi Haan Kabhi Naa* (Sometimes Yes, Sometimes No, 1994). With television, SRK built a network alongside other film producers and directors who were now working simultaneously in film and television, and this symbiotic television–film network helped kickstart his career. Also, their networks enabled SRK's move from state-led television to commercial cinema.

In parallel, a state-led network through institutional nodes like the NFDC, which rose to prominence in the 1980s, was hoping to cultivate a global presence. Having co-produced two successful global films, *Gandhi* (1982, dir. Richard Attenborough) and *Salaam Bombay!* (1988, dir. Mira Nair), the NFDC's strategic expansion of television and video sought soft power in neighbouring nations.[22] Mainstream Hindi cinema, although outside the official discourse of good cinema, was accessible via television in India and neighbouring countries.[23] Television was the ubiquitous and favoured mass medium, and practitioners of mainstream and parallel cinema hoped television would support films.[24] In a seminar on the topic at the International Film Festival of India in 1990, practitioners of parallel or art cinema like Girish

Karnad, Ketan Mehta (director of SRK's early television shows and films), Gautam Ghosh, and Mrinal Sen argued for a BBC-inspired television model that would encourage the creation of better cinema for the small screen.

SRK's career got its start through the NFDC circuit of directors, who were trying to make parallel cinema more commercially viable through television. As polemical battles were being fought over the question of art and commerce, the Indian state supported the high art cinema being produced by graduates of the Pune-based FTII, which was established in 1960 by the government to develop 'suitable teaching' of film and television.[25] SRK, however, gravitated towards commercial and populist Bombay cinema, which lacked state support. The state derided it as a cinema that was forever 'grappling with remoulding the so-called formula [for success]' and completely mired in 'violence and sex'.[26] Khan, on the other hand, was born into filmdom: his father, Tahir Hussain, and uncle, Nassir Hussain, were established film producers. Khan also began his career with Ketan Mehta, a director who was part of the NFDC circuit. The *New York Times* described their film *Holi* (1984), about hazing in Indian colleges, as 'very decently and exuberantly performed'.[27] During this phase, formal global forays had been largely centred on state nodes, such as the NFDC and the FTII.

Gradually, staid government attitudes and policies toward commercial cinema changed, and SRK was crucial in creating a new global circuit and market for Indian Hindi films.[28] His foray into mainstream filmdom through films like *Dilwale Dulhaniya Le Jayenge* (*DDLJ*) (The Brave Hearted Will Take the Bride, 1995, dir. Aditya Chopra) and *Pardes* (Foreign Land, 1997, dir. Subhash Ghai) made him the star of the Indian diaspora, a dedicated audience segment and a source of foreign revenue. Both SRK and Khan were, at the start of their careers, part of the state-sponsored impetus to create 'good', 'educational', socially driven cinema with niche international film festival appeal. In contrast, little is known about the distribution or export figures of mainstream popular Hindi cinema. According to the Federation of Indian Chambers of Commerce and Industry's (FICCI) 2001 report on the entertainment sector, until the 1990s, data reports pertaining to mainstream Hindi cinema exports were nominal to non-existent.[29] Entanglement with mafia networks and a lack of formal process and structure accounted for the absence of data. In the late 1990s, after the Indian state revamped its policies and recognized cinema as a legitimate industry, the Hindi film industry began to acquire a global network structure.[30] This policy directive came about partly because the Indian state recognized that films could generate an inflow of foreign capital and bolster the economy. As a result, the state-run FICCI instituted FICCI Frames, a forum to bring cinema policy, export concerns, and international collaboration into the conversation.

The film that helped illuminate Bollywood cinema's global economic potential was SRK's *DDLJ*. Following its immense success, the film's producer, Yash Chopra, was promptly anointed the chair of FICCI Frames. *DDLJ*'s success was imperative in establishing SRK's centrality within the Bollywood network, with the Indian diaspora emerging as a key market in the evolving industrial network.

DDLJ is arguably the most successful Hindi film of all time. It broke all exhibition records in India and ran continuously from October 1995 to February 2015 at the Maratha Mandir theatre in Mumbai.[31] It is the longest-running film in the history of Indian cinema.[32] The film's enduring popularity occasioned a re-release in October 2020 in India, Europe, the Middle East, Africa, Australia, and New Zealand, despite the Covid-19 pandemic, to celebrate twenty-five years of the film. *DDLJ*'s success can be attributed to its presentation of a fluid national identity, in which SRK played a key role.[33] At a time marked by constant debates and negotiations over the relationship between the local and the global, *DDLJ* presented a 'reconceptualization of Indianness' that projected a 'portable' and global Indian identity.[34] In the film, SRK's character is a diasporic Indian born and brought up in the UK, who dexterously negotiates his 'Indianness' in a global world—an identity that he re-conceptualized for the diaspora as nationalist affect and belonging. The film, for many differently positioned viewers, 'mediated a cultural logic of citizenship' that was simultaneously Indian and global.[35]

DDLJ was groundbreaking for a variety of reasons. The most significant—from a network perspective—was the introduction of a new parallel diaspora network for Bollywood. SRK's embodiment of the film's protagonist, Raj Malhotra, led to a coalescence of SRK's affective charismatic appeal with the effective economies of the industry, state, and consumer. His stardom's affective power emanated from the magnetism of his romantic, affable, macho, yet goofy character, Raj Malhotra. In the film, Raj is introduced to the viewers as the 'unknown' and 'unseen' romantic partner whom the heroine, Simran (a second-generation diasporic British-Indian), fantasizes about. Her coming-of-age reverie about her dream partner is intercut with shots of Raj displaying physical prowess and 'desirability': playing rugby (on an all-white team), go-karting, running alongside a chartered plane, bowling, playing basketball, and swimming. The montage introduces Raj as an amalgamation of attractions onto whom viewers can project their affective desires for commodities, identity, and belonging—specifically, the desire for diasporic Indians to be accepted by white communities and performatively lay claim to their adopted homeland. Raj is 'cool' and 'masculine' and, unlike the heroine, does not fit the stereotype of the 'geeky', 'obedient' model-minority, second-generation immigrant. Beyond his charm and hyphenated identity, Raj is the ideal expatriate Indian. He lands in Punjab's lush mustard fields, secretly hoping to win over his beloved Simran, who is betrothed to Kuljeet—a native-born 'dunce'. Kuljeet welcomes Raj into the 'native' fold and befriends him because Raj reveals himself to be the ideal investor; he wants to set up a Stroh's beer factory in rural Punjab.[36] Throughout the film's narrative, Stroh's beer and its prominence presage a *neoliberal cinematic turn* that resonated with the Indian state's economic and pedagogical mission.[37] In this on-screen representation of the diasporic Indian, SRK embodied a neoliberal 'consumability' that was modern and globally acceptable.[38] Concurrently, his on-screen persona instantiated the ideal diasporic consumer for this emergent state–industry global corporate network, one that was Punjabi, rich, and conformist.[39] *DDLJ* set the tone for how SRK's affective persona would morph into a consumable brandscape that magnified his star switching power in this moment of neoliberal transition for the other two critical nodes in the Bollywood network: the state and the industry.

The global success of *DDLJ* initiated crucial policy and structural changes for the industry. In its cinematic refrain, 'Ghar aaja pardesi tera des bulaye re' (Come back home, stranger, your country beckons), the film echoed the zealous state rhetoric that the '[g]overnment of India does sincerely care for NRIs'.[40] This intersection of cinematic affect with policy changes was primarily triggered by the foreign exchange crisis that the country was attempting to avert. As opposed to the earlier ideology of 'brain drain',[41] which painted NRIs as burdens on the nation, the state now beckoned diasporic Indians back to their roots, seeing NRIs as a '"bank" from which the parent country [could] borrow both capital and new skills and technology'.[42] Diasporic Indians now became untapped resources of financial, intellectual, and technological capital. The Indian government saw NRI remittances as a solution to the foreign exchange crisis. In 1993, in an early gesture of bonhomie, the government organized a conference that included Indian passport holders residing in other countries—that is, NRIs—and people of Indian origin who were nationals of other countries. Influential diasporic Indians such as British politician and business magnate Swraj Paul and Guyanese premier Cheddi Jagan were invited. The conference served a twofold purpose. First, it aimed to make India's economic and foreign policy outward-looking, as Nehru had originally envisioned. Second, it wanted to 'evolve a strategic economic and foreign policy that [built] on the strength of its vibrant and varied diaspora'.[43] Mainstream Bollywood films became consequential to that effort because at the height of the foreign exchange crisis, when the rupee was swiftly devalued, and all government effort was focused on foreign-capital inflow to prevent currency collapse, *DDLJ* grossed over INR 1,220 million (roughly equivalent to USD 16 million) in domestic and foreign markets.[44] The film's success made the state realize that films had the economic and soft power potential to lure the diaspora to reconnect with the 'homeland'. *DDLJ* was a precursor to the Indian state's formal legitimization of the film industry, which made visible cinema's potential and primacy within the state and industry networks.

DDLJ made SRK into a megastar. The film catalyzed cinematic collaboration; furthermore, the overlap between state and industry interests only magnified this effect. The famous Bollywood film critic Anupama Chopra points out that *DDLJ* marked a 'generational shift' in Bollywood.[45] Rajshri Productions, Yash Raj Films, Mukta Arts, Dharma Productions, and other leading family-led film-production clusters all began creating films for the diaspora market, which often featured the NRI hero SRK in the lead role.[46] *DDLJ*'s global success had altered the family-led studios' vision and ambition. The producer, Yash Chopra, felt that '*Dilwale* ... changed Yash Raj films [forever].... Apart from fame and money, [*DDLJ*] gave our company new dreams.'[47] The film created a formula of storylines, distribution models, and star casts that the industry would replicate.[48]

GLOBAL DREAMZ

My logic very humbly is that I would like to make a Hindi film which is accepted worldwide. As an actor and a producer, I'd like the whole world to see a Hindi film and accept the fact that from the next one onwards, a Hindi film gets at least half of a British film opening—or even one fourth a British film opening. That would be nice, but I don't really see myself having a realistic chance of being James Bond.

—Shah Rukh Khan[49]

In the early 2000s, SRK and Khan, much like their predecessors, attempted to create and distribute global films. The post-liberalization generation of Bollywood stars was presented with possibilities because their production entities could now register as legitimate business corporations and receive bank financing.[50] It was a paradigm shift, and corporate leaders like Amit Khanna, who later spearheaded the domestic media conglomerate Reliance Entertainment, noted the industry's quandary irrespective of regulatory changes: '[W]hy will banks step up to fund films. Ninety percent of the people have no collateral to offer.'[51] In a star-driven industry like Bollywood, stars again became the catalysers for this structural change. Their affective agency and brand power turned into the guarantee of a project's profitability needed by financial institutions. The banks' 'ego massaging multi-crore rupees payments [could] only be made when a star [was] worth it'.[52] The megastars' extensive star switching power in this moment of structural change thus emanated from their symbolic power. Nick Couldry describes this type of prominence as the transversal effects of media, whereby 'media capital', or a celebrity's symbolic power, works across various fields: social, political, and cultural.[53] Megastars like SRK and Khan possessed this symbolic power and commanded non-symbolic and tangible commercial power because of integral roles that enabled them to exceed industrial constraints and innovate. The early 2000s were an instantiation of switching power where family clout, individual ties, and positional embeddedness within the industry were concretized with the stars' affective appeal as a commercial brand. This put the stars in a position where their individual production ventures became bankable as well.

SRK and Khan both attempted to create global projects soon after setting up their production companies. Dreamz Unlimited, SRK's first venture with his female co-star Juhi Chawla and director Aziz Mirza, mainly targeted the Indian and diaspora market with *Phir Bhi Dil Hai Hindustani* (But the Heart Is Still Indian, 2000, dir. Aziz Mirza). The film was met with a lukewarm response. Although Dreamz Unlimited was a partnership that involved another prominent female star, her agency, and prominence in industrial and journalistic discourse remained limited, underscoring the different treatment of women within this industry and business discourse.[54] In an interview about the redefined model of star-led productions in Bollywood cinema, Chawla highlighted her family's background in television production. She detailed how star brands could be leveraged in the emergent model:

It is not that we have to put in our personal funds or anything of the
sort.... We sold the music rights of the film [*Phir Bhi Dil Hai Hindustani*]
to Sony Music and the money ... was invested in the production of the
film.... [T]he overseas rights were sold to Eros International, so they
put in their money. That's how we financed the film.[55]

Chawla's interview highlighted her understanding of the new framework. She
emphasized the novelty of this synergistic model for Bollywood financing,
which until then had operated on an informal *hundi* system, as described in
earlier chapters.[56] The article's description of her vision, however, is replete
with references to her 'giggling' and 'laughing' before broaching these serious
topics, undercutting the authoritative industry power that Chawla now
possessed as the co-owner of a production company.[57] This was a moment of
industrial transition, and despite the industry's masculinist norms, space for
female stars to move beyond their traditional roles had opened—but these
spaces were not unconstrained by sexism. The nascent changes for female
stars at this moment followed Cecilia Ridgeway's contention that when new
kinds of work occur in environments that are in a state of flux, the combined
novelty of the changes creates capacity and space for re-negotiating gendered
expectations through industrial or organizational frameworks.[58] Nevertheless,
the rhetorical media construct around Dreamz Unlimited often fashioned
Chawla's role as a limited participant in the venture. As the novelty wore
off, however, institutional entropy returned to existing endogenous gendered
biases. As a consequence, several burgeoning female star-led production
ventures quickly petered out.[59]

SRK and Chawla's second project for Dreamz Unlimited, *Aśoka* (2001, dir.
Santosh Sivan), a historical drama about Emperor Ashoka (268–232 BCE),
who is credited with popularizing Buddhism throughout Asia, a topic of
potential widespread appeal, was more expansive in scope. The film, made
on a budget of INR 130 million, was one of the first Indian films to get a
major UK release across eighty-four theatres.[60] The UK distributor, Martin
Myers, reported the film was released like a Hollywood film and should have
been 'the biggest Asian film ever made'.[61] It had a US release as well and
was screened at the Venice and Toronto Film Festivals. The film's marketing
budget was more extensive than any other international Bollywood release
thus far. Publicity investment for *Aśoka* on the UK was close to GBP 150,000,
with multiple ads appearing on London's subway system.[62] SRK envisioned
the film as global in scope: 'The film's message is universal. [With interest

in] *Aśoka* on the Eastern side also. So, we did go and meet up with some distributors in Japan who are interested in taking the film.'[63] SRK parted ways with Chawla after a three-film partnership to set up his independent production, Red Chillies Entertainment. Concurrently, Khan, under the banner of Aamir Khan Productions, created *Lagaan* (Agricultural Tax, 2001, dir. Ashutosh Gowariker).

At this moment, a new kind of industrial spatial logic appeared. Stars became the key industrial and social actors propelling the film industry towards global flows through networks established via spatio-historical, institutional, natural, and cultural linkages. While *Aśoka* vied for a pan-Asian logic of cultural proximity and Buddhism-oriented soft power, Aamir Khan Productions's *Lagaan* operated on the spatio-historical and cultural logics of a post-colonial amalgam of a global and national identity. *Lagaan* offered three critical aspects to the Bollywood network, star switching power, and cinema's global flows: First, it was a project of innovative storytelling, market conceptualization, and business strategies spearheaded by Aamir Khan Productions, a star-led enterprise. Second, it came when the Bollywood network had structurally evolved to include globally networked home-grown organizations like Reliance Entertainment with the potential to accelerate the export of cinema to new international markets. Third, despite minimal state support, this film became crucial to India's nation-branding as an emergent Asian power, like the villagers in *Lagaan*, willing to fight for its rightful place.

Lagaan was one of the first films to come out of the newly formalized Bollywood industry. It not only 'captured the Indian imagination' but 'spilled over into the global mindscape'.[64] It received a wide international release and an Oscar nomination; it furthermore had higher international than domestic box-office earnings.[65] A historical drama set in colonized India, *Lagaan* centres on a motley group of villagers who defeat British colonialists at their own game: cricket. A suspenseful cricket match determines a drought-stricken village's fate; their win helps the villagers get rid of the exorbitant taxes the British colonial rulers had imposed. Khan attempted to create a universal story: '[*Lagaan* is about] the triumph of the human spirit and about the underdog achieving the impossible', which was also locally resonant in key ways.[66] Its theme concretized India as a nation poised to find its rightful place in the world order despite its colonial past. Cricket, having been de-colonized and indigenized by the villagers, becoming a part of India's vernacular was the film's most resonant theme.

The ensuing global popularity of *Lagaan*—and the fact that the film involved cricket, a sport seen as an antipodal inversion of post-colonial hierarchies because of India's emergence as a cricketing superpower—added to India's cinematic soft power and nation-branding as it entered the new millennium.[67] *Lagaan* was the first Indian film to be released in China after multiple political and military disputes, including the Sino-Indian wars in 1962 and 1967, India's stance over Tibet, and the Pokhran nuclear tests. Many Chinese touted the film as resonant with China's parallel experiences as a country that had also been colonized and oppressed. As a Chinese viewer noted on Douban, '[*Lagaan*] was a battle of honor for the colonized.'[68] Evidently, *Lagaan*'s cinematic narrative presented a critical cultural branding of India's ambitions in a positive light with vital implications for the nation state and the entertainment industry.

From a narrative and business perspective, *Lagaan* went a step beyond *Aśoka*. The film had an international cast and a story about British rule in India, and by using British actors, it created a ready market in the UK. Additionally, Khan took his home production to film festivals worldwide, including Locarno, Chicago, Toronto, Damascus, Pusan, and Bergen.[69] The Bollywood network was poised for global expansion, and critical star switching nodes like SRK and Khan worked towards redefining industry goals and practices. *Lagaan* was an early instance of convergent marketing practices led by star-owned business entities that paved the way for advertising and marketing firms like Leo Burnett within this nascent networked structure.[70]

Khan's production house was the first to apply a conscious business strategy of a *film as a brand*. The film as a brand is intrinsically artistic and commercial and includes people brands such as the star and other creatives. In Bollywood, the star remained the primary brand that largely determined the film's success.[71] In their perceptive theorization of the film brandscape, Daragh O'Reilly and Finola Kerrigan note that films offer multiple branding signifiers.[72] Studio brands, genre, and country of origin, as well as product placement, can entice audiences and fans to watch a film. Character brands, in the case of franchises, become essential to the film brandscape as well. As Mark Lorenzen and Florian Arun Täube have emphasized, Bollywood's informal industry lacked an understanding of branding and marketing as formal processes before this moment.[73] *Lagaan* was thus seen as an innovative 'marketing blitzkrieg'. The domestic promotions included, among other things, a chance to play a cricket match with Khan on the 'invincible' Britannia–*Lagaan* cricket team; this tactic leaned into the colonial background of the movie to partner with one of India's biggest food-processing companies with a resonant name. The film included merchandizing in a big way. *Lagaan* comics, games, letter pads, and autograph books sold by Archies, a gift and greeting card company, flooded the market. Veteran film producer Yash Johar acknowledged the star's unique acumen and prospicience by asserting that through marketing and lobbying, Khan 'singlehandedly brought attention to *Lagaan*' in a way that 'never occurred to others before'.[74] The switching power and agency of stars like Khan and SRK thus initiated significant changes in business practices at a time of structural change for the industry.

While filming *Lagaan*, Khan commissioned the documentary *Chale Chalo: The Lunacy of Film Making* (2003, dir. Satyajit Bhatkal), which later won a national award. Before *Lagaan*'s release, the company launched its website, a practice that would 'in time become the standard [business and marketing] practice'.[75] In another first for Bollywood, Khan adapted *Lagaan* as a comic book.[76] Khan's venture, however, had its most significant impact on the distribution sector, changing the global perception of the Indian film industry. It increased the likelihood that large distributors would take up Indian films for worldwide distribution. '*Lagaan* [was] an example of organized filmmaking', and industry analysts like Bobby Bedi, who co-produced *Bandit Queen* (1994, dir. Shekhar Kapur), the prior decade's global film, hoped *Lagaan* would popularize that model in an industry notorious for its lack of transparency.[77] *Lagaan*'s international distributors were Sony International and Columbia TriStar. It was the third Indian film ever to be nominated for an Oscar, thus marking a milestone for the Indian film industry. Along with *DDLJ*, its global success spurred initiatives and policy changes leading to the creation of platforms like FICCI Frames, which, chaired by *DDLJ* director Yash Chopra, brought together government and industry interests to facilitate an exchange between industry figures, influencers, and policymakers.[78] Following *Lagaan*'s successful global run, the FICCI Frames convention of 2002 announced that the Industrial Development Bank of India (IDBI) had now set aside an INR 1 billion (equivalent to USD 14 million) corpus fund for film financing.[79] As industry leaders repeated calls to 'corporatize or perish', structural and policy changes took place in film financing, marking a structural paradigm shift for Bollywood's small-world, family-led film-production clusters. It was, as KPMG's industry analysts noted, a learning curve that would re-engineer processes of distribution before sale and private funding structures for organized financing. It would be 'unfair to expect

Hollywood standards of transparencies, efficiencies, and sophistication overnight', but the industry was on its way.[80]

Television remained pertinent to this circuit of exchange and corporatization. Television and neo-corporate organizations associated with the industry, such as Zee Telefilms and UTV Motion Pictures, enabled and sustained the film industry's ambitions.[81] In its 2001 summit, FICCI addressed the synergy between film and television in the long-term viability of both industries. As bank-funded financing for films was still being explored, 'big television' and 'media corporates' appeared to be the critical engine of future financing.[82] *Lagaan's* immense popularity globally and domestically led the change in this domain as well when UTV acquired it for distribution. Ronnie Screwvala, UTV's chief executive officer (CEO), foresaw this as a new industry trend that was now structurally factored into television and corporate media entities like Zee, Reliance, and UTV. Screwvala insisted that

> TV immortalizes the movies. TV networks need films for revenue as well as TRPs [television rating points]. Barely two years ago, 80 percent of Indian content was movie-related. Today 50 percent of our TV channels themselves are film driven including TNT, HBO, Star Movies and Star Gold. Moreover, in the West, the movie business itself is one of the biggest advertisers of television.[83]

Close on the heels of *Lagaan*, Sunny Deol, a less famous but still important star, co-produced *Gaddar* (Rebellion, 2001, dir. Anil Sharma) with Zee Telefilms. *Gaddar's* financial practices were a far cry from the *hundi* system of yesteryear. Zee Telefilms issued the team formal cheques and sold territorial music and distribution rights to its subsidiary Zee Music and other overseas entities. The experimental model adopted with *Asoka* and *Lagaan* was being materialized, and international distributors like Sony were taking on Indian films for global distribution.[84]

What megastars SRK and Khan possessed at this moment, however, was relational agency and power. Other changes were underway through nodes like UTV, Zee, and Reliance that helped accentuate star switching power in this moment of transition. Preceding *Lagaan's* success, UTV was already producing and distributing other films like *Bade Miyan, Chote Miyan* (Big Mister and Little Mister, 1998, dir. David Dhawan), *Mission Kashmir* (2000, dir. Vidhu Vinod Chopra), *Sarfarosh* (Fervent, 1999, dir. John Matthew Matten), *Hyderabad Blues* (1998, dir. Nagesh Kukunoor), and *The Terrorist*

(1997, dir. Santosh Sivan). However, it was primarily *Lagaan* that affirmed the viability of this strategy, and Khan's ambitions via *Lagaan* served to globalize it.

The relational power that informed Khan and SRK's ability to instigate novel business practices and network effects stemmed from their powerful brandscapes. Considered in its totality, the term refers to an imaginary market landscape that situates particular brands in relation to others and connotes the brand's total experiential reach and engagement.[85] Star brandscapes are meta-constructions that encompass the seductive desirability of stars and star bodies. They constitute an evocative embodied reaction to the star, in tandem with the allure that materializes through the star body's evocations in the staged offerings of other brands associated with them. Hence, star brandscapes are embodied and affective because the star brandscape essentially is transitively constructed by the desiring, affective, pleasure-seeking body and, by extension, star values and ideoscapes—what the star represents ideologically—as we consume the star on-screen, off-screen, and through other consumption spaces. Therefore, the star brandscape is culturally constructed through a complex interplay of on-screen and off-screen identities and the experiential universe of brand associations. The affective aspects of star brandscapes serve only to bolster the star's established pre-eminence in Hindi cinema's industrial structure, thus lending them and their organizations immense direct effective power within the industry business (see Figure 3.1).

In this emergent networked structure marked by the debut of star brandscapes, Bachchan's earlier novel attempts to capitalize on his stardom's brand equity through his organization, ABCL, was now consciously being built upon by SRK and Khan. Brandscapes for Indian stars are distinctive from Western paradigms because, through star-led organizations, the stars exceed the brandscapes. Indian megastars like SRK and Khan are not simply commodities indistinguishable from their charismatic visual presence, but they are also the corporations hoping to extract more value through their ubiquitous consumable brandscapes. This dichotomous agency is critical in understanding the relational affective and effective components of star switching power. Thus, their power and brandscapes are constructed through an iterative process between various actors, be it key individuals, film industry corporations, or other corporate, political, or state actors. Within this network, their brandscapes' relative strength and pervasiveness provide them with the ability to exceed and work across the various actors and networks to accomplish their organizations' goals (see Figure 3.2).

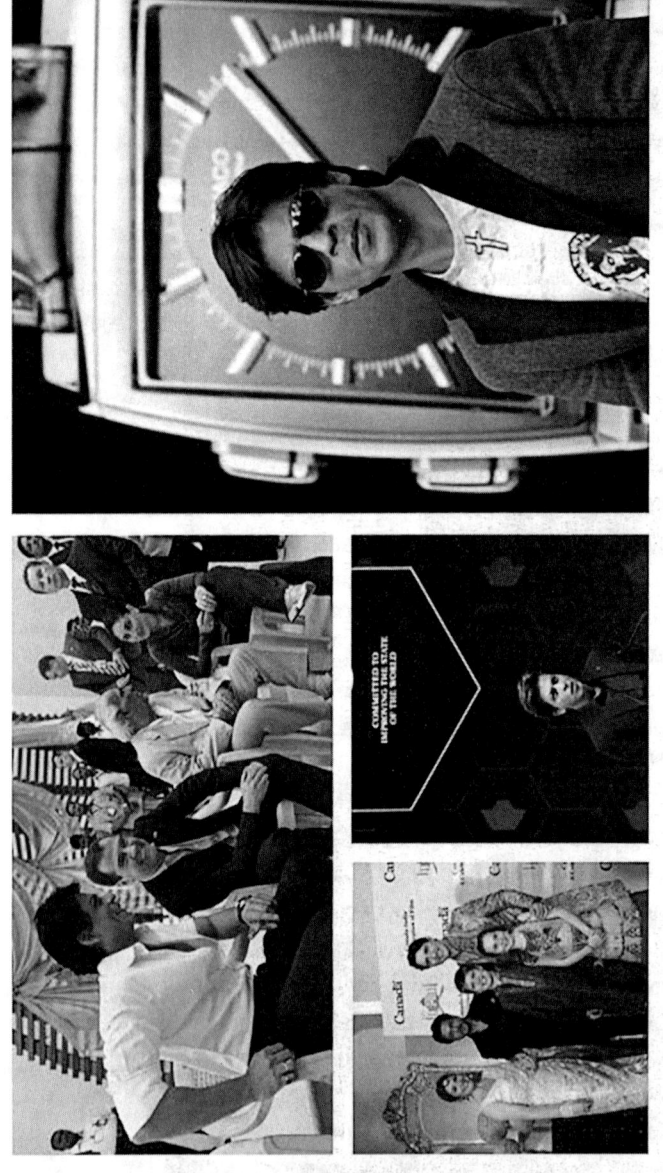

Figure 3.1 The *consumable switching power* of Shah Rukh Khan (SRK): (*clockwise from right*) SRK posing during the launch of the Swiss watch TAG Heuer, 2006; SRK speaking after receiving a Crystal Award from Hilde Schwab, chairperson and co-founder of Schwab Foundation for Social Entrepreneurship, during the World Economic Forum's (WEF) annual meeting in Davos, 2018; Canadian prime minister Justin Trudeau, wife Sophie Gregoire Trudeau, daughter Ella Grace, and son Xavier posing with SRK in Mumbai, 2018; SRK talking to Russian president Dmitry Medvedev during the latter's visit to a Bollywood studio, 2010

Source: (clockwise from right) Reuters/Adnan Abidi; Reuters/Denis Balibouse; Reuters/Danish Siddiqui; Reuters/Dmitry Astakhov/RIA Novosti/Kremlin.

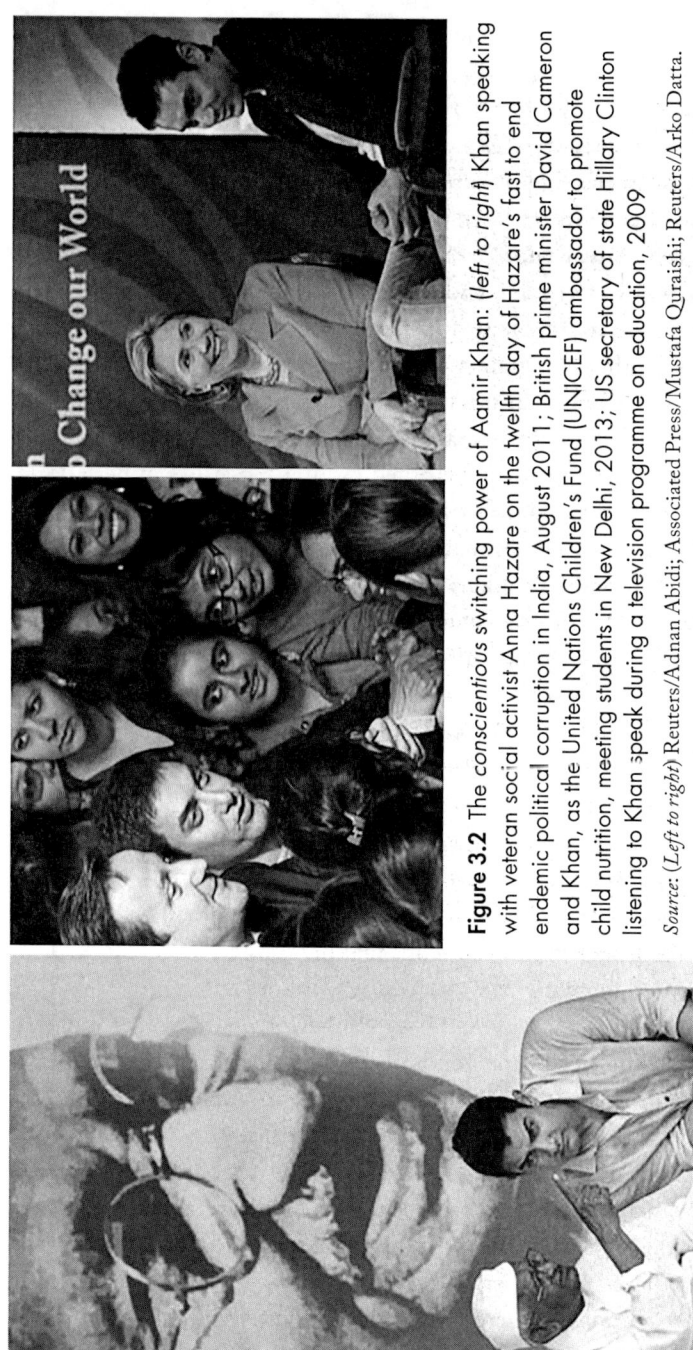

Figure 3.2 The *conscientious switching power* of Aamir Khan: (*left to right*) Khan speaking with veteran social activist Anna Hazare on the twelfth day of Hazare's fast to end endemic political corruption in India, August 2011; British prime minister David Cameron and Khan, as the United Nations Children's Fund (UNICEF) ambassador to promote child nutrition, meeting students in New Delhi, 2013; US secretary of state Hillary Clinton listening to Khan speak during a television programme on education, 2009

Source: (*Left to right*) Reuters/Adnan Abidi; Associated Press/Mustafa Quraishi; Reuters/Arko Datta.

Oscar-lobbying for *Lagaan* unfolded in a complex interplay of brandscapes. Corporate nodes and social, personal, and industrial networks all needed to come together for *Lagaan*'s success. Moreover, the global success and circulation of *Lagaan* would have to instantiate star switching power through a composite of social ties and direct corporate power mediated through star brandscapes and affect. An article in the *Economic Times* noted that 'corporate India's aristocracy is involved in … [ensuring] the film gets its fair share of visibility'.[86] Parmeshwar Godrej, India's premier socialite and power broker, and industrialist Adi Godrej's wife, took *Lagaan* under her wing. The Godrej Group, a diverse Indian conglomerate, also became a sponsor for the film through its consumer brand Britannia. 'I am helping to create buzz around the film in a very small way by contacting friends in California.… *Lagaan* is a great movie, Aamir, a great actor,' argued Godrej.[87] Because of her efforts, Hollywood actors Goldie Hawn and Peter Rawley 'championed the film [and] helped the *Lagaan* cause immensely'.[88] Diaspora networks were directly leveraged through prominent nodes like wellness guru Deepak Chopra, as were the industry nodes of producers Ashok Amritraj and Shekhar Kapoor and political entities like Swraj Paul, baron and member of the UK's House of Lords.[89]

Here we see star affect most clearly in how Godrej canvassed for *Lagaan* at the Oscars and mobilized corporate nodes and networks. Often, the association is mediated through a star's brand value, but with Bollywood, it is also based on the star's power to influence individuals and collectives, a benefit Khan enjoyed because he was part of a well-established Bollywood family-led film-production cluster. In addition to using his brand and networking power, Khan possessed direct network-making power, as evidenced by Godrej's Hollywood lobbying.[90]

In his 2013 book *Hollywood Stardom*, Paul McDonald points out that feature films are 'complex cultural goods' that require collaborative efforts and 'multiple inputs for their production' and circulation.[91] McDonald's analysis in the Hollywood context points to the star's primacy in the production process and industrial exchange. It posits a move away from the charismatic theory of stardom that recognizes stars in public culture as only symbolic figures whose identities are primarily textual. McDonald recognizes the integration of the star's symbolism and commercial aspects. The limitation is that 'Hollywood stardom is filtered through the tight oligopoly of the major studios, which hold economic and cultural dominance' over the industry.[92] In the instance of *Lagaan*, a corporatized Bollywood network at a moment of emergence—with collaborating corporate, state, and individual nodes—yet again consolidated around a star-led organization, Aamir Khan Productions, leading to a culmination of industry, corporate, and state interests. Thus, the Indian Film Commission and FICCI sat up and took notice, and individual nodes such as Godrej and Mira Nair (a Hollywood-based Indian director) became interested in the film's marketing and circulation. More importantly, as organic Bollywood film clusters inched their way towards a formalized collaborative network, the star figure at the helm always led the change, effectively or affectively, and often both.

With the stars offering innovative business strategies, they received a competitive advantage and showed other stars and industry nodes that change was feasible. Star-led organizations thus set off a series of network effects. In business, direct network effects occur when more people adopt a product, platform, or service, leading to an increase in value. Innovative business models and production practices also tend to create network effects on the production side, wherein other companies opt for similar strategies and models.[93] Up until this point, Bollywood was a small-world network with close ties among family-led production clusters. Stars possessed a distinctive centrality within this industry structure because of their direct role in the industry as producers of successful films. The microstructure of an underlying network of connections often influences how much network effects matter. That Bollywood was such a small-world network led to organizations like Aamir Khan Productions and Dreamz Unlimited communicating to others in the network that this neoliberal global landscape presented opportunities. These organizations connected hitherto local Bollywood to the global, encouraging other stars and prominent directors to see themselves in similar roles as businessmen and producers. Several factors went into the creation of strong network effects. Most prominently, star brandscapes again emerged as the relational agency that determined whether business or production practices would generate network effects. The world of Bollywood in this moment of transition consisted of clusters of densely connected individuals and production entities with strong ties. However, only stars with dynamic and successful brandscapes, a condition derived from their charisma and affective power, could create substantive network effects.

Network effects can be distilled from charisma, which becomes an essential component of business transformations or leadership.[94] Business management scholars Raina Brands, Jochen Menges, and Martin Kilduff point out that gender becomes an important determinant of whose charisma leads to leadership. Women's charisma is perceived differently and does not necessarily lead to visionary or leadership roles.[95] Evidently, female stars were at a disadvantage despite equivalent charisma and affective power.

The network effects instigated by SRK and Khan arose in multiple production and business practices. The early efforts of Red Chillies Entertainment and Aamir Khan Productions influenced and provided a model for new kinds of content, new global markets for Hindi cinema, and novel business practices in film promotion, marketing, distribution, and corporate partnerships. In the wake of an evolving industrial landscape, these prominent organizations expanded the scope of cinema from film to an entertainment landscape and helped Bollywood conglomerates converge industrially. Many of their early production and business choices proved visionary and were quickly adopted by other star-led and traditional Bollywood businesses.

Subhash Ghai, a director with an established brand, endeavoured to create the next international project with *Kisna: The Warrior Poet* (2005), a romantic saga of an Indian boy and a British girl set during the Indian independence struggle in the 1930s. The film starred British actor Antonia Bernath and featured music by the celebrated A. R. Rahman, a Bollywood music director who had begun to gain international fame after *Lagaan*'s and *Asoka*'s success. Ghai acknowledged that he was following the new trend: 'Today, India is a global phenomenon. Everyone, right from the media to the corporate world, is busy selling India abroad. It's important for a filmmaker to grow with the times. How long can I make the same stuff?'[96]

Driven by the same impetus for globality, Ghai wrote *Kisna* in collaboration with Farrukh Dhondy, an Indian-born British playwright and screenwriter known for his role in 'shaping British television viewing habits', and script doctor Margaret Glover.[97] The hiring of Bernath, according to Ghai, 'automatically [gave] the movie global appeal'.[98] Hiring international talent evolved into a common strategy that was adopted to break into the international market—'a passport to global success' (see Table 3.1).[99]

This trend in film-making was also the genesis of a new kind of nationalism and industry-driven nation-branding where India was claiming a global space. In *Kisna*, set in 1947, Bernath is not the 'other'; she is the devoted beloved. In *Mangal Pandey: The Rising* (2005, dir. Ketan Mehta), a quasi-sequel to *Lagaan*, starring Khan, the East India Englishman is not the evil oppressor but an honourable friend. Film critics noted that *Mangal Pandey* 'trie[d] to match *Lagaan*'s grandeur and emotional resonance … [but failed

Table 3.1 List of Indo-British ventures following *Lagaan* (Agricultural Tax, 2001, dir. Ashutosh Gowariker)

Film	Year	Director
Bride and Prejudice	2004	Gurinder Chadha
Kisna: The Warrior Poet	2005	Subhash Ghai
Mangal Pandey: The Rising	2005	Ketan Mehta
Before the Rains	2007	Santosh Sivan

in] whipping up the lather'.[100] Similar to *Lagaan*, the film explores India's struggle against tyrannical British rule, albeit through a historical lens with a global vision and ambition evident from the first *mahurat* (inaugural) shot,[101] clapped by none other than Prince Charles (see Figure 3.3).[102] The story could travel, the cast was international, the film had Rahman's music and a hybrid 'glocal' sensibility through its style and sound, and in the lead was Khan, whose success with *Lagaan* bolstered his confidence in the project. The film won recognition at international film festivals like Locarno but failed to replicate *Lagaan*'s success.[103]

Lagaan's director, Ashutosh Gowariker, concurrently ventured into another self-produced globally ambitious project *Swades* (Homeland, 2004), starring SRK, the indisputable diaspora hero. *Swades* was built on the premise of diasporic longing, with SRK playing a NASA scientist enticed to return to his impoverished village. With an incipient sense of belonging, he resolves to work for 'the people' in a place where he can make a real difference. *Swades* was, according to Gowariker, about what 'India is today', a 'shining' nation brimming with potential.[104] 'India Shining' was the 2004 government-launched nation-branding slogan to showcase the country's rapid economic growth and emphasize policy measures to promote a globalized environment.

The period marked the emergence of a new kind of content, selling a new kind of India in a new way to a global and domestic audience in tune with India's arrival on the global stage. Financial institutions like Goldman Sachs touted the early 2000s as the moment of ascendance for the Global South, especially Brazil, Russia, India, China, and South Africa (BRICS). They were 'the leading stars of many capitalist growth stories unfolding in post-colonial and post-communist contexts'. Within this global spectacle, India emerged as a 'prominent nerve center of unbridled capitalism'.[105] *Aśoka* and *Lagaan* were precursors to this kind of national spectacle and branding and presented a marker for India's 'shining' new identity.[106]

Figure 3.3 Britain's Prince Charles (now King Charles) holding a clapper board in front of Aamir Khan for the *muhurat* (inaugural) shot of *Mangal Pandey: The Rising* (2005, dir. Ketan Mehta)

Source: Reuters/Stephen Hird.

The Bollywood narratives triggered through these films built affective frameworks around globality, devotion to the nation, and India's emergence as a distinctive power that had overcome its colonial, 'third world' past. *Lagaan*, *Kisna*, and *Mangal Pandey*, which soon followed, all evoked a presentist history, filtering historical episodes through a contemporary lens and targeting dual markets, the global and the local. The 'formula' for globalization was thus crystallized; it was defined by a collaborative international cast and crew, a story that straddled the East and the West, Rahman's alchemy of global and local sounds, and a cast of Bollywood stars with expansive brandscapes and switching power, some marked by their racial indeterminacy: ergo, globality. The formulas for garnering global visibility and distribution deals were also concretized, and film festivals and markets like Cannes came to be critical entryways to international markets.

Prominent journalist and industry consultant Meenakshi Shedde, writing in the context of *Lagaan*'s Oscar nomination, related the global success of other Asian cinemas from China, Iran, Korea, and Japan to European film festivals. She underscored that Bollywood's arrival would signal a truly global industry when

> our films earn unstinted praise from critics worldwide, snag big laurels at the Oscars and in Europe, and have Miramax and Sony putting their weight behind us internationally. [T]hen we can consider ourselves on par with Iranian cinema. India's domestic market is huge. But in the face of globalization, and the uncertainty of the local box office, it is best to cultivate the overseas market as well.[107]

Film festival networks now structurally occupied a prominent place in the distribution process.

Yash Raj Films, the producer of the 1990s SRK breakout hit *DDLJ*, had now become a vertically integrated media corporation and distributed Khan's *Mangal Pandey*. According to Avtar Panesar, the long-standing head of Yash Raj Films's international operations,

> Cannes and Berlin had always attracted filmmakers, but around the 2000s we actively started making movies that were more palatable for the west. A lot of the Indian companies started going public and the festivals and film markets became a way to also be seen to be reaching out to non-core audiences and expanding the footprint.[108]

After SRK and Khan modelled a new kind of global film, the network consolidated. Already the formula and structure for globality were emerging. The producer of *Bandit Queen* (arguably the most global film of the 1990s), Bobby Bedi, also produced Khan's *Mangal Pandey*. Other personnel who contributed to the global formula, like screenwriter Dhondy and music composer Rahman, remained a constant factor in the new globally ambitious film ventures. In this emergent networked structure, the impact and propulsion of other film industry nodes towards the new model led by SRK and Khan are amply evident.

Although *Mangal Pandey* failed to be a global hit, it had a record opening in niche multiplexes in India.[109] Within the domestic market, it pointed to the viability of global films for the cosmopolitan middle class, riding the wave of India Shining. Khan shut down his critics by playing up the film's success: '[M]ultiplex owners will go on record that the film's opening was not just good, but earth-shattering.'[110] The Bollywood network was now shifting and evolving as it moved away from individual star-led efforts to an integrated set of actors and networks that would ensure a global presence and create a sustainable business model for films.

Khan's *Lagaan* created another marked shift in the Bollywood network, which led to a string of Indo-British ventures, including Aishwarya Rai's *Bride and Prejudice* (2004), directed by the British-Indian director Gurinder Chadha. This venture marked the second wave of experimentation wherein Indian stars like Aishwarya Rai (a former Miss World) lent the films visual globality by embodying a very high degree of racial indeterminacy. The active incorporation of the beauty pageant network initiated by Bachchan within Bollywood's new network structure was now overtly conspicuous, with a marked preference for Indian stars that possessed this 'corporeal malleability'. Their 'bronzed' whiteness was targeted at the convergent logic of the global market. The deliberate deployment of 'white-passing' ethnic bodies was to broaden market appeal; anyone could identify with them.[111] The next phase of the global film product was thus an innovation that deployed racially indeterminate star bodies like Aishwarya Rai and Hrithik Roshan (see Figure 3.4).[112]

Jodhaa Akbar (2008) was directed and produced by *Lagaan*'s director, Ashutosh Gowariker, who described Rai and Roshan as his dream cast. A *New York Times* article hailed them as 'paradisically beautiful' consummate actors who, with their ethnically indeterminate looks and impeccable English, were poised to be India's first international movie stars.[113] Buoyed by the success of *Lagaan*, Gowariker had set up his own production company and produced *Swades*. *Jodhaa Akbar* was his second attempt at creating a globally viable film. The deliberate positioning and success of *Jodhaa Akbar* highlighted the burgeoning Bollywood network and its global ambition, and Gowariker's collaboration with UTV exemplified Bollywood's new corporatized domestic nodes that now wanted a piece of the Bollywood pie. Entrepreneur Ronnie Screwvala founded UTV Software Communications in 1990, at the moment of liberalization, and gradually moved from television to film production as the benefits of liberalization trickled down to the film industry. Unlike the film industry's existing family-led clusters, nodes like UTV were more corporatized and had the infrastructure to create global projects.[114] We see a collaborative network solidifying with individual nodes attempting to create global film projects in collaboration with corporate media nodes, a step forward in expanding the network as Bollywood nodes

Figure 3.4 (*Left*) Aishwarya Rai walking the red carpet at the Cannes Film Festival; (*right*) Hrithik Roshan walking the ramp for India Couture Week

Source: (*Left*) Associated Press/Villard/Niviere/Sipa; (*right*) Associated Press/Rafiq Maqbool.

moved away from their small-world ties and unsavoury connections with the mafia.[115] Within the context of star switching power and their star-led network effects, Khan's and SRK's business and product innovations led to other individual nodes (such as stars and directors) within the industry and family-led film-production clusters to replicate them.

In the classic story of network externality or network effects, demand and economies of scale lead to growth; consequently, a product is valued more as more consumers are drawn to it. This moment created network economies wherein more producers wanted to attract those audiences. The network effect thus ran across markets and affected not simply consumers but content creators as well.[116] SRK's and Khan's initial experimentation and forays set off these network effects in production. Other stars saw that they could replicate this new production model, and many star-led productions were set up during this time (see Figure 3.5).

Shah Rukh Khan
Dreamz Unlimited
Red Chillies Entertainment

Aamir Khan
Aamir Khan Productions

Akshay Kumar
Hari Om Entertainment

Hrithik Roshan
Filmkraft Productions

Ajay Devgn
Ajay Devgn Films

Farhan Akhtar
Excel Entertainment

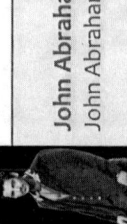

Saif Ali Khan
Illuminati Films

Salman Khan
Salman Khan Films
Salman Khan Productions
SK TV

John Abraham
John Abraham Entertainment

Sanjay Dutt
White Feather Film Productions

Anil Kapoor
Antila Ventures
Anil Kapoor Films

Amitabh Bachchan
Amitabh Bachchan Corporation
Limited
AB Corp

Figure 3.5 Star-led media and production companies: male stars

Source: Prepared by the author using various news sources.

One prominent star who emerged at this time was Hrithik Roshan. His portrayal of the Mughal emperor Akbar in *Jodhaa Akbar* won him international acclaim. Like Khan, he was part of a family-led film-production cluster, Filmkraft Productions—started by his actor-turned-director father, Rakesh Roshan, and music-director uncle, Rajesh Roshan—a company that was corporatizing and vying to create yet another film for the global market. *Kites* (2010, dir. Anurag Basu) was an experiment that tested the limits of Bollywood's globality and built on the model that would be propounded by Khan's next film, *3 Idiots*. This film not only incorporated global nodes like Reliance into the fold but also led the expansion of Hindi films to other lateral markets like China.

The success of Khan and Reliance's collaboration on *3 Idiots* can be seen in how the Roshans attempted to create similar film projects. Their global film, *Kites*, in partnership with Reliance, was similar to Dev Anand's *Guide* (1965, dir. Tad Danielewski [English version] and Vijay Anand [Hindi version]), with two different versions of the film produced, one for the domestic audience and another for international viewers. The international version, *Kites: The Remix* (2010), was edited and partly directed by Hollywood filmmaker Brett Ratner, with an English and a Spanish rendition. *Kites* cast Mexican actress and model Bárbara Mori as the female lead, and Roshan channelled his ethnic ambiguity into projecting a transnational identity. An article in the *New York Times* called the film 'a carefully calibrated assault on resistant international markets.... [T]he movie harnesses English, Hindi, and Hispanic talent to an everything-but-the-kitchen-sink plot, replaces dancing with explosions, and choreographers with stunt specialists.'[117]

Despite the massive effort and expectations, the film did not garner the success the Roshans had been hoping for, but as the *New York Times* emphasized, *Kites*, in many ways, epitomized Bollywood's global ambition in this phase, underscoring the historical centrality of star-led productions in taking Indian cinema global. Megastars created new trends and models that exceeded other nodes in the industry and enabled network effects adopted by a 'second rung' of stars, often without similar success. These stars, though, lacked the switching power to initiate change in ways that SRK's and Khan's brandscapes could.

Another example of a 'second-rung' superstar who adopted the new industry model is Akshay Kumar, who, with Shree Ashtavinayak Cine Vision, a publicly listed corporate entity, attempted to produce a global project. Like UTV, Ashtavinayak got its start in television production in the

1990s and then gravitated to film. The company envisioned and produced a global film, *Blue* (2009, dir. Anthony D'Souza), written by American writers Joshua Lurie and Brian Sullivan, with Australian singer and actor Kylie Minogue as the film's global hook. Like SRK and Khan, this was Kumar's attempt to widen his global popularity. Through his production company, Hari Om Entertainment (now Cape of Good Films), incorporated in 2008 in partnership with his wife, Bollywood actress Twinkle Khanna, and in collaboration with other nodes of the Bollywood network, Kumar attempted interesting global ventures. Although Khanna hailed from a Bollywood film family—her mother and father were Bollywood superstars of the 1960s and 1970s—her in-house productions were discursively criticized in condescending terms or dismissed outright. A newspaper article emphatically noted that although 'Twinkle has always been credited as a co-producer for all Hari Om Entertainment Films, … Twinkle was not involved in any aspect of her home productions'.[118] In 2016, Khanna launched her independent production house, Mrs Funnybones Movies, which generated press headlines such as 'Akshay's wife Twinkle starts her production house'.[119] Cynthia Enloe astutely points to the tendency among social commentators, policymakers, and journalists (predominantly female journalists, who are often left to cover women) to dismiss women's efforts. Women and their endeavours are not seen to possess the same gravitas, and their ideas are presented as 'lightweight' or a 'passing whim' not to be taken seriously.[120] In the larger discourse of female switching power, perception of the star's industrial ambitions and the discourse about it is a recurrent barrier to their success. Like Chawla (in the case of Dreamz Unlimited), Twinkle's contributions were construed as peripheral to Hari Om Productions's success.[121]

Similar to SRK, Kumar's star brand was built around the Indian diaspora, specifically the Punjabi and Sikh communities. As someone who was born in Punjab and had lived in South-East Asia for several years learning martial arts and making a living as a part-time cook, Kumar's captivating immigrant narrative became the mainstay of several film projects featuring him. An emphasis on national identity and belonging stand out in several of his films that possess a quintessential 'Indianness' the diaspora was loath to lose—a remnant of *DDLJ*'s hyphenated diasporic identities. Kumar's diasporic character embodies nationalistic jingoism while simultaneously foregrounding a distinctive Sikh or Punjabi identity. His comedic and romantic features, like *Singh Is Kinng* (2008, dir. Anees Bazmee), *Singh Is Bliing* (2015, dir. Prabhu Deva), and *Namastey London* (2007, dir. Vipul Shah), tell the story of a Punjabi immigrant bumpkin who undergoes growth and assimilates well into his new environment. Reminiscent of earlier Bollywood tropes, Kumar's character lives in a moment of surging nationalistic pride. In *Namastey London*, after hearing India being disparaged as a land of snake charmers, Kumar jingoistically asserts,

> We are a 5,000-year-old culture. When we greet one another, we fold our hands in namaste because we believe that God resides in the heart of every human being. We come from a nation where we allow a lady of Catholic origin to step aside for a Sikh to be sworn in as prime minister by a Muslim president to govern a nation of over 80 per cent Hindus.

Kumar's character projects a branding narrative about India as an ancient secular tradition that has found its place in the global world and should be respected as such. Predictably, Kumar gradually emerged as the sine non qua around contemporary nation-branding discourses initiated by the current conservative ruling political party, the Bharatiya Janata Party (BJP).[122]

Kumar's film narratives drew from his personal life in appealing to niche diaspora networks. His early *Khiladi* series (1992–2000) focused on his martial arts skill and blended action and comedy.[123] In an initial effort to create pan-Asian films, Warner Bros. produced *Chandni Chowk to China* (2009, dir. Nikkhil Adjani) with Kumar as the lead. As the Bollywood network was expanding, it was an early attempt by Hollywood studios to create Indian films for a larger lateral market that included China. The movie was a poorly executed narrative about an Indian cook living in China whom the Chinese claimed was a reincarnation of war hero Liu Shen. The story is reminiscent of *Kung Fu Panda* (2008, dir. Mark Osborne and John Stevenson); however, it failed to garner the same success. It was a big blow to Warner Bros. and their planned franchise with Kumar (he was set to take on a new adventure to Africa). The Hollywood studio's attempt to cater to markets proximate to Bollywood by leveraging Kumar's stardom failed. However, Kumar, through his own production company and other collaborations, continued to create films in his niche action-comedy genre. Through his global film-production efforts, two interesting trends gained prominence. The first was casting an international star in a cameo to give added global appeal to a Bollywood film. This trend was apparent in most of Kumar's films, starting with *Blue* (2009, dir. Anthony D'Souza), *Kambakkht*

Ishq (Damned Love, 2009, dir. Sabbir Khan), and *Singh Is Kinng* (featuring Kylie Minogue, Sylvester Stallone, and rapper Snoop Dogg). Along with a few other comedy films—for example, *Fool N Final* (2007, dir. Ahmed Khan), which featured Mike Tyson in a guest appearance—these efforts, however, had few large-scale network effects.

After Warner Bros.'s failed attempt at a pan-Asian film, Sony Pictures tried their luck with newcomer actors in the film *Saawariya* (Beloved, 2007, dir. Sanjay Leela Bhansali), based on Fyodor Dostoevsky's short story 'White Nights', and Disney collaborated with the newly corporatized Yash Raj Films for an animated feature, *Roadside Romeo* (2008, dir. Jugal Hansraj). The attempts were a curious medley that failed to retain either a Hollywood or Bollywood identity. Because the Bollywood industry's evolution was built around small-world networks and family-led film-production clusters, the network that now included Hollywood nodes necessitated Hollywood studios to collaborate with established local film clusters, predominantly star-led production entities. Thus, all early Hollywood ventures failed until Fox Searchlight Pictures collaborated with SRK's Red Chillies Entertainment and Dharma Productions (another prominent family-led production house) and came up with a new global strategy for *My Name Is Khan* (2010, dir. Karan Johar).

The collaborative production *My Name Is Khan* told the story of an autistic Indian American Muslim, played by SRK, who faces racism in the wake of 9/11. He embarks on a journey across the US to meet president Barack Obama just to tell him, 'My name is Khan, and I am not a terrorist.' The film was a typical Bollywood melodramatic narrative in the style associated with SRK, although the appeal of the subject was global. *My Name Is Khan* was the highest-grossing film in India that year. It collected USD 17.6 million globally and USD 23.1 million in the Indian market, surpassing Khan's *3 Idiots*'s global success, which had been released the year before.[124]

This partnership and strategy redefined the operation model for Hollywood studios in India. They no longer attempted to create their own experimental content; instead, they backed prominent productions led by stars, directors, or other established Bollywood production studios. According to PricewaterhouseCoopers (PwC) analyst Smita Jha, *My Name Is Khan*'s global success helped Indian film-production houses see that Hollywood studios were skilled at content-based marketing strategies, especially in reaching Bollywood's non-traditional markets. This was the first instance when an Indian film had a day-and-date release in Egypt, Jordan, and Lebanon. The studio leveraged SRK's star appeal in the Middle East, collecting USD 4.1 million in the Middle East alone.[125] After Bachchan's ubiquity in the Middle East, especially in Egypt, SRK was the next star to ignite an interest in Indian films. Like most SRK ventures, *My Name Is Khan* redefined the collaborative business model between Hollywood studio nodes and Bollywood production houses to create a mutually beneficial business synergy.

By the 2010s, in addition to Hollywood studios, several other global nodes had emerged that helped build global celebrity brands and enabled other stars to access audiences abroad. Beyond globally ambitious productions and distribution, some of these nodes brought together Bollywood events, awards, and thereby 'liveness' as Bollywood expanded beyond films. Bollywood was now expanding as an entertainment network through nodes like the IIFA, FICCI Frames, and the Times of India Film Awards (TOIFA), which sought to establish Bollywood cinema in transnational spaces and leverage the industry in a transitive way for other business, economic, and cultural exchanges. Stars remained the central figures to inspire this change and around whom the events' success was crystallized. According to an IIFA marketing executive, 'IIFA is like Bollywood's date party with the global film fraternity.'[126] Ranjani Mazumdar contends that the 'liveness' of these events added to the signage of stardom, transforming it into a mediated spectacle. The star became the node around which industrial, state, and corporate interests converged. Replicating the pattern of network effects, this change was yet again instigated by SRK. Following his immense success as the diaspora's favourite star, SRK organized his Red Chillies-produced 2004 concert tour, *Temptation*, which encompassed twenty-seven cities across the US and the UK, where SRK, along with other Bollywood stars, performed live stage shows. The euphoric reception for SRK in these global diasporic enclaves was likened to Beatlemania in a BBC documentary about the show.[127]

In a film culture, and structure wherein music and dance are pivotal components of the narrative structure, SRK, via Red Chillies, envisioned and morphed Bollywood into a broader cultural form that expanded the scope of the industry to bring music, dance, and live stage performance into its fold. Mazumdar notes that the event signalled the genesis of a hyper-visual culture that brought entertainment through a dense network of circuits across continents. This entertainment, mediated through technology, emerged into a

The SRK Empire

Kolkata Knight Riders

- Sports franchise where SRK owns 55 per cent stake through Red Chilies
- First IPL team to turn profitable (in Mar 2012), won IPL 5 (2012)
- Want to scale up brand merchandising, build an official fan base on the Manchester United model

Red Chillies Entertainment

VFX
- One of India's largest visual effects studios
- Popular project – *Krrish 3* (2013, dir. Rakesh Roshan)
- Looking for MPAA certification to bid for more Hollywood projects

Production
- Film production house with many blockbusters to its name
- Contributes the most to Red Chillies
- Popular projects: *Chennai Express* (2013, Rohit Shetty), *Happy New Year* (2014, dir. Farah Khan)

KidZania India

- Mexican edutainment brand, which opened its first theme park in India in June 2013
- SRK owns 26 per cent stake in the company and promotes the brand in India
- Three self-funded centres to be opened in Mumbai, Delhi NCR, and Bangalore

SRK's future business interests
Restaurants and other sports like hockey

SRK's failed ventures
Dreamz Unlimited, srkworld.com, Idiot Box

Figure 3.6 The Shah Rukh Khan (SRK) empire

Source: Prepared by the author.

Note: MPAA stands for Motion Picture Association of America; IPL stands for Indian Premier League, a cricket league held annually in India.

new economy of stardom generated through event management companies.[128] As the instigator of this change, Red Chillies was a critical component of this emergent Bollywood network in the early 2000s (see Figure 3.6). Stars with switching power existed not simply as nodes acted upon, but they produced significant change within the industry's structure and led to Bollywood's evolution as an entertainment industry.

As we got closer to the turn of the decade, by the 2010s, the evolution of Bollywood had extended to sports. Again, Red Chillies generated considerable network effects. SRK's company (alongside Chawla, his former collaborator who is again visibly absent from the popular discourse on his team's success) bought a majority stake in the Indian Premier League (IPL), bringing together two of India's biggest passions: Bollywood and cricket. Bollywood morphed into another spectacular entertainment form, a complex network that brought together sports, television, film, and music anchored by the glitz of stardom and celebrity. The symbiosis of Bollywood and cricket followed the neoliberal economic turn in state policy and governance. It led to televised cricket in India's remotest rural areas.[129] Investments flowing from Bollywood spurred the sport's evolution into a diffused cultural entertainment form that now included stars like SRK and Bollywood music and dance, thereby creating a commodified spectacle that could synergize and promote both Bollywood and cricket. This SRK-initiated network effect led to other Bollywood stars acquiring stakes in sporting leagues. Furthermore, the Kolkata Knight Riders—the most valuable IPL brand—because of SRK's ownership, was the first IPL team to break even (see Table 3.2 for ownership details).[130] While sports leagues have been popular in Europe, the IPL and other star-led sporting leagues like Kabaddi are brilliantly glocal, if not uniquely Indian, entertainment vehicles.

Through Red Chillies, SRK also started a successful visual effects (VFX) company, exploring media distribution possibilities through mobile and other digital platforms. While scholars Kavita Karan and David Schaefer have termed this an adoption of Western models, the centrality of stars within Bollywood and star ownership of independent production houses is, actually, diametrically opposed to the Hollywood model. Stars have become initiators of trends and business models around which industry practices crystallize. This leads us to ask, how do stars possess this power when industry structures are moving away from small-world networks towards powerful corporate nodes? The first answer to this enquiry is that change is a gradual process and small-world network ties still exist in Bollywood.

Table 3.2 Star-owned sports teams

Star	Sports league	Team
Shah Rukh Khan	Indian Premier League (cricket)	Kolkata Knight Riders Trinbago Knight Riders Cape Town Knight Riders Abu Dhabi Knight Riders
Juhi Chawla	Indian Premier League (cricket)	Kolkata Knight Riders (with SRK)
Preity Zinta	Indian Premier League (cricket)	Punjab Kings
Shilpa Shetty	Indian Premier League (cricket)	Rajasthan Royals
Bonnie Kapoor with Sridevi (deceased)	Celebrity Cricket League	Bengal Tigers
Sohail Khan	Celebrity Cricket League	Mumbai Heroes
Abhishek Bachchan	Pro-Kabaddi League Indian Super League (soccer)	Jaipur Pink Panthers Chennaiyin FC
Sonakshi Sinha	World Kabaddi League	United Singhs
Akshay Kumar	World Kabaddi League	Bengal Warriors Khalsa Warriors
Ranbir Kapoor	Indian Super League (soccer)	Mumbai Team
John Abraham	Hockey India League Indian Super League (soccer)	Delhi Wave Riders Northeast United FC
Hrithik Roshan	Indian Super League (soccer)	FC Pune City
Tapsee Pannu	Premier Badminton League	Pune 7 Aces
Riteish Deshmukh	Celebrity Cricket League	Veer Marathi
Sohail Khan	Celebrity Cricket League	Mumbai Heroes
Sunny Leone	Premier Futsal	Kerala Cobras

Source: Prepared by the author using various news sources.

The second answer derives from the relative relationship, introduced earlier, between star brandscapes and switching power, which the following section elaborates on.

THE POWER AND AFFECT OF STAR BRANDSCAPES

Stars possess an inordinate amount of power within the Bollywood industrial structure. However, not all of them possess the same kind of power, and conversations with industry insiders helped me theorize the relationship of star brandscapes to direct corporate power. The president of corporate relations for a large conglomerate in India revealed, on the condition of anonymity, that SRK's stake in his IPL team was largely based on his brand equity—that is, he invested very little capital, and his majority share and ownership in the league was based on the revenue-generation potential of his brand. This is reminiscent of Bachchan's earlier endeavour; however, this time, SRK was able to monetize the enormity of his stardom. A variety of factors determine star switching power. Most importantly, from an industry standpoint, it is determined by the centrality of the star and their production company within the industry structure. Star brandscapes become a potent mediator of this industrial centrality, which explains why some stars possess the power to exceed the network's constraints to create new business models and pathways for globalization. Avtar Panesar, the vice president of special projects at Yash Raj Films, notes that consistent popularity determines the star's brand value, the extent of their brandscapes, and the sustained success of their production and distribution ventures:

> The thing with the star system is that unless there is an absolute consistency to your star power, you are not going to be able to pull in or have the clout every Friday [new movies in India are released in theatres on Fridays]. Changing fortunes of the star also mean a change in the fortunes of their production company, a case in point being Sunny Deol. Around the same time that some of these changes were going on with stars setting up their production companies in the 2000s, he tried to set himself up as a business vertical but failed because, by that time, his stardom and fortunes had changed.[131]

In contrast, Panesar adds, is SRK's consistency, which made Red Chillies one of India's top production companies. Unlike other star-led production entities that failed to present a consistent roster of releases, because they only produce films with their single star, Red Chillies is a full-fledged production company that produces a wide range of films and other media. That a leading star, SRK, runs it is incidental.[132] This perspective foregrounds some of the limits of stardom; in other words, a sustainable and consistent business model is critical for any business to work. However, as the industry structure was evolving into a networked model, the kind of direct agency and power that a star like Bachchan possessed was not exactly the same for SRK and Khan, although it was similar. For instance, following the success of *Lagaan* in the post-liberalization era, people compared Khan to Bachchan:

> Aamir is easily the most admired brand—I would put Aamir and Amitabh Bachchan at the same level. This has been possible through consistently good performances, which have been varied rather than stereotyped. Most recently, he has reinvented the whole process of delivery through *Lagaan*. He has all the essentials of a strong brand, retaining freshness, relevance, and promise for his target audience.[133]

Brandscapes and the multiplicity of corporate nodes at this moment had changed the nature of star switching power. Saibal Chatterjee, a veteran film journalist, emphasizes,

> In this era, instead of one star like Bachchan driving the industry, you have Shah Rukh, Aamir, Salman, Akshay, Hrithik, and to a certain extent Ajay Devgn. They all have their niche fan following and their kind of cinema that they do. Their brands don't overlap.... They all have their own turfs. Once you know your target, you create your own company, and you push that brand and make the most out of it. Here [in India], it's not the producer, the writer, or the director that's central; it's the star. The name of the lead actor determines how big the project will be. If it's Aamir or Shah Rukh Khan, it will be very big because they will also look at an international market. Salman Khan will be slightly smaller because he is more Indian than global. Akshay Kumar will have his Punjabi diaspora audience, and Hrithik will be global too, at least he is trying.[134]

Stars with switching power, like SRK, Khan, and Bachchan, configure networks and can programme them and redefine their goals. SRK and Khan, through their critical positions within the network, define goals and business practices for a global Bollywood industry. They also redefine a star's position within the Bollywood network wherein the star becomes a key industry stakeholder, integral to business decisions and practices. Other stars with somewhat influential brandscapes soon follow in their footsteps, setting up star-led production companies. However, the star brand becomes the relational agency mediating the switching power that individual stars and their business clusters possess; that is, what distinguishes stars like Bachchan, SRK, and Khan is their ability to create new pathways for the Bollywood business and their ability to adopt transformative business practices with a global vision. Due to the small-world nature of Bollywood and the star's centrality to the success of the Bollywood film, they possess high relational industry power.

Earlier stars such as Bachchan and Raj Kapoor were central to industry networks because of their close political, social, and cultural ties. Conversely, stars like SRK and Khan prospered as the industry structure was shifting. They possessed industrial power relationally derived from their brandscapes but also from power derived through their star personas. Together they constructed brandscapes that spilled over to the realms of industry, politics, and diplomacy, lending them switching power as change-makers for Bollywood business.

Khan's conscientious brandscape is constructed around scarcity, whereas SRK's brand persona is built around abundant consumability. Both star brandscapes have generated affective sensoria that inspired fandoms and affect that spilled over to the realms of industry and politics. The last part of the polyptych delves into how the sensorium associated with Khan or SRK appears in transnational fandoms, politics, and diplomacy. This is influenced by important qualities that define each star's brandscape and distinguish them from each other.

THE AFFECTIVE SENSORIUM OF SRK

My fieldwork journey during the sultry July of 2016 from New Delhi to the Red Chillies office in Bandra Bandstand, Mumbai, abounded with the techno-visual sensorium of SRK. He was on the back of my boarding pass, endorsing Vi-John shaving cream as 'a smooth way to take off'; he was on the airport television selling Nerolac Paints and Pepsi; and he was on the numerous billboards I encountered on my unremitting cab ride through the sluggish and seemingly unending rush-hour traffic of Mumbai to Bandra Bandstand. I was there to meet Karuna Badwal, the business manager for Red Chillies Entertainment. However, more than the physical encounter with the people related to Red Chillies, the accentuated affect and ubiquity of SRK in the space inspired a reflective pause. I was taken in by the enormity of his brandscape, which encompasses everything from Pepsodent toothpaste, hair oil, colas, and fairness cream for men to luxury TAG Heuer watches. Until 2017, SRK had the highest number of brand endorsements among all Bollywood stars and consistently made the *Forbes* global list of 100 highest-earning celebrities.[135] His position since 2016 has been shifting as he moves away from the realm of stardom to being more of an industrial node through his expansive business empire, which structurally aligns with the changes in Bollywood. That said, the resounding global success of his recent film *Pathaan* (2023, dir. Siddharth Anand) has brought SRK back into the realm of stardom, even if temporarily.

SRK's star brand and persona, as it emerged at this time, was global, urban, and consumable across geographies. Rajinder Dudrah describes SRK as the 'literal and metaphorical embodiment of an actor-cum-star who is able to perform most successfully the anxieties, hopes, and fantasies of urban India and its related South Asian diasporas'.[136] *DDLJ*'s resounding success placed him at the helm of diaspora networks. The affective economy created by *DDLJ* conflated urban India with the South Asian diaspora. Recognizing this is critical to understanding how a typical SRK film has since been positioned and marketed. His films appealed to the global consumerist fantasies of young urban India and the diaspora ostensibly living this aspirational reality. SRK's on-screen personae, which includes Raj Malhotra (*DDLJ*), Arjun Saagar (*Pardes*), and Aman Mathur (*Kal Ho Naa Ho*), simultaneously enact a relatable and aspirational diasporic identity and a chic urban Indianness. SRK articulated this aspect of his branding in a *Filmfare* interview: 'In the 1970s, the hero was anti-establishment, but I promise a better world. *The yuppie* doesn't bash a truck full of *goondas*. He kills in the stock market.'[137] SRK's assessment of his characters raises the question of his stardom's 'symbolic commerce', the forms through which his stardom and brand circulate in cultural markets within and outside India.[138] He gradually became the symbol of 'India's ascent to the global stage and of a new access to the luxurious goods of the metropolis'.[139] According to veteran journalist Alaka Sahani,

> In the last couple of decades, everything has become very Bollywood-centric. In America, you probably won't find George Clooney selling a toothpaste or Navratna Tel or Rajnigandha pan masala. The ad world here is extremely star-centric. About a decade ago, we had Shah Rukh Khan taking a bath covered in rose petals for Lux soap, a brand that was so far endorsed by only female stars. If you switch on the TV, most of the endorsements are done by stars, especially Shah Rukh. Here, stardom is so huge that stars can sell anything, even insignificant things. I can understand if Shah Rukh endorses a good watch, but it is so many random things.[140]

In his analysis of Western stardom, Richard Dyer has emphasized that stars express particular ideas of individuality, of what it is to be human in our contemporary society. For SRK, that notion revolved around consumability, 'consumo ergo sum'. He is India's first 'consumable hero'; 'the emblem or mascot of the NRI' who embodies a cool globalism; a 'yuppie', equally at ease at home and in the world; 'a feeling'; and 'an embodiment of the male desire to be desired', which advertising agencies ensure readers can be accomplished through consumption.[141] SRK's affective appeal is centred on a melodramatic emotional pitch and a sensitive masculinity that coalesce around India's newfound neoliberal cosmopolitanism. More importantly, how did the industry leverage this affective brandscape to achieve its global agenda via the political and diplomatic realms? As it turns out, this relationship exhibited a reciprocal dynamic.

THE NETWORKED GLOBAL SPACE OF FLOWS AND THE BOLLYWOOD STAR

[SRK is a] cult phenomenon … let's forget about the Bollywood name. In Germany, it's a Shah Rukh Khan market. He is a guarantee for [the] box office.[142]

—Stephan Holl, proprietor of Rapid Eye Movies
(Bollywood's German distributor)

I realized that you cannot imitate Shah Rukh Khan. He is such a perfect actor. We wanted to show our respect to Bollywood and these fantastic actors. They are very popular in Germany. Bollywood is a cultural institution. This is the one instrument to connect to the world, and it is a very good instrument. Me and my wife are Bollywood addicts.[143]

—Michael Steiner, former German ambassador to India (2015)

The two statements above encapsulate feelings about SRK's popularity in Germany and its primacy in both industrial and diplomatic contexts (see Figure 3.7). Hindi cinema's globalization in the 2010s through star figures instantiated the remarkable convergence of industrial, governmental, and diplomatic logics initiated by their effective and affective embeddedness. While SRK bedazzled the Germans, Khan inspired dedicated fandoms

Figure 3.7 Shah Rukh Khan (SRK) being greeted by enthusiastic fans at the sixtieth Berlinale Film Festival in Germany, 2010

Source: Reuters/Mark Blinch.

in China. Both countries were new and non-traditional markets for Bollywood.

The genesis of Bollywood's industrial relationship with Germany happened in the 1930s and 1940s with Himanshu Rai and Devika Rani and flourished because of Rani's exceptional switching power.[144] The relationship was focused on 'industrial knowledge' and exchange with directors Mohan Bhavnani, Himanshu Rai, and actress Rani all training and working in Berlin's Universum-Film-Aktiengesellschaft (UFA), one of Germany's leading film studios.[145] The German market, however, remained indifferent to future Bollywood collaborations and films. The tenor was more of a mentoring relationship wherein Germany, 'Europe's leading country', was nurturing artistic growth and exposing Indians to European arts.[146]

The dynamic in the 2010s was starkly different. SRK and his globality became the node around which the flows of Bollywood to Germany were mobilized. The early 2000s defined the moment when the affective power of Bollywood stars worked in conjunction with the institutional goals of the state and global and local industries. Within this formative network structure, film festivals were imperative nodes for the circulation of Hindi cinema beyond Indian shores. SRK—who had established his global marketability early on as the 'star of the Indian diaspora' alongside Aishwarya Rai, former Miss World and the global face of Indian beauty (the subject of the next chapter)—was the cynosure of the Cannes Film Festival in 2002. The special screening of their film *Devdas* (2002, dir. Sanjay Leena Bhansali) in the non-competition section of the festival was repackaged as India Day and celebrated with aplomb and spectacle. The stars made their way to the screening in a horse-drawn carriage. Sushma Swaraj, the Indian minister for information and broadcasting, several Indian global business leaders like the Hindujas, and the Indian ambassador to France were in attendance. The event was managed by Eros International (now Eros Media World), the largest international distributor of Hindi films. The screening represented a moment where multiple nodes, networks, and interests converged around stars whose affective iconicity situated them as central nodes. This spectacular moment of visibility led to a film distribution deal for SRK's *K3G* with German independent distributor Rapid Eye Movies. *K3G* turned out to be a successful release theatrically as well as on television and DVD. Asian store owners reported an increasing demand for Bollywood films after *K3G* premiered on television, and SRK blockbusters dominated sales.[147] An article in the *Hollywood Reporter* described SRK's star power at the Berlinale Film Festival following his newfound success in Germany: '[The appeal of] SRK ... equals that of Tom Cruise + Brad Pitt x 10 to his loyal [German] admirers.'[148] SRK expeditiously became the central node that defined the 'mattering maps' of Bollywood in Germany from both an audience and industry perspective. There was a viable shift in the perception of Indian cinema in Germany that had now expanded in scope from 'artistic' Bengali films, the good cinema propounded by the Indian state, to commercially oriented mainstream cinema starring SRK.[149]

The affective economies mobilized in the mid-2000s led to a contemporary global Bollywood that was set in motion by technology and policy changes. SRK and Khan inspired fandoms that acted as 'grassroots intermediaries', moulding media content's circulation and enabling the logic of affective economics.[150] Henry Jenkins contends that fandoms can impact marketing-driven economic ratiocination to commodify and quantify fan desire, enabling fandom agency within this larger economy. SRK's fandom in Germany led to the emergence of the Bollywood magazines *Ishq* and *BNA Germany* as crucial industrial nodes. These publications provided Bollywood content in glossy magazine formats, but also evolved to provide event management and marketing, film promotion, and production consultancy.[151] Regarding German and other fans, SRK confessed to being 'a feeling that they could not resist'.[152] Praseeda Gopinath identifies SRK's avowal as an affective shift in male stardom that aligned with the star's figuration as a neoliberal cosmopolitan man.

The feeling that SRK inspired in fans like Julia Wessel triggered affective economies and new nodes that added to the Bollywood network and an expansion of Bollywood films on German television. This fandom for Bollywood cinema evolved as a gendered fandom wherein the affective pull of SRK put him at the centre of his female fans' 'mattering maps' and prompted them to act. Monika Jones, a news anchor for Germany's global television broadcaster Deutsche Welle, emphasized the collective 'feeling' around SRK: '[H]e has given us Germans the opportunity to show our feelings. Everything here always has to be so serious; no one shows any feelings. So, it's just good to let it out.'[153] SRK's fandom and fan affect via multiple fan-led and Bollywood-based nodes made inroads into the German-speaking market, furthering Bollywood's transformation globally. This expansion included events and award shows. The television-driven success of Bollywood films in Germany, Austria, and Switzerland also stimulated the DVD market. Rapid Eye Movies bought the rights for Indian films that were then sold to television stations, which in turn spurred DVD sales.[154] SRK's Red Chillies remained a primary bridging node in the process. Following the success of his early films, Germany and the European market were quickly integrated into Red Chillies's global expansion strategy. A press briefing about SRK's film *Om Shanti Om* (2007, dir. Farah Khan) noted that the film set the record for the highest number of prints any Indian movie had ever released. The film earned Red Chillies an INR 750 million (approximately USD 10.7 million) distribution agreement (inclusive of worldwide rights but excluding music and satellite rights). It was, at the time, the highest-paying Hindi movie deal. SRK stated that besides Germany, the film generated interest in Poland, Australia, South Africa, and Malaysia, all new non-traditional markets.[155]

SRK's German stardom connected his work to other nodes, such as Eros, Bollywood's leading global distributor. The company's chief operating officer (COO) underscored her confidence in this new broader distribution strategy by anchoring it around SRK and his power in non-traditional markets: 'He [SRK] has markets which no other star has, from Poland to

Australia to Germany of course.'[156] Germany surfaced as the strongest non-traditional market for SRK; the German television channel RTL2, known for its pioneering experimental role with new kinds of content, became a vital space for Bollywood in the German televisual landscape. With *In guten wie in schweren Tagen*, the German title for *K3G*, the channel began its new innovation—broadcasting edited-for-television Bollywood films. In November 2004, RTL2 broadcast the first dubbed Bollywood film for German television audiences and achieved a 15.1 per cent rating among 14–29 year-olds and 12.2 per cent among 30–49 year-olds. There was, however, a substantive skew in this demographic; around 70 per cent of this viewership was female. For the next few years, several television channels across Germany, Austria, and Switzerland (and a Turkish-language cable channel) were broadcasting Bollywood movies.[157] In 2011, SRK's Red Chillies produced *Don 2* (2011, dir. Farhan Akhtar), which was filmed in Germany and received funding of EUR 550,000 from Germany's regional film support agency, Medienboard Berlin-Brandenburg.[158]

SRK in the German market and Khan in the Chinese market mobilized fan networks to expand Bollywood. Vera Wessel—editor-in-chief of the German Bollywood magazine *Ishq* and Julia's sister who joined her sister's magazine venture (2006–present)—emphasized the role that fandoms and fan labour played in Bollywood's German expansion: 'We hadn't done a magazine before, we didn't have a big company behind us. We were just a couple of fans getting together and starting this.'[159] Wessel notes the role of mediated technology in Bollywood's reception among German speakers: '[T]hose were the early days, and we did not have social media, but there was a big Internet forum run by a fan and film critic. The forum was on a Swiss server where all Shah Rukh Khan fans from Germany, Austria, and Switzerland interacted.'[160] Several competing German-language Bollywood magazines cropped up to cater to this niche fandom.

Jenkins uses the term 'affective economics' to describe how media industries exploit fan labour.[161] SRK's fandom in Germany shows that affective fan economies were directly transformed into industrial nodes, such as *Ishq* or *BNA Germany*. Bollywood did not necessarily have the strategy to exploit this fan labour, but SRK's popularity presented an opportunity for German fandoms to be structurally bound into Bollywood's expanding global network as intermediary industry nodes. Wessel reiterates this change in her organization: 'We got into it because of SRK, and then we watched a lot of other films as well. Pretty quickly, we moved past Shah Rukh. But the market

didn't. Everyone else was watching just his films and every film he did, ever.'
Ishq is currently Germany's only long-standing Bollywood magazine, and
Wessel hopes that the fandom expands beyond SRK 'because he is getting
older and not making as many films'.[162] Evidently, Hindi cinema's presence in
Germany was affectively mediated through SRK.

Sara Ahmed reminds us that affective economies rooted in fan or industry
networks are, among other things, psychic. The psychic appeal of SRK
relates to his vulnerable masculinity—'a man who can cry and is witty,
humorous and romantic at the same time'.[163] He thus instigated a strong
affective pull for German female audiences. In the German context, this fan
desire and agency were leveraged relationally by the industry and anchored
by SRK and Red Chillies as the primary node. Fan desire triggered German
investment in other industrial nodes, such as the globally networked Indian
media conglomerate Zee, which started a new German television channel in
2016 to showcase Bollywood content for German audiences. SRK mobilized
a catalytic pull around which varied business and state interests created
new and non-traditional inroads for Indian cinema and entertainment in
Germany.[164]

The affective contours of SRK's impact on diplomacy were evident in the
German ambassador's tribute to Bollywood. Clearly, the critical component
of star switching power is its ability to exceed the networks to which it
belongs and create new connections. In the German context, SRK's affective
power permeated the diplomatic discourse between India and Germany.
Recurrently, Bollywood cinema and entertainment as a more extensive
cultural and industrial network led to an amalgamation of industrial and
diplomatic interests. Hindi cinema and stars led by SRK became the means
to deepen cultural ties. A close analysis of the cultural outreach by the Indian
embassy in Berlin reveals recurring events like 'Bollywood & Samosa', which
tout Bollywood films as 'colorful, dynamic … and the most important export
product of India'.[165] Calling attention to the film industry's emplacement
as the most prominent cultural exchange platform, 'Bollywood & Samosa'
predominantly showcases SRK films.

Like SRK, Khan mobilized his star persona to create affective economies
centred around industrial, political, and cultural diplomacy networks, which
allowed Hindi cinema to circulate in new ways. Social media and film
platforms launched between 2005 and 2009, such as Douban, Weibo, and
MTime—the newest technologies for cultural absorption—became the key
mediators for Khan's affective appeal in China.

AFFECTIVE ECONOMIES OF KHAN'S
STARDOM IN CHINA

This movie [*3 Idiots*] is not simply a movie. It has become some sort of religion.

—Bā sī tè dé, a Douban user (2010)[166]

Khan's *3 Idiots* became a blockbuster hit for Bollywood, the highest-grossing Indian film of all time, collecting USD 62 million in global box-office sales.[167] Fandoms were created through the informal pirated economy when *3 Idiots* made its way to China via Hong Kong. Khan's socially conscious star persona—evinced in his films, refracted and performed through interviews, and displayed in his association with social causes, such as female foeticide, domestic violence, and treatment of the elderly—was at the core of his resonance with Chinese audiences. His appeal also derived from 'parallel modernities'—modernities in the developing world that run parallel to modernities in the West. The films mirrored the realities of Indians and Chinese alike (see Figure 3.8).[168] For example, *3 Idiots* received a rating of 9.2 out of 10 on the Chinese film website Douban. Its appeal—as described in the context of parallel infrastructures, development, social issues, and progress—revolved around its socially conscious star, Khan.

In a move that reflected converging film and television mediascapes, Khan extended his brand equity and value to television by producing a show for the first time: *Satyamev Jayate* (Truth Alone Triumphs, 2012–2014). Here, he performed his socially conscious star persona on television, conveying moral authority through the 'trope of his sacrificial stardom'.[169] *Satyamev Jayate*, according to Star TV's creative director, Monika Shergill, gave their channel 'a social agenda, a conscience. For the first time, Indian television has used its strength for something important. We consider it a landmark.'[170] Mobilizing anti-consumerist and social-value-driven moral authority created Khan's affective power. For the television show, his in-house production entity, Aamir Khan Productions, did not permit advertising: 'I just felt that while I'm doing this show, I didn't want to be selling something. I don't know how to say it. It didn't feel right to me.'[171] His decision points to an effective–affective mobilization of a star brand or persona that exceeds individual brand associations in favour of surpassing consumerist capital. Industry discourse about him cemented the idea. Reliance Entertainment's chairman noted

Figure 3.8 Aamir Khan posing with Chinese fans dressed in Aamir Khan Productions merchandise during the promotion of his film *Thugs of Hindostan* (2018, dir. Vijay Krishna Acharya)

Source: Associated Press/Imaginechina.

this inherent contradiction between possessing a higher social purpose and being a star, a persona that is innately consumable and on display: '[Aamir] is a throwback to a ... [previous] era when filmmakers lived for cinema and believed it had a higher social purpose beyond making money.'[172]

It is a truism, Barry King points out, that stars 'develop out of' and 'sustain capitalist production and consumption'.[173] Stars like Khan are 'manufactured by the industry and endowed with a scarcity value', which creates a political surplus that highlights the star's ability to mobilize passions.[174] Khan, beyond his star persona, is a central node in the industry. As a producer, he has effective power to mobilize his scarcity value and political surplus to solidify his socially conscious image and create inroads into the Chinese market. This ability, however, was relationally tied to structural changes in the industry, such as the concurrent emergence of home-grown, globally ambitious media conglomerates like Reliance Entertainment. Reliance Entertainment was a subsidiary of India's mammoth industrial conglomerate, Reliance Industries Limited, which famously bailed out DreamWorks Pictures at the height of the 2008 recession. The company undertook the distribution of *3 Idiots*, releasing it on 2,126 screens, including 366 screens overseas. The film was screened simultaneously in India, the US, the UK, Australia, New Zealand, and Malaysia.[175] The massive box-office returns and word-of-mouth publicity prompted a second release in non-traditional Bollywood markets: Hong Kong, China, Japan, and South Korea. It received the coveted New Year's release slot in China two years after its original release.[176]

Evidently, despite China's strict quotas for foreign films and strained cultural ties with India, Khan's star power, combined with the film's socially relevant subject matter created a fandom for *3 Idiots*, leading to a new distribution network in China. Given their strained political history with three open military conflicts (1962, 1967, 1987) and India's continued asylum for the Dalai Lama and displaced Tibetans, entertainment and cultural exchange between India and China had been severely restricted. Despite these barriers, Khan's socially conscious stardom enabled a new circuit for the flow of Hindi cinema. It arose from his affective power and capital accumulated together with his direct collaborations with entertainment conglomerate networks like Reliance. Star switching power is premised on the ability to create connections and flows where none existed before. The circulation of *3 Idiots* was an exemplary instantiation of star switching power within industry-oriented networks.

Khan's industry-oriented star power gradually spilled over into the realm of diplomacy and soft power. The Indian state's alliance with the film industry has historically been precarious. However, Khan's dominance in the Chinese sociocultural sphere through technology-mediated fandoms brought the star to the helm of Indo-Chinese political diplomacy networks. He arranged film promotions for his subsequent film, *PK* (2014, dir. Rajkumar Hirani), in coordination with Indian prime minister Modi's China visit to encourage goodwill in the wake of escalating border tensions.

'NI HAO, UNCLE MI': STAR SWITCHING POWER AND CULTURAL DIPLOMACY NETWORKS

The popularity of Khan's star persona in China can be delineated within a 'socially conscious glocal cosmopolitanism' framework. 'Glocal cosmopolitanism', according to Esther Chin, constitutes the relational ways we experience diverse 'global interdependencies'.[177] Khan's star persona and the extended star text are built around his socially conscious films that foreground glocal and parallel developmental interdependencies between India and China. Given the similar roadblocks, such as population control, infrastructure, environmental degradation, and urbanization, in the two growing southern economies, Khan's films found resonance in neighbouring China. Additionally, despite their cultural differences, the films reflected shared value proximities related to family structure, respect for elders, and collectivism (versus Western individualism). Moreover, the political excess driving Khan's star affect stems from a desire for social change. Viewers relate to Khan because his films perform a 'doubling' of his socially conscious star image.[178] In *3 Idiots*, he speaks against a hypercompetitive educational system. *Taare Zameen Par* (Like Stars on Earth, 2007, dir. Aamir Khan and Amole Gupte) delves into dyslexia within the discourse of neurodivergence. *Dangal* addresses gender disparities, the rural–urban divide, and a lack of sports and athletics infrastructure in developing countries. A desire for social change drives each narrative, and this desire finds credence in Khan's star persona, the source of his affective appeal and power. The fandom around Khan can be distilled into similar issue-driven discourses that are easily translatable within cultural diplomacy networks. Khan's films offer a novel way to engage with India. A Chinese viewer points out on the microblogging site Douban:

> The way we look at India is like how the Western world had looked at China for many years. In the past, when Western journalists traveled to China and discovered a piece of human trafficking, they made a big fuss out of it, causing the Western world to think that China was very backward.[179]

Another viewer commiserates with the plight of Indian women and urges others to empathize with the Indian point of view:

> We should not judge India from the Chinese mode of thinking. It is not that we can think Indian women's [lives have] infinite possibilities just because we as Chinese people do. We should look at this film from an Indian point of view—we should see that it is women's fight for justice that opens up infinite possibilities.[180]

Khan's socially conscious glocal cosmopolitanism evokes empathy and cultivates a discourse of parallel modernities and commonalities. The star switching power thus vested in Khan already navigates the realm of soft power. Hence, within this discourse of public diplomacy, star switching power becomes the central operative framework. Khan's socially conscious glocal cosmopolitanism lets him mobilize networks that led the state to seek him out for diplomatic exchange, both during a peaceful cultural exchange and in the context of a spiralling conflict like Doklam in 2017.

The Chinese context demonstrates how star switching power is relational and enables stars to exceed the industry and configure new networks and influence in social, cultural, and political realms, most prominently in diplomacy and soft power. This is a different paradigm of soft power compared to top-down models that rely on and emphasize state initiative because although it benefits the state eventually, it is not state-centric or generated by the state. It points to the pre-eminence of stardom and star power within the Bollywood industry structure and the interconnected realms of industry and politics because stars can leverage political relationships for industrial growth and development.

In summary, this chapter explained the rise of a networked Bollywood industry structure that now incorporates a diverse set of global and local nodes and institutional networks including home-grown but globally influential organizations like Reliance that helped realize post-millennial Bollywood's global ambitions. It enumerated the switching power of SRK and Khan as business leaders and change makers who helped shape the evolving industry ecology either directly or inadvertently through network effects. Additionally, it explicated the progression of star brands, which were a novelty when Bachchan initiated the idea (recall Chapter 2), to numerously mediated brandscapes that entailed a range of colourful spectacles from global awards shows and live events to television, digital, and social media platforms. This helped percolate their influence beyond the industry into the realm of cultural diplomacy, unpredictably intersecting with digital fandoms and helping pave the way for Bollywood to enter hitherto inaccessible markets like Germany and China.

Some female stars in this era have similarly been able to foster industry and diplomacy connections through their affective star power. Most prominently, Aishwarya Rai—the recipient of France's highest civilian honour, Knight of the Order of Arts and Letters—falls into this category. However, within this rapid structural change in the industry, female star switching power remained disjunct from direct industrial power. Despite appearances, Bollywood remained hierarchical and masculinist, wherein women's power manifested itself predominantly in the affective realm. Few female stars had a direct presence as producers or directors, although stars like Juhi Chawla and Hema Malini attempted to establish themselves in the industry business. However, with rapid structural changes, women's switching power began to change, especially for crossover stars. Star agency begins to be wielded indirectly via industrial or institutional nodes ranging from talent agencies, established star-led entertainment organizations, and Hollywood studios to create direct industrial power. The next chapter tells the story of female stars such as Aishwarya Rai, Priyanka Chopra, Anushka Sharma, and Deepika Padukone in contemporary networked Bollywood.

4

GLOBAL BEAUTY QUEENS

Aishwarya Rai, Priyanka Chopra, and Female Star Switching Power

Winning Miss World in 1994 opened up new worlds for Aishwarya Rai, and her meteoric rise from beauty queen to celluloid goddess was swift and assured. After Bollywood, Hollywood beckons. The celestial beauty of Miss World 1994, Indian actress Aishwarya Rai, is about to light up Western screens. She is poised to star in her first English-language movie, *Bride and Prejudice*. Already, she has received four offers from Hollywood, 'but I couldn't fit them into my schedule', declares Rai.... She is now a veteran of more than 20 movies. Her latest blockbuster was *Devdas*, a lush cinematic spectacle starring Shah Rukh Khan and Madhuri Dixit. The first Bollywood production to be screened at the Cannes Film Festival last year, it kick-started a Bollywood craze in Europe.[1]

Aishwarya Rai, India's triumphant Miss World, was now Bollywood's reigning queen and global crossover star. *Time* magazine listed her among the world's most influential people and noted that Rai gets the

> sort of web adulation that even Britney Spears might envy. [There are] '17,000 sites in her honor' including poetry sites, a Hindu shrine, even a site dedicated just to her eyes. Her hope, she says, is to lead an Indian invasion, to 'catalyze' Bollywood's crossover to the West, and 'open the doors for everybody else'.[2]

This was the early 2000s, and Bollywood's global momentum was cresting. With the success of Aamir Khan and SRK via films like *Lagaan* and *Devdas*,

Bollywood cinema was prominently visible around the world. While the discourse of Bollywood's global success was generally male-dominated, the ethereal presence of Rai's culturally transcendent beauty, ergo the possibility of her becoming Bollywood's first crossover star, dominated the discourse about industry globalization. The beauty pageant network, fuelled by Rai and Sushmita Sen, winners of the Miss World and Miss Universe crowns, respectively, in 1994, followed by Amitabh Bachchan's attempt to integrate the beauty pageant industry into the globalizing Indian entertainment sector, was now firmly entrenched in the Bollywood network. The beauty pageant industry and Hindi cinema were organic partners for one another, as both were similarly constituted by global flows of capital, industrial and institutional collaborations, and national cultural influence that were deeply ensconced in debates about gender and national and cultural identity. The turn of the twenty-first century represents an important chapter in the history of networked Bollywood and more extensive processes of Bollywoodization through international connections and industry expansion that accelerated in subsequent years. In this process, a few female stars, especially international beauty pageant winners, came to constitute new nodes of influence and power in the industry, wielding star switching power that had in the past been limited almost exclusively to elite men. This chapter explores the kinds of star switching power these figures possessed and the ways Bollywood's beauty queens catalysed new directions and modes of international connection in an era of changing state–industry relations shaped by Indian nationalism and neoliberal globalization.

As beauty queens made their way to Bollywood stardom, what kind of star switching power did these women possess? To examine this question, in this chapter, I focus on Aishwarya Rai and Priyanka Chopra, two of Bollywood's most prominent global female stars. Rai, as we have seen, gained global prominence alongside SRK and Khan in the early 2000s to the 2010s following her run as an international pageant queen. A few years later, Chopra, the winner of the 2000 Miss World pageant, picked up the global baton and continued her way to Hollywood, hoping to fulfil her 'quest to try and influx Hollywood with Indian talent as much as [she] can'.[3] Together, these two stars become significant markers to bookend this conversation of the female star's switching power from the 2000s to the contemporary networked Bollywood of the 2020s.

In Chapter 2, I analysed how Bachchan helped formally incorporate the beauty pageant network and the accompanying influx of consumerist, capitalistic global modernity by bringing together ideas of star equity and branding into the industry. Chapter 3 traced the development of the industry's global ambitions through the star figures of SRK and Khan, elaborating on their switching power in furthering the industry's global presence to yet uncharted markets. In this chapter, I turn to the affective regimes and effective industrial changes and processes instigated by the coalescence of the international beauty pageants' global ecosystem and individual beauty queens like Rai and Chopra into the agglomerated Bollywood network. I point to the variable nature of switching power possessed by the stars Rai and Chopra and the relative construction of that power. I argue that unlike SRK, Khan, or Bachchan, who were prominent in the industry network beyond their affective stardom, Rai and Chopra's female star switching power was transformed into a power that was predominantly rooted in the gendered constructions of national embodiment. This embodiment is premised on their personal, social, and industrial power and ability to become a switching node. Rai and Chopra epitomize the ways in which feminine-coded beauty facilitates globalization. As their global careers demonstrate, immense power is embodied in that ideal. Their agency, however, is negotiated through a gendered dynamic and at a time when the networked industry was incorporating powerful global corporate industrial nodes into its rapidly evolving ecosystem as well as state nodes that were invested in propelling these changes. In this context, their switching power was decidedly different from that of their male forebears. Their industrial and cultural power is grounded in affective regimes and intertwined in global networks of commodity-consumption-permeated brandscapes and the beauty-queen story brand. Nonetheless, while Rai's and Chopra's star brands were encapsulated within global, affective, and commoditized regimes, their personal brand power at the same time exceeded those regimes and therein lay their power and ability to affect industrial and diplomatic flows.

Additionally, Chopra emerged on the horizon when the industry was restructuring, and global nodes like Hollywood studios, international talent agencies, and streaming platforms were becoming entrenched in Hindi cinema and entertainment's industrial structure. As this agglomerated and intensely networked configuration emerged (it is still emerging), it altered traditional star switching power but, at the same time, created fissures and a space to assert new forms of agency for the female star. Chopra, I argue, is the star of networked Bollywood, whose global foray was structurally supported by multiple global nodes ranging from talent agencies to Silicon Valley venture capitalists. She won her Miss World crown almost a decade after Rai, and her globality became the lens to access the emergence of contemporary networked Bollywood. As Cecelia Ridgeway asserts, structural flux in industries creates new kinds of work and agency for women. Thus, a multivalent structure existed to support Chopra's global crossover and production efforts that can only prevail in transitional, emergent industrial forms. On the other hand, Rai, and others, such as Sen, registered their presence on the global stage first only as beauty queens with excessive aesthetic capital that buoyed their visibility in other areas, including Bollywood and Hollywood, at a time when there was not a pre-existing industrial infrastructure to support their global crossover. Yet all these women were critical to the structural transformation and recognition of Hindi film and entertainment into a globally networked industry. This chapter maps the shifts and transitions of structure, female star node agency, and the mobilization of that structure, all of which provided a catalyst for industry globalization and the establishment of covalence between Bollywood and India as a strong, emergent global brand.

What follows is an intertwined yet chronological account of the evolution and expansion of the Bollywood network from the late 1990s to the early 2020s, filtered through the lens of gendered switching power in industrial, diplomatic, and cultural contexts. These changes to Bollywood's industrial structure are instantiated through the agentic power of Rai and Chopra, the primary case studies. The first part of the triptych that this chapter situates is the history and incorporation of beauty pageants into the Bollywood network. The second part looks closely at beauty queens' power and how global female star switching power evolved, placing that power in a context where bodily affect is, in many instances, more pronounced than the industrial narrative. Finally, it asks, what did Rai signify, what role did her star persona play in the global expansion of the industry, and how did her affective power mobilize international economic and diplomatic ties? The third part similarly examines Chopra's agency as a global star in Bollywood's iteration of a contemporary network connected through two-way flows to an increasingly Bollywoodized Hollywood.

THE BEAUTY PAGEANT IN INDIA

Pageants have deep roots starting in Greek mythology where, during the Trojan War, there was a prize for the fairest.[4] In its current form, it was P. T.

Barnum who recognized the potential of the beauty spectacle. He organized a contest where, alongside flowers and babies, women would parade in front of judges to win a prize.[5] The beauty pageant form primarily proliferated in the so-called *Third World* countries when they de-colonized and gained independence after the Second World War. The contests' internationalization, however, started after the inauguration of the Miss World pageant in 1951. The Miss Universe pageant, a beauty spectacle of 'galactic proportions', soon followed, having been created by a swimwear company in dispute with the Miss America pageant over photographic rights.[6] The synergistic relationship between India's Hindi film industry and the nascent pageant network started early.

During the International Film Festival of 1952, hosted by India for the first time and well attended by international filmmakers like Frank Capra, Miss India honoured the delegates with a bouquet.[7] The festival gathered key stakeholders for the Bollywood network, with India hosting the event explicitly to provide the popular industry with a model for how to be a proper industry. The minister of information and broadcasting emphasized that cinema was both an industry and an art: 'I hope that ... those who wish to mould the future of this great country would ... take a more intelligent and critical interest in this industry.'[8] This was a formative moment for stakeholders whose roles were being formalized through state-sponsored cinema, and the already established mainstream Hindi film industry was being positioned tenuously in relation to the state exhortation that cinema is high art and popular Hindi films were neither art nor a structured industry. In the absence of any 'leading Indian actresses', because the event was a snub to the mainstream film industry, Miss India was asked to fill in for the actresses.[9]

The respectability and positioning of Miss India within the Bollywood industry network shifted and evolved gradually. A leading Bollywood actor of the 1950s, Nutan—whose mother, Shobhana Samarth, was one of Hindi cinema's founding female actors, directors, and producers—also participated in and earned a top spot in the Miss India contest.[10] There was a spate of beauty queens in the decades that followed. In the 1950s and 1960s, a few actors like Nutan and Leela Naidu possessed centrality in industrial, political, and social networks. Nutan emerged as a prominent star in the 1950s, and her success was followed by Naidu. Naidu hailed from an illustrious political family and made *Vogue*'s 1964 list of the 10 most beautiful women in the world. Some of the noteworthy individual beauty queens in the transitional decades of the

1970s and 1980s, who sought careers in the film industry included Meenakshi Sheshadri, Zeenat Aman, Persis Khambatta, and Juhi Chawla. Aman and Khambatta stood out in this emergent dynamic as embodiments of the global at a time when popular Hindi cinema was decidedly marked as plebian by the state and middle-class audiences alike. Khambatta moved to Hollywood and starred in a minor role as Lieutenant Ilia in *Star Trek*, and Aman, the second Indian woman to win an international beauty pageant, Miss Asia Pacific, was hailed as Hindi cinema's sex siren. Aman marked a representational shift in the Bollywood heroine vis-à-vis the vamp, albeit with caveats. Jyotika Virdi and Nasreen Munni Kabir note that in Aman's incarnation, the 1970s' heroine was now the 'vamp transformed into the gangster's moll but with fewer and fewer scenes until she disappeared from the Hindi screen altogether'.[11] Aman's foray into Hollywood with Krishna Shah's *Shalimar* (1978) was similarly fleeting. As a global beauty queen, she embodied a *Westernized, liberated femininity* as someone who could be *unashamedly sexual*.[12] The 1970s beauty queen's positioning in Bollywood was that of a sexualized heroine, a model turned actor who was bold enough to bare and, therefore, also expendable. The following decade saw Chawla, another Miss India, make her foray into Hindi films. Unmarked by any sexualized global victories, Chawla personified the girl next door and starred in and produced successful films with Khan and SRK. From the 1990s, all beauty queens began to seek careers in the Indian Hindi film industry.

This historical recounting of beauty queens and the incorporation of the local and global beauty queen network in the Bollywood industry highlights how the meanings and perceptions of a beauty queen and an international beauty pageant winner had drastically shifted in 1994 when Rai and Sen won the Miss World and Miss Universe crowns, respectively. First and foremost, the understanding of the beauty pageant became transnational because the Indian state and the people, now enamoured by globalization and its promises of mobility and recognition, wanted to partake in it. Thus, the 1990s were the decade when the import of a transnational beauty contest like Miss World became a media spectacle, a 'modern ritual of feminine achievement' that 'heralded the nation's endorsement of global capitalism'.[13]

As beauty queens like Rai and Sen came into the industry, they, unlike Bachchan or Raj Kapoor, did not have insider networks or industry and political connections. However, like SRK, who was admitted to filmdom when the Indian television network got incorporated into the film industry,

Rai and Sen were voted in because of the tacit incorporation of the beauty queen network within Bollywood's emergent global entertainment network.[14] The explicit validation of the primacy of the pageant network to Bollywood's globalization ambitions came via Bachchan's ABCL endeavours. ABCL hosted the Miss World pageant in 1996, despite intense opposition and protests, and it was hailed as a historic event that would signal to the world that India was receptive to globalization and all that it entails. Additionally, it marked the globalization of Bollywood via ABCL and its structural transformation into an entertainment network.[15]

Noting the tenor of the industrial transformation in business practices and structure at this defining moment when the beauty queens and the pageant network were integrated into the industry, a 1996 article in *India Today* asserted,

> For once, the ultimate professional Amitabh Bachchan was upstaged. '… Sushmita Sen smashed everything in sight with her professionalism. Amitabh Bachchan was almost rusty compared to her.' For the apparently newly reconstituted former Miss Universe with her assets more upfront, Bollywood is small change—the world having been her oyster. Neither Sushmita nor [Aishwarya] Rai are losing their designer composure when they ask, and even get, Rs 50 lakh–75 lakh [5–7.5 million] for each film. 'I was a working girl and am used to doing my own thing,' says Aishwarya. The new image-driven breed has tremendous marketing sense. 'This is the first time that you are getting professional actresses in the industry. These girls are like men,' says director Mukul Anand.[16]

The quote instantiates several aspects of the *new breed* of the global beauty queens Rai and Sen; bathed in the aura of their embodied globality, Rai and Sen's switching power is submerged in the affective. In the absence of ties to the small-world Bollywood networks, Rai and Sen's arrival marked and was defined by a transformative moment in the film industry, wherein their embodied global affect situated them as central star nodes. The discourse about them was similarly empowering and euphoric. In contrast, recall the discussion of the journalistic coverage of Chawla in the previous chapter; she was giggly and excited, traits hardly professional despite her partnership with SRK in a production company. The journalistic narrative about the global beauty queens, on the other hand, starting with Rai and Sen and leading to the next decade with Chopra, was consistently empowering and awe-inspiring.

Compared to the starlet Miss Indias of the 1950s, the new global beauty queens of liberalizing India possessed symbolic capital in abundance. Rai and Sen were a class apart from the Miss Indias of yesteryear, who were diminutive starlets, less than Bollywood actresses. These beauty queens came into the industry with an abundance of embodied affect, which lent them power that was built upon their abounding sociocultural capital. According to Pierre Bourdieu, this cultural capital exists in three primary forms: as skills and dispositions; objectified in cultural objects or things; and, more importantly, through institutions that certify the existence of that embodied form, thereby overdetermining it and lending it that power.[17] This affective power, which predominantly constituted the switching power of beauty queens like Rai and Sen, was derived from embodied cultural capital, which possessed all the characteristics that Bourdieu articulates.

One of the most significant moments of Rai's arrival on the world stage, wherein she increased Bollywood's global appeal through her association, was at the Cannes Film Festival. Her skills and disposition as a beauty queen— her voice, diction, height, clothes, and ability to project her superlative beauty—garnered her attention and cultural capital. After an interview with Rai at Cannes, London's *Screen Daily* editor, Matt Mueller, noted, 'Rai speaks English with such precise, clipped diction that interviewing her is like receiving a grammar lesson from a royal.'[18] Although couched in a colonial incredulity, the British journalist's statement externalizes the cultural capital inherent in her voice and diction and her composure and poise. Celebrating her pageant win, another article noted, 'Aishwarya is beautiful in every sense of the word.' Rai's 'translucent green eyes', 'modulation of voice cadence from low purr to a rich timbre', and a 'height of 5'7"' encapsulate 'everything one needs to make it on the international platform'.[19] Evidently, Rai possessed the skills and disposition to 'make it' and garner cultural capital through the beauty pageant network that recursively positioned her as a consequential node in attracting global attention and sociocultural capital to the Bollywood network that had now enthusiastically incorporated Rai into its fold.

This sociocultural capital is also represented in cultural objects or things, and Rai, as an actor, beauty queen, and purveyor of luxury brands, was also the embodiment of neoliberal consumer capital and desirability. Soon after her Miss World victory, Rai was anointed the brand ambassador of the Swiss luxury watch brand Longines. Global cosmetics giant L'Oréal soon

Figure 4.1 Aishwarya Rai posing for photographers at the Cannes Film Festival, 2014

Source: Associated Press/Villard/Niviere/Sipa.

followed. Rai has continued to represent these brands for over two decades amid a plethora of other endorsements, including Pepsi, Coke, Lux, De Beers, and several domestic brands. However, Rai's brand associations and related affect evoke a specific tenor of global luxury. Her Longines campaign asserts that 'elegance is an attitude', marking an exclusivity to the globally relevant elegance that only a few can possess. India's top advertising executive Prahlad Kakkad reinforces the global exclusiveness of Rai's story brand and, by extension, her sociocultural capital derived from it, which is in equal parts exclusive and global:

> Aishwarya was never a big or major endorser of Indian products. She has
> an impressive list of international brands to her name, and that's because
> she is not *just an actress* who can be judged on hits and flops, but the fact
> that she is a representative of the Indian woman and an ambassador of
> the country.[20]

In her exclusivity, she gets to possess cultural and economic capital in a
distinctive form by consuming goods that are socially scarce and fit with
the global cultural elite. Embodying this perspicacious quality, she exceeds
her position within domestic or industry networks and gets to represent
and perform Indian identity in the global arena. Her story brand establishes
these pecuniary distinctions wherein her cultural capital is established
through consumption enacted in aesthetic and interactional styles that fit
with an exclusive social class.[21] In other words, Rai, through branding, has
established herself as an elite representative of Indian culture; her world and
the structures surrounding her—in other words, her habitus, in Bourdieuan
terms—is elite.

The third form that solidifies cultural capital is validation through
institutions that certify, endorse, and create new forms of cultural power.
For Rai, this accruing of cultural capital and her resultant affective power
within India's burgeoning entertainment industry happened through
various networks. The Indian state, the global beauty pageant network, the
associated multinational corporations, and Hindi cinema's industrial network
convergently created, endorsed, and certified Rai's centrality and sociocultural
capital. At this moment in the 1990s and early 2000s, Rai emerged as a key
node, a resplendent pageant winner, the epitome of cosmopolitan beauty and
desire. Her embodied presence stood to fortify all said networks that could, in
turn, mobilize her globality and recursively their own global positioning, be it
the Indian state or the film and entertainment industry. Rai's return to India
after winning the Miss World crown in Sun City, South Africa, bespoke the
political significance of her win. Immediately after her return, Rai was invited
to meet with prime minister Narasimha Rao, president Shankar Dayal
Sharma, and the opposition leader Sonia Gandhi. At the press conference
that followed, Rai remarked, 'I had a very congenial meeting with the Prime
Minister, I conveyed Mr. Nelson Mandela's message to him.'[22] Already, she
was elevated to a national brand ambassador (see Figure 4.2).

The beauty pageant in India, Susan Dewey points out, had emerged
in the late 1990s and early 2000s as a space of empowerment and social

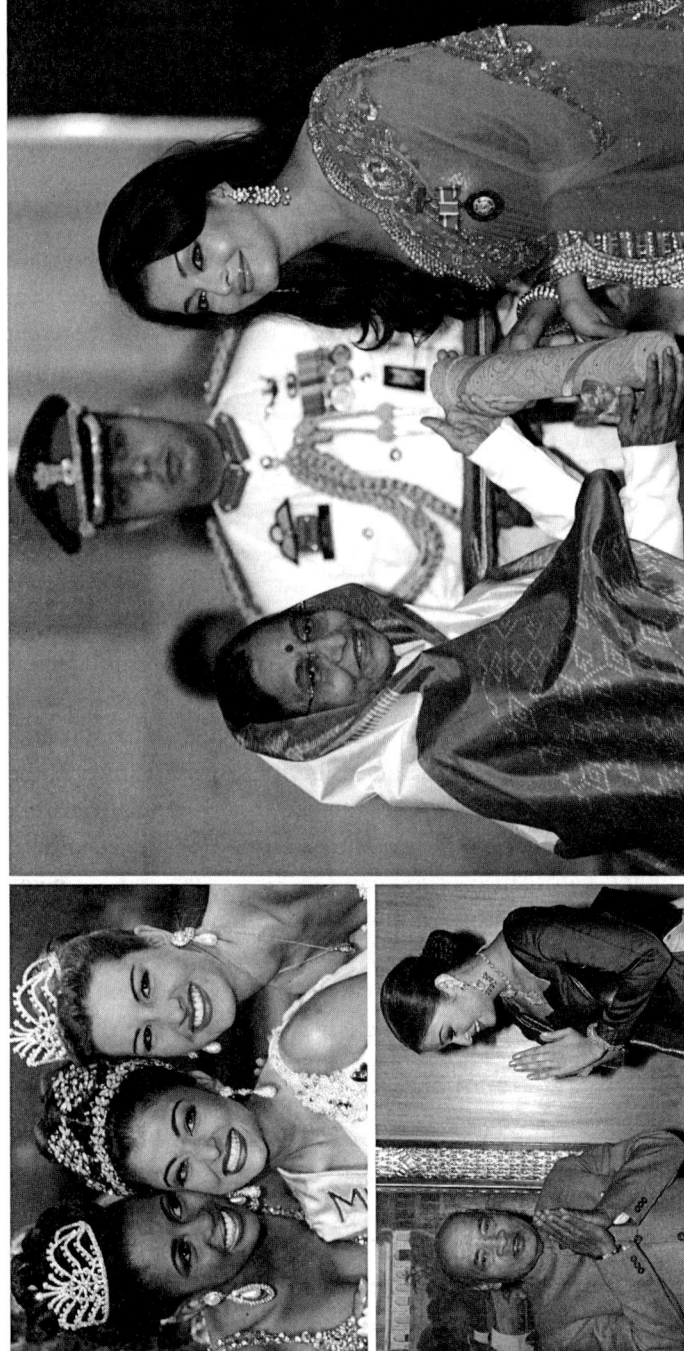

Figure 4.2 Aishwarya Rai heralded as the brand ambassador for the nation: (*top left*) Rai being crowned Miss World in Sun City, South Africa, 1994; (*bottom left*) Rai greeting Indian prime minister P. V. Narasimha Rao upon her return from the Miss World contest, 1994; (*right*) Rai receiving India's fourth highest civilian honour, Padma Shri, from Indian president Pratibha Patil, 31 March 2009

Source: (*Top left*) Reuters/Juda Ngwenya; (*bottom left*) Reuters; (*right*) Reuters/B. Mathur.

and individual mobility that reveals a complex nexus of state policies, entertainment, and visual media's post-liberalization explosion. The pageant, she notes, revealed the complex workings of a Foucauldian power that exists at once inside and outside of situations through complex processes of positioning. While Dewey's remarks are targeted at the Miss India pageant, as it evolved after Rai's and Sen's wins and the explosion of the culture of pageant-winning celebrities that it created in its wake, they are crucial to understanding how the complex interworkings of state agendas and policies, Bollywood's global ambitions, and multinational corporate motives worked together to incorporate beauty pageants into the larger Bollywood network where all their cumulative interests converged.[23] The star switching power that emerged for beauty queens in this context, however, speaks of the exceptional abilities of some stars to exceed the networks to which they belong. Rai, in this instance, emerges as a catalytic node for a globalizing industry and liberalizing state. Her embodied affective power catalysed new pathways and bridges for the networks themselves. Beyond the symbolic sociocultural capital cultivated through skills, objects, and institutions that fortified her affective power and agency, Rai embodied a transnational corporeality that lent her stand-alone affective power. While her and Sen's first-place finishes equally revealed the potential of beauty queens in facilitating the globalizing agendas of the industry, state, and global corporations alike, Sen as a stand-alone figure fell by the wayside because her embodiment in many ways was not ideal. Sen was, in her own words, too tall and lanky for Bollywood and too Indian for Hollywood.[24] Rai's exceptional affective power was validated through the local and global institutions early on and proceeded to enable many new circuits for industrial and cultural flows that facilitated industrial collaborations and cultural diplomacy. Unlike the contemporary male stars who came to possess direct institutional power or effective power, Rai's agency is delineated primarily in the affective realm, wherein her embodied affect functions as institutional brand power to enable the global ambitions of Bollywood and the global cultural branding of the nation state.

There are two parallel threads to be explored as we unpack Rai's embodied affect as institutional brand power. The first is to analyse how she functions as this brand assemblage in both state and industrial contexts, and the second is to analyse what goals she accomplishes for the Bollywood network and the Indian state. Rai's affective agency functions through her brand assemblage. The idea of a star brand as an assemblage refers to the diverse trajectories, technologies, institutional ideas, and processes that converge to create a star persona brand like Rai. I deploy Celia Lury's idea of brand as an assemblage to a star persona because it helps foreground two key aspects of the evolution of Bollywood as a veritable network in the 1990s through the 2010s: First, it acknowledges that sociological categories of race—or, rather, racial malleability—gender, and class in the process of developing a star brand identity for Rai and her embodied switching power. Second, it articulates a brand assemblage as a distinctive spatio-temporal construct to communicate that Rai's brand, while distinctive, is also auto-spatial and constructed institutionally. 'Auto-spatial' for Lury refers to the set of possibilities a brand presents and the multiple ways in which they can be presented and mobilized in different marketing spaces or used experimentally to extend other brands and recalibrated to extend beyond a limiting geo-demographic.[25] Rai's affective pull, the global value in her distinctiveness and superlative beauty during this spatio-temporal moment, helped create a structure for the industry and corporate networks—state, local, and multinational—to sustain star brand assemblages like Rai. As a star brand, her auto-spatial quality offered a superlative moment for the mobilization of global flows of collaboration and visibility for both the industry and the state. Her rise marks a turning point. While Bachchan declared himself a brand and failed in his endeavour for lack of a structural, institutional assemblage to sustain his branding, Rai, who serendipitously went on to become Bachchan's daughter-in-law, marked a moment of cultural industrial change. Inherent within the discourse of star branding is this idea of larger commodification and global equity of said star personas. Rai's presence enabled a new pathway and possibility that led other contemporary stars like Chopra, who emerged from a similar nexus of the beauty pageant network and the Hindi film industry, to be global stars—and particularly stars associated with Bollywood as a capacious global industry and national brand—in a more prominent way.

The next section will explain the process of developing Rai's global star brand assemblage and how her persona gets defined and cultivated, marketed, mediated, and reinforced through institutional structures, technological mediations, fandoms, and Rai's own on- and off-screen star performativity. It reflects the affordances created by Rai's brand assemblage for the evolution of the Bollywood entertainment network and the implicit discourse of nation-branding and cultural soft power in Europe and North America because, as a cultural-ambassador beauty queen and a Bollywood actor, she simultaneously represents both.

CULTIVATING AND MARKETING RAI'S GLOBAL STAR PERSONA AND HER MALLEABLE SWITCHING POWER

Deepa Shah, a *Sunday Times* journalist, describes her encounter with Rai through her charismatic affect, 'her blue-green eyes, voluptuous lips, willowy doll like frame render her ethereal', other-worldly. Moreover, she is not the first to describe Rai in these terms. Julia Roberts reportedly declared Rai 'the most beautiful woman in the world'.[26] The domestic and international coverage of Rai consistently frames her in this manner. The essence of Rai's switching power, I therefore argue, is foundationally grounded in this malleable, ethereal beauty that she embodies. She epitomizes a persona that is neither purely Western nor purely Eastern but an unexplored interstitial space between the global and the local— sometimes referred to as the 'glocal'. The deferential gestures to her beauty, and the power imbued within this discourse, stem from her malleable charismatic embodiment of the glocal. Rai occupied a medial and flexible space where her transfiguration, the projection of her star persona and the resultant affective power, could be simultaneously global and local, a quality repeated, emphasized, and constructed within her star persona. Her global malleability was instantiated through her brand assemblage and further actualized in the industrial, journalistic, and state discourse surrounding her persona.

Longines was one of the earliest transnational brands that Rai endorsed. The campaign advertised their watches with the tagline 'Elegance is an attitude'. Personifying the embodiment of effortless elegance and timeless beauty propounded by the brand, Rai, in an ad campaign that unveils a day in her life, asserts, 'Elegance is an attitude, is something that resonates naturally with me. To be a spokesperson for that … comes naturally to me. It is not even an effort.' Of course, just another day in the life of Rai is at the Prix de Diane, Longines's horse race for fillies in Chantilly, France. The ad opens with an establishing longshot of the sixteenth-century historic château and cuts to Rai's arrival on a grand French estate. Seated in a chauffeur-driven vintage automobile, Rai is dressed in a flowy white ensemble with a black fascinator adorning her sophisticated chignon hairdo. She gently waves to the onlookers and disembarks. Each shot is bathed in a soft light, filmed in slow motion, and accentuated with sustained orchestral scoring to emphasize Rai's elegant yet effortless arrival. In a melodic, enunciated voice, Rai goes on to articulate the timelessness of time and la dolce vita that should evoke elegance, luxury, and tradition. Her philosophy evokes the brand's purported values of tradition, elegance, and performance. Prestigious equestrian venues have been a core association for the luxury watchmaker because 'the sport reflects our philosophy and values of performance, elegance and tradition', says Charles Villoz, the vice-president of sales for the company.[27]

As a brand ambassador for Longines, Rai is equally at ease embodying Indian traditional elegance and luxury in a saree as she is espousing elegance as a life philosophy in a lacy dress and floral hat at Ascot, London's most royal and traditional venue for glamour, or the similarly elite French Prix de Diane (see Figures 4.2 and 4.3). Villoz attests to Rai's malleable embodiment and the aesthetic capital she is imbued with:

> Aishwarya has been associated with us since 1999, and it is a big help. Not only in this country [India] but also globally. Wherever we have travelled (with Aishwarya), the response has been overwhelming. She is a global face, and we would like to continue this association as long as possible.[28]

Rai's malleable, flexible aesthetic capital, however, represents a limited form of power, one that can only be put to specific ends. While the rhetoric of the empowered and superlatively attractive beauty queen personifying la dolce vita is seductive, feminist scholars like Sarah Banet-Weiser point to the appropriation of second-wave liberal feminist ideas of individual choice and gender equality into the identity construction of beauty queens. It is an appropriation that concretizes the idea of the pageant winner's beauty as capital—something that lends mobility and access to an exclusive, elite class.[29] Morena Figuero confirms the ambiguous precarity in the positioning of beauty queens. She notes that negotiating beauty is difficult and that beauty is simultaneously 'a resource and a feeling, an unavoidable lure that does different kinds of work'.[30] While it can be empowering in a way that elevates previously marginalized individuals, beauty also performs the work of stabilizing and enabling hierarchies. However, in the larger discourse of power, specifically gendered switching power within the context of Bollywood's globalization, I want to emphasize the ability that elite class inclusion and the possession of beauty capital lends to a persona like Rai. As a globally desirable persona who emerges from India at a moment when the entertainment industry and the state are looking outward, it imbues her with

Figure 4.3 Aishwarya Rai launching Swiss watchmaker Longines's bridal collection of watches, 2007

Source: Associated Press/Mustafa Quraishi.

the ability to mobilize global collaboration and influence to achieve key goals for both the Indian entertainment industry and the state.

Rai became a part of the Hindi film industry when her presence helped integrate new and critical networks like the Cannes Film Festival, where Bollywood had been vying for visibility. On the special screening of Rai's *Devdas* (2002, dir. Sanjay Leela Bhansali) at Cannes, an article from Agence France Presse noted, '[Bollywood] has at last won international respect ... one of its emotional song-and-dance features will appear at the Cannes film festival.'[31] It was the first mainstream Bollywood film invited to the elite French film festival and key marketplace for global distribution of international content. The screening of *Devdas* was distinctive because it was an out-of-competition world premiere, marking an endeavour by Cannes to welcome Bollywood. This was brought about due to various factors, and earlier efforts of SRK and Khan also played a role in creating this moment of acknowledgement. Thierry Frémaux, the artistic director of Cannes, in his interview with *Variety*, noted the burgeoning festival visibility of Bollywood. Locarno screened *Lagaan*, and *Aśoka* played at the Venice and Toronto film festivals: 'It is a hugely productive industry that Cannes had not welcomed in a long, long time.'[32] In the space of the film festival, Rai represented a bridging node. She embodied an auto-spatial persona that brought visibility to Bollywood, appropriating and performing a global modernity for legitimacy and thus recursively lending legitimacy to India's Hindi film industry's arrival on the global stage. Her beauty again functioned as the conduit for the recognition of Bollywood at the Cannes festival.

Rai was the cynosure for the industry and Cannes's coverage of *Devdas*. Newspapers gushed about Rai 'conquering hearts', onlookers gathered outside the screening venue to 'catch a glimpse of the former Miss World', and reviews of *Devdas* described Rai as 'unforgettable and sublime'.[33] Her malleable beauty and Bollywood's global visibility emphatically blended in an interview with London's *Sunday Times*. Rai asserted, 'I've had people come up to me and say: "You've got light hair and light eyes. You're not really Indian".' She then goes on to elaborate on her innate Indianness through her roles in films like *Hum Dil De Chuke Sanam* (I Have Given My Heart Away Beloved, 1999, dir. Sanjay Leela Bhansali) and *Devdas*: 'We made *Devdas* to the best of our abilities as an Indian classic.... But its entry at Cannes has obviously opened up other possibilities.... Maybe this heralds a new beginning for Indian cinema.'[34] As a new globally ambitious Bollywood industry emerged at the turn of the millennium, Rai evolved into an efficacious bridging node that linked the film industry to other global networks. Hence, apart from Cannes and the global film festival circuit, Rai's presence also heralded a new interest from Hollywood. As she notes in the same interview, a meeting with Martin Scorsese, who asked her for a print of *Devdas*, was, as Rai describes it, an exhilarating moment for the film's director, Sanjay Leela Bhansali.[35]

In places such as Cannes, Rai, due to her globally marketable, malleable beauty, carried the weight of the industry's global ambitions in ways that were specific to her identity as a woman. As an industry's intermediary, she became the bridging node in whose globality other industrial entities— local, global, or diasporic—could agree on and become invested in. Ashok

Amritraj, a diasporic film producer and the chairman and CEO of Hyde Park Entertainment Group, a Hollywood-based production company, proclaimed that casting Rai for his crossover film *Jeans* (1998, dir. S. Shankar) was 'something of a minor coup'. Rai became the star vehicle for launching Amritraj's crossover East–West film, which he envisioned would raise the 'ante in Indian cinema'.[36] As if epitomizing and proclaiming the film's industrial globality and ambitions mirrored through Rai, the film's most spectacular and lavish song, 'Adisayam', finds Rai ensconced in all key global geographic markers. She is at the Grand Canyon in one shot and in front of the Egyptian pyramids or the Great Wall of China in another. She is equally at home dancing on top of the Empire State Building, at the Colosseum in Rome, and at the Taj Mahal. The metaphor of Rai as the global beauty was deployed in an idiomatic way by both the film industry and the Indian nation state in projecting an acceptable global identity. So Amritraj, a diasporic Indian, an established Hollywood producer but wary of global or collaborative Indian projects thus far, takes the leap with Rai's *Jeans*. With Rai, the industry experimented with global firsts. *Jeans* was the most expensive Tamil film that Amritraj funded, and similarly *Devdas* was the most expensive Hindi language film, which similarly wielded Rai's affective centrality as a global bridging node that helped pitch both films ambitiously for a larger global audience.

Rai, because of her racial malleability and excessive aesthetic capital, materialized as an industrial anchor and bridge not only for India but also for the West; she was at the centre of global media flows, those that originated in the global media core and reached out to the peripheral nations as well. Her racially ambiguous yet superlative beauty ordained her as the emblematic global face of beauty desired by the cosmetic industry and coveted by filmmakers both within domestic and transnational spaces of economic, cultural, industrial, and material flows. Will Smith approached Rai for roles in his productions *Hitch* (2005) and *Seven Pounds* (2008), though she turned them down. He opined, 'I really wanted to work with her.... She has this powerful energy where she doesn't have to say anything, do anything, she can just stand there. Anything she's making, I'll be there.'[37] In the early 2000s, Rai appeared in several English language films, including *The Mistress of Spices* (2005, dir. Paul Mayeda Berges), *Bride and Prejudice* (2004, dir. Gurinder Chadha), *Provoked* (2006, dir. Jug Mundhra), *The Last Legion* (2007, dir. Doug Lefler), and *The Pink Panther 2* (2009, dir. Harald Zwart). Many diasporic directors, like British-Indians Gurinder Chaddha and Jug

Mundhra, who cast Rai in titular roles in their projects (like Amritraj before them), took an opportunity to showcase a global Indianness.

In the iteration of networked Bollywood that was forming in the early 2000s, Rai possessed a 'betweenness centrality' that could bring together global and local industry interests. Betweenness centrality situates an actor or node in a favourable position so that they create a short geodesic path for other actors in a network or two, hitherto unconnected networks, to come together.[38] Her structural position as a reigning beauty queen and the perception of the global persona in the domestic and global spheres lent her a distinctive structural position premised upon who she was—that is, the global promise of success she represented as well as the multiple networks to which she was connected, ranging from Hollywood to the French, British, and Italian film industries (see Figure 4.4). How centrally one is situated within a network, and how influential one can be in that bridging position,

Figure 4.4 Aishwarya Rai, a jury member for the fifty-sixth Cannes Film Festival, posing with fellow jury members, American actor Meg Ryan and director Steven Soderberg, 2003

Source: Reuters/Eric Gaillard.

according to Elihu Katz, is a factor of who one is, what one knows, and whom one knows. Rai's position lent her an affective excess and switching power to make other nodes cognizant of her presence and abilities, and, in this sense, she served as a central node connected not only to Bollywood but also to the Indian state at a time it was reconfiguring its relationship with the Hindi cinema industry.

In the year following the screening of Devdas—Bollywood's opulent saga wherein industry and state interests came together, with Rai being the brand that launched this global ambition—she was chosen as a judge at Cannes. Thus, in 2003, she earned the unique distinction of being the first Indian actor ever to be selected as a jury member for the festival. These mediascapes that Rai participated in intersected with the Indian state's global branding objectives, in which Rai, being a part of the beauty queen network, was firmly entrenched. As Rai notes in an interview, '[A]cting in Hollywood is about representing India at an international level.'[39] Like sports, the contestants on a beauty pageant platform represent a larger national imaginary. The beauty queens are, as Michelle Rocío Nasser de La Torre remarks, 'a national feminine beauty' that represents the 'nation as a unified, homogeneous whole'.[40] It logically follows that a persona like Rai would invite the projection of the nation and national identity onto herself. Due to her structural and temporal position, Rai seamlessly embodied the national identity project on the global stage. She thus became the emblem and brand for the nation and film and media industry networks, both arduously vying to be global.[41] Within the persona of the beauty queen herself is the symbolic role of the cultural diplomat that brings attention to the nation state through superlative aesthetic capital. Rai actualized this symbolic persona, as can be seen in her emerging role as a recognized cultural ambassador for India abroad in places of strategic importance to the entertainment industry's expansion.

France has been one of the regions where Rai, as a cultural ambassador, has been most influential in creating new connections for the entertainment industry as well as larger trade and commerce with the French state. In recognition of 'her contribution to the world of cinema and to the development of Franco-Indian co-operation in the film industry [and] art and culture', Rai was made a Knight of the Order of Arts and Letters, the Chevalier dans l'Ordre des Arts et des Lettres, on her birthday on 1 November 2012. Beyond her contribution to the fields of cinema, arts, and culture, Rai became the literal embodiment of cultural diplomacy when, moved by her transcendent beauty, the Dutch named a tulip after her. Authenticating the tulips with their new name—Aishwarya Rai—the director of the Netherlands Board of Tourism announced, 'Herewith I give you the tulip—the symbol of the tourist destination of Holland. This tulip represents all the beautiful things of Holland ... named after one of the most beautiful women in the world—Aishwarya Rai.'[42] There is a political economy of this embodiment that tugs at both notions of power and labour, and therein lies the difference in the switching power of beauty queens like Rai. Their excessive aesthetic capital establishes them as bridges and conduits, and their presence creates new cultural and industrial connections. In the instance of Holland, Rai became a bridging node that enabled multivalent flows. On the one hand, it was a way for the Netherlands to lure in the Bollywood industry for location shooting and other production collaborations. On the other hand, Rai's recognition, in turn, solidified the positioning of India and Bollywood as global. She is positioned at the helm in a way that she becomes visible to the world trying to find its way into India's rapidly globalizing, ascendant economy. Star switching power is a framework that examines the power that exists in excess and achieves desirable outcomes, but the gendered nature of it comes to the fore when instantiated through stars like Rai. So, while she possesses that excessive power, which is primarily affective, she is the bridging node that is acted upon, whose power is leveraged by institutional nodes in the multivalent processes of global exchange, not the direct actor. In the flows of global culture and capital, the relational circuits of power are evidently gendered. Because Rai does not possess direct industrial power—unlike the male stars—her globality and beauty capital can also be construed as labour in the service of the larger institutional structures. Rai's switching power, therefore, straddles between both gendered power and gendered labour.

Rai's body, therefore, becomes the site for the nation and national identity to be performed; yet her presence is construed in different ways, and her agency is gendered. As Oluwakemi Balogun and Kimberly Kay Hoang note, '[W]omen's bodies are differentially positioned to represent their nations either as cultural bearers of tradition or as countries on the assent in the new global economy.'[43] Clearly, Rai becomes the marker of an ascendant nation. The political economy of this embodiment by a beauty queen like Rai has implications for the material, cultural, and economic exchange value of her body as an emblem and brand. This positioning of Rai as a national and industry brand is networked in the way that she emerges to lead the facilitation of connections between elites, institutions, and various other stakeholders. This is all the same laborious cultural work that is embedded in the industry's political economy. Rai's empowerment is dependent on her role as a labouring conduit for global cultural and capital flows.

Speaking in the context of Nigerian beauty queen diplomats, Oluwakemi Balogun notes that the embodied Nigerian beauty queen destabilizes hierarchies at multiple levels. She shatters Western superiority, privileged notions of beauty, and local hierarchies of gender and class.[44] Rai's centrality manifests itself more as affective networked power. It contrasts with the radically embodied labour that challenges post-colonial, Western hierarchies regarding ideals of beauty. Her positioning is different because her beauty, unlike the radical non-conformism of Nigerian beauty queens, is racially malleable. Her ability to embody a culturally ambiguous and racially malleable beauty positions her at the apex of the industry and state cultural networks in a way that she can attract flows of cultural capital and influence from both the Western core and the peripheral Global South. This is the quality that lends her switching power, and this powerful betweenness and duality help her exceed networks. New connections get created around her. Her in-betweenness does not challenge or threaten global hierarchies but becomes a means to indicate that India as a nation brand and Bollywood are ready to compete on the global stage by projecting a superlative same-ness. Or perhaps she embodies a desirability and accessibility that is foreign but also familiar, including in a colonial sense. Her flexible beauty and malleability are not without their problems and are steeped in Bollywood's gendered hierarchies; their networked affect, however, lends an empowering quality to the industry and state stakeholders that deployed it.

Ultimately, Rai's presence was crucial to the dissemination of Bollywood's presence as a global brand and malleable cultural form that could be deployed in the neoliberal space of flows to sell everything from films to De Beers diamonds to eye-donation campaigns. In being 'the face that could launch a thousand brands', Rai was the literal embodiment of political, economic, and cultural flows, and therein lay her networked power. Yet, although things happened because of her presence, unlike a male megastar like Bachchan, she did not have direct industrial clout. Neither she produced films nor did she affect or direct change to industry production practices, although her mere presence did lead to several international cinematic co-productions. Perhaps, fittingly, Rai later married into the Bachchan family, the most pre-eminent and influential star family in the Bollywood network (recall Chapter 2 on Bachchan) (see Figure 4.5).

Figure 4.5 (*Left to right*) Amitabh Bachchan, Jaya Bachchan, Abhishek Bachchan, and Aishwarya Rai Bachchan—Rai married Amitabh Bachchan's son, Abhishek Bachchan, in 2007

Source: Reuters/Sukree Sukplan.

THE COMING TOGETHER OF NETWORKED BOLLYWOOD (2010S–PRESENT)

In a rapidly globalized world, coupled with technological advances, it's only natural that filmmaking is becoming a truly global enterprise. India is unique in that it has a huge film industry with a sizable audience. The Hollywood studios are looking to broaden their market in India, while Indian films are seeking to gain more market share in the U.S. One of the ways to do that is to co-finance and co-produce films. This is growing steadily given that, over the last couple of years, Hollywood studios have forayed into Indian film production while Indian companies are now being seen as serious sources of co-financing by Hollywood players.

—Dan Glickman, chief of the Motion Picture Association of America (MPAA), September 2009[45]

After Rai, the next most prominent beauty-queen-turned-Bollywood-star who would position brand Bollywood and brand India on the global stage is Priyanka Chopra. Chopra's emergence as a star took place within an industrial structure that had significantly evolved since Rai's rise. This structure involved new local and global multimedia conglomerates, talent agencies, Hollywood studios, and more. It also took place within a changing political–economic context of the rise of India's conservative right-wing party, the BJP, which has had a consistent neoliberal economic agenda. These transformations would shape Chopra's role as a node in networked Bollywood and the possibilities and limitations of her own star switching power.

By the end of the decade of the 2000s, the desire for industry globality that was expressed at the turn of the millennium was now visible in Bollywood's industrial structure. Glitzy multiplexes replaced single-screen theatres, allowing for more diversity in the types of content produced, and pulled in new audiences: the post-globalization consuming class. The multiplex phenomenon significantly changed film financing and distribution and had an impact on the film form and aesthetic, leading to a new conceptualization of the film industry. The multiplexes enjoyed state support and favourable state policies. It was a moment when the state's ideological directives dovetailed with the multiplex phenomenon, which reflected the neoliberalized urban transformation of 'India Shining'—a slogan coined by the ruling BJP government. The slogan encompassed a globalized urban imaginary where utopian visions of urbanization and development (*vikas*) for the consuming class and 'the phantasmagorias of wealth'[46] attracted new industrial nodes in the Bollywood network in an unprecedented way.

Hitherto, only companies like UTV and Pritish Nandy Communications, which had tasted earlier success when the global flows reached Indian television, had embraced the offerings in the film industry. The coming of the multiplex evoked interest from mega organizations. Among the most iconic of these is the Indian telecommunications and oil and gas corporation Reliance, whose entertainment enterprise was set up as a private media and entertainment company in 2005. As a convergent media conglomerate, Reliance's interests ranged from films, music, sports, gaming, the internet, and mobile to digital content delivery platforms. Similarly, Zee Entertainment, which was until now only interested in television, emerged as another globally networked entertainment conglomerate. With the addition of these powerful nodes with business clout, the Indian film and entertainment industry's mediascape looked significantly different. This kind of diversified globalization, according to Amelia Arsenault and Manuel Castells, leads to the formation of a global network of interlocked media businesses that form the core of a contemporary, networked global media business landscape.[47] The emergence of Reliance as a strong business node came to the fore most prominently when the company decided to invest in Steven Spielberg's DreamWorks Pictures in 2008. The company invested USD 825 million to own a 50 per cent stake in DreamWorks.[48] Given the changing globalization landscape and the rise of India as one of the world's largest markets, many Indian firms ranging from communications to oil and gas, were doing similar mergers and acquisitions globally to 'bring home new products and build competitive strength in India'.[49] The Reliance acquisition, however, was by far the largest merger and acquisition deal in this period and brought considerable attention to the burgeoning film and entertainment sector.[50] Additionally, this global expansion of Indian firms to Hollywood augmented the Bollywood industry brand as global.

As illustrated by the example of Reliance, in this historical moment, there is a distinctive shift in the network.[51] Networks, as Peter Dicken, Philip F. Kelly, Kris Olds, and Henry Wai-Chung Yueng note, are neither purely organizational forms nor pure structures. They are relational processes that evolve and are empirically realized in different structural configurations based on spatio-temporal contexts. As the global economic structure changes, the networks shift relationally in the context of those changes. A network lens helps emphasize the interconnectedness and hybridities of how individuals, firms, and the nation state function within it. How they function within the context of the changes in the economic order determines a particular manifestation of the network. In the 2010s, firms like Reliance and Zee emerged as strong networked domestic industry nodes because the economic reforms initiated by the Indian state—opening its doors to foreign investment and collaboration—had taken root, and in addition to international investment in India, Indian firms across all industrial sectors acquired a global outlook. Thus, Reliance, aspiring to situate itself as a leading company in world entertainment, signed deals with several leading Hollywood stars, including Brad Pitt, George Clooney, Tom Hanks, Julia Roberts, and Jim Carrey.[52] The company further invested in post-production facilities and acquired over 200 movie theatres in the US, expanding its business footprint in a vertically integrated way.[53] The primacy of India as a burgeoning market and the visibility created through firms like Reliance boosted foreign direct investment and collaborations with foreign entities.

Key Hollywood studios that had already registered a presence in India in this period were joined by other industry nodes like talent agencies. Agencies like the Creative Artists Agency (CAA) and William Morris Endeavor (WME) staked a claim in the Indian market by joining forces with local pre-existing talent companies. These changes were significant in that they structurally pushed the boundaries for the informal industry practices that had existed until now. Not only was the culture moving away from handshake deals, but the industry was also structurally evolving into a networked configuration with various intermediaries and stakeholders that overlapped with state power and national paradigms of expansion.

On top of changing distribution avenues, production practices, and multiplex exhibition venues that were outward looking and in pursuit of global markets, another industry change, which would have a huge impact on stars and their power, was brought about through talent agencies. The concept of talent agencies was new for Bollywood, and it was only in this ascendant agglomerated network phase (the 2010s) that talent agencies began to surface. One of the earliest talent agency nodes that embodied the global–local dialectic and reconfigured the industry landscape and star presence was CAA KWAN. The company was a joint venture between Hollywood's CAA and India's largest talent agency, KWAN Entertainment & Marketing Solutions. CAA KWAN executive Purti Chaturvedi underscores the drastic transformation in the industry dynamic as well as the emergence of talent agencies as a new structural addition to the Bollywood network:

> [In India,] we saw certain agencies try celebrity management as a more corporate or systematic thing only 8–10 years ago. They were agencies like Percept, Matrix Entertainment, and GloboSport that came into play. These were the pioneers trying to solidify the presence of a talent management system in India because, before them, there was no such concept in India.[54]

The joint venture, CAA president Richard Lovett noted, was a tremendous opportunity for CAA to step into 'India's robust entertainment industry'. The venture would provide 'tremendous opportunities for talent across multiple platforms'. As mentioned earlier, being glocal in its embodiment, the venture would also provide opportunities for talent across global regions.[55] The structural transformation with the coming of talent agencies was significant because, until now, stars had operated through personal managers that were also critical to the functioning of their production ventures. Talent agency nodes reconfigured this industrial dynamic, cementing the move away from family- or star-led industrial production clusters that were trying to adopt corporate business practices and structures. The unfolding industrial space was being re-scaled as glocal, and within it, older practices were being reconfigured. Suresh Iyer, senior marketing and advertising consultant for Wizcraft Entertainment—the company that conceptualized and organized the IIFA, an event that marked a symbolic and global manifestation of Bollywood—asserted that talent agencies were a key change in the structural transformation. From a 'single manager does it all' model, Bollywood has moved to an era where every area (endorsements, appearances, and film-script reading) is covered by agencies:

> Talent agencies have now become like a necessary evil. It works for the film stars because these are more ways for them to make money. It works for the talent agencies because they, too, are getting a piece of the pie. But to the business, it is unnecessary because you have an extra doorman fee to pay.[56]

Male stars with switching power responded to this structural change in a different way. Stars like SRK, Amitabh Bachchan, Aamir Khan, Salman Khan, and Akshay Kumar continued to work through managers, but manager roles had been folded into production and media entities, or individual managers functioned outside of the formal talent-agency structural matrix. SRK, for instance, is managed by an in-house agency that takes care of PR and other deals for the star and his production company, Red Chillies. Salman Khan is individually managed by Reshma Shetty, the co-founder of Matrix Entertainment.[57] Advait Chandan, a director from Khan's production team, also doubles as his manager. Talent agencies like CAA and KWAN, however, represent Bollywood's new crop of actors, including Deepika Padukone, Shahid Kapoor, Ranbir Kapoor, Farhan Akhtar, Sonakshi Sinha, and Shraddha Kapoor.[58] The new generation of stars, therefore, has had a different set-up and thus a different global exposure because of what the networked talent agencies can enable. The Bollywood network is rapidly changing. Agencies such as CAA KWAN are putting in place Western 'best practices' and a systematic method of managing celebrities and 'packaging' and selling films to production houses. The agencies have brand advisors like Chaturvedi for each star client to ensure that 'they don't endorse a random brand and get the value they are supposed to get'.[59] This evolving ecosystem is conducive to the branding theories outlined earlier, where the star image and the brand need to be congruent. It is within this transitional zone, as Bollywood is acquiring a flexible, networked structure that a new crop of Bollywood stars emerges who could now avail themselves of institutional and industry nodes structurally embedded in the network to help mobilize their global presence and switching power. This is the context in which Chopra's star presence and switching power get created and defined.

CHOPRA: THE STAR OF NETWORKED BOLLYWOOD

When Rai started her global career, she was represented by Simone Sheffield, the owner of the UK-based Canyon Entertainment. It was not a bad representation for Rai, but the scale of the game changed drastically with Chopra who became one of the first Indian stars to be represented by CAA, one of the top US talent agencies. India was a market expanding with global opportunities, and after taking on Chopra, CAA invested in a joint venture with the Indian talent agency KWAN. Unlike Rai's entry, Chopra's move into the Hollywood and international market was a result of a premeditated strategy. Chopra possessed the 'affective agency' and 'switching power' to exceed the network and create global synergies. As Nyay Bhushan, the India correspondent for the *Hollywood Reporter*, points out,

> Chopra's introduction to the US was built in stages. She was first signed as a music artist to Universal Music/Interscope Records and released some singles. She was then signed as the first Indian to model for Guess clothing. After her television breakthrough with *Quantico*, the next step was a major film like *Baywatch*. It's probably the first time a mainstream Indian actor was introduced in this manner to Hollywood. Also, in her formative years, Chopra had spent time in the US as a student, so she was attuned to American culture in some way at an early age.[60]

Chopra's presence was structurally built and was the result of the coming together of many new nodes and the intensification of the now agglomerated and highly interconnected global network that did not exist in the Indian industrial landscape prior to this time, what I have termed as contemporary networked Bollywood.

Desi Hits, a company founded by Anjula Acharia, a diasporic British Indian, materialized as a key node in Chopra's crossover journey to the US and global recognition. Like in the early 2000s phase prior to this, diasporic nodes and institutions emerged as the most invested catalysers. Desi Hits sought to 'bridge cultures' and produce common industrial investment interests in Bollywood's global networked structure, which was clearly visible at this time. 'India [had become and] is an extremely attractive market for American Companies', and Acharia envisioned her organization as a way to bridge the talent gap.[61] Acharia, a South Asian-origin venture capitalist, talent scout, and entrepreneur—whose organization anticipated 'pop culture shifts'—was invested in pairing South Asian stars with Hollywood and bringing Hollywood talent to India.[62] Through her platform Desi Hits, Acharia hoped to present the best fusion of Eastern and Western content. Doing so fulfilled a personal quest, part of living in the global South Asian community.[63] Prior to Chopra, Acharia paired Britney Spears with Indian singer Sonu Nigam and brought Lady Gaga to India. Chopra, however, has been Acharia's most exemplary pairing:

> When I met Priyanka, I thought she's incredibly disruptive. I really care about diversity and women. There's been a handful of South Asians in mainstream American pop culture, and they've really never represented me. To me, she's as disruptive as a startup, and she is inspiring other women to go and live their dreams and go and build a company.[64]

Chopra's embodiment and switching power were different, and, therefore, she emerged as a different kind of star. Like Rai, she won the Miss World pageant, and her global presence was first created through the beauty industry network. However, Chopra's career peaked at a time when the Indian industry structurally evolved as an interconnected global network wherein the industry was looking outward, and the world was looking towards India. While Rai's presence was globally dispersed and more relevant in the context of the UK and Europe, Chopra became the first Indian star to register a mainstream presence in the US entertainment industry. When Chopra signed up for ABC's FBI drama series *Quantico*, Bollywood distribution company Eros featured *Quantico* spots before their online film screenings, and ABC cross-promoted a collection of Chopra's films targeted at the US market.[65] The mere presence of Chopra in a US television project led to this synergy between ABC and Eros. The disruptive switching power of Chopra needs to be framed within the larger discourse of the industry structure because her success parallels the disruptive ambitions of the Indian and US entertainment industries that were invested in globalizing their business and collaborations. The synergy that Chopra's presence cemented was possible because she became the conduit to vitalize an expansion that Eros and ABC were already keen on. The disruptive switching power of Chopra was defined by three key factors: her embodiment of interstitial disruption in the US–India context, the relational evolution of the network, and the temporality of when she emerged on the horizon. In other words, her relational power within this network, which had significantly evolved during this time, was crucial in defining and situating her disruptive switching power.

Acharia signed Chopra in 2010 and worked to get her deals in every area of the entertainment sector, starting with her music single, followed by an advertising campaign with the American fashion brand Guess, and later a chance to perform for the National Football League (NFL). Acharia sought out Chopra because she was looking not just for South Asian talent but for a talent 'who would understand American pop culture as well'.[66] That Chopra had spent some teen years in the US meant that she understood American culture, and she could sing too. She possessed an interstitial star affect and persona that could work in global and local markets and across a variety of entertainment sectors. Chopra never fails to acknowledge the support of Acharia in most of her social media posts marking her global milestones. Evidently, in the current situation, when Bollywood is already global and networked, we see the emergence of nodes like Acharia, who are connected to diasporic networks and talent agencies like CAA and WME, which are specifically focused on crossover talent and have represented Chopra on the global platform. Unlike Rai, who was moving in previously unexplored and unchartered territory and possessed the switching power to create new networks based largely on her affective appeal, for Chopra and other female stars succeeding her, a network is already in place to enable them to navigate the global entertainment arena.

Why such a network emerged has much to do with the interest of Western media organizations in India and their strategies to expand their reach in the burgeoning Indian market. It also has to do with ambitious global media corporations like Reliance, Zee, and UTV (now owned by Disney) emerging from India, as well as the corporatization and globalization of the entertainment and media sector at large. The story of ABCL in Chapter 2 points to Bachchan's early vision for Indian entertainment. After 2005, following the industry gaining formal government status, it finally achieved a shape that echoed this early vision. The presence of American and international organizations in India, too, has had an important influence on the global flows of Bollywood and the global forays of Indian talent. As veteran actor Kabir Bedi—one of India's earliest global stars to work in Europe and America—points out, much has changed for Indian cinema, and Hollywood, too, has changed and evolved at the same time. The reason why more Indian stars can find parts in American projects is

> [t]he range of people that Hollywood is looking for has expanded. The range of roles has expanded, so there is not just an opening of doors but a greater willingness to look internationally on the part of Hollywood and international television. That is a sea change of difference, and the presence of a star in such a project makes a lot possible.... Co-productions are possible ... different versions of the films are possible.[67]

Thus, as the Bollywood network expands with transnational nodes like Hollywood studios in India and a global network of PR and talent agencies, the global forays of Indian stars create the anticipation and expectation of transnational industry collaborations and synergies. This trend, however, perhaps predicted a decided shift in the nature of 'star switching power' that would become less pronounced and would perhaps operate on a more diffuse affective plane. Yet Chopra represents an interstitiality within this global space of flows because of her disruptive embodiment and industrial positioning. The industrial positioning of her star persona came together with her interstitial and disruptive embodiment in a deliberate way.

While Rai's beauty and the global Miss World platform were the main enablers of her global crossover and appeal, Chopra's persona and appeal were deliberately constructed. Every PR piece, news story, and television show in the US—ranging from *Live! With Kelly and Michael* to *The Tonight Show Starring Jimmy Fallon* to *The Ellen DeGeneres Show*—repeated a similar narrative about Chopra: that she went to school in the US (albeit for only a couple of years, a detail often elided in the reports), that she bested the competition at Miss World, and that her stardom in Bollywood was enormous. It was a narrative of an already popular star from a prolific and exotic industry, Bollywood, but one who was also familiar with US culture. Throughout public appearances, Chopra went about relating specifics about her US experience: her love for New York, her teenage idolization of Tupac

Shakur, and her enthusiasm for hotdogs that she devoured with talk show host Jimmy Fallon. It is a measured construction of a star persona that is exotic yet familiar and well versed enough in American culture to be acceptable to US audiences. Rai, in her early years, had been caught off guard on the David Letterman show when she was questioned about why she lived with her parents despite being an adult, well-off popular star. Chopra, in contrast, was able to project an American identity and successfully assimilate within the US mediascape to the point of being able to bob apples on television—a quintessentially American activity. Although originally perceived as an exotic beauty, her brand identity was reframed as a 'cultural insider' who was at home in the world—specifically the US.

As new international PR and talent agencies found a new breeding ground in India, the network power, agency, and management of the star persona shifted from individuals to institutions. In the case of Chopra, CAA KWAN executive Purti Chaturvedi explains,

> Priyanka wants to be recognized more as a global icon than an Indian icon, and her PR agencies help her construct that imagery. It is about the PR team she has put together; they help her come up with the narrative. Look at Aishwarya, she too was a global icon, but her narrative was just one of beauty. She was the most beautiful woman in the world who is an Indian, and look, none of her Hollywood ventures did well. So, it is all about the PR narrative.[68]

Speaking from the trenches of talent management and PR networks, Chaturvedi underscores that shift in the Bollywood network. The new nodes and institutions like CAA, KWAN, and Bling possess the agency and network power to shape and define the star's narrative. Unlike Rai, who spearheaded an individual effort to 'strengthen the Indian identity on the global platform', Chopra marks the next phase of that identity, 'the global Indian', who is bolstered by a management team who helps her to specifically perform a South Asian American identity that merges discourses of cosmopolitanism and global citizenship. With this notion of the global Indian, she defined her industrial agency and brand in the current context of a South Asian and a person-of-colour (POC) identity shifting across political and sociocultural vectors due to mass protests like Black Lives Matter and the election of Kamala Harris, America's first South Asian and Black vice-president. Given that Chopra's brand evolved into a performative South Asian

Figure 4.6 A visible transformation in Priyanka Chopra's looks: (*left*) Chopra, newly crowned Miss World, at her first press conference, 2000; (*right*) Chopra at a promotional event for the Disney film *Planes*, 2013

Source: (*Left*) Reuters/Str Old; (*right*) Reuters/Mario Anzuoni.

American cosmopolitan identity, let us map the two phases and evolution of Chopra's brand identity.

Unlike Rai, Chopra does not possess the racial malleability that would make this new entertainment sector naturally accessible (see Figure 4.6). However, as I have underscored, behind Chopra was a veritable network sustaining and crafting strategies for her success. Chopra's first Hollywood project was voicing the character of the Indian plane Ishani for Disney's animated feature *Planes* (2013, dir. Klay Hall).

Casting Chopra was a strategic move by which Disney strengthened its presence in the Indian market. Chopra's voice in this feature kick-started the branding narrative of her global identity. Unlike Appu from *The Simpsons*, Chopra's character, Ishani, does not have a pronounced Indian accent. As Chopra herself points out,

> I wanted her [Ishani] to be the way we speak, you know, which is the way I speak. And [Klay Hall] was totally cool with that. But I did add a

few Indian words here and there. Hindi words and expressions because I wanted her to be very unique to the culture that we come from. I wanted to keep it real.[69]

Almost simultaneously, Chopra launched her music single 'Exotic' with Pitbull, an American rapper of Cuban origin. The music video shows Chopra appropriating a Latinized look, a visual identity easily accessible to her. Chopra did not possess the easy racial ambiguity that Rai epitomized, however. Furthermore, she faced friction due to her endorsement of skin-lightening products and plastic surgery, which highlighted racialization as an important aspect of media industry globalization.

Chopra's next international campaign, for Guess, had her channelling her 'inner Sophia Loren'. Through numerous other television appearances, interviews, and magazine covers in the West, Chopra's star persona and 'glamour' have been constructed as global. While tentatively rooting herself in an Indian identity that was interspersed throughout the PR-orchestrated discourse, Chopra foregrounded her 'global-ness' and peppered it with a hint of the 'exotic'. Rai, in contrast, projected herself as an envoy of India on a global platform and avowedly worked towards strengthening the voice of the Indian film industry and Indian identity. Chopra eschews a focus on identity discourse: she strategically uses a flexible Indianness as an embellishment, foregrounding her identity as a global citizen. From her controversial magazine cover for *Condé Nast Traveller*, where she claimed the identity of a global traveller, to her association with the United Nations's Global Citizen platform, Chopra has identified as a global citizen: 'I think the globe has become a really small place now, and we are all global citizens, at least I think I am. The girl next door's face has changed. She does not come from a particular place.... She can be from anywhere.'[70] The narrative of Chopra's entry into American entertainment is tailored to this globalized identity. Speaking of her ABC show, *Quantico*, Chopra explains, 'When I was asked what kind of a show I was looking for, I said, "I will do anything that has nothing to do with my ethnicity." I want to be an actor first, and later, we will see how "Indianness" comes into it.'[71] Chopra then goes on elaborate that her character, Alex, on *Quantico*, is half-Indian and wears an Om bracelet, but those details are just incidental to the character.

There are two central threads to the PR-driven discourse that builds Chopra's public face that are essential to understanding her nodal role in networked Bollywood and star switching power. The first is the enormity of her Bollywood stardom—hence, a step forward to Hollywood for her is a step forward for Bollywood–Hollywood synergy. In this instance, the 'globality' of the Bollywood brand is leveraged to establish Chopra's stardom in the American entertainment industry, where she was a relative newcomer. Chopra nonchalantly expressed to Kelly Ripa on the *Kelly and Michael* show that her ride to the Oscars was in a Rolls-Royce and that '[her] car in India is a Rolls-Royce, the best thing about it is the rug, you take your shoes off, and it feels like a hug'.[72] Mentions of her Rolls-Royce, her many bodyguards, and easy transatlantic flights on her private jet are tangential and sometimes direct references to her Bollywood superstardom. Through depicting the luxurious aspects of her stardom, recounting a slumber party in the sky for *Travel + Leisure* magazine, or donning USD 5 million worth of diamonds on the Oscar red carpet, Chopra's star persona is layered with luxury and excess.[73] There is an individualistic and elitist exceptionalism built into the Western discourse of her Bollywood-associated star persona that buoys her and enables her to navigate the Western entertainment industry on an equal footing.

The other crucial aspect of Chopra's American star persona is her status as a fashionista and style icon. The narrative of her initial encounter with American culture is constructed within the fashion frame:

> She [Chopra] decided to give Queens a try after, while visiting her cousins, she noticed their school didn't require a uniform. 'For a 12-year-old, not wearing a uniform was very important,' she said. Her parents agreed to let her stay with her extended family in New York City, and Chopra lived there and in the outskirts of Boston until she was 16.[74]

Whatever the real reasons for her four-year stint in US schools, this narrative is built on Chopra's embodiment of distinctive style and fashion, which is a different type of embodiment than Rai's.

Chopra, in her post-*Quantico* phase, has emerged as a disruptive brand and industry node whose agency within the industrial network is more than that of other female stars of networked Bollywood. As we have seen throughout earlier chapters, star switching power is moulded by connections to, and positionality within, political and sociocultural dimensions. Her disruptive power and agency stem from relational changes within the US political climate where a cosmopolitan South Asian identity has gained currency due in part to the emergence of figures such as vice-president Kamala Harris on the political

Figure 4.7 American vice-president Kamala Harris (*right*) arriving to speak with Priyanka Chopra Jonas (*left*) at the Democratic National Committee's Women's Leadership Forum in Washington, DC, 30 September 2022

Source: Associated Press/Jacquelyn Martin.

horizon (see Figure 4.7). They also stem from the ways her brand identity is informed by her personal life, which has been marked by her marriage to American singer and songwriter Nick Jonas, enhancing her positioning around celebrity that remains at the core of her brand representation. This celebrity is tied to wealth and luxury, which intersects with fashion. Chopra wore drop earrings worth USD 3.2 million when presenting the 2020 Oscars and a 75-foot tulle veil with a dress made up of 2,380,000 mother-of-pearl sequins on her wedding.[75] Her bold fashion choices, according to CNN, have established her as '[the] polished and glamorous … queen of the red carpet'.[76] At the same time, the recent privileging of diversity within the American entertainment and media industries has lent the Chopra brand a new racialized relevance as well—one that can associate her, albeit across stark class divides, with POC groups and identities.

Chopra's effective and affective power is the conjoined manifestation of these multiple sociocultural and political aspects that make her a disruptive node in the industry as well as the cultural and political landscape. A disruptive start-up is a business idea that challenges the status quo and embodies audience and consumer desires before they become desires. Structurally, disruptive start-ups have evangelizers within the industrial structure and fervent fans and consumers for their brands that help in mainstreaming their identity. Not only does Chopra have a similar supportive industry network through nodes like Acharia, but her celebrity brand identity has undergone a deliberate shift. She is no more touted as a global nomad but is represented as a South Asian American. Moreover, in the contemporary performance of her celebrity brand, her bicultural position is emphasized wherein she celebrates—and uses social media to show that she celebrates—the Hindu festival Diwali and Thanksgiving with equal fervour and aplomb.

The temporality of her industry presence was opportune, which lent Chopra a switching power that is interstitial and between two worlds yet can affect industrial change and bring to fruition a Bollywood-like star businessperson model to her crossover industrial positioning in Hollywood and Bollywood. Like SRK and Bachchan, Chopra has leveraged her growing global brand equity for business partnerships and investments. Acharia reframes their recent relationship not as talent and manager but as 'business partners'.[77] Currently, Chopra is a co-investor with Acharia in Bumble, a women-centric online dating app where Chopra is the face of the brand. In addition, Chopra has been co-producing content for Netflix. Most recently, she co-produced *The White Tiger* (2021, dir. Ramin Bahrani) with Shonda Rhimes. In the beginning, says Acharia, 'I invested in Priyanka [because] partnering with Chopra was figuratively like a single that became a hit. I love ... women who can become brands themselves because they stand for something and can move an industry.'[78]

Chopra's effective and affective power worked in a way that it is bringing about some form of Bollywood-like agency to stars as businesspersons within her crossover Hollywood–Bollywood media sphere, which is clearly an intersection of disruptive switching power in the sociocultural, economic, and political realms. Moreover, disruptive industrial changes propelled by new nodes like streaming platforms in Covid-19 times have reconfigured industry structures where women like Chopra can assert more direct and indirect clout.

This chapter historicized a contemporary moment when we were all enamoured with and curious about Chopra's Hollywood crossover and rise to global fame. This contemporary moment, the chapter has argued, was created due to the integration of the global beauty pageant and cosmetic industry into the expanding Hindi film and entertainment business at the turn of the millennium, a change that marked a significant restructuring of gender and power in a post-liberalized and nationalizing India.

Female beauty queens became symbolic national icons with affective power that could be ostensibly mobilized. An evolving industry structure flooded with new institutional nodes, and local and global stakeholders further supported this change. The explosion of streaming platforms, talent, casting, and marketing agencies structurally altered gendered power hierarchies and global access for contemporary stars. The female star's agency was thus significantly altered. Simultaneously, the structural access to global markets was also altered because now a host of global investors and stakeholders were looking toward India (and its 1.5 billion people) as a coveted market. A rising nationalistic, neoliberal, media-savvy state, no more indifferent to the film and entertainment industry, further fuelled these changes. The concluding chapter reflects on the changing industry structure amid the multitude of global and local nodes, a media-savvy celebritized state, and incipient global models of star power that Bollywood might resemble in the future. Alternatively, does this moment mark a coalescence, where gendered and established conglomerate hierarchies are disrupted, a Bollywoodizing of Hollywood, of which Chopra is an early case study?

5

BARDS OF CHANGE

How Streaming Platforms and State–Industry Alliance
Are Reconfiguring Star Power in Networked Bollywood

I just wanted to get into this [streaming] world [and] understand how
[it] worked. The digital platform has opened up avenues for everybody.…
OTT [over-the-top streaming platforms like Netflix] gives you great
freedom to work without any pressure.… And most importantly, if your
film is released on an OTT platform, there is no pressure from the box
office. I feel it is like a revolution that is taking place, and I am lucky to
be a part of that revolution.[1]

—Anil Kapoor, Bollywood star

Anil Kapoor, the Bollywood star whom we first encountered in the
Introduction, recently released his first Netflix film, *Thar* (2022, dir. Raj Singh
Chaudhary), a Hindi-language neo-Western thriller.[2] The above statement by
Kapoor acknowledges the novelty of changes to the contemporary industrial
structure in the age of streaming. In its current iteration, the Bollywood
landscape has been rapidly transforming, with the film industry becoming
increasingly 'networked' with global and local streaming platforms. The
contemporary industrial ecosystem is teeming with streaming platforms,
including vernacular regional, national, and global entrants like Netflix
and Amazon Prime Video. In India, these streaming services are referred
to as 'over-the-top' (OTT) platforms because they bypass traditional media
services and many regulatory constraints to reach consumers directly through
the internet.

Kapoor's comment reflects broad changes in the industrial landscape and Bollywood's position and influence on globalized entertainment culture in the third decade of the twenty-first century. At the 2014 IIFA, the Tampa conference recounted in the Introduction, Bollywood was hoping to make a splash in the US, wherein stars like Kapoor, who had created some presence in the US market, were leveraged as anchors. The story of India's Bollywoodized market and industrial network, however, only a decade later, appears strikingly different. Now we see Netflix pulling out all stops to create a strong presence in India, closely followed by Amazon Prime Video and Disney+. OTT platforms like Netflix and Amazon Prime Video are just the newest contenders. They have drastically altered the entertainment industry structure not just in India but also in Hollywood, where long-established conglomerate monopolies are being broken up or reconfigured. Through its multidirectional global ties, the Indian entertainment industry has been transforming into a veritable global network. Contemporary networked Bollywood currently is a more collaborative, agile, and transnationally interconnected ecosystem, challenging established structural and organizational hierarchies in the industry while also repositioning the significance of Indian producers and consumers of films and entertainment globally. This conclusion carries the story told in this book about the importance of star switching power to the structural transformations, development, and globalization of networked Bollywood up to the present moment. This book has narrated the relational story of star switching power and the Bollywood network, wherein some megastars possessed a superseding agentic power that made them strategic industrial actors. It has presented Indian Hindi cinema and entertainment's industrial history from the 1950s to the present. In doing so, it has explicated how certain male megastars got to be situated as the key vectors in initiating important business models and industrial changes owing to their ability to exceed the networks to which they belonged and their critical role in making the industry global. This industry structure, as this book has amply illustrated, was always-already global and networked. Yet what changed over time, as global economic and technological flows to India were amplified, was the intensity, the multiplicity, and the granular interconnectedness of the industry's organizational and business structure that I have termed 'networked Bollywood'.

Using networks as a heuristic for examining the industrial–organizational and business structure and the relational gendered, classed, and affective workings of power within it that operates through powerful star nodes was a generative framework in multiple ways. It allowed me to narrate this history of Bollywood's globalization and the encompassing structural and industrial change while articulating sociological networks of power possessed by elite megastars and how they leveraged that power through their primacy in these sociocultural and geopolitical networks. The multiplicity of networks built around a flexible and perpetually inclusive framework allowed me to articulate the reconfiguration and transformation of the industry's structure and business over time as new nodes like the beauty pageant, the cosmetic industry, or technology-driven fan networks augmented and refashioned the Bollywood network. A network heuristic thus helped me capture the poly-dimensional ontology where I could bring the sociocultural, geopolitical, affective, and industrial into a relational discussion about individual nodal power possessed by the star businessmen, the change-makers in Bollywood.

In the evolution of Hindi cinema's nascent networks to an industry replete with multiple global or local participants and stakeholders, some things have transformed. In contrast, some others have remained consistent over time. One of the consistent factors has been the agentic power possessed by stars within this industrial structure, which the previous chapters mapped historically through key stars. The other factor has been the dominance of small-world ties that still overwhelmingly inflect the business and organizational structure. This concluding chapter maps the transformation and immutability of contemporary power structures and practices, which it situates within the unfolding contexts of a rapidly transforming industrial ecology and an increasingly media-savvy state.

I follow this conclusion through the three main categories of nodes, stakeholders, and networks that I have traced throughout this narrative of Bollywood's globalization—namely, the star, the state, and the structure of the Hindi film and entertainment industry. What has changed, what remains the same, and what do recent changes signal in terms of the star's agentic power? How are the industry's evolving structure and the new Indian celebritized state's influence over a previously overlooked and excluded industry impacting agentic star power within it?[3] The Indian entertainment industry's contemporary formation as networked Bollywood is an evolving structure with multiple nodes possessing varying nodal power, which changes how the star nodes exist within it. Revealing both important continuities and marked changes from previous decades, the remainder of this chapter examines agentic star power and the limits of its excess in contemporary networked Bollywood, which is gradually transforming into a conglomerate Hollywood-like industrial formation, even as Hollywood itself is becoming Bollywoodized with stars similarly possessing industrial agency in the wake of conglomerate hierarchy disruptors like Netflix. Since this book's narrative has been filtered through the lens of star switching power, the star, the state, and the industry are the three critical actors in a relational dynamic. This conclusion, therefore, lays out the continuities and changes in star agency in relation to a transforming industry and elucidates the changes in star switching power with regard to an ideologically driven, media-savvy state. It ends, therefore, with a provocation about power: namely, what does the heuristic of star-switching reveal—beyond the operational levels of power possessed by stars as industrial actors—about structures of epistemic power that undergird not only the entertainment industry but also global relations more broadly?

STAR SWITCHING POWER AND THE INDUSTRY

The central vector in this story has been star power in the business and industrial realms. The book has articulated star switching power as a superseding agentic power that makes some key stars strategic industrial actors. What are the conditions and factors that foster agentic star power and imbue them with an excess that allows them to forge new paths and imagine and implement new entrepreneurial changes? Bollywood stars, compared with other industries, could be more strategic business actors because of their relational embeddedness within the industrial structure, a structure that was dispersed and polysemous—an agglomeration of multiple independent production clusters of different scales. Unlike a top-down conglomerate industry structure (such as Hollywood), this bottom-up structure gave the star-led family clusters an advantage because of the star-driven nature of the Hindi film product. Also key was the lack of state support and, by extension, a lack of surveilling machinery beyond stringent taxation measures that were implemented upon this liminal industry.

Moreover, this agentic switching power begins to change as the industrial structure transforms into a network with multiple global and local stakeholders in the form of domestic corporations such as Reliance, Zee, and UTV and international production and business entities ranging from Netflix and Apple to Viacom and Sony. Contemporary networked Bollywood, therefore, is an evolving structure, with multiple individual and agglomerated nodes and clusters possessing varying nodal power that changes how the star nodes exist within it. However, the star nodes within the Hindi film and entertainment industry still have residual structural dominance. Although with the industry's evolution towards a conglomerate Hollywood-like industrial formation, the limits of agentic star power and its excess are transforming.

Ergo, to assess star agency and power within an industrial structure in flux, I examine three groups of actors who provide insights into the contemporary workings of Bollywood star power and how it shapes the industry's globalization. The first set includes the established star proprietors of large business entities, such as SRK and Aamir Khan. The second set includes established female stars with some industrial and much affective power. Finally, the third set includes the new crop of stars who have found fame and established their careers within the current industrial structure, thus offering insights into its potential future. The critical question then to revisit in this conclusive and forward-looking chapter is: As the means and conditions of the structured industry patterns are changing and evolving, how are the agency of the star node and its power changing within it? What does an agentic structure look like for each of these sets of actors?

Various vectors that impact star agency and switching power are changing, including the social structural and political contexts encompassing those network patterns of social ties that comprise interpersonal, inter-organizational, or transnational settings of action. In the context of Bollywood star power, this interplay between structure and agency and which stars can possess the ability to switch is varied. It is critical, then, to reflect on how this power is changing with respect to industry hierarchies, gender, and established power structures embedded within these networks. The established megastar businessmen still dominate the top rung in the three-rung hierarchical structure I have outlined. For instance, Netflix first started its foray into the Indian market by establishing partnerships with prominent star-led production companies such as Red Chillies Entertainment. Ted Sarandos and Reed Hastings marked their entry into the Indian market with a remarkable tweet by Netflix India featuring a photo of Sarandos and Hastings with two of the most popular Khans in Bollywood, SRK and Aamir, captioning the image as 'Last night got pretty Khantastic'.[4]

Predictably, beyond Red Chillies, Netflix's first stage of expansion included deals with significant stars, producers, and directors such as Aamir Khan, Anil Kapoor, and Karan Johar to cement its position in the Indian market.

The early stage of its India strategy was concentrated on capitalizing on pre-existing global resonances of Bollywood films and stardom. The case of Red Chillies offers a notable exemplar of the structural dominance of established star proprietors in this dynamic and helps us understand the interconnected multitiered organizational structure and the effective industrial power of an organization like Red Chillies.

Helmed by Bollywood megastar SRK, Red Chillies Entertainment was the first organization that Netflix partnered with in 2017 in its bid to create inroads into the Indian market. Speaking about the partnership, Netflix's CEO, Ted Sarandos, emphasized that

> Shah Rukh Khan is the most sought-after actor in the Indian film industry and has played a huge role in bringing Indian cinema to the world stage. His moniker 'King Khan' speaks to his status as a cultural icon and to the incredible popularity of his films among audiences worldwide.[5]

The Netflix partnership with Red Chillies was articulated as extending SRK's global vision, underscoring the relative power of Red Chillies in India with regard to the partnership. Netflix's co-founder, Reed Hastings, affirmed his belief in 'the global vision of Red Chillies to create groundbreaking content out of India' that would 'deepen [Netflix's] relationship with Red Chillies and expand [its] slate of originals in India'.[6] Netflix's initial impetus for the Indian market was to capitalize on the global iconicity of SRK's stardom to create a recursive fandom. Hence, the first deal inked with Red Chillies was to acquire a library of SRK films.

Concurrently, SRK's 'global dreamz [sic]' were solidifying through his expansive production and entertainment company, Red Chillies, which was producing not only films and television shows but also curating events as well as managing SRK's brand endorsements and multiple sports franchises owned by the star. Articulating his vision for further expansion, SRK acknowledged his collusive agreement with Netflix to expand the breadth of his organization: 'We have always tried to create world-class content and entertainment from India. Netflix has shown that Indian stories have a global audience, and we would love to use this platform and its reach to tell more stories.'[7] The deal with Red Chillies came on the heels of Netflix's global announcement that the streamer would ramp up international investments and that India was a 'super priority market' for them. This partnership existed alongside their prior content deal with Red Chillies, inked in 2016, to become the exclusive streaming home for SRK and Red Chillies movie titles across the world.[8]

The idea of a networked industrial structure formation denotes increased global competitiveness because it creates strong and spread-out inter-organizational networks that are global and local and operate at different scales. A networked industrial formation has the following characteristics: collusive agreements, formation of trade and distribution networks, and formation of cost-reducing alliances that are mutually profitable—also important is the presence of a multitiered organizational structure.[9] As this book has variously established, the contemporary Indian film and entertainment industry landscape is an agglomeration of multiple interconnected stakeholders beyond the family-led independent film-production clusters. The Red Chillies–Netflix arrangement exemplifies collusive agreements and coalitions typical of a networked organizational structure within an industry. The deal exemplifies market sharing and exclusive territories agreements. The objectives of this alliance were similarly multifold, mainly targeted at co-producing content and increasing the market demand and distribution of Indian content globally and, consequently, the demand for the Netflix platform in India. Netflix is but one prime example of how business synergies in a networked industry structure manifest. Such synergistic strategic alliances often lead to reduced or shared production costs or equivalently help to expand the scale, the parameter of demand, or markets for the product.[10] Additionally, a contemporary networked Bollywood entertainment industry is also emphatically *Bollywoodized* in its expansion and appeal across industrial sectors and entertainment registers.

A defining element of a networked industry organizational structure is that it is flexible—with nodal players that have varying powers where some transform into key hubs and others are minor in scale but critical and dominant. Trust, power, and flexibility in the context of network partnerships and structural power are some core elements within this formation. Furthermore, as this book has demonstrated, following the demise of the studio system after independence, the Hindi film industry has consistently been structurally networked but dominated by some critical nodal actors like the megastar or the director-businessman. Contemporaneously, in Netflix's partnerships with companies like Red Chillies or Dharmatic Entertainment (owned by Johar, SRK's close friend and a director with excessive industrial clout), the local partners or nodes have substantial leverage in determining the content and nature of the partnership. Hence, Netflix, in its first collaborative deal, acquired an extensive library of SRK's films, including flops from the 1990s, such as *Chahat* (Desire, 1996, dir. Mahesh Bhatt) and *Oh Darling Ye Hai India* (Oh Darling, This Is India, 1995, dir. Ketan Mehta). In the more contemporary context, Netflix has also acquired SRK's flops, such as *Zero* (2018, dir. Anand L. Rai), which failed to create any ripples at the box office. Based on the industrial clout of these production partners, Netflix has become a repository for content created by the top rung of producers that could not find distribution elsewhere. So how is contemporary networked Bollywood a measure of the new?

The fundamental changes lie in the scale and scope of the networked alliances that are far more developed and constituted by global and local alliances and partnerships. This structure has efficiency advantages: Netflix and Amazon Prime Video neither have to produce nor do they necessarily need the infrastructure to produce content in India. A partnership with SRK's Red Chillies helps both parties co-produce, distribute, and brand content like *Bard of Blood* (2019) to their unique advantage. As mentioned earlier, in many ways, such alliances have always existed to varying degrees. However, after the 2010s, as the industry got more integrated into the global flows, the nature, pace, and scope of the networked model expanded. Inevitably, SRK solidified his position as more than a Bollywood icon. Beyond the media industry, he is a business mogul in the sporting world of cricket, as the owner of private cricket teams in India, the Caribbean, the US, and the United Arab Emirates (UAE), epitomizing a synergistic culmination of Bollywood and cricket.

Similarly, Priyanka Chopra, Bollywood's leading global female star, whom we encountered in the last chapter, is an entrepreneurial producer and investor whose investments (apart from her production company, Purple Pebble Pictures) include Bumble, a dating website; Genies, a virtual avatar firm; Anomaly, a line of sustainable hair-care products; and, most recently, Sona, an Indian restaurant in New York, and more.[11] Touting Sona as the place where you go 'to have really great Indian food with a cool [global] vibe', an article in *Vogue* emphatically situated the appeal of Chopra's restaurant within her story brand: 'There's nobody that personifies global Indian more than Priyanka, and she has broken down boundaries in a way that no one from Bollywood has today.'[12] Much emphasis is placed on Chopra's story brand of effortless global luxury, which is consistently incorporated in her marketing narrative in the US. Whether it is her Rolls-Royce that she pointedly emphasized on a talk show or her luxury wedding at an Indian palace where she wore the world's longest veil, her story brand encompasses an affective evocation of global luxury.[13] At the recent launch of Sona Home, a product line built on her now-established restaurant, Chopra reasserted the essence of the Sona product line thus: '[T]he roots are entrenched in Indian culture [but] being able to be global and to be able to just be beautiful on any table setting was really important to us.'[14] It parallels her globally malleable affective star persona, which I have discussed in Chapter 4. For contemporary female stars, structural and industrial power in Bollywood is often initiated in the affective realm and leveraged as direct industrial effective power, as in the case of Chopra.

The convergent story brand of female stars like Chopra somewhat parallels the understanding of how star power operates in Hollywood. Martin Barker has addressed this phenomenon of convergent star story brands in Hollywood from the perspective of movie franchises.[15] Geoff King further advanced the argument in the Hollywood context by declaring that a star like Will Smith, who was a film, television, and music star rolled up in one, is a franchise in himself and, as such, exceeded his star text.[16] Paul McDonald offered a tempering take on Smith, pointing out his 'dependent independence' within the conglomerate Hollywood structure. The story that this book has presented is somewhat congruous but different. It situates the Bollywood male megastar's exceptional power, which exceeds the limits of industrial networks and is derived from their on-screen and off-screen star texts but also their industrial centrality. Industrial centrality is the key determinant of why Will Smith's agentic excess is different from that of SRK. It is also the key element in how we comprehend Chopra's agency and the boundaries of her star excess that oozes into and is informed by the networked industrial structure of contemporary Bollywood.

In their theorization of what constitutes agency, Mustafa Emirbayer and Ann Mische emphasize the interrelationship between agency and structure. Agency and, by extension, power in a given context, they argue, is temporally constructed as actors engage with different structural environments.[17] That process is interactive. It changes based on historical conditions. Yet the situation, too, is constitutive of action and defines how the actors can be agentic in a changed industrial or historical context.[18] The kind of contemporary glocal hybridity that manifests through Netflix or Amazon Prime Video within this context establishes the power hierarchy within the industrial structure that situates established star-owned companies at the top of the industrial stratum. How do we then unpack the agency of female stars like Chopra?

In thinking through this hierarchical structure, as Cecilia Ridgeway astutely reminds us, we must infuse a gendered frame into the context of organizational and institutional structures. The gendered frame of networked Bollywood reveals a new kind of negotiated agency that follows Ridgeway's contention that when new kinds of work occur in environments that are in a state of flux, the combined novelty of the changes creates capacity and space for re-negotiating gendered expectations through industrial or organizational frameworks. The current phase has similarly created a moment of agency for leading female star producers and entrepreneurs. Following Chopra's success, the industrial structure is equipped to support this kind of agency, so presently, we have a spate of Indian female stars and second- and third-rung male stars attempting their Hollywood crossover (see Table 5.1). Digital streaming platforms, talent agencies, casting agencies, and PR infrastructure are but some of the critical emerging nodes that have fundamentally altered the industry's structural landscape.

Consequently, male superstars, heretofore the central repositories of power within the industrial structure, do not possess it in the same way anymore. The new generation of male and female stars is structurally embedded in the networked industry structure differently. At the same time, female stars within this transitional phase have acquired a differential agency. Beyond Chopra, whose presence is more global, stars like Anushka Sharma, outsiders to the small, networked Bollywood family-business clusters, are able to find interstitial power within this changing environment.

Sharma turned producer in 2015 with her film *NH10* (dir. Navdeep Singh), under her independent production entity, Clean Slate Filmz. *NH10* was a misogynistic slasher film highlighting the issue of honour killings in India and women's complicity in upholding patriarchal oppression. Speaking about her interstitial position of power in a male-dominated industry, Sharma emphasizes both her leverage as a famous star and the impediment of her gender:

> I have built a position for myself as an actor. I wanted to leverage that for myself, to be able to back content and ideas which are truly phenomenal and path-breaking in the stories that we tell as producers.... I did not start producing films for myself per se. I just wanted to tell good stories. I would be sitting and talking to writers, discussing things with them and I would wonder why a certain type of film was not being written.

Then I realized that it is not very common in our industry for great roles to be constantly written for women. So, I wanted to take this step.[19]

The evolving landscape of the industry is fluid. Structural disruptions through streaming platforms like India's Hotstar (recently acquired by Disney+) that preceded global entrants like Netflix, Amazon Prime Video, and Apple TV further led to network effects, creating an explosion of global, local, vernacular, and niche OTT streaming services—in other words, agglomerated, globally and locally interconnected, scalar industry clusters (see Figure 5.1).

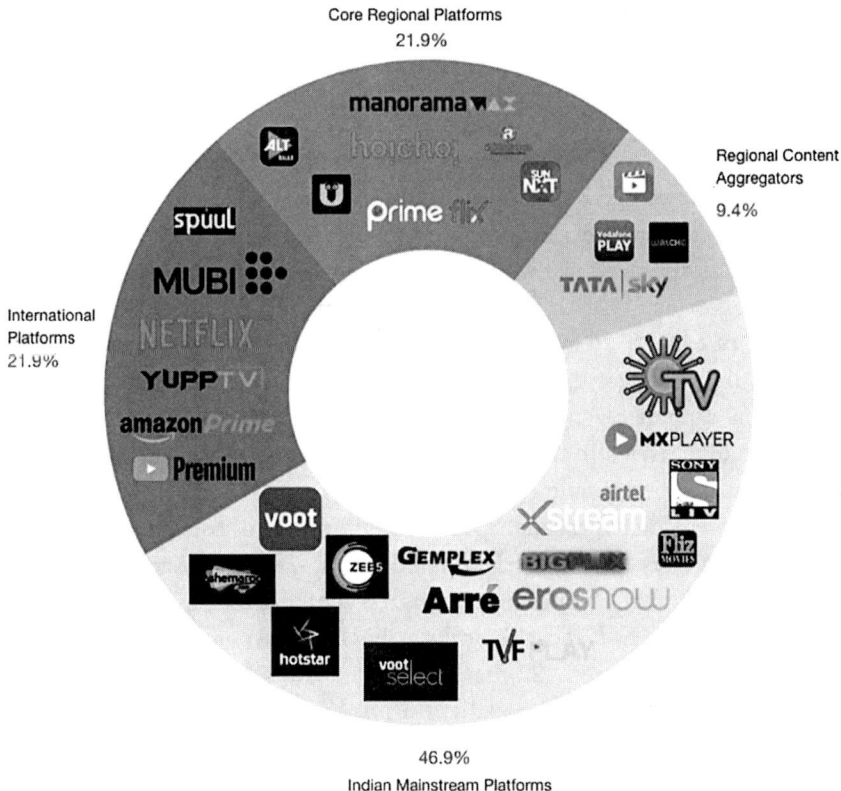

Figure 5.1 Global, local, and regional streaming platforms in India

Source: Meha Agarwal, 'Mapping The Market: India's Regional OTT Video Streaming Landscape', Inc 42, 27 March 2020, https://inc42.com/features/mapping-the-market-indias-regional-ott-video-streaming-landscape (accessed 4 May 2022).

This moment of structural metamorphosis has accorded agency to female stars that, as Anthony Giddens notes, 'goes beyond intentions people have in doing things, but in their capability of doing those things in the first place'.[20] This metamorphosis transforms agency into power, albeit a negotiated form of power. Fittingly, Sharma's Clean Slate Filmz recently announced that it would launch an OTT video-streaming platform in the first quarter of 2023 called Clean OTT. The announcement, emphasizing the company's women-oriented focus, noted that 'the service will place women-driven storylines, actors, directors, and producers at the heart of its content library for global audiences'.[21]

In the context of an evolving, agglomerated, interconnected, and (as the book terms it) contemporary networked industrial landscape, there is an evident osmosis of local and global discourses and industrial practices. The diversity discourse that an organization like Netflix propounds has found its way into the Indian film and media landscape. The impetus and negotiated agency possessed by a female actor-producer like Sharma, or even Chopra for that matter, is tied to the diversity discourse. Agency and discourse have a mutually constitutive relationship. As Michel Foucault notes, discourses guide selection processes and determine what is retained and valued versus what is forgotten.[22] Judith Butler further claims that 'possibilities of agency arise out of existing webs of power and discourse'.[23] While an organization like Netflix's push for diversity in content and producers of that content is driven by capitalistic brand-driven performativity that caters to its left-leaning audiences, it still creates an interstitial moment of structural power for women producers and actors. This alignment of interest and negotiated power can be best articulated through Derrick Bell's theory of convergent interests, wherein to address unequal relations of power, there needs to be a mutual convergence of interests for both parties.[24] Women actors and producers like Chopra, Sharma, and, most recently, Alia Bhatt, who announced her own production company in 2022, have leaned into this convergent moment to assert their industrial clout globally. *Darlings* (dir. Jasmeet K. Reen), Bhatt's first film under her own production banner, Eternal Sunshine Productions, in partnership with SRK's Red Chillies, was released on Netflix on 5 August 2022.[25] Her business investments and star brand extend beyond film to Nykaa, an app for beauty products, and Style Cracker, a fashion-styling platform. She also launched a children's clothing brand called Ed-a-Mamma, which creates products for children aged between two and fourteen.[26] Additionally, Bhatt signed with WME and was onboarded onto her first Hollywood project,

Heart of Stone (2023, dir. Tom Harper), with Gal Gadot and Jamie Dornan. Her entrepreneurship, business trajectory, and expansion look very similar to that of Chopra, which signals an established model and pathway that now exists in Bollywood for female stars with the affective power to leverage it in the industrial or business domain. Her journey also reflects an established infrastructure supporting Indian stars' crossing over to Hollywood. It is another instance of network effects, sustained infrastructural change, and a network of talent and PR management nodes that support this change. See Table 5.1 for stars who have been able to make a similar crossover to Hollywood since Chopra.

Bhatt, however, becomes an interesting case to study the power differentials within the negotiated agentic power of female star entrepreneurs in the contemporary moment. Bhatt's agentic power within the industrial structure exemplifies how the family-driven small-world ties or networks that determined Bollywood's early organizational hierarchy remain at the industry's core despite its transformation to a global networked structure.

Table 5.1 Indian stars who have crossed over to Hollywood

Bollywood stars' Hollywood debut	Project/Talent agency
Hrithik Roshan	Details not yet announced/Gersh
Kubbra Sait	*Foundation* (series for Apple TV+)
Alia Bhatt	*Heart of Stone* (2023, dir. Tom Harper) with Gal Gadot (Netflix film)/WME
Sikandar Kher	*Monkey Man* (2023, dir. Dev Patel) (acquired by Netflix)
Ali Fazal	*Death on the Nile* (2022, dir. Kenneth Branagh) and *Victoria & Abdul* (2017, dir. Stephen Frears)/WME
Dhanush	*The Gray Man* (2022, dir. Anthony Russo and Joe Russo) (acquired by Netflix)
Huma Qureshi	*Army of the Dead* (2021, dir. Zack Snyder)/United Agents
Deepika Padukone	*XXX: Return of Xander Cage* (2017, dir. D. J. Caruso)/ICM Partners
Dimple Kapadia	*Tenet* (2020, dir. Christopher Nolan)/Lavin Entertainment
Farhan Akhtar	*Ms. Marvel* (series for Disney+)/Do It Talent Ventures
Nargis Fakhri	*Spy* (2015, dir. Paul Feig)/Coconut Talent Management

Source: Prepared by the author using various news sources.

While some things change, some stay the same—one of which is the residual structural dominance of the megastars and the small-world ties formed through family-led film-production clusters. The hypervisibility of Bhatt, in contrast to the general structural invisibility of female stars, points to an institutionalized configuration of power wherein the social location and structural embeddedness within the small-world industrial networks render female actors like Bhatt more powerful. The social location of female stars within the industry's small-world social structure confers them with advantages and opportunities. However, as I have written about elsewhere, historically, female stars of yesteryear, like Nargis, for instance, who were similarly embedded in the industrial small-world hierarchy, could not avail themselves of opportunities in similar ways.[27] Bhatt's entrepreneurial rise, therefore, is especially indicative of this current temporal moment of industrial flux and its intersection with Bollywood's residual small-world close ties and networks. The case of Bhatt thus warrants a closer look.

Bhatt is the daughter of popular director and producer Mahesh Bhatt, who owns a family-led production company with his brother, Mukesh Bhatt. In an extension of these small-world ties and family networks, Bhatt recently married Ranbir Kapoor, Raj Kapoor's grandson, whom we discussed in Chapter 1. Bhatt and Kapoor's wedding pictures epitomize the deep-seated, endogamous, in-group homophilic small-world network ties that define the Bollywood network at its core—a reminder, as Raymond Williams has contended, of residual and dominant practices that influence the emergent structures.[28]

The pictures feature stars Kareena Kapoor and Karishma Kapoor, cousins of Ranbir Kapoor and grandkids of Raj Kapoor, as well as Kunal Kapoor (former actor and producer), son of Shashi Kapoor. Most descendants of the Kapoor clan have built their careers in Bollywood. Also featured is Amitabh Bachchan's daughter, Shweta Nanda, who is married to Nikhil Nanda, Raj Kapoor's maternal grandson. Figure 5.2 instantiates how the central nodes, stars with switching power, such as Raj Kapoor and Amitabh Bachchan, and now their progeny, are deeply embedded within these small-world family-network clusters through endogamous ties.

Star switching power, or the effective component of this power, is created and reproduced through elite sociocultural positioning, which is inflected by class, caste, and religion. Part of this hierarchical practice feeds into a stratification logic wherein maintaining a lineage within the industry helps power be concentrated around specific, powerful nodes. At the same time, it

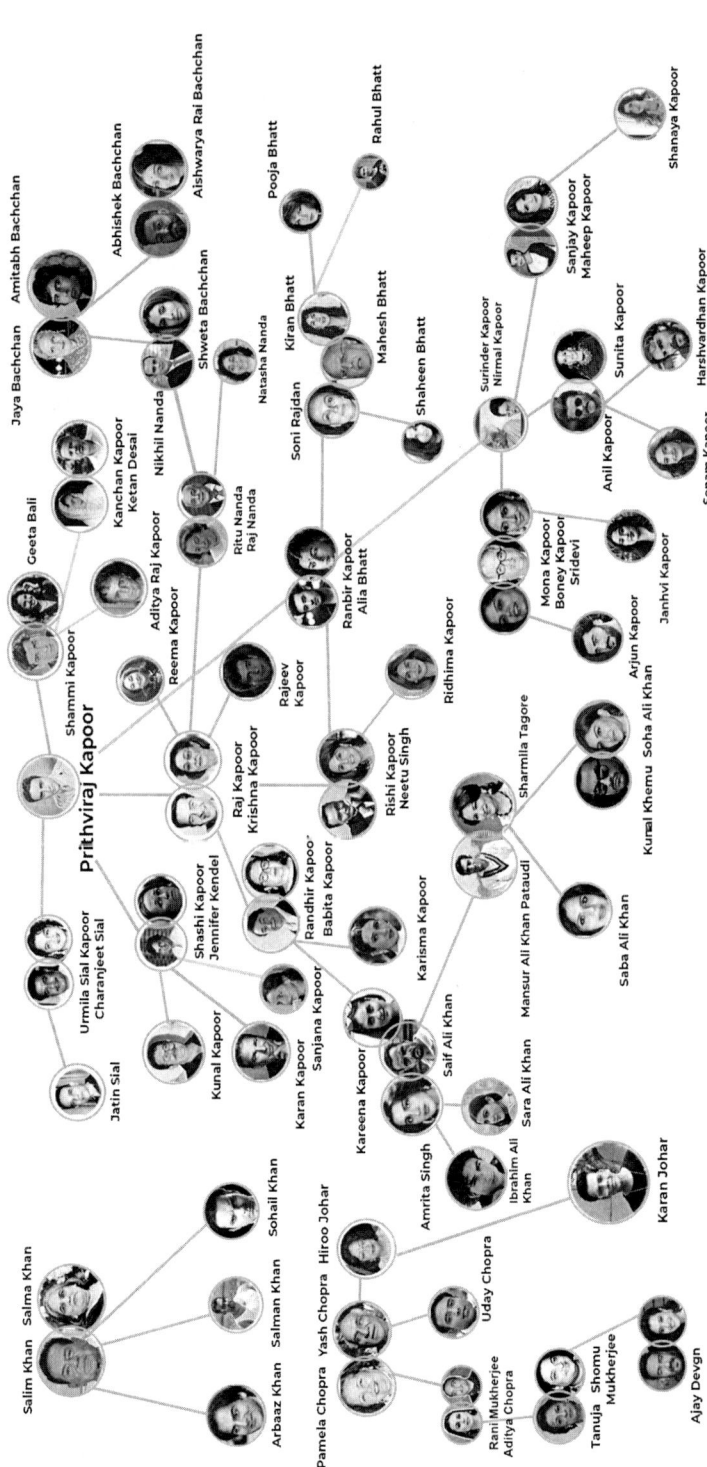

Figure 5.2 Endogamous ties in Bollywood

Source: Prepared by the author.

recreates nepotistic barriers to entry and the acquisition of similar power for other star nodes within the existing structure. There is also considerable affect in the success stories of star progeny that bring together collective identities of the star clan, an extension of the affective story brand of male stars like Raj Kapoor and Amitabh Bachchan. The weddings as public spectacles also feed into the Bollywoodization discourse wherein these personal events function as mediated spectacles to generate affect for the next generation of star descendants, which has its own charm with fan networks and supplements the brand value of the star clan. Hence, a star like Bhatt, whose family owns an established family-led production company, possesses the effective centrality, despite her gender, to start her own production and related businesses. Her efforts are further supported by another strong business node in the Bollywood network, SRK's Red Chillies, and by Netflix's offers to be their distribution platform.

While Netflix and Amazon Prime Video are considered disruptors within the global media landscape, as I noted earlier, within the Indian market, they structurally conform to the dominant star- or family-led business network structure. Within a 'corporate' framing, the dynamic replicates the same stratified power hierarchies wherein power remains concerted and functions through key male actors and business nodes within this network. A simple instance of this power working within the contemporary networked Bollywood structure is encapsulated in Netflix's recent announcement of a Bollywood adaptation of the American comic book series *Archies* (2023). *Archies* previously spawned the CW hit *Riverdale* (2017–present) in the US, which was later acquired by Netflix.

To launch its high-profile musical remake of *Archies* in India, Netflix hired Zoya Akhtar, part of Bollywood's multigenerational film family, to direct and produce the film under the aegis of Tiger Baby Films, her home production. The main protagonists of the film, Archie, Betty, and Veronica, will be essayed by the next generation of Bollywood stars from established star-led film clans, namely Agastya Nanda (Bachchan's grandson), Suhana Khan (SRK's daughter), and Khushi Kapoor (Sridevi—also known as 'female Bachchan' for her box-office pull, recall Chapter 2—and producer Boney Kapoor's daughter). As an Indian journalist covering this announcement commented, 'the stars invariably belong to what has been described as the Bollywood banyan tree, which symbolizes the interconnectedness of the different branches of an Indian family distinct from the birch tree of Hollywood'.[29] Such structural embeddedness of star nodes within the industry network helps cement and sustain alliances as well as production and distribution partnerships that aid them in pursuing their self-interest and producing joint benefits.[30] Hence, partnering with Bollywood's star-led production system and fitting within its structure, which is evolving yet remains dominated by family and close ties, makes business sense even for so-called disruptors like Netflix and Amazon Prime Video.

While Bollywood's structural model of small-world, star-led, family-oriented ties that have been absorbed into the networked corporate structure is distinctive from Hollywood, it is also similar in that nodes like Netflix have created interstitial spaces for agency and diverse voices, especially for stars. Though the new crop of actors possesses a different type of agency and relational power, it is not a stand-alone excessive power that would enable them to be a 'switch' to turn on new connections. However, the interconnected organizational web that I term 'contemporary networked Bollywood' stands to relatively support their power and build on it in its bid for global expansion. From Huma Qureshi to Ali Fazal, even the second rung of Bollywood actors can now access Hollywood and perform in global crossover films because, given the evolution of industrial structure, there now exists an infrastructure in the form of talent and casting agencies to support that crossover. As Qureshi herself notes, 'My agents [at CAA] asked if I'd want to meet a casting director who was working on a big [Hollywood] film', and she landed a role in Zack Snyder's zombie heist film, *Army of the Dead* (2021).[31] Fazal similarly credits the happenstance of his agent knowing the opportunity that helped him get crossover Hollywood roles. The industrial flux with other structural disruptors like Netflix also makes production ventures accessible to some of these stars. After repeated Hollywood casting and critical acclaim in *Victoria & Abdul* (2017, dir. Stephen Frears), Fazal recently launched a production company, Pushing Buttons Studios, with his partner and co-actor, Richa Chadha. Their first venture, *Girls Will Be Girls*—currently under production and being directed by a debutant female director, Suchi Talati—is an Indo-French collaboration, a prospect that has Fazal enthused. With his ambitious production house, Fazal aims to create a

> mutually beneficial ecosystem of artists. [Pushing Buttons Studios] is more like a portal for artists to come and jam and collaborate and not to get held back because that was the biggest issue we faced when we were starting off. We are also ensuring that artistes get a piece of the pie to the point of even having shares in the profit.[32]

Crediting the rise of OTTs, Fazal notes that 'it is because the business models have opened up … there are more opportunities for everybody'.[33]

On the one hand, the multiplicity of streaming platforms in India has become a leveller in democratizing opportunities for the second rung of stars, retired Bollywood actors, and even character actors who have benefitted from the explosion of OTT content and platforms. Currently, there are over fifty streaming services in India representing the spectrum of global, national, and regional companies. According to PricewaterhouseCoopers (PwC), India is the fastest growing market for video-streaming platforms, 'set to power global growth'.[34] Netflix has invested over USD 400 million to license or co-produce Indian content in the hopes that their next 100 million users would come from India. Amazon Prime Video has a similar strategy. On the other hand, these changes have created an interesting power dynamic wherein a newer lower rung of stars also can mobilize a managed and negotiated agency alongside the megastars. In the past, as this book has illustrated, agency or switching power was possessed aplenty by individual megastars and demonstrably operated in different ways. The newer nodes like streaming platforms and a plethora of nodes such as talent, marketing, and casting agencies are recalibrating that structure wherein certain pre-existing elite formations are being reproduced. Although it is creating interstitial spaces of negotiated agency for a broader swathe of actors who are not necessarily stars with the ability to be switches or catalytic mobilizers. The industry structure itself has transformed (albeit currently in a fluid state) to support the embedded practices where stars have a distinctive centrality in the industry hierarchy. The contemporary Bollywood network is geographically expansive and more globally pertinent today than it has been in the past. Thus, recursively, streaming disruptions in the global space are creating a Bollywoodization of Hollywood. It is an osmosis of industrial formations wherein we see structural and formation mobilization where stars in Hollywood, too, are gaining more agency within the business.

The structural changes in conglomerate Hollywood due to the disruptions by streaming platforms are creating an industrial structure like Bollywood, with stars like Reese Witherspoon asserting that with the pent-up demand for content, now is the time for a change: 'Now we're going to have the ability to tell more stories, to hire more female filmmakers, to promote and lift up even more authors.'[35] The star as the producer and businessperson is gaining primacy in the Hollywood industrial discourse in what the *Hollywood Reporter* identified as the moment when 'streaming wars [are] further disrupting Hollywood hierarchies and upend[ing] conventional wisdom about audiences, creators and distributors [in the] dynamic landscape of entertainment power'.[36] The *Hollywood Reporter* list included, apart from Witherspoon and Will Smith, twenty-four actor-producers like Leonardo DiCaprio, Jennifer Lopez, Tiffany Haddish, Lin-Manuel Miranda, Margot Robbie, Issa Rae, and Phoebe Waller-Bridge. Brad Pitt's Plan B Entertainment was especially highlighted for its two Oscar contenders, *Vice* (2018, dir. Adam McKay) and *If Beale Street Could Talk* (2018, dir. Barry Jenkins).[37] Pitt's Plan B has since produced an Oscar winner in *Minari* (2020, dir. Lee Issac Chung). Perhaps fittingly, when SRK and Pitt got together for an interview while the latter was in India to promote *War Machine* (2017, dir. David Michôd), Plan B's first collaboration with Netflix and SRK's Red Chillies had just released their globally ambitious *Dilwale* (2015, dir. Rohit Shetty) and signed a post-theatrical run release agreement with the streamer. Predictably, Netflix self-branded itself at this Indian event as 'Netflix: Home to King Khan [as SRK is popularly known for his ubiquitous presence and popularity]'.[38]

The moment of acknowledgement of the deep-seated difference in industrial structure between the Indian and American contexts occurs when the interviewer, Rajeev Masand, addresses both stars' production efforts and notes the length of time SRK has been in the business of production. It is followed by an anecdote by SRK about his first production business venture, Dreamz Unlimited, with Juhi Chawla and Aziz Mirza in the 1990s (recall Chapter 3). Their film, he notes, was financed by a construction company owner, who agreed to lose money on SRK because SRK was so good.[39] Whether it is the Hindujas, India's industrial conglomerate distributing Raj Kapoor's films internationally when there was no infrastructure for international distribution, or a construction company owner financing SRK's first film, the affective pull that engenders and mobilizes elite fan networks has been endemic to the story of Bollywood's male megastars' switching power. However, the structural disruptions brought about by new nodes like talent agencies, casting agencies, and streaming platforms within India and the momentary disruption caused by streamers in the Hollywood context have challenged power hierarchies in both contexts. Albeit momentarily, the presence of Netflix, Amazon Prime Video, and other platforms has created an interstitial agency for stars like Pitt and Witherspoon to carve a space for themselves as businesspersons within the conglomerate Hollywood structure. Pitt notes in the interview this democratization of film-making in that he can now back 'risky' films as a producer, something that the studio system in Hollywood cannot support. Does this moment represent a structural

Bollywoodization of Hollywood? Perhaps it is a juncture of momentary agency. Netflix's currently flailing position within this structure brings into question this interstitial moment of power for stars beyond a 'dependent independence' that is being structurally resisted in Hollywood. One key instance of this apparent change, at the same time that some of the dominant power structures still remain strong, would be the sale of Witherspoon's Hello Sunshine to Candle Media, a company owned by two former Disney executives and backed by Blackstone, one of the US's largest private equity firms.[40]

In contrast, in Bollywood, where star productions have been structurally dominant since the 1950s, the coming of talent agencies and global and local streaming has changed the balance of power but differently across various rungs of stars. For the new crop of Bollywood actors who do not have the wherewithal to own an entertainment or media entity and to afford in-house PR, marketing, and talent management, their representative agencies define their careers. In the words of Vijay Subramaniam, the CEO and co-founder of Collective Artists Network, India's leading talent agency, 'the agency makes the star'.[41] They make 'the best infrastructure available to make their talents shine. We have created an entire infrastructure that interacts with the world of entertainment. We manage not just stars. We manage writers, directors and so we do literally everything from financing to script doctoring to putting together [an] entire project'.[42] Subramaniam's language reveals the corporatization of an industry ecosystem that, until a couple of decades ago, was reliant on one manager to take care of everything, a mantra that most stars relied on. Leading stars like Bachchan, SRK, and Aamir Khan still operate within the older model, although their business operations themselves are corporatized. Several of the now-corporatized family film-production clusters like Yash Raj Films, Karan Johar's Dharma Productions, and Bollywood star Salman Khan have started their talent agencies: YRF Talent, Dharma Cornerstone Agency, and Uniworld Being Talented, respectively. In the contemporary networked structure within Bollywood, the multiplicity of nodes brings in many variables altering or even challenging the power structures. While some structures are changing to be more Hollywood-like, others are corporatizing in a distinctive Bollywood way, where male megastars and established family-led industry nodes retain their effective industrial (albeit corporatized) power and impart a negotiated power to the next rung of stars and actors mentioned earlier. However, the very multiplicity also creates interstitial moments of structural agency that challenge the gendered dynamic of this star-driven and family-cluster network structure. This transitionary concursion offers female stars like Anushka Sharma and Deepika Padukone, outsiders to Bollywood family clusters, the power and ability to exist as significant nodes within the networked industrial dynamic. However, how this structure further develops and unfolds remains to be seen. At the beginning of this narrative about Bollywood globalization, I identified the star, the state, and the industry as the critical actants within Bollywood's structural transformation, likening them to a scalar, global network with multiple stakeholders. Despite the transformations that are evident and many that are still to unfold, the established stars—the Khans, Bachchans, Kapoors, and so on—are firmly embedded in positions of power within the industrial–organizational networked structure. Another vector that has changed simultaneously is the industry's relationship with the Indian state. Since 2014, under Modi's leadership, the Indian state has been savvy in understanding the soft power and media-power discourse and manipulating it to their advantage, leading up to moments like the now-famous Bollywood selfie with Modi.

STAR SWITCHING POWER AND THE STATE

On 10 January 2019, popular Bollywood director Karan Johar tweeted a selfie of Indian prime minister Narendra Modi flanked by Bollywood stars and directors. The tweet marked the moment as an 'incredible opportunity to interact with [Modi]', positioning the Hindi film industry as 'the world's largest industry' that, together with the Modi-led state, '[hoped] to inspire and ignite positive changes towards a transformative India'.[43] This selfie posted by Johar, which consisted largely of the new crop of Bollywood stars, is emblematic of the power of the state, the deliberate harnessing of 'star power', and Bollywood's affective brand association to relationally and osmotically create affect for the Indian national leader, Modi. The affect of the image is distinctive in that Modi is flanked by the new crop of stars: Varun Dhawan, Ranveer Singh, Ayushman Khurana, Bhumi Pendakur, Ranbir Kapoor, Rajkumar Rao, Vicky Kaushal, and Siddharth Malhotra.[44] The aesthetic of the selfie that positions the political leader, Modi, at the centre of the frame, surrounded by a multitude of Bollywood stars whom Modi termed 'popular film personalities' in his follow-up tweet, eclipses the affective potential that any of the stars possess individually. There is a transference of their cumulative affect onto the political leader, Modi, who stands aggrandized by the adulatory framing. The purpose of recounting this social media transaction at the end of this book is twofold. The first is to highlight the visible shift in Bollywood's position vis-à-vis the state. Whereas Hindi cinema has historically narrated the nation, its liminality in relation to the government and the government's consequent disdain for Bollywood helped stars with elite sociopolitical networks and excessive affective power emerge as switches that could work around the state and make new circuits and connections visible. In the wake of a political leader like Modi entrenched in propagandizing through media and leveraging existing marketing, PR, and media and entertainment networks, the potential for the kind of stand-alone switching power that someone like Bachchan or SRK could possess is dwindling. For the new generation of stars, switching power does not exist in the same way because they are often being mobilized through political networks; the obverse, which was true for the existing megastars, is not necessarily true for them. Second, this selfie points to a convergent Hollywood-like transmedia stardom that is fashioned through social media but is increasingly orchestrated and controlled not by the stars themselves but rather, as talent agency CEO Subramaniam construes his ilk, 'the star makers'.[45]

The contemporary Indian state under Modi epitomizes a deliberate *celebritization* of the political sphere, which is now deeply intertwined with the media. Compared with governments of the past that either derided or ignored Bollywood, the celebritized Indian state under Modi is media-savvy.[46] Elsewhere, I have theorized about what is the celebritized political sphere and how the notion applies to the Indian context.[47] A celebritized media-savvy Indian state under Modi marks a coming together of celebrity, media, and the PR and marketing machinery, which can be mobilized to serve political, national, and global geopolitical interests. A Modi-led celebritized Indian state exemplifies a perspicacious politic that understands and can mobilize the power of media across multiple valences. The Bollywood industry and its megastars have consistently been vital to this media mobilization for political imperatives. Hence, at the height of a border skirmish between India and China in 2017 over the disputed territory of Doklam, which is claimed by Bhutan and supported by India, Modi utilized Aamir Khan's *Dangal* as a means to de-escalate the brewing geopolitical tension. At an ensuing political rally, Modi proudly proclaimed that 'China's President told me … that he had watched the movie "Dangal," which made him feel pride in the state of

Haryana [the setting for the movie]'.[48] Aware of Khan's growing popularity in China, Modi timed his visit to China to coincide with Khan's film promotion tour, although Khan claimed he had no knowledge of Modi's plans and that it was a coincidence that they were in China at the same time.[49] Later, Modi also hoped to appoint Khan as a brand ambassador to promote trade between the two countries, which also could not materialize. Between the Bollywood selfie, an impromptu diplomatic move anchored to a Bollywood megastar, and more deliberate brand construction for Modi himself through the transference of celebrity affect by orchestrating interviews and events conducted by stars, the role of the state within networked Bollywood is decidedly different.

How are these deep relational changes apropos the state altering the power hierarchies and star switching power? Two significant Bollywood events and their political imbroglio point to the media-savvy Modi state's strategy to use Bollywood as a tool for political distraction channelled through stars and star affect. First, I think it is vital to state that under Modi, the media, technology, PR, and marketing have a newfound relevance in the Indian political sphere, which marks a distinctive break from past governments. Second, Bollywood, India's most prominent cultural industry, is gradually and noticeably becoming integrated with the Indian state's power, influence, and agenda, sometimes overtly and sometimes in a nebulous way, as a tool for political distraction in a nation of ardent Bollywood followers.

At the peak of the Covid-19 pandemic in 2020, when cases in India were rising by nearly 100,000 a day, and simultaneously a bellicose China was amassing troops on the Indian border, the Indian media had shifted its concerted attention to a group of Bollywood stars. The pandemic and Chinese border incursions were ignored in favour of solving the mysterious suicide of Bollywood actor Sushant Singh Rajput, who was a part of the new crop of rising Bollywood actors. His suicide provoked a media frenzy with multiple tales about the prevalence of drugs in Bollywood and assertions of foul play managed by Bollywood's small-world nodes to oust Rajput because he was a rising star. The fact that Rajput was an outsider from the state of Bihar— where state elections were impending for Modi's political party, the BJP—is a revealing lens to access this story. The story gained mammoth proportions in the news, positing a simple rustic Bihari (high-caste Rajput) whose virtue was corrupted by the wickedness of the big city and the degenerate Mumbai film world. Kangana Ranaut, a contemporary female star and supporter of the BJP, in characteristic performative women's empowerment move emblematic of Modi's BJP, added further intrigue and glamour with her public opinions about nepotism in Bollywood. The Supreme Court waded in, and three federal agencies investigated the case. Eventually, the actor's death was confirmed to be a suicide. However, the incident diverted public attention and garnered enough sympathy in Bihar for Modi's political party to win the state elections.

The second significant event was the arrest of Bollywood megastar SRK's son Aryan Khan for consuming drugs at a party. The event happened amidst the massive ongoing farmer protests in India, which were exacerbated when a BJP worker ran over a group of protesting farmers. The incident evoked multiple responses from various quarters, including the conservative BJP faction that favours an aggressive Hindutva nationalism, which is a distortion of the tenets of Hindu beliefs created by careful orchestration of the Indian state under Modi.[50] SRK, of course, being at the nexus of sociocultural and political power, received immense support from other political parties such as the Shiv Sena in Maharashtra, also a Hindu-oriented party, as well as from the film industry and his fans in India and abroad. His son's arrest in the context of the Modi government thwarting a Muslim actor was covered by major national and international news outlets such as the *Washington Post* and CNN, although SRK's star persona is the embodiment of secular India: he is married to a Hindu wife, was educated in a Catholic school, and is publicly known for having a shrine of all gods in his home. The more pertinent question then becomes: is mapping political agendas onto powerful stand-alone megastars like SRK a foreboding of pernicious political power and influence that could create new hierarchies of star switching power? In an industry that traces its roots to a syncretic amalgamation of Sanskrit dramaturgy and folk forms with Parsi theatre and whose formative structure was built on the labour of the practitioners of Parsi theatre, Muslim identities are as prevalent as Hindu identities and are curiously intermeshed. All top stars in the industry are Muslim with deep-seated Hindu family ties.[51] In the contemporary iteration of star switching power in networked Bollywood, various questions inflect the future morphosis of that power. Will the star nodes who possess it be the ones who collaborate with the now media-savvy Indian state in specific ways to reflect its larger goals nationally and internationally? While the stand-alone power of certain megastars like SRK is questioned, it still stands to reason that they are the core of the industry. Despite the state's newfound interest in utilizing Bollywood as a distraction strategy or in the interest of geopolitical soft power, will it transform or impact the well-established small-world ties and hierarchies? What space do the women stars occupy in this masculinist industry's emerging hierarchy? Would it be one of performative empowerment projected by the Modi state's new agendas that anchor their solipsistic politics to aggrandize the divine feminine in Hinduism to turn female stars like Ranaut into mouthpieces? Or does breaking up hierarchical power through disruptions in industry structure and renewed state interest create spaces for a real interstitial agency? How is the state interest creating different dimensions of star switching power and celebritized state power that is similarly vested in stand-alone individual political actors like Modi and new types of stratified power of film-industry actors like Aamir Khan?

STAR SWITCHING AND POWER IN A NETWORKED WORLD

In sum, what does the heuristic of star switching that this book theorized help us see about power? That is, what insights does it offer into the ways power operates through and beyond individuals? Moreover, what do star power's epistemic centrality and its ability to 'switch' across multiple realms of the industrial, sociocultural, and geopolitical—realms that the entertainment industry actively interconnects—let us see about macro power structures? While the main focus of this book has been on power within Hindi cinema's evolving entertainment industry, the story told here illuminates forms of power that exceed the operational power of industrial actors. It emphasizes the self-realization of power at an epistemic level by these stars in question. The conjunction of epistemic power and the self-realization of potential new directions for this power were critical to the stars' ability and willingness to be the switches that would illuminate the global pathways of Hindi cinema and its expansion across various industrial and political borders.

For instance, star switching power as a heuristic helps reveal a form of geopolitical, cultural power centred on stars as non-state actors. This form of power blurs the boundaries between public or cultural diplomacy and creative or content industries because, despite operating in a non-state-centric framework, stars facilitate the projection of appealing images of a nation state. Aamir Khan in China provides an exemplary case where lateral cinematic ties that started with pirate flows of cinema and social media networks become an empowering anomaly. It establishes that fan or audience agency, and thereby star affect, can forge an alternate framework for cultural attractions and power that works through individual social actors outside of state-centric discourses. Despite the Hindi film industry remaining peripheral for the state and not legitimized as an industry for over eight decades of its existence, stars carved out a discursive space for cultural diplomacy. The fandom economy for stars like Kapoor, Bachchan, or contemporary megastars SRK, Khan, and Chopra delineates how the circulation of Bollywood's malleable cultural form, channelled through these stars, mobilized the Indian nation's intangible soft power. Furthermore, this epistemic power and centrality in the contemporary moment are attaining a new form through affective sensoriums of digital technology that are vital conduits in influencing and shaping opinion across an interconnected globe. One follower of Khan, pointing to his own myopic understanding of India, called on other liberal-minded Chinese voices to understand that 'the way we look at India is like how the Western world had looked at China for many years', and it was time for that to change.[52] As this example shows, star switching power in the realm of cultural diplomacy has a more meaningful impact than top-down formulations of 'soft-power'-centring state objectives.

Significantly, every iteration of power that star switching reveals, including the realm of cultural diplomacy, unmasks deep-seated gendered structures where men get the hierarchy-enhancing roles. Parsing the gendered industrial power illuminates how gender inequality is dynamically related to other forms of group-based inequality, such as social class, caste, and religion. Yet the case of beauty queens offers additional information about the gendered dimensions of power in cultural diplomacy and how it changed over time. For instance, in the 1950s, Bollywood male megastar Raj Kapoor, during his travels to Russia, was allocated a coupe reserved for the czars, while Nargis, also a stunning and charismatic star, was ignored by the Russians during her state-sponsored visit to Moscow and not even provided the basic courtesy of an airport pickup and drop-off, largely because of her gender.[53] Later, however, the female star and beauty queen's embodiment of aesthetic capital, beauty, and charm was overtly translated into a global cache for nation-branding. While elements of exceptional beauty and auratic charm have always been central to affective star power for both male and female stars, these elements overdetermined the female star's agency. What the global beauty queen or Bollywood star could do with this agency, however, took on new meanings when the Indian nation state began actively vying for a place in the global economy in the 1990s. This gendered power in cultural diplomacy is grounded in affective regimes and intertwined in global commodity consumption networks that have accelerated and assumed larger proportions in the contemporary context.

The structural change in gendered power became demonstrably visible in the late 1990s and 2000s when beauty-queens-turned-Bollywood-stars like Aishwarya Rai were being conferred the highest civilian honours by the French or had the Dutch name tulips after them. The newfound affective agency of certain female stars, as seen through international beauty pageant winners like Rai, was negotiated through a gendered dynamic and at a time when the networked industry was incorporating powerful, global, corporate industrial nodes into its rapidly evolving ecosystem alongside a state that was actively invested in propelling these changes. In this process, a few female stars, like Rai and Chopra, came to constitute new nodes of influence and power in the industry, wielding star switching power that had previously been limited almost exclusively to elite men. Although sometimes limited by gendered institutional hierarchies, this period does represent a significant evolution in the female star's switching power.

Most importantly, this book theorized that power is constituted by a dynamic relationship that is never static and changes contextually. It has done this by sculpting an analytic that helped examine power relations from micro to macro structures. Star switching power, we have seen, is a power that emanates as industrial and sociocultural star power, expands to the realm of soft, national, or political power, and manifests as a deeply gendered phenomenon across these multiple variegated yet interwoven domains. This book has presented the story of the globalization of the Indian Hindi film industry across eight decades as more than an industrial, business, or cultural history. The story it has told also offers a meta-reflection on the dynamics of power, tracing its interdependence with political, sociocultural, industrial, and geopolitical systems, consistently locating individual agency within these structures. It grappled with the dynamics of individual star power, locating specific stars' embeddedness in institutional structures and the micro workings of power filtered across class, caste, gender, and affective capital that culminates as star switching power. The book compels us to reflect on who gets to have this sticky hierarchical power giving them the ability to influence the global trajectory of an industry.

NOTES

INTRODUCTION

1. The IIFA, Bollywood's international award show, had chosen Tampa as its 2014 venue because, according to the IIFA organizers, Wizcraft, the city had shown an appetite for Indian glamour, and its tourism leaders were aggressive in their willingness to host the event, beating the other contenders, Orlando and Miami. Moreover, the United States (US), especially Florida, has a significant Indian-American population. For more, see Tamara Lush, 'Indian Film Awards Arrive in Tampa, Fla., but Why?' Yahoo Finance, 23 April 2014, https://finance.yahoo.com/news/indian-film-awards-arrive-tampa-110627041.html (accessed 21 December 2022).

2. For more on the types of business events and forums held in Tampa, see University of South Florida, 'FICCI-IIFA Global Business Forum 2014', Muma College of Business, University of South Florida, 1 April 2014, https://www.usf.edu/business/documents/iifa/iifa-schedule.pdf (accessed 20 December 2022).

3. On 'Bollywoodization', see Ashish Rajadhyakshya, 'The "Bollywoodization" of the Indian Cinema: Cultural Nationalism in a Global Arena', *Inter-Asia Cultural Studies* 4, no. 1 (2003): 25–39, which uses the term to explain the phenomenon of the expansion of Bollywood from cinema to a global culture industry.

4. Press Trust of India, 'IE Entertainment', *Indian Express*, 8 April 2014, http://indianexpress.com/article/entertainment/bollywood/anil-kapoor-to-launch-entertainment-firm-in-dubai/ (accessed 28 February 2017).

5. Nyay Bhushan, 'Bollywood Star Anil Kapoor Launches Production Company', *Hollywood Reporter*, 10 April 2014, 1–2.

6. The formal announcement to include Bollywood in the state-approved industries eligible for state support and benefits was made in 1998, but it took a few years for the regulations to be implemented and for the benefits to trickle down. By 2001, some support infrastructure was in place, and banks were allocating loans to filmmakers and producers. For more, see Shankar V. Aiyar and Anupama Chopra, 'Bollywood Hazy about New Industry Status but Expects Business to Get Streamlined Now', *India Today*, 25 May 1998, 1–3.

7. When 'industry' is used in this book, it refers to not only a meta-formation that includes the prominent actors I just described but also other actors and stakeholders that get added as critical participants within the more extensive global network.

8. Megastars are worshipped by fans and ardent followers. There are many temples in India dedicated to stars like Amitabh Bachchan. However, there is more significant scholarship on stars as 'celluloid deities' in the context of south Indian films. For more, see Preminda Jacob, *Celluloid Deities: The Visual Culture of Cinema and Politics in South India* (Washington, DC: Lexington Books, 2009).

9. This approach is distinct from Bruno Latour and Michel Callon's actor–network theory (ANT). ANT understands human and non-human actors as equally able to act. In contrast, relational sociology considers non-human actors as unable to create meaning, even though they are part of social networks. Furthermore, in relational sociology, the analyst assigns who and what counts for the analysis, whereas ANT follows an open interpretative approach, letting the actors studied make the connections themselves. For more, see Sophie Mutzel, 'Networks as Culturally Constituted Processes: A Comparison of Relational Sociology and Actor–Network Theory', *Current Sociology* 57, no. 6 (2009): 871–887.

10. The understanding of sociocultural power is derived from sociological network theories building on scholars like Amelia Arsenault, Manuel Castells, Celia Ridgeway, and others like Stephen Borgatti, whose work on organization networks and power informs my understanding of how star power functions within the industry business. Besides other film and media studies, scholars like Patrick Jagoda, Elena Gorfinkel, and Tami Williams have emphasized the need to frame and understand contemporary film and media aesthetics and business formations as networks. This book

positions Bollywood as an industry where a networked model was germane to the industry structure and evolved from a modest, global network to an intensified networked structure with multiple global nodes and hubs.

11. According to Manuel Castells, a sociologist renowned for his work on globalization, communication, and information society, switchers are social actors who, because of their position in the social structure, hold network-making power—the paramount form of power in the network society. Manuel Castells, 'A Network Theory of Power', *International Journal of Communication* 5 (2011): 773–787.

12. Aswin Punathambekar's excellent work is critical to understanding the 'corporatization' of the Indian Hindi film industry starting in the early 2000s. He defines corporatization as 'a moment of industrial transformation whose broader discourse and derivativeness has haunted the Bollywood film industry'. Broadly, corporatization is a heterogeneous 'media space being shaped by a productive, if at times uneasy, coexistence of capitalistic practices defined as much by kinship networks and interpersonal relations as by modes of speculative practices and risk management that Hollywood has rendered globally recognizable'. For more, see Aswin Punathambekar, *From Bombay to Bollywood: The Making of a Global Media Industry* (New York: New York University Press, 2013).

13. Raymond Williams, 'Dominant, Residual, and Emergent', in *Marxism and Literature*, 121–127 (Oxford: Oxford University Press, 1977).

14. Mats Forsgren, Ulf Holm, and Jan Johanson, *Knowledge, Networks, and Power: The Uppasala School of International Business* (Basingstoke: Palgrave Macmillan, 2015). The authors at the Uppasala School have conceptualized the idea of a market as a business network that is based on the assumption that long-term business actors engage in long-lasting relationships that become important for business growth and internationalization.

15. For more on history as method, see Roy Suddaby, 'Toward a Historical Consciousness: Following the Historic Turn in Management Thought', *Management* 19, no. 1 (2016): 46–60; Wim Van Lent and Gabrielle Durepos, 'Nurturing the Historic Turn: "History as Theory" versus "History as Method"', *Journal of Management History* 25, no. 4 (2019): 429–435.

16. Ibid.

17. Ashish Rajadhyaksha, 'The "Bollywoodization" of the Indian Cinema: Cultural Nationalism in a Global Arena', *Inter-Asia Cultural Studies* 4, no. 1 (2003): 25–39.

18. Ravinder Kaur, *Brand New Nation: Capitalist Dreams and Nationalist Designs in Twenty-First-Century India* (Redwood City, CA: Stanford University Press, 2020).

19. *The Guardian*, 'Millennium Dome Hosts the Bollywood Oscars', 26 June 2000, https://www.theguardian.com/film/2000/jun/26/bollywood.news (accessed 10 June 2023).

20. For more on ideas of the push, pull, and squeeze of the global, see Keri E. Iyall Smith, *Sociology of Globalization: Cultures, Economies, and Politics* (New York: Routledge, 2013).

21. David Held, Anthony McGrew, David Goldblatt, and Jonathan Perraton, *Global Transformations: Politics, Economics and Culture* (Redwood City, CA: Stanford University Press, 1999).

22. For more on relational sociology, see Mustafa Emirbayer, 'Manifesto for Relational Sociology', *American Journal of Sociology* 103, no. 2 (1997): 281–317; Mustafa Emirbayer and Jeff Goodwin, 'Network Analysis, Culture and the Problem of Agency', *American Journal of Sociology* 99, no. 6 (1994): 1411–1454. Emirbayer's perspective brings together a range of studies under the heading of relational sociology, also including and analytically building on Pierre Bourdieu, Andrew Abbott, and Charles Tilly.

23. An interdisciplinary understanding of networks from sociology, social network analysis, and business management organization are germane to my articulation of a network framework in this discourse of media industries and star power. For the relevance of a network framework to film and media studies, see Patrick Jagoda, *Network Aesthetics* (Chicago: University of Chicago Press, 2016) and Elena Gorfinkel and Tami Williams, *Global Cinema Networks* (New Brunswick, NJ: Rutgers University Press, 2018).

24. For more, see Forsgren, Holm, and Johanson, *Knowledge, Networks, and Power* and Michael Keane, 'Cultural Technology Transfer: Redefining Content in the Chinese Television Industry', *Emergences: Journal for the Study of Media & Composite Cultures* 11, no. 2 (2001): 223–236.

25. For more on network ontology, refer to communication studies scholars Alexander R. Galloway and Eugene Thacker, *The Exploit: A Theory of Networks* (Minneapolis, MN: University of Minnesota Press, 2007), 60.

26. Networks as a concept and heuristic have been used in economics, social theory, technology, management, and various contemporary theorizations of network society, including media aesthetics and distribution. See Vincent August, 'Network Concepts in Social Theory: Foucault and

Cybernetics', *European Journal of Social Theory* 25, no. 2 (2022): 271–291. See also Jagoda, *Network Aesthetics* for media aesthetics and networks, and Gorfinkel and Williams, *Global Cinema Networks* for cinema distribution and networks.

27. For more on spreadable media and convergence, see Henry Jenkins, Joshua Green, and Sam Ford, *Spreadable Media: Creating Value and Meaning in a Networked Culture* (New York: New York University Press, 2013).

28. Nandini Raghvendra, 'Ashok and Ambika Hinduja Combination All Set to Change Rules', *Economic Times*, 16 January 2010, https://economictimes. indiatimes.com/business-of-bollywood/ashok-and-ambika-hinduja-combination-all-set-to-change-rules/articleshow/5450566.cms (accessed 29 June 2022).

29. Wendy Hui Kyong Chun, 'Networks Now: Belated Too Early', in *Postdigital Aesthetics: Art, Computation and Design*, ed. David Berry and Michael Deiter, 289–315 (London: Palgrave Macmillan, 2015).

30. A recent example of thinking of a network as a form in literary theory is Caroline Levine, *Forms: Whole, Rhythm, Hierarchy, Network* (Princeton, NJ: Princeton University Press, 2015).

31. Elena Gorfinkel, 'Introduction: Global Cinema in a Time of Networks', in *Global Cinema Networks*, by Gorfinkel and Williams, 1–20 (New Jersey: Rutgers University Press, 2018).

32. Jennifer A. Starr and Andrea Larson, 'A Network Model of Organization Formation', *Entrepreneurship: Theory and Practice* 17, no. 2 (1993): 5–15, 5.

33. Janet Staiger, Ann Cvetkovich, and Ann Reynolds, *Political Emotions: New Agendas in Communication* (London: Routledge, 2010), 4.

34. A hub is a node with a number of links to other nodes that greatly exceeds the average.

35. Rani belonged to the crème de la crème of Indian society. She was the grandniece of Nobel laureate Rabindranath Tagore, daughter of the first Indian surgeon general, M. N. Chaudhary, and educated at the Royal Academy of Dramatic Arts and Music in London. At a time when female actors were conspicuously outside the realm of bourgeois, nationalist, and patriarchal 'respectability', Rani possessed significant social and cultural capital that could help her overcome the taboos associated with women actors in Hindi films. She also possessed an elite 'globality' that was markedly different from other female actors at the time.

36. Cecilia L. Ridgeway, 'Framed before We Know It: How Gender Shapes Social Relations', *Gender and Society* 23, no. 2 (2009): 145–160.

37. Sean Redmond, 'The Whiteness of Stars: Looking at Kate Winslet's Unruly White Body', in *Stardom and Celebrity: A Reader*, ed. Sean Redmond and Su Holmes, 263–275 (London: Sage Publications, 2007).

38. Carolyn Pedwell, 'Affective (Self-)Transformations: Empathy, Neoliberalism, and International Development', *Feminist Theory* 13, no. 2 (2012): 163–179.

39. For instance, Satyajit Ray, arguably one of the most renowned Indian filmmakers in the West, was a part of this state-initiated parallel cinema network. His films were an integral part of all of the state-initiated international cultural exchanges and festivals.

40. Aseem Chhabra, 'Raj Kapoor, The Relentless Romantic, Was India's First Crossover Filmmaker', *India Today*, 16 September 2017, https://www. indiatoday.in/magazine/news-makers/story/20170925-raj-kapoor-joseph-stalin-delhi-nehru-prithviraj-kapoor-rajya-sabha-1045131-2017-09-16 (accessed 2 July 2021).

41. For more see, Jan Melissen, *The New Public Diplomacy Soft Power in International Relations* (London: Palgrave Macmillan, 2005).

42. Susanna Paasonen, Ken Hillis, and Michael Petit, *Networked Affect* (Cambridge, MA: MIT Press, 2015), 3.

43. For more on the enormity of SRK's stardom, see David Letterman's *My Next Guest Needs No Introduction*, aired on 25 October 2019 (season 2, episode 14).

44. Paasonen, Hillis, and Petit, *Networked Affect*.

45. Sara Ahmed, *The Cultural Politics of Emotion* (Oxfordshire: Routledge, 2014).

46. Paul Booth, *Digital Fandom: New Media Studies* (New York: Peter Lang, 2010).

47. There is a space–time compression that, the geographer David Harvey notes, characterizes contemporary globalization. Castells argued that this space–time compression created a new kind of space for interaction in society that has distinctive characteristics. This space of flows is comprised of interactions and the material characteristics that make up those interactions possible, and the space is shaping up our society's organization both materially and immaterially. However, this book predominantly focuses on material factors through powerful human actors within a global space of flows. For more on space of flows, see Manuel Castells, *The Information Age: Economy, Society, and Culture*, vol. 1: *The Rise of the Network Society* (Cambridge, MA: Blackwell Publishing, 1996).

48. Abhilekh Patal is a digital portal to access a more extensive collection of documents from the National Archives of India.

49. For more on agglomerated networks, see Börje Johansson and John M. Quigley, 'Agglomeration and Networks in Spatial Economies', Regional Science: Working Papers, University of California, Berkeley, 16 August 2004, 1–14.

50. For more on the economy and evolution markets in India, see Vibodh Parthasarthy and Adrian Athique, 'Market Matters: Interdependencies in the Indian Media Economy', *Media, Culture and Society* 42, no. 3 (2020): 431–448.

51. The 1980s and 1990s were transitional decades when criminal economy networks became central to Bollywood financing and Hindi cinema circulated through pirate networks. As this book will reveal in detail, the Indian state's relationship with the film industry had been tenuous from the start. The state treated popular Hindi cinema 'at worst as a reprehensible, though unavoidable, social catastrophe, at best a barbarous pastime for the uncultured'. The state did not recognize film-making as a formal industry eligible for government benefits until 2001, but it was heavily taxed at the same time. In the 1980s and well into the 1990s, Hindi films obtained financing from the Dubai-based mafia through a network of 'formerly obscure small businessmen and well-known pirates' who became film producers and started financing big projects. The dovetailing of pirate circulation through informal criminal economy networks was brought to the fore in the late 1990s after the death of Bollywood music producer Gulshan Kumar, whom the mafia extorted and murdered. Following several high-visibility cases of threats and extortion, the state was forced to act, which eventually led to formal industry status. For more, see Adrian Athique, 'The Global Dynamics of Indian Media Piracy: Export Markets, Playback Media and the Informal Economy', *Media, Culture and Society* 30, no. 5 (2008): 699–717.

CHAPTER 1

1. Shyam Benegal, personal interview with the author on Indian cinema in the Soviet Union, 23 June 2016.

2. India gained independence from British rule in 1947.

3. For more on the pre-1990s market structure, see R. Vaidhyanathan, *India Uninc* (New Delhi: Westland Books, 2014).

4. Uday Bhatia, '120 Years of Watching Movies: The First Picture Show', *Mint*, 22 February 2017, https://www.livemint.com/Leisure/YovgiRxYB wmx9yo54M1scL/120-years-of-watching-movies-The-first-picture-show. html (accessed 18 July 2022).

5. Some scholars claim that there were films produced before *Raja Harishchandra* but are not mentioned in British records. See Jigna Desai and Rajinder Dudrah, *The Bollywood Reader* (London: McGraw-Hill Education, 2008), 3.

6. Laura Fish, 'The Bombay Interlude: Parsi Transnational Aspirations in the First Persian Sound Film', *Transnational Cinemas* 9, no. 2 (2018): 197–211.

7. Priya Jaikumar, *Cinema at the End of Empire: A Politics of Transition in Britain and India* (Durham, NC: Duke University Press, 2006), 5.

8. Jaikumar, *Cinema at the End of Empire*, 5.

9. Brian Shoesmith, 'Changing the Guard: The Transition from Studio-Based Film Production to Independent Production in Post-Colonial India', *Media History* 15, no. (2009): 439–452.

10. Sean P. Holmes, 'The Hollywood Star System and the Regulation of Actor's Labour, 1916–1934', *Film History* 12, no. 1 (2000): 97–114.

11. Shoesmith, 'Changing the Guard'.

12. Jaikumar, *Cinema at the End of Empire*.

13. Public Record Office, Britain Board of Trade 64/91, letter from R.D. Fennelly at the Britain Board of Trade to R.A. Wiseman, Dominions Office (17 February 1938), n.p.

14. Ibid.

15. Bombay Talkies Studios, 'Himansu Rai', n.d., https://www.thebombay talkiesstudios.com/himanshu-rai (accessed 15 September 2021).

16. See Jaikumar, *Cinema at the End of Empire*, 72, 260.

17. Y. A. Fazalbhoy, *The Indian Film: A Review* (Bombay: Bombay Radio Press, n.d.).

18. Madhava Prasad, 'The Economics of Ideology: Popular Film Form and Mode of Production', in *The Bollywood Reader*, ed. Rajinder Dudrah and Jigna Desai, 33–44 (Maidenhead, Berkshire: Open University Press, 2008), 52.

19. Eric Barnouw and S. Krishnaswamy, *Indian Film* (London: Oxford University Press, 1980), 69.

20. Prasad, 'The Economics of Ideology'.

21. Chidananda Das Gupta, 'Indian Cinema Today', *Film Quarterly* 22, no. 4 (1969): 27–35, 30.

22. Prasad, 'The Economics of Ideology', 48.

23. Tino Balio, *United Artists*, vol. 1: *1919–1950: The Company Built by the Stars* (Madison, WI: University of Wisconsin Press, 2009), xi.

24. In 1938, the US Department of Justice filed an antitrust lawsuit alleging that eight major motion picture companies had conspired to control the motion picture industry through their ownership of film distribution and exhibition. The decrees mandated a separation between film distribution and exhibition by requiring the defendants (Paramount Pictures, Twentieth Century Fox, Loew's Incorporated [now Metro-Goldwyn-Mayer, or MGM], Radio-Keith-Orpheum [dissolved in 1959], Warner Bros. Pictures, Columbia Pictures, Universal Studios, and United Artists) to divest either their distribution operations or their theatres. Going forward, the decrees prohibited those defendants from distributing movies and owning theatres without prior court approval. US Department of Justice, 'The Paramount Decrees', https://www.justice.gov/atr/paramount-decree-review (accessed 1 May 2021).

25. Denise Mann, *Hollywood Independents* (Minneapolis: University of Minnesota Press, 2008).

26. Charles Higham, 'Meet Whiplash Wilder: Billy Wilder Interviewed in 1967', British Film Institute, 1967, https://www.bfi.org.uk/sight-and-sound/interviews/meet-whiplash-wilder-billy-wilder-interviewed-1967 (accessed September 2021). The bureaucratic labour entailed in production discouraged Wilder and held back what he saw as the creative spirit.

27. For more on the idea of dependent independence, see Paul McDonald, 'The Will Smith Business', in *Hollywood Stardom*, 155–177 (Sussex: Blackwell Publishing, 2013).

28. McDonald, *Hollywood Stardom*.

29. Ben Fritz, 'Will Smith, Adam Sandler and How Sony Suffered through the Collapse of the A-List Star', *Hollywood Reporter*, 28 February 2018, https://www.hollywoodreporter.com/lifestyle/arts/will-smith-adam-sandler-how-sony-suffered-collapse-a-list-star-book-excerpt-1088418 (accessed 9 August 2021).

30. Jawaharlal Nehru, *Soviet Russia: Some Random Sketches and Impressions* (Allahabad: Allahabad Journal Press, 1928).

31. Paul M. McGarr, *The Cold War in South Asia: Britain, the United States, and the Indian Subcontinent, 1945–1965* (Cambridge, UK: Cambridge University Press, 2013), 32.

32. Nargis's given name at birth was Fatima Rashid. She adopted Nargis as her screen name. In 1958 she married fellow actor Sunil Dutt and changed her name to Nargis Dutt. She is referred to as Nargis throughout the book.

33. *Variety*, '14 Leaders of India's Pix Industry Feted in H'wood', 8 October 1952, 4.

34. Ivan Spear, 'Hollywood Report', *Boxoffice*, 18 October 1952, 26.

35. Nitin Govil, 'In and Out of Alignment: Cold War Sentiment and Hollywood-Bombay Film Diplomacy in the 1950s', in *A Companion to Indian Cinema*, ed. Neepa Majumdar and Ranjani Mazumdar, 391–413 (Hoboken, NJ: John Wiley and Sons, 2021), 393.

36. Baburao Patel, 'A Burlesque Delegation', *Filmindia*, October 1952, 3.

37. Victor J. Danilov, president emeritus of the Museum of Science and Industry, Chicago, makes this assertion in an article published in 1988.

38. Museum of Modern Art Department of Film, 'Film Utsav-India: Profile Schedules', New York, 25 October 1985.

39. *Times of India*, 'Russian Fairy Tale in Color', 20 June 1948, 12.

40. Bunny Reuben, *Raj Kapoor: The Fabulous Showman* (Bombay: Virgo Books, 1988), 116.

41. Reuben, *Raj Kapoor*, 116.

42. Stein Kristiansen, 'Social Networks and Business Success: The Role of Subcultures in an African Context', *American Journal of Economics and Sociology* 63, no. 5 (2004): 1149–1172.

43. Museum of Modern Art Department of Film, 'Film Utsav-India: Profile Schedules', 5.

44. Quoted in Kapoor's biography by his daughter Ritu Nanda. See Ritu Nanda, *Raj Kapoor: His Films and His Life* (Moscow: Iskusstvo Publishers, 1991), 67.

45. Dina Iordanova, Juan Goytisolo, Gàjendra K. Singh, Asuman Suner, Viola Shafik, and P. A. Skantze, 'Indian Cinema's Global Reach: Historiography through Testimonies', *South Asian Popular Culture* 4, no. 2 (2006): 113–140.

46. Ministry of External Affairs, 'Cultural and Goodwill Mission to China under the Leadership of Mrs. Pandit', Public Record, National Archives of India, New Delhi, 1952.

47. Ravi Vasudevan, *The Melodramatic Public: Film Form and Spectatorship in Indian Cinema* (Basingstoke: Palgrave Macmillan, 2010).

48. *India Today*, 'Remembering Prithviraj Kapoor: 10 Facts You Must Know about the Father of Bollywood', 3 November 2016, https://www.

indiatoday.in/education-today/gk-current-affairs/story/prithviraj-kapoor-birthday-349871-2016-11-03 (accessed 7 February 2022).

49. Press Trust of India, 'No Abolition of Capital Punishment: Pandit Pant Turns Down Suggestions', *Times of India*, 26 April 1958, 8.

50. Press Trust of India, 'Hindu Succession Bill: Opposition to Provision', *Times of India*, 23 November 1955, 6.

51. 'Bourdieuan' pertains to Pierre Bourdieu's theorization of social capital based on the recognition that capital is not only economic and that social exchanges are not purely self-interested and need to encompass 'capital and profit in all their forms'. Pierre Bourdieu, 'The Forms of Capital', in *Handbook of Theory and Research for the Sociology of Education*, edited by J. Richardson, 241–258 (Westport, CT: Greenwood Publishing), 241. Bourdieu's conceptualization is grounded in theories of social reproduction and symbolic power. His work emphasizes structural constraints and unequal access to institutional resources based on class, gender, and race.

52. *Times of India*, 'Film Seminar on February 27: Inauguration by Mr. Nehru', 8 February 1955, 11.

53. *Times of India*, 'Film Seminar', 6 March 1955, 8.

54. *Times of India*, 'Undue Interference in Arts Opposed: Premier Explains Stand at Film Seminar', 28 February 1955, 7; *Times of India*, 'The Social Whirl', 23 January 1955, 10.

55. Sanjoy Hazarika, 'Raj Kapoor, Top Indian Film Star, Is Dead at 64', *New York Times*, 3 June 1988, A19.

56. McGarr, 'A Rather Tedious and Unfortunate Affair: The Rahi Saga and the Troubled Origins of Indo-Soviet Cinematic Exchange', *Historical Journal of Film, Radio and Television* 36, no. 1 (2016): 5–20.

57. Natalya Fedotova, 'Russia's All-Time Favourite Bollywood Films', Ministry of External Affairs, Government of India, 10 May 2013, https://www.mea.gov.in/outoging-visit-detail.htm?21693/Russias+alltime+favourite+Bollywood+films (accessed 10 September 2021).

58. Oxana Naralenkova, 'Bollywood Returns to Russian Screens', Russia beyond the Headlines, 10 September 2009, https://www.rbth.com/articles/2009/09/10/100909bollywood.html (accessed 1 May 2015).

59. Yudhishthir Raj Isa, 'Cultural Diplomacy: India Does It Differently', *International Journal of Cultural Policy* 23, no. 6 (2017): 705–716.

60. Gautam Chakrabarti, 'From Moscow with Love: Soviet Cultural Politics across India in the Cold War', *Safundi: The Journal of South African and American Studies* 20, no. 2 (2019): 239–257, 246.

61. *Times of India*, 'Russian Fairy Tale', 12.

62. N. Koulebiakin, 'Films for Russia: To the Editor, Times of India', *Times of India*, 9 October 1953, 6.

63. McGarr, 'A Rather Tedious and Unfortunate Affair'.

64. S. Sen to Vijaya Lakshmi Pandit, 'Notes on Communist Propaganda in India', 24 April 1952, Subject File 24, pp. 47–56, Nehru Memorial Museum and Library.

65. *Times of India*, 'Forum to Discuss Film Artistes' Problems: Seminar to Be Held in Delhi in February', 8 December 1954, 5.

66. Khwaja Ahmad Abbas, '"МЕНЯ ЗОВУТ КЛОУНОМ" НОВЫЙ ФИЛЬМ РАДЖА КАПУРА ["Mera Naam Joker" A New Film by Raj Kapoor]', *Sovetskaia Kul'tura*, 8 December 1967, 4.

67. I. Rachuk, 'Administration of Film Productions', Official Letter, Ministry of Culture of the Union of Soviet Socialist Republics (USSR), Moscow, 1959, 10.

68. Rachuk, 'Administration of Film Productions', 10.

69. Kardashev Makarov, Folder (1950–1960), 'To Com. Stepanov V. T.', Official Letter, Ministry of Culture of the USSR, Moscow, 113.

70. Durga Khote, *I, Durga Khote: An Autobiography* (New Delhi: Oxford University Press, 2006), 34–35.

71. Maurizio Lazzarato, 'Immaterial Labor', in *Radical Thought in Italy: A Potential Politics*, ed. Virno Paolo and Michael Hardt, 133–148 (Minneapolis, MN: University of Minnesota Press, 2006), 133.

72. Michael Hardt, 'Affective Labor', *Boundary 2* 26, no. 2 (1999): 89–100.

73. Pierre Bourdieu, 'The Contradictions of Inheritance', in *Weight of the World: Social Suffering in Contemporary Society*, ed. Pierre Bourdieu, Alain Accardo, and Priscilla Parkhurst Ferguson, 507–513 (Cambridge, UK: Polity Press, 1999), 511.

74. Johanna Oksala, 'Affective Labor and Feminist Politics', *Signs: Journal of Women in Culture and Society* 41, no. 2 (Winter 2016): 281–303, 284.

75. Michael Hardt and Antonio Negri, *Multitude: War and Democracy in the Age of Empire* (London: Penguin Books, 2004), 96.

76. G. Aleskandrov, 'The Art of the People of India', *Pravda*, 24 September 1954.

77. *Times of India*, 'Good Reception in Moscow: Indian Film Festival', 8 August 1963, 5.

78. *Times of India*, '8th International Film Festival Opens', 4 January 1981, 1.

79. Official letter, 6 October 1954, Moscow Department, Ministry of culture of the USSR.

80. Abbas, '"Mera Naam Joker"'.

81. Raj Kapoor and Ritu Nanda, *Raj Kapoor Speaks* (New Delhi: Penguin Books, 2002).

82. *Times of India*, 'Undue Interference in Arts Opposed'.

83. Ibid.

84. *Times of India*, 'State Control of Film Industry Opposed', 21 December 1956, 3.

85. P. K. Ravindranath, 'Bungling Film Exports', *Times of India*, 17 September 1972, A5.

86. *Variety*, 'Pictures: India's "Aan" as Yankee Wedge for US Dates', 24 September 1952, 7, 20.

87. Ibid., 20.

88. *Boxoffice*, 'Aslan Khan to Distribute Five Pictures from India', 27 May 1963, SE-2.

89. Ibid.

90. *Boxoffice*, 'Group from India Seeks Film Market in U.S', 12 October 1964, E-5.

91. The Film Producers Guild of India Limited was established in 1954 by key figures in the industry, such as Raj Kapoor, Mehboob Khan, Sasadhar Mukerji, B. N. Sircar, V. Shantaram, Vijay Bhatt, and B. R. Chopra. The guild incorporated the television sector within its fold in 2004 and assumed its current nomenclature as the Film & Television Producers Guild of India. Since 2017 it assumed the role of an all-pervasive industry body incorporating producers from all three mediums—film, television, and new media—and is now commonly known as the Producers Guild of India; however, it continues to formally operate as a registered company: the Film & Television Producers Guild of India Limited. The guild collaborates with various trade bodies and federations such as the Federation of Indian Chambers of Commerce and Industries (FICCI) and the Confederation of Indian Industries (CII). For more, see http://producersguildindia.com (accessed 9 June 2023).

92. Vincent Canby, 'Indian Film Industry Team Here; Many Vexations, Lack of Theaters; Difficulties in Breaking Even', *Variety*, 21 October 1964, 24.

93. The state-sponsored parallel-cinema filmmakers like Satyajit Ray, in contrast, enjoyed a good distribution network. Ray's films were consistently distributed in the West through Edward Harrison.

94. See Canby, 'Indian Film Industry Team Here'.

95. Joan Crosby, 'Music Makes Heart Grow Fonder – in India Anyway', *Times Recorder*, 13 September 1964, 2-B.

96. *Variety*, 'No Pension for Pearl Buck: Her Reel Life Begins at 72', 29 January 1964, 5.

97. Ibid.

98. *Variety*, 'Film Reviews: The Guide', 10 February 1965, 6.

99. Bosley Crowther, 'Pearl Buck Is Adapter of Scenic "Guide"', *New York Times*, 10 February 1965, https://www.nytimes.com/1965/02/10/archives/pearl-buck-is-adapter-of-scenic-guide.html (accessed 2 March 2022).

100. Dev Anand, 'The Stars in Their Place', interview with *Times of India*, 7 April 1968.

101. Wilderness Film India Archive, 'Dev Anand on "Guide" and "Evil Within" and Manohar Malgonkar's Book Influences', YouTube, August 2017, https://www.youtube.com/watch?v=Pkb7nE1StS4 (accessed June 2019).

102. *Variety*, 'International Sound Track: London', 28 March 1979, 38.

103. Peter Noble, 'In Confidence: Peter Noble', *Screen International*, 16 October 1982, 4.

104. *Screen International*, 'International Sound Track: New Delhi', 13 July 1983, 34. The film was shown in the non-competition section of the festival.

105. *Variety*, 'Pictures: Dev Anand from India Scouting NY for Distrib', 8 August 1962, 18.

106. N. Dayasindhu, 'Embeddedness, Knowledge Transfer, Industry Clusters and Global Competitiveness: A Case Study of the Indian Software Industry', *Technovation* 22, no. 9 (2002): 551–560.

107. Shashi Kapoor, 'Are We Ashamed of Our Cinema?' interview with Khalid Mohamed, *Times of India*, 2 January 1983, A1.

108. Nyay Bhushan, 'A Major Star at Home, He Made a Name for Himself in the US with His Work for Merchant-Ivory', *Hollywood Reporter*, 10 May 2015, http://www.hollywoodreporter.com/news/shashi-kapoor-indian-hollywood-crossover-794675 (accessed 29 October 2015).

109. Structural equivalence is the most 'concrete' form of equivalence. Two nodal actors in a network are structurally equivalent if they have precisely the same ties to the same individual actors. Pure structural equivalence can be pretty rare in social relations, but approximations to it may not be so rare. In studying a single population, two actors who are approximately structurally equivalent are facing pretty much the same sets of constraints and opportunities. Commonly, we would say that two nodal actors who are

approximately structural equivalent are in approximately the same position in an organizational structure or network.

110. Madhu Jain, *Kapoors: The First Family of Indian Cinema* (New Delhi: Penguin Books, 2006).

111. Robert Emmett Long, *James Ivory in Conversation: How Merchant Ivory Makes Its Movies* (Berkeley, CA: University of California Press, 2005).

112. Long, *James Ivory in Conversation*, 69. Merchant Ivory's first Indo-US feature, *The Householder*, was sold to Columbia Pictures, and the studio paid Merchant Ivory in 'frozen rupees'.

113. Nikhil Govil, *Orienting Hollywood: A Century of Film Culture between Los Angeles and Bombay* (New York: New York University Press, 2015).

114. Nandini Raghvendra, 'Ashok and Ambika Hinduja Combination All Set to Change Rules', *Economic Times*, 16 January 2010, https://economictimes. indiatimes.com/business-of-bollywood/ashok-and-ambika-hinduja-combination-all-set-to-change-rules/articleshow/5450566.cms?from=mdr (accessed 7 March 2021).

115. Raghvendra, 'Ashok and Ambika Hinduja'.

116. Wilderness Films, 'Shashi Kapoor on Merchant Ivory Productions', YouTube, https://www.youtube.com/watch?v=vm_aSshRCbE (accessed 5 May 2021).

117. Amelia Arsenault and Manuel Castells. 'Switching Power: Rupert Murdoch and the Global Business of Media Politics: A Sociological Analysis', *International Sociology* 23, no. 4 (2008): 488–513, 490.

118. Bhushan, 'A Major Star at Home'.

119. Gitanjali Roy, 'Shashi Kapoor's Suhana Safar: The Story of Bollywood's Raja Saab', NDTV, 9 May 2015, http://movies.ndtv.com/bollywood/shashi-kapoors-suhana-safar-the-story-of-bollywoods-raja-saab-760125 (accessed 1 November 2015).

120. Kuldeep Singh, 'Obituary: Geoffrey Kendal', *The Independent*, 22 October 2011, http://www.independent.co.uk/arts-entertainment/obituary-geoffrey-kendal-1165113.html (accessed 4 November 2015).

121. Aseem Chabbra, 'An Excerpt from Biography of Shashi Kapoor: India's First Crossover Star', *Hindustan Times*, 13 May 2016, 1.

122. Michael Keane, 'Cultural Technology Transfer: Redefining Content in the Chinese Television Industry', *Emergences: Journal for the Study of Media and Composite Cultures* 11, no. 2 (2001): 223–236.

123. Kunal Kapoor, 'Shashi Kapoor: Popular Actor "of Course" but Shashi Kapoor Was a Maverick Producer Too', interview with Nandini Ramnath, *Mint*, 6 May 2013, 1–3.

124. Ibid.

125. World Public Library, 'Junoon (1978 Film)', http://www.worldlibrary.org/articles/junoon_(1978_film) (accessed 9 November 2015).

126. Pamela G. Hollie, 'Manila Film Festival Proves All Out Spectacular', *New York Times*, 7 February 1982, http://www.nytimes.com/1982/02/07/movies/manila-film-festival-proves-all-out-spectacular.html (accessed 15 November 2015); Roy Stafford, '"36 Chowringhee Lane": The Case for Global Film: Discussing Everything That Isn't Hollywood (and a Little That Is)', 27 August 2008, https://itpworld.wordpress.com/2008/08/27/36-chowringhee-lane-india-1981/ (accessed 9 November 2015).

127. Philip Bergson, 'UK News: Oxford Revival under New Management', *Screen International*, 9 June 1984, 24.

128. *Los Angeles Times*, 'There's Lots to Remember about Filmex', 1 November 2006, http://articles.latimes.com/2006/nov/01/entertainment/et-aficopy block1 (accessed 24 November 2015).

129. *Variety*, 'International: Kapoor to Hawk Utsav at Filmex', ProQuest Entertainment Industry Magazine Database, 27 June 1984.

130. *Times of India*, 'What's a Bit of Sauce between Friends?' 25 September 1983, A2, para. 17.

131. Khalid Mohamed, '"Utsav": Bawdy Entertainment?' *Times of India*, 29 September 1985, 5.

132. Shashi Kapoor, '"West Doesn't Understand Our Films"', *Times of India*, 26 May 2002, 2.

133. Kunal Kapoor, 'Shashi Kapoor', 1–3.

134. The masala genre has its roots in Sanskrit dramaturgy and aesthetic tradition, where Bharatmuni, in his book *Natyashashtra* (Treatise on Performing Arts), argues for nine *rasa*s that represent the essence of human emotion in drama or any expressive form. He argues that an aesthetic performance is incomplete without *rasa*s. The idea of masala as a blending of action, romance, comedy, song, dance, and so on, that evoke different emotions in the audience has cultural roots in this Vedic treatise.

135. Karen Anand, 'India's Screen Dreams', *Screen International*, 7 May 1988, 344.

136. Kunal Kapoor, 'Shashi Kapoor', 1–3.

137. Jain, *Kapoors*.

138. Wild Films India, 'Shashi Kapoor: Raj Kapoor Was a Real Bhagat of Charlie Chaplin', 27 May 2017, https://www.youtube.com/watch?v=FpEChEsMU3s&t=96s (accessed 15 May 2018).

139. See Arsenault and Castells, 'Switching Power'.

CHAPTER 2

1. Press Trust of India, 'Our People Love Indian Movies: Afghanistan's Ambassador', 13 September 2013, New Delhi (Dow Jones, Factiva Database).

2. Members of a number of guerrilla groups operating in Afghanistan that opposed invading Soviet forces and eventually toppled the Afghan communist government during the Afghan War (1979–1992). Rival factions thereafter fell out among themselves, precipitating the rise of one faction, the Taliban.

3. S. Gupta, 'How Amitabh Bachchan Floored the Afghan Mujahideens', *Indian Express*, 4 October 2012, https://www.youtube.com/watch?v=iECf SCXxraU (accessed 2 August 2025).

4. Ibid.

5. Tejaswini Ganti, *Bollywood: A Guidebook to Popular Hindi Cinema* (New York: Routledge, 2004).

6. *Times of India*, 'Egypt's AB Mania', 2 December 2005, 2.

7. BBC, '*Bollywood Star Tops the Poll*', 1 July 1999, http://news.bbc.co.uk/2/hi/entertainment/381017.stm (accessed 1 January 2019).

8. Sanjoy Hazarika, 'India Relaxes after Film Idol Escapes Death', *New York Times*, 26 September 1982, 1–2.

9. Vibodh Parthasarthy and Adrian Athique have theorized on scalar change in the Indian media market in their recent work: 'Market Matters: Interdependencies in the Indian Media Economy', *Media, Culture and Society* 42, no. 3 (2020): 431–448.

10. For more on corporatization and convergence in the 2000s, see Aswin Punathambekar's excellent work *From Bombay to Bollywood: The Making of a Global Media Industry* (New York: NYU Press, 2013).

11. Richard Dyer, *Stars* (London: British Film Institute, 1998).

12. Neepa Majumdar argues that the 'star-as-real-person' is replaced by a second 'star-as-image', in the twin role popularized in Indian films, which is eventually revealed to be false. The authentication process is carried out on-screen, even when the roles might be framed in terms of extra-filmic information. Bachchan's switching power performed a doubling of on-screen and off-screen identities, informing his power within the Bollywood network. Neepa Majumdar, 'Doubling, Stardom, and Melodrama in Indian Cinema: The "Impossible" Role of Nargis', *Post Script* 22, no. 3 (2003): 89–103.

13. Arvind Panagariya, *India in the 1980s and 1990s: A Triumph of Reforms* (New Delhi: International Monetary Fund, 2003).

14. Sreya Mitra and Meheli Sen both express the idea of Bachchan's transfiguration as a benevolent patriarch. Mitra, 'From "Angry Young Man" to "Benevolent Patriarch": Amitabh Bachchan, Bollywood Stardom and the Remaking of Post Liberalization India', *South Asian Popular Culture* 18, no. 1 (2020): 63–77; Sen, 'Introduction', in *Figurations in Indian Film*, ed. Meheli Sen and Anustup Basu, 1–20 (New York: Palgrave Macmillan, 2013).

15. Bridges make networks small-world networks by reducing the overall path between nodes in a network.

16. David S. Grewal, 'Network Power and Globalization', *Ethics and International Affairs* 17, no. 2 (2003): 89–98; David S. Grewal, *Network Power: The Social Dynamics of Globalization* (New Haven, CT: Yale University Press, 2008).

17. *Hindustan Times*, 'Amitabh Bachchan's 77th Birthday: From His Struggle with TB to the Meaning of His Name, 77 Lesser Known Facts about Actor', 11 October 2019, 1; Susmita Dasgupta, *Amitabh: The Making of a Superstar* (New Delhi: Penguin Books, 2006).

18. Dorothy Norman (1905–1997), a photographer, writer, and social activist, first met Indira Gandhi when Gandhi visited the US with her father, Jawaharlal Nehru, in 1949. Their friendship spanned 35 years.

19. These were letters to her friend Dorothy Norman. Indira Gandhi, *Indira Gandhi, Letters to an American Friend 1950–1984* (San Diego, CA: Harcourt Brace Jovanovich, 1985).

20. Pierre Bourdieu, 'The Forms of Capital', in *Handbook of Theory and Research for the Sociology of Education*, ed. J. G. Richardson, 241–258 (New York: Greenwood Press, 1986).

21. Dasgupta, *Amitabh*.

22. Chidananda Das Gupta, 'Indian Cinema Today', *Film Quarterly* 22, no. 4 (1969): 27–35.

23. Madan Gaur, *Other Side of the Coin: An Intimate Study of Indian Film Industry* (Delhi: Trimurti Prakashan, 1973), 114.

24. Gaur, *Other Side of the Coin*, 114.

25. Indira Gandhi, *Selected Thoughts of Indira Gandhi: A Book of Quotes* (New Delhi: Mittal Publications, 1985), 115, 59.

26. Gandhi, *Selected Thoughts of Indira Gandhi*, 114. This was said in 1966.

27. Pierre Bourdieu, *Distinction: A Social Critique of the Judgement of Taste* (Boston, MA: Harvard University Press, 1984).

28. Government of India, 'Lok Sabha Debates: Fifth Series, Vol XII - No 13', Lok Sabha Debates, Lok Sabha Secretariat, New Delhi, 29 March 1972.

29. Ibid.

30. Gandhi, *Indira Gandhi*.

31. Filmfare, 'IK Gujral: Presidential Address to 17th Filmfare Awards', 22 May 1970, 29–33, quoted in Madhava Prasad, *Ideology of Indian Film* (New Delhi: Oxford University Press, 1998).

32. Government of India, 'Report of the National Institute of Public Finance and Policy on Aspects of Black Money in India', Lok Sabha Proceedings, New Delhi, 22 August 1985, 673.

33. Imke Rajamani, 'Pictures, Emotions, Conceptual Change: Anger in Popular Hindi Cinema', *Contributions to the History of Concepts* 7, no. 2 (2012): 52–77.

34. Ranjani Mazumdar, 'From Subjectification to Schizophrenia: The "Angry Man" and the "Psychotic" Hero of Bombay Cinema', in *Making Meaning in Indian Cinema*, ed. R. S. Vasudevan, 238–264 (Delhi: Oxford University Press, 2000), 243.

35. Ashis Nandy, 'Indian Popular Cinema as a Slum's Eye View of Politics', in *The Secret Politics of Our Desires: Innocence, Culpability and Indian Popular Cinema*, ed. Ashis Nandy, 1–18 (Chicago, IL: University of Chicago Press, 1999); Rajamani, 'Pictures, Emotions, Conceptual Change', 52, 54.

36. Dasgupta, *Amitabh*.

37. TEDx Talks, 'Cinema in Society', 28 November 2017, TED×IIFT Delhi.

38. Rasheed Kidwai, *Neta Abhineta: Bollywood Star Power in Indian Politics* (Gurugram: Hachette, 2018), 149.

39. J. P. Dutta, 'The … Der … Bollyw', *Times of India*, 14 August 1997, B8.

40. Priya Joshi notes Indira Gandhi's family psychodrama is reflected in *Deewar*. Like the character of Maa in the film, Gandhi prospered with an absent husband, made her younger son her heir, and 'commissioned the murder of the nation's youth'. While Joshi's observations are spot on, these similarities and evocations were intended as a cathartic critique, not a scathingly dismissive look at the system, because the state and system were all too powerful, and Bachchan's personal alliance was clearly with the social and political elite. Priya Joshi, 'Cinema as Family Romance', in *The 1970s and Its Legacies in India's Cinemas*, ed. Priya Joshi and Rajinder Dudrah, 8–22 (London and New York: Routledge, 2014), 14.

41. Neepa Majumdar, 'Doubling, Stardom, and Melodrama in Indian Cinema: The "Impossible" Role of Nargis', *Post Script* 22, no. 3 (2003): 89–103.

42. Dasgupta, *Amitabh*, 70.

43. Nandy, *The Secret Politics of Our Desires*, quoted in Rachel Dwyer's essay 'Bollywood Bourgeois', India International Centre Quarterly 33, nos. 3–4 (Winter 2006–Spring 2007): 222–231, 227.

44. Dasgupta, *Amitabh*, 87.

45. Madhava Prasad, *Ideology of the Hindi Film* (Delhi: Oxford University Press, 1998), 141.

46. Prasad, *Ideology of the Hindi Film*, 138.

47. Dasgupta, *Amitabh*, 87.

48. *Times of India*, 'From Guddi to Retiring Ma', 9 December 1999, 1.

49. Zothanpari Hrahsel, Vir Sanghvi, and Surender Bhatia, 'Amitabh Bachchan Towers over the Indian Film Firmament Like No Other Star in Recent Memory', *India Today*, 15 May 1980, 1–4. According to film critic Aruna Vasudev, film journals could not comment on or even mention films that were refused a censor-board certificate or made any reference to individual actors or producers.

50. S. Kirpekar, 'Cinematic Amitabh Drive', *Times of India*, 16 December 1984, 9. There was also a sympathy wave that favoured Bachchan and sympathy for the demise of Indira Gandhi.

51. Sunil Sethi, 'Allahabad to Witness Fight between Political Grit and Celluloid Stardom', *India Today*, 31 December 1984, https://www.indiatoday.in/magazine/nation/story/19841231-political-battle-between-hemvati-nandan-bahuguna-and-amitabh-bachchan-in-allahabad-803526-1984-12-31 (accessed 1 May 2020).

52. *Times of India*, 'It's Chance to Work for People: Amitabh', 30 December 1984, 12.

53. K. Sandeep Kumar, '35 Years On, Amitabh's "Big" Victory Record Still Unbeaten', *Hindustan Times*, 24 April 2019, https://www.hindustantimes.com/lok-sabha-elections/35-years-on-amitabh-s-big-victory-record-still-unbeaten/story-Gunch0IJIfEGA6NgfAdLvO.html (accessed 1 May 2020).

54. Nimisha Misra, 'What Amitabh Bachchan Means to a Person from Allahabad', Film Companion, 5 May 2018, https://www.filmcompanion.in/features/bollywood-features/what-amitabh-bachchan-means-to-a-person-from-allahabad.

55. Misra, 'What Amitabh Bachchan Means'.

56. Bachchan's veneration as an icon in India is almost divine; scholars like Bishnupriya Ghosh, Vijay Mishra, and Madhava Prasad have expounded on this idea.

57. Lawrence Grossberg has argued that fandom constitutes an 'affective sensibility' through which fans construct 'mattering maps' of the cultural world with which to determine where to invest time, money, and self. Given that everyone's relation to culture is affective and we all map the cultural world in different ways, what makes fandom unique, according to Grossberg, is that fans redefine their identities in relation to those maps. Grossberg, 'Is There a Fan in the House? The Affective Sensibility of Fandom', in *The Adoring Audience: Fan Culture and Popular Media*, ed. Lisa A. Lewis, 50–68 (New York: Routledge, 1992).

58. Mattering maps, according to Grossberg, are imagined communities that redefine fan identities by creating maps that determine their sensibility and cultural world where they choose to invest time, money, and self.

59. Saibal Chatterjee, 'Cannes 2019: Afghan Film Brings Bollywood and Amitabh Bachchan to the Film Festival', NDTV, 25 May 2019, https://www.ndtv.com/entertainment/cannes-2019-afghan-film-brings-bollywood-and-amitabh-bachchan-to-the-film-festival-2042841 (accessed 1 July 2019).

60. Ministry of External Affairs, 'Public Diplomacy: History and Evolution of Non-Aligned Movement', Government of India, 22 August 2012, https://mea.gov.in/in-focus-article.htm?20349/History+and+Evolution+of+NonAligned+Movement (accessed 1 May 2019).

61. Afghanistan slowly faltered in its non-aligned geopolitical resolve as the Soviets intervened in Afghanistan's civil war in 1979. Ministry of External Affairs, 'Public Diplomacy.

62. *Kabul Times*, 'India Offers 30 Scholarships to Afghanistan', 7 April 1973, 1.

63. Hamid Mowlana and Yahya R. Kamalipour, *Mass Media in the Middle East: A Comprehensive Handbook* (Westport, CT: Greenwood Press, 1994).

64. *Kabul Times*, 'Provincial Press', 12 April 1973, 3.

65. Karishma Upadhyay, 'Afghanistan: A Bollywood Flashback', *Times of India*, 8 October 2001, A1. Even before the film's shooting schedule started, the king and the royal family were deported to Italy. Their deportment was followed by a bloodless coup.

66. D. Chopra, 'Isn't Amitabh a Pathan? He Is So Tall', *Times of India*, 20 March 2004, 18.

67. For more see Klaus Dodds, '"Have You Seen Any Good Films Lately?" Geopolitics, International Relations and Film', *Geography Compass* 2, no. 2 (2008): 476–494.

68. Raj Chengappa, 'For Most Afghanis, War Is Just Another Day', *India Today*, 31 December 2001, https://www.indiatoday.in/magazine/special-report/story/20011231-for-most-afghanis-war-is-just-another-day-774758-2001-12-31 (accessed 1 May 2016).

69. Taran N. Khan, 'Encounters with Bollywood in Kabul', *Himal Magazine*, 15 September 2013, https://www.himalmag.com/encounters-bollywood-kabul (accessed 15 May 2016).

70. *Al-Kawakib*, 'Khatawat Jadida Tuqawwi al-Rabt Baynana wa Bayna Ahl al-Hind' (New Steps to Strengthen Ties between Us and the People of India), 5 November 1957, 16, cited in Walter Armbrust, 'The Ubiquitous Nonpresence of India: Peripheral Visions from Egyptian Popular Culture', in *Global Bollywood: Travels of Hindi Song and Dance*, ed. Sangita Gopal and Sujata Moorti, 200–220 (Minneapolis, MN: University of Minnesota Press, 2008).

71. *Al-Kawakib*, 'Khatawat Jadida', 16.

72. Gabika Bockaj, 'Nostalgia and the Mediatic Imagination in Tito's Yugoslavia', in *Media and Utopia: History, Imagination and Technology*, ed. Arvind Rajagopal and Anupama Rao, 171–188 (New York: Routledge, 2016).

73. Armbrust, 'The Ubiquitous Nonpresence of India', 201.

74. Ibid., 210.

75. Andrew J. Flibbert, *Commerce in Culture: States and Markets in the World Film Trade* (London: Palgrave MacMillan, 2007), 111.

76. Lehren Retro, 'Egyptian Fans for Big B', YouTube, 27 April 2012, https://www.youtube.com/watch?v=QJNKTtR0SRw (accessed 1 May 2020).

77. H. E. Banna, 'Bachchan Fans in the Nineties Write His Name with Their Blood and Memorize His Songs', Filfan, 31 March 2015, https://www.filfan.com/news/details/46157 (accessed 1 May 2020); A. Algafsi, 'Jwlh Amytab Batshan Kamlh Fy Msr Aljz [Amitabh Bachchan's Complete Egypt Tour Part 2]', YouTube, 14 May 2012, https://www.youtube.com/watch?v=zv67EXCejU8&feature=youtu.be (accessed 1 May 2020).

78. Sadat was assassinated in 1981.

79. Agence France Presse, 'Bollywood Steams Back to Egypt with "Chennai Express"', Arab News, 11 October 2013, https://www.arabnews.com/news/467358 (accessed 20 June 2019).

80. K. Abdelmaq Suud, 'Contractor Movies and Amitabh Bachchan', *Al Ahram*, 4 July 1988, 9.

81. *Al-Ahrar*, 'Movie Stars and Amitabh Bachchan Face to Face', 9 March 1987, 1.

82. Ibid.

83. Ibid. This is a translation of the original text, which was in Arabic.

84. Ibid.

85. Ibid.

86. Adrian Athique, 'The Global Dynamics of Indian Media Piracy: Export Markets, Playback Media and the Informal Economy', *Media, Culture and Society* 30, no. 5 (2008): 699–717, 703–704.

87. Khan, 'Encounters with Bollywood in Kabul'.

88. *Economic Times*, 'Afghanistan and the Popularity of Bollywood Are Inseparable', 17 June 2012, https://economictimes.indiatimes.com/industry/media/entertainment/afghanistan-and-the-popularity-of-bollywood-are-inseparable/articleshow/14209348.cms?from=mdr (accessed 20 June 2019).

89. Manmohan Singh, 'Budget Speech of Minister of Finance Manmohan Singh', Government of India, New Delhi, 24 July 1991, 1–31, 31.

90. William Mazzarella, 'Locations: Advertising and the New Swadeshi', in *Shoveling Smoke Advertising and Globalization in Contemporary India*, 3–36 (Durham, NC: Duke University Press, 2003), 5.

91. Rupal Oza, *The Making of Neoliberal India: Nationalism, Gender, and the Paradoxes of Globalization* (New York: Routledge, 2006); Shanti Kumar, *Gandhi Meets Primetime: Globalization and Nationalism in Indian Television* (Urbana, IL: University of Illinois Press, 2006); Leela Fernandes, *India's New Middle Class Democratic Politics in an Era of Economic Reform* (Minneapolis, MN: University of Minnesota Press, 2006); Rupal Oza, 'Showcasing India: Sexuality and the Nation in the 1996 World Pageant', in *The Making of Neoliberal India*, ed. Rupal Oza, 79–101 (New York: Routledge, 2006).

92. Ibid.

93. Arvind Panagariya, 'Phase IV (1988–2006): Triumph of Liberalization', in *India: The Emerging Giant*, ed. Arvind Panagariya, 95–109 (New York: Oxford University Press, 2008).

94. Miriam Salzer-Mörling and Lars Strannegård, 'Ain't Misbehavin': Consumption in a Moralized Brandscape', *Marketing Theory* 7, no. 4 (2007): 407–425. Their idea of the brandscape is closely related to Appadurai's conceptualization of the flows of meanings and symbols that form the global world; see Arjun Appadurai, *Modernity at Large: Cultural Dimensions of Globalization* (Minneapolis, MN: University of Minnesota Press, 1996).

95. Priyanka Sinha, 'Action Jackson', *Indian Express*, 16 June 2011, http://archive
.indianexpress.com/news/action-jackson/804525/5 (accessed 20 June 2019).

96. 'French producer Alain Chamas who tried unsuccessfully to sign Bachchan
for his film *Crossings* opposite Jon Voight and Richard Dreyfus finally
remarked in sheer exasperation: "This man is not just a star. Amitabh
Bachchan is an industry"', *India Today*, 25 December 2000, https://
www.indiatoday.in/magazine/indiascope/story/20001225-issue-date-
may-1-1980-751505-2000-12-25 (accessed 1 January 2020).

97. Paul McDonald notes that despite owning production entities, Hollywood
stars are bound by the power of Hollywood's conglomerate system in a
way that their production companies are 'working for the studios' and
are reliant on them even though the studios do not own their companies.
This, according to McDonald, characterizes 'the working contradictions of
stardom in conglomerate Hollywood' and the star production company's
'dependent independence'. The Indian star, in contrast, was an agent of
change within the emergent industry structure. Paul McDonald, 'The
Will Smith Business', in *Hollywood Stardom*, ed. Paul McDonald, 155–178
(Malden, MA: Wiley-Blackwell, 2013), 155.

98. Vimla Patil, 'Muqaddar Ka Sikandar', *The Tribune*, 4 March 2001, 1.

99. Douglas B. Holt, *How Brands Become Icons: The Principles of Cultural
Branding* (Boston, MA: Harvard Business Press, 2004).

100. Mitra, 'From "Angry Young Man" to "Benevolent Patriarch"'.

101. Kajri Jain, *Gods in the Bazaar: The Economies of Indian Calendar Art*
(Durham, NC: Duke University Press, 2007), 21.

102. Marina Bernadette Victoria Martin, 'An Economic History of Hundi,
1858–1978', PhD thesis, London School of Economics, January 2012.

103. The Companies Act was first passed in the parliament of India in 1956. It
was amended in 1988, 1990, 1996, 2000, 2011, and 2013. Considering that
the framework for regulation of corporate entities had to be in tune with the
emerging economic scenario that encourage good corporate governance and
enable protection of the interests of the investors and other stakeholders,
major changes were made to the Act after the 1980s when the Indian
economy started liberalizing. For more, see Ministry of Corporate Affairs,
'Ministry of Corporate Affairs: Background', https://www.mca.gov.in/
MinistryV2/background.html (accessed 13 June 2023).

104. India Brand Equity Foundation, *Corporatisation of Indian Film Industry*
(New Delhi: Department of Commerce, Ministry of Commerce and
Industry, Government of India, 2013).

105. For more, see Tejaswini Ganti, *Producing Bollywood: Inside the Contemporary Hindi Film Industry* (Durham, NC: Duke University Press, 2012), 260.

106. Sucheta Dalal, 'Amitabh Firm Set to Create a New Trend', *Times of India*, 14 January 1995, 15.

107. Dalal, 'Amitabh Firm Set to Create a New Trend', 15.

108. Ashok Banker, '"Big B" Dream of Showbiz Supershop Comes Unstuck', *Rediff Business*, 22 June 1999, https://www.rediff.com/business/1999/jun/22abcl2.htm (1 May 2019).

109. Uday Kotak, interview with Sucheta Dalal, in Dalal, 'Amitabh Firm Set to Create New Trend', 1.

110. Celia Lury, *Brands: The Logos of the Global Economy* (London: Routledge, 2004).

111. McDonald, 'The Will Smith Business', 42.

112. Jean-Noel Kapferer, *The New Strategic Brand Management: Creating and Sustaining Brand Equity Long Term* (London: Kogan Page Limited, 1997).

113. *Times of India*, 'Zee Cinema to Start', 25 March 1995, 15.

114. Amitabh Bachchan, interview with Allen J. Mendonca, 'If My Friends Happen to Be Politicians, Then So Be It', *Times of India*, 28 August 1996, 13.

115. Nabeel Abbass, 'Sad View to a Thrill', *Times of India*, 2 January 1996, A8.

116. Rashid Irani, 'Something to Talk about Late Night Shows in the City', *Times of India*, 19 May 1996, 5.

117. Khalid Mohamed, '"Bandit Queen" Draws Crowds and Protests', *Times of India*, 15 February 1996, 1.

118. Nikhat Kazmi, 'The Film as Hero: Bollywood's Big Comeback', *Times of India*, 24 December 1995, 13.

119. Ashley D'Mello, 'Article 5', *Times of India*, 11 April 1997, 15.

120. William Callahan makes this argument for the organization of Miss World in Thailand. I think it applies similarly to the Indian context, albeit mediated through Bachchan and his organization, ABCL. William Callahan, 'The Ideology of Miss Thailand in National, Consumerist, and Transnational Space', *Alternatives* 23 (1998): 29–61.

121. Radhika Parmeshwaran, 'Global Media Events in India: Contests over Beauty, Gender and Nation', *Journalism & Communication Monographs* 3, no. 2 (2001): 52–105.

122. *Business Today*, 'Mega Events', 7–21 November 1996, 30–31.

123. Neville Hoad, 'World Piece: What the Miss World Pageant Can Teach about Globalization', *Cultural Critique* 58, no. 1 (February 2004): 56–81, 14.

124. Christopher Thomas, 'Beauty Contest Veils Ugliness of Indian Poverty', *The Times*, 25 November 1996, 1.

125. George Ritzer, *The McDonaldization of Society* (London: Sage Publications, 1993).

126. Agence France-Presse, '"Bandit Queen" Condemns Miss World Pageant', 30 September 1996.

127. Miss World, 'Miss World Organization Press Conference', New Delhi, 4 November 1996.

128. Hoad, 'World Piece', 63.

129. Oza, 'Showcasing India'.

130. Ibid., 81.

131. Manuel Castells 'Space of Flows, Space of Places: Materials for a Theory of Urbanism in the Information Age', in *The City Reader*, ed. Richard T. LeGates, and Frederic Stout, 229–239 (New York: Routledge, 2020).

132. Saskia Sassen, *The Global City: New York, London, Tokyo* (Princeton, NJ: Princeton University Press, 1991).

133. Doreen Massey, 'General Introduction', in *Space, Place and Gender*, ed. Doreen Massey, 1–16 (Cambridge, UK: Polity Press, 1994), 5.

134. Manuel Castells, *The Rise of Network Society* (Malden, MA: Wiley Blackwell, 2000), 220.

135. *Times of India*, 'Pageant Protestors Display Nude Amitabh Cut Out', 23 November 1996, 7; *Times of India*, 'Indian Touch Will Be the Hallmark of Beauty Show', 26 October 1996, 1; Sonora Jha Nambiar, 'Bachchan Fails to Play Santa Claus: Spastics Society of Karnataka Still Waiting for ABCL Cheque', *Times of India*, 27 December 1996, 1; *Times of India*, 'Six "Angry Young Men" Ransack ABCL's Bangalore Office', *Times of India*, 28 October 1996, 1.

136. Khalid Mohamed, 'After Payback Bachchan Back to Movie Action', *Times of India*, 29 April 2001, 1.

137. Rakshande Italia, 'Zee TV Soon to Enter US Homes', *Times of India*, 27 April 1996, 13.

138. Abhay Vaidya, 'Desk-Top Glut', *Times of India*, 20 February 1994, 17.

139. Girish Dikey, 'For the Big B It's Bombay First', *Times of India*, 18 October 1995, A1.

140. Seema Sinha, 'Jack of All Trades', *Times of India*, 29 November 2002, A9; Ajita Shashidhar, 'Who Dares Wins', *Outlook Business*, 16 May 2009, 66–68; Meenakshi Shedde, 'Synergy of Films and TV Is Key to Entertainment Boom', *Times of India*, 10 June 2001, 5.

141. Tridwip K. Das, 'Girl with the Mike: Anuradha Prasad's Bhartiya Avataar Sees Her Assume Various Forms', *Times of India*, 19 June 1998, A6.

142. S. Kumar, *Gandhi Meets Primetime*.

143. Shyam Benegal, interview with Nalini Uchil, 'Where Art Thou?' *Times of India*, 13 July 1991; Amitabh Bachchan, 'In the Company of the Nehrus', *Times of India*, 17 February 1991, 11.

144. Uchil, 'Where Art Thou', A1.

145. *Times of India*, 'H…: In … Boney … … Producer', 4 July 2004, ProQuest Historical Newspapers, A2.

146. Virginia Valian, *Why So Slow? The Advancement of Women* (Boston, MA: MIT Press, 1999).

147. *Times of India*, 'Careless Whisper', 7 January 1990, A4.

148. Meera Joshi, 'Movie Matter: Film Personalities Venturing into Corporate finance', *News India Times*, 19 May 1995, 1.

149. Ibid., 1.

150. Over the five years following the Miss World contest, India witnessed a 25 per cent growth in its cosmetics and personal care sectors. In 2000, the size of the cosmetic market had grown to USD 160 million.

151. Anita Anand, *The Beauty Game* (New Delhi: Penguin Books, 2002).

CHAPTER 3

1. Anupama Chopra, 'Bollywood Is Dancing Far Abroad; Global Fortunes Advance for Hindi Films, but US Market Is Still Resisting', *International New York Times*, 27 September 2014, 1.

2. Wessel's magazine, *Ishq*, has a circulation of 30,000 copies in Germany, Austria, and Switzerland. A. Chopra, 'Bollywood Is Dancing Far Abroad'.

3. Baanyan Tree Productions, 'Making of "Kal Ho Na Ho: Lebe Jetzt"', YouTube, 10 December 2015, https://www.youtube.com/watch?v=2Rey NYwfrs8&list=PLdIOK2roOEqza2FCVixe2qJeJX3uDtScR&index=81 (accessed 12 January 2016).

4. Asian News International, 'Chai to Cha and Jackie Chan to Aamir Khan: Chinese Envoy Talks about Close Cultural Ties with India', 8 October

2019, https://www.aninews.in/news/national/general-news/chai-to-cha-and -jackie-chan-to-aamir-khan-chinese-envoy-talks-about-close-cultural- ties-with-india20191008170040 (accessed 1 November 2019).

5. *Financial Express*, 'Chinese President Xi Jinping Watched Aamir Khan- Starrer "Dangal" on Multiple Occasions, Says China Envoy to India', 18 June 2018, https://www.financialexpress.com/india-news/chinese- president-xi-jinping-watched-aamir-khan-starrer-dangal-on-multiple- occasions-says-china-envoy-to-india/1211038/ (accessed 20 June 2018).

6. Kate Berbano, '5 Indian Film Stars Who Made It Big in China: From Aamir Khan of 3 Idiots Fame, to Fatima Sana Shaikh and Hong Kong- Born Katrina Kaif', *South China Morning Post*, 22 July 2020, https:// www.scmp.com/magazines/style/celebrity/article/3094191/5-indian- film-stars-who-made-it-big-china-aamir-khan-3 (accessed 1 September 2020).

7. Douban, 'Douban Top 250', IMDb, 27 September 2016, https://www. imdb.com/list/ls066077036 (accessed 22 October 2017); Douban, 'Three Silly Havoc in Bollywood: 3 Idiots (2009)', 2010, https://movie.douban. com/subject/3793023 (accessed 22 October 2017).

8. Wei Xi, 'Bollywood Superstar Aamir Khan Softens Sino-India Communications', *Global Times*, China, 29 January 2018, https://www. globaltimes.cn/content/1086932.shtml (accessed 12 April 2019).

9. India considered appointing Khan as its brand ambassador to China. Asit Ranjan Mishra and Lata Jha, 'India Tap Aamir Khan to Boost Trade with China', *Mint*, 2 April 2018, https://www.livemint.com/Politics/WNFg7 BkwAp7BVpMkKhbZ6N/India-may-tap-Aamir-Khan-to-boost-trade- with-China.html (accessed 1 January 2019).

10. There is a space–time compression that, geographer David Harvey notes, characterizes contemporary globalization. Sociologist Manuel Castells argued that this space–time compression created a new kind of space for interaction in society that has distinctive characteristics. This space of flows is comprised of interactions and the material characteristics that make up those interactions possible, and the space is shaping up our society's organization both materially and immaterially, although this book predominantly focuses on material factors through powerful human actors within a global space of flows. For more on space of flows, see Manuel Castells, *The Rise of the Network Society*, vol. 1: *The Information Age: Economy, Society, and Culture* (Cambridge, MA; Oxford: Blackwell Publishing, 1996).

11. Mark Lorenzen and Florian Arun Täube, 'Breakout from Bollywood? The Roles of Social Networks and Regulation in the Evolution of Indian Film Industry', *Journal of International Management* 14: 286–299, 292.

12. The Reserve Bank of India (RBI) issued broad guidelines to commercial banks regarding bank finance for film production in August 2001. The policy stated,

> Under the RBI scheme, Banks may provide finance to film producers (corporate as well as non-corporate entities) with good track record in the relevant field. Banks may also provide finance to these entities for production of films in participation with National Film Development Corporation Limited. Banks can finance up to 50 per cent of the project cost on merits. Producers are required to bring in at least 35 to 40 per cent of the budget of the film. Banks may provide finance to such projects where the total cost of production of a film does not exceed Rs. 10 crores [100 millions].

Government of India, 'Policy on Film Finance', Archive Press Information Bureau, 20 August 2001, https://archive.pib.gov.in/archive/releases98/lyr2001/raug2001/20082001/r2008200124.html (accessed 30 December 2022).

13. Vibodh Parthasarathi and Adrian Athique, 'Market Matters: Interdependencies in the Indian Media Economy', *Media, Culture and Society* 42, no. 3 (2020): 431–448.

14. Castells, *The Rise of the Network Society*, vol. 1, 442.

15. Yash Chopra, interview with Uday Chopra, 'Dilwale Dulhaniya Le Jayenge', *Dilwale Dulhaniya Le Jayenge* (DVD, Collector's Edition), Yash Raj Films, 1995. Eventually, ABCL was relaunched as Amitabh Bachchan Corporation in 2003, now solely focused on film production, with the help of Bachchan's influential industrial and political coterie that included India's largest oil and telecom company, Reliance.

16. Shankar V. Aiyar and Anupama Chopra, 'Bollywood Hazy about New Industry Status but Expects Business to Get Streamlined Now', *India Today*, 20 March 1998, https://www.indiatoday.in/magazine/economy/story/19980525-bollywood-hazy-about-new-industry-status-but-expects-business-to-get-streamlined-now-828244-1998-05-25 (accessed 1 May 2019).

17. Laya Maheshwari, 'How India Is Shaping Hollywood', BBC Culture, 9 October 2017, https://www.bbc.com/culture/article/20171006-how-india-is-shaping-hollywood (20 June 2019).

18. Rahul Bhatia, 'The Curious Case of Saawariya', *Open*, 14 April 2010, https://openthemagazine.com/features/business/the-curious-case-of-saawariya (1 June 2018).

19. While I am using Susan Strange's term 'relational power', her usage implies the power two actors possess relative to each other to exert control or domination over the other. I foreground the relational power that two actors can possess because they are allied with each other. Their ability and power are additive. Susan Strange, *States and Markets* (London: Pinter, 1988).

20. Edward A. Gargan, 'TV Comes In on a Dish, and India Gobbles It Up', *New York Times*, 29 October 1991, A4.

21. Jitesh Pillai, 'It's Talent That Talks', *Times of India*, 30 March 1997, A6.

22. Coined by Jospeh Nye in the late 1980s, the term 'soft power' is the ability of a country to persuade others to do what it wants without force or coercion. While stars and power wielded by stars have not been discussed within this discourse on soft power, it factors into this discourse. The Indian government attempted to create influence in the neighbouring counties of Pakistan, Bangladesh, Nepal, and Sri Lanka by wielding the soft power of Bollywood stars.

23. Doordarshan was freely available in Nepal, soon followed by Hutchinson Wampoa's satellite venture, Star TV. Martin Piotrowski, 'Mass Media and Rural Out-Migration in the Context of Social Change: Evidence from Nepal', *International Migration* 51, no. 3 (2013): 169–193.

24. *Times of India*, 'TV Must Support Cinema', 16 January 1990, 11.

25. Government of India, *Manual of the Film and Television Institute of India* (Pune: Right to Information Act, 2005).

26. National Film Development Corporation, *Indian Cinema: A Visual Voyage Conceived by National Film Development Corporation* (New Delhi: Ministry of Information and Broadcasting, Government of India, 1998).

27. Vincent Canby, 'Holi, about a High School in India', *New York Times*, 8 April 1985, C14.

28. Government policies changed for two reasons: First, Bollywood's entrenchment in the criminal economy networks was revealed. Second, state policy changed due to liberalization, which tangentially trickled down to the film industry as well.

29. FICCI and Arthur Andersen India Private Limited, *Indian Entertainment Industry: Envisioning for Tomorrow* (Annual Industry Report) (New Delhi: Federation of Indian Chambers of Commerce and Industry, 2001).

30. A network is a set of interconnected nodes. A node is a point where a curve connecting two points intersects itself. A network has no centre, just nodes. Nodes may be of varying relevance for the network. Nodes increase their importance for the network by absorbing more relevant information and processing it more efficiently. The relative importance of a node does not stem from its specific features but from its ability to contribute to the network's goals. Manuel Castells, 'Informationalism, Networks, and the Network Society: A Theoretical Blueprint', in *The Network Society: A Cross-Cultural Perspective*, ed. Manuel Castells, 3–45 (Cheltenham: Edward Elgar Publishing, 2004).

31. Divya Goyal, 'The End: Maratha Mandir Shows Dilwale Dulhania Le Jayenge For Last Time', NDTV, 20 February 2015, http://movies. ndtv.com/bollywood/the--end--maratha--mandir--shows--dilwale-- dulhania--le--jayenge--for--last--time--740769 (accessed 1 January 2018).

32. Sharin Bhatti, '1,009-Week Run Proves Too Short for Fans of DDLJ Bollywood Classic', *The Guardian*, 27 February 2015, https://www. theguardian.com/world/2015/feb/27/protests-prompt-return-to-indian-cinema-of-film-that-ended-run-after-1009-weeks (accessed 15 February 2018).

33. Sharmistha Gooptu, 'Transcending Nationalism: Bollywood Films Redefine Idea of Indianness', *Times of India*, 10 February 2006, 30.

34. Purnima Mankekar, *Unsettling India: Affect, Temporality, Transnationality* (Durham, NC: Duke University Press, 2015), 39–70.

35. Ibid.; Aswin Punathambekar, *From Bombay to Bollywood: The Making of a Global Media Industry* (New York: New York University Press, 2013), 235.

36. Stroh was a beer brewery located in Detroit, Michigan. The presence of Stroh's beer was one of the earliest instances of product placement in Bollywood films. This trend was taken up in a big way by subsequent Bollywood productions like *Kuch Naa Kaho* (Don't Say Anything, 2003, dir. Rohan Sippy) and *Kaante* (Thorns, 2002, dir. Sanjay Gupta).

37. Ashish Rajadhyaksha, 'The "Bollywoodization" of the Indian Cinema: Cultural Nationalism in a Global Arena', *Inter-Asia Cultural Studies* 4, no. 1 (2003): 25–39; Jigna Desai and Rajinder Dudrah, *The Essential Bollywood* (London: Open University Press; McGraw-Hill Education, 2008).

38. Susan Koshy argues that the diaspora has been typically seen as exemplary neoliberal subjects defined by flexibility, high human capital, and opportunistic mobility, but also identified as a subgroup that can reproduce

and replicate that human capital. Susan Koshy, 'Neoliberal Family Matters', *American Literary History* 25, no. 2 (2013): 344–380.

39. Raj was the ideal target consumer. For more, see Sudhanva Deshpande, 'Hindi Film: The Rise of the Consumable Hero', *Himal Southasian*, 1 August 2001, https://www.himalmag.com/hindi-film-the-rise-of-the-consumable-hero.

40. For more, see S. Venkitaramanan, 'Between Cheers and Jeers', *Times of India*, 7 June 1998, 15.

41. 'Brain drain' refers to the phenomenon whereby people who avail themselves of the best higher education funded by the Indian taxpayer use those skills for personal gain and to benefit the foreign Western nations where they migrate.

42. *Times of India*, 'Banking on a Drain', 4 December 1995, 12.

43. *Times of India*, 'A Varied Diaspora', 29 December 1993, 12.

44. Steven Baker, 'Shah Rukh Khan, Kajol's "DDLJ" Completes 900 Weeks', Digital Spy, 12 January 2013, http://www.digitalspy.com/bollywood/news/a450513/shah--rukh--khan--kajols--ddlj--completes--900--weeks/#~p6yUcN52Y8PI0w (accessed 17 January 2017).

45. Lata Jha, 'Of Millions and Multiplexes: Bollywood's Liberalization Story', *Mint*, 22 July 2016.

46. Some examples include *Pardes*, *Swades*, *Yaadien*, *Taa*, *Namastey London*, *Singh Is Kinng* (franchise), *Salaam Namaste*, *Hum Tum*, and *Dostaana*, among others.

47. Y. Chopra, 'Dilwale Dulhaniya Le Jayenge'.

48. The success of *DDLJ* led to many films, such as *Pardes*, *Swades*, and *Kal Ho Naa Ho*, with SRK as the diasporic hero. His films arguably also perform better in foreign markets than in the domestic market. For more data on his films' performance in foreign markets, see Lata Jha, 'Why Shah Rukh Khan Remains the Ultimate NRI Hero', *Mint*, 10 February 2017, https://www.livemint.com/Consumer/ZLahUQiFIQKYz2MSeo1JDN/Why-Shah-Rukh-Khan-remains-the-ultimate-NRI-hero.html (1 February 2018).

49. Shah Rukh Khan, interview with Stephen Dalton, 'Indian Hope Trick', *The Times*, 25 October 2001.

50. This change in financing and corporatization was initiated by information and broadcasting minister Sushma Swaraj in 1998. Before these changes were initiated, banks shied away from lending to Bollywood projects. Films were funded by a *hundi* system (money raised against promissory notes) to fund their projects. The infamous underworld sources fund less than 15 per cent of the films. The remaining 85 per cent of odd producers

get their money from assorted businessmen—builders, jewellers, traders—who, attracted by the glamour, pump in money. Following this legislative change, the films could register themselves as business corporations and get loans from banks. For more, see Aiyar and Chopra, 'Bollywood Hazy about New Industry Status'.

51. Aiyar and Chopra, 'Bollywood Hazy about New Industry Status'.
52. Ibid.
53. Nick Couldry, 'Celebrity, Convergence, and the Fate of Media Institutions', in *A Companion to Celebrity*, ed. P. David Marshall and Sean Redmond, 98–113 (Malden, MA: Wiley Blackwell, 2016).
54. Chawla's businessman husband, Jai Mehta, assisted with the venture.
55. Sukanya Verma, 'Juhi Chawla on Why She Turned Producer, Rediff, 16 December 1999, https://www.rediff.com/movies/1999/dec/16juhi.htm (accessed 15 June 2023).
56. A promissory note system (locally called *hundi* system) was the most widely prevalent source for film financing. It was an informal system that often involved money from the underworld criminal economy—one of the key reasons the Indian state legitimized film making as an industry.
57. For more, see Juhi Chawla, interview with Sukanya Verma, 'We Want to Make Nice Film', Rediff.com, 16 December 1999, 1–3.
58. Cecilia L. Ridgeway, 'Framed before We Know It: How Gender Shapes Social Relations', *Gender and Society* 23, no. 2 (2009): 145–160.
59. Manisha Koirala attempted to start her own production company. Pooja Bhatt launched her production venture in the late 1990s and actively started directing films. It is important to note that Pooja's father, Mahesh Bhatt, is a prominent Bollywood producer and director. Sushmita Sen, a former Miss Universe, also launched her production venture, Tantra, in 2005. Shilpa Shetty expressed a similar ambition a few years down the line in 2008. It is important to note, however, that despite the efforts, none of these ventures were successful and gradually petered out.
60. Suresh Nair, 'Arc of Triumph: Chat', *Times of India*, 19 October 2001, A6.
61. Rashmee Z. Ahmed, 'Asoka Is Set to Make It Big in the West', *Times of India*, 26 October 2001, 16.
62. R. Ahmed, 'Asoka Is Set to Make It Big'.
63. Sunil Kataria, 'India Star Hopes Peace Film Will Touch War-Torn World', *Reuters*, 25 October 2001, 1.
64. Christina Daniels, *I'll Do It My Way: The Incredible Journey of Aamir Khan* (New Delhi: Om Books International, 2012).

65. Lifetime gross of *Lagaan* in the international market was USD 1,546,734. Domestic lifetime earning was USD 909,043. Box Office Mojo, 'Lagaan: Once Upon a Time in India (2001)', https://www.boxofficemojo.com/title/tt0169102/?ref_=bo_se_r_1 (accessed 1 June 2019).

66. Daniels, *I'll Do It My Way*, 103.

67. Alyssa Ayres, 'How You Play the Game: Cricket, World Order, and India's Rise', *Octavian Report*, 2017, https://octavianreport.com/article/how-you-play-the-game-cricket-world-order-and-the-rise-of-india (accessed 10 December 2019).

68. Iron-wing Gadfly, 这片子很象京都球侠 (This movie is very similar to Kyoto Ballman). Douban, 25 February 2014, https://movie.douban.com/review/6561641/.

69. Kajal Wallia, 'Bollywood Out to Woo Crossover Audience in Europe, US', *Times of India*, 12 January 2002, 5.

70. Bollywood scholar Aswin Punathambekar noted that *Kaante* hired the global advertising firm Leo Burnett in an early instance of changing corporatized marketing practices within Bollywood.

71. Lorenzen and Täube stress that the star plays a greater role in mainstream film success in Bollywood than in Hollywood. Lorenzen and Täube, 'Breakout from Bollywood?'.

72. Daragh O'Reilly and Finola Kerrigan, 'A View to a Brand: Introducing the Film Brandscape', *European Journal of Marketing* 47, nos. 5–6 (2013): 769–789.

73. For more, see Lorenzen and Täube, 'Breakout from Bollywood'.

74. Anna M. M. Vetticad and Anil Padmanabhan, 'Lagaan: As Race for Oscars Draws to a Close, Aamir Khan Proves His Marketing Acumen', *India Today*, 25 March 2002, https://www.indiatoday.in/magazine/society-the-arts/films/story/20020318-lagaan-as-race-for-oscars-draws-to-a-close-aamir-khan-proves-his-marketing-acumen-795737-2002-03-25 (accessed 2 June 2022).

75. Daniels, *I'll Do It My Way*, 112.

76. Renuka Methil, 'Despatch, Golden Pumpkins, Signposts', *India Today*, 18 March 2002, 1.

77. Shyam G. Menon and Latha Venkatraman, 'A Lagaan Oscar Will Boost Film Industry', *Hindu Business Line*, 2 March 2002, 1.

78. Embassy of India, Paris, 'Brief Note on Frames 2019', https://www.eoiparis.gov.in/docs/1544680191Brief%20note%20on%20Frames%202019.pdf (accessed 10 August 2020).

79. IndianTelevision.com, 'FICCI Frames 2002 Concludes; Need for Corporatisation, Stamping out Piracy the Principal Thread of the Convention', 17 March 2002, https://www.indiantelevision.com/special/y2k2/ficci/ficsp16.htm (accessed 10 August 2020).

80. Richa Mishra, 'Film financing Still In Learning Stage: Study', *Hindu Business Line*, 8 September 2003, 1.

81. Avtar Panesar, personal interview with the author, 'Bollywood in the 1990s and early 2000s', 2 January 2021.

82. Meenakshi Shedde, 'Synergy of TV and Films Is Key to Entertainment Boom', *Times of India*, 10 June 2001, 5.

83. Ibid.

84. Ibid.

85. David A. Aaker and Alexander Biel, *Brand Equity & Advertising: Advertising's Role in Building Strong Brands* (Hillsdale, NJ: Lawrence Erlbaum Associates, 2003).

86. Tina Tandon and Rahul Joshi, 'From Bhuvan to Oscar', *Economic Times*, 27 February 2002, https://economictimes.indiatimes.com/brand-equity/from-bhuvan-to-oscar/articleshow/2203652.cms?from=mdr (accessed 10 August 2019).

87. Ibid.

88. Christy Grosz, 'Playing on Global Stage: For Int'l Filmmakers, Getting Selected Is the First Step in the Game', *Variety*, 14 November 2011, 21.

89. Swraj Paul, Baron Paul, PC, is an Indian-born British business magnate and philanthropist. In 1996, he was appointed a life peer by Conservative Party prime minister John Major and sat in the House of Lords as a cross-bencher with the title Baron Paul. Ashok Amritraj is a Hollywood producer, chairman, and CEO of the Hyde Park Entertainment Group. Shekhar Kapoor is a Bollywood director who moved to the US following his film *Bandit Queen*'s success.

90. Vetticad and Padmanabhan, 'Lagaan'.

91. Paul McDonald, *Hollywood Stardom* (Chicester: Wiley Blackwell, 2013), 20–23.

92. Ibid., 283.

93. Arun Sundarajan, 'Network Effects', New York University, 2003, http://oz.stern.nyu.edu/io/network.html (accessed 22 October 22 2020).

94. Bernard M. Bass, 'Leadership: Good, Better, Best', *Organizational Dynamics* 13, no. 3 (1985): 26–40; Raina A. Brands, Jochen I. Menges, and Martin Kilduff, 'The Leader-in-Social-Network Schema: Perceptions of Network

Structure Affect Gendered Attributions of Charisma', *Organization Science* 26, no. 4 (2015): 1210–1225.

95. Brands, Menges, and Kilduff, 'The Leader-in-Social-Network Schema'.

96. Gautam Buragohain, 'Growing with the Times', *Times of India*, 31 January 2005, A8.

97. Kaveree Bamzai, 'Patriotic Films: The New Nationalism', *India Today*, 11 October 2004, 34.

98. Ibid.

99. Krishna Shah, interview with the Times News Network, 'Foreign Stars Give Bollywood a New Shine', *Times of India*, 28 October 2004.

100. Jitesh Pillai, 'Film: Picks & Pans', *Times of India*, 21 August 2005, C4.

101. A *mahurat* ceremony announces Bollywood films. The ceremony marks the first day of shooting.

102. *Times of India*, 'Royalty Kicks off the Mutiny', 5 November 2003, B1.

103. *Times of India*, 'Aamir Khan Does an Encore at Locarno', 6 August 2005, A12.

104. Ibid.

105. Ravinder Kaur, *Brand New Nation: Capitalist Dreams and Nationalist Designs in Twenty-First Century India* (Redwood City, CA: Stanford University Press, 2020), 5. However, scholars and critics emphasized the ensuing disproportionate growth that favoured the middle classes and created a more profound chasm aggravating the socio-economic conditions of other 'subaltern classes'. Leela Fernandes, *India's New Middle Class: Democratic Politics in an Era of Economic Reform* (Minneapolis, MN: University of Minnesota Press, 2006).

106. The term was used to indicate a move away from monopolistic and restrictive trade practices.

107. Meenakshi Shedde, 'Beyond the Oscars: Chale Chalo to Asian Audiences', *Times of India*, 23 March 2002, 10.

108. Avtar Panesar, personal interview with the author (email), 19 January 2020.

109. The culture of multiplexes (as opposed to single-screen theatres)—a product of post-liberalized India—has changed the business of movie-making. With multiple screenings in a single theatre, cinemas can afford to run more 'niche' cinema alongside popular films, ensuring good business alongside critical acclaim. This means that commercial cinema subsidizes the cost of running niche films, which would not run in a single-screen theatre on their own merit.

110. Omar Qureshi, 'Aamir's Mutiny against Critics', *Times of India*, 16 August 2005, 10.

111. This type of plasticity is often employed in the study of biopower and racial politics.

112. In the next chapter, I will delve into Rai's comparable switching power and clout that remains confined to the affective realm and its intersections with newer corporate nodes like the cosmetics industry and Hollywood and its implications.

113. Anupama Chopra, 'Bollywood Princess, Hollywood Hopeful', *New York Times*, 10 February 2008, https://www.nytimes.com/2008/02/10/movies/10chop.html (accessed 15 January 2020).

114. UTV's successful film production strategy made UTV an attractive acquisition for Hollywood studios. Disney acquired UTV in 2012.

115. *Lagaan* was produced by Aamir Khan Productions and financed by long-term Bollywood financier Jhamu Sugandh. Hence, it demonstrated an essential first step wherein the will to corporatize came from within. Khan and Sugandh were still threatened by the Mumbai and Dubai mafia, whose impact on the industry has not gone away completely. For more, see *Times of India*, 'Abu Salem Gangsters Shot Dead', 15 October 2001, https://timesofindia.indiatimes.com/city/mumbai/4-Abu-Salem-gangsters-shot-dead/articleshow/1232590518.cms (accessed 15 January 2020).

116. Geoffrey G. Parker and Marshall W. Van Alstyne, 'Two-Sided Network Effects: A Theory of Information Product Design', *Management Science* 51, no. 10 (2005): 1494–1504.

117. Jeannette Catsoulis, 'Bollywood Does Vegas', *New York Times*, 20 May 2010, https://www.nytimes.com/2010/05/21/movies/21kites.html (accessed 1 February 2020).

118. Meena Iyer, 'Twinkle Khanna Launches Production House, Mrs Funnybones Movies', *Mumbai Mirror*, 14 December 2016, https://mumbaimirror.indiatimes.com/entertainment/bollywood/twinkle-khanna-launches-production-house-mrs-funnybones-movies/articleshow/55970238.cms (accessed 1 January 2017).

119. *Dainik Bhaskar*, 'Akshay's Wife Twinkle Launches Her Production House Mrs. Funnybones Movies', 14 December 2016, https://daily.bhaskar.com/news/ENT-BOW-twinkle-khanna-productions-5481015-NOR.html (accessed 22 February 2019).

120. Cynthia Enloe, *Seriously! Investigating Crashes and Crises as if Women Mattered* (Berkeley: University of California Press, 2013).

121. Like his co-stars SRK and Khan, Kumar does not produce all of his films under his home banner, Hari Om Productions. Several of his productions are in collaboration with other companies.

122. Kumar was bestowed with the rare honour of conducting a non-political interview with Modi, the current Indian prime minister, in 2019, just before the Indian general elections. The interview was similar to Jimmy Fallon's engagement with Donald Trump's hair, humanizing the candidate and creating an affective narrative about his persona.

123. Early Khiladi films included *Khiladi* (1992), *Main Khiladi Tu Anari* (1994), *Sabse Bada Khiladi* (1995), *Khiladiyon Ka Khiladi* (1996), *Mr. and Mrs. Khiladi* (1997), *International Khiladi* (1999), and *Khiladi 420* (2000).

124. Nyay Bhushan, 'India', 6 May 2010, http://www.hollywoodreporter.com/news/india--23346 (accessed 1 January 2016).

125. Ibid.

126. Suresh Ramalingam, personal interview with the author. 'Celebrity in Bollywood', 1 June 2016.

127. See *The Inner and Outer World of Shah Rukh Khan*, directed by Nasreen Munni Kabir and Peter Chappell and produced by Hyphen Films, Eros International, 2005.

128. Ranjani Mazumdar, 'Film Stardom after Liveness', *Continuum: Journal of Media and Cultural Studies* 26, no. 12 (2012): 833–844.

129. Azmat Rasul and Jennifer M. Proffitt, 'Bollywood and the Indian Premier League (IPL): The Political Economy of Bollywood's New Blockbuster', *Asian Journal of Communication* 21, no. 4 (2011).

130. Shuvaditya, 'Kolkata Knight Riders Is the Most Valuable IPL Brand Due to SRK Effect', Crictracker, 30 May 2017, https://www.crictracker.com/kolkata-knight-riders-valuable-ipl-brand-due-srk-effect (accessed 30 March 2018).

131. Avtar Panesar, personal interview with the author, 'Bollywood in the 1990s and early 2000s', 2 January 2021.

132. Ibid.

133. Tandon and Joshi, 'From Bhuvan to Oscar'.

134. Saibal Chatterjee, personal interview with the author, 'Celebrity in Bollywood', 20 June 2016.

135. *Mail Today*, 'King Khan Is Badshah of 2015 Forbes' Celebrity 100', 12 December 2015, 1.

136. Rajinder Kumar Dudrah, *Bollywood: Sociology Goes to the Movies* (New Delhi: SAGE Publications, 2006), 84.

137. Anupama Chopra, *King of Bollywood: Shah Rukh Khan and the Seductive World of Indian Cinema* (New York: Grand Central Publishing, 2007), 161.

138. McDonald, *Hollywood Stardom*, 7.

139. Alessandra Consolaro, 'Who Is Afraid of Shah Rukh Khan: Neoliberal India's Fears Seen through a Cinematic Prism', *Governare La Paura* (2014): 1–31, 10.

140. Alaka Sahani, personal interview with the author (research fieldwork), 15 June 2016.

141. Gopinath Pillai, *The Political Economy of South-Asian Diaspora: Patterns of Socio-Economic Influence* (New York: Palgrave Macmillan, 2013).

142. Mira Advani, 'Berlin Ballyhoo over Bollywood', *Hollywood Reporter*, 12 February 2008, https://www.hollywoodreporter.com/news/berlin-ballyhoo-bollywood-104610 (accessed 1 November 2018).

143. *Deccan Chronicle*, 'German Ambassador, His Wife in Love Triangle with Salman Khurshid a la "Kal Ho Naa Ho"', 25 April 2015, https://www.deccanchronicle.com/150425/nation-current-affairs/article/watch-salman-khurshid-plays-saif-ali-khan-german-version-kal (accessed 1 September 2016).

144. See Chapter 1.

145. Sifra Lentin, 'A German Renaissance in Bombay', Indian Council on Global Relations, 1 December 2016, https://www.gatewayhouse.in/a-german-renaissance-in-bombay (accessed 1 November 2019).

146. Ibid.

147. Florian Krauss, 'Bollywood's Circuits in Germany', in *The Magic of Bollywood: At Home and Abroad*, ed. Anjali Gera Roy, 295–317 (New Delhi: SAGE Publications, 2012).

148. Advani, 'Berlin Ballyhoo over Bollywood'.

149. Krauss, 'Bollywood's Circuits in Germany'.

150. Henry Jenkins, *Convergence Culture* (New York: New York University Press, 2006).

151. 'About Us', 1 January 2021, http://upd.bna-germany.com/index.php?id=about (accessed 1 January 2022).

152. Interview with Shah Rukh Khan, Filmfare 2012, quoted in Praseeda Gopinath, '"A Feeling You Cannot Resist": Shah Rukh Khan, Affect, and the Re-Scripting of Male Stardom in Hindi Cinema', *Celebrity Studies* 9, no. 3 (2018): 307–325.

153. Deutsche Welle, 'Shah Rukh Khan: The Face of Bollywood', 17 April 2013, https://www.dw.com/en/top-stories/s-9097 (accessed 1 September 2018).

154. Brigit Pestal, *Faszination Bollywood: Zahlen, Fakten, und Hintergründe zum 'Trend' im Deutschsprachigen Raum* (Marburg: Tectum Verlag, 2007).

155. Nandini Raghavendra, 'SRK to Release 2K Prints of Om Shanti Om', *Economic Times*, 8 September 2007, 1.

156. Ibid.

157. Pestal, *Faszination Bollywood*, 130–137.

158. Nyay Bhushan, 'Khan's "Don 2" Gets German Support', *Hollywood Reporter*, 31 August 2010.

159. Vera Wessel, personal interview with the author, 'Popularity of Shah Rukh Khan and Bollywood in Germany', 5 February 2021.

160. Ibid.

161. Henry Jenkins, 'The Moral Economy of Web 2.0', Pop Junctions, 21 March, http://henryjenkins.org/blog/2008/03/the_moral_economy_of_web_20_pa_2.html (accessed 5 June 2023).

162. Vera Wessel, personal interview with the author, 'Popularity of Shah Rukh Khan and Bollywood in Germany', 5 February 2021.

163. Sara Ahmed, *The Cultural Politics of Emotion* (New York: Routledge, 2004), 46.

164. Anjali Roy Gera, *The Magic of Bollywood: At Home and Abroad* (New Delhi: SAGE Publications, 2012); Sangita Gopal and Sujata Moorti, *Global Bollywood: Travels of Hindi Song and Dance* (Minneapolis, MN: University of Minnesota Press, 2008).

165. 'Bollywood & Samosa at the Indian Embassy', Berlin Global: Cultural Diplomacy News from Berlin, 12 August 2015, https://www.berlinglobal.org/index.php?bollywood-samosa-at-the-indian-embassy&highlight=Shah%20Rukh%20Khan (accessed 10 October 2019).

166. 巴斯特德, 'If There Are Ten Stars, I Want to Give Ten Stars; If There Are One Hundred Stars, I Give One Hundred!', Douban, 29 August 2010, https://movie.douban.com/review/3608774 (accessed 1 September 2012).

167. Rob Cain, 'How A 52-Year-Old Indian Actor Became China's Favorite Movie Star', *Forbes*, 8 June 2017, https://www.forbes.com/sites/robcain/2017/06/08/how-a-52-year-old-indian-actor-became-chinas-favorite-movie-star/#64db10fb516e (accessed 1 June 2020).

168. Brian Larkin, 'Indian Films and Nigerian Lovers: Media and the Creation of Parallel Modernities', *Africa: Journal of the International African Institute* 67, no. 3 (1997): 406–440.

169. Akshaya Kumar, 'Satyamev Jayate: Return of the Star as a Sacrificial Figure', *South Asia: Journal of South Asian Studies* 37, no. 2 (2014): 239–254.

170. Sunaina Kumar, 'The Sky Divers', *Tehelka*, 18 August 2012, https://web. archive.org/web/20130424073150/http://tehelka.com/the-sky-divers (accessed 1 September 2020).

171. Shoma Chaudhury, 'We've Been Through So Much Raw Emotion, Our Whole Team Feels We Need Some Counselling', 19 May 2012, http:// www.shomachaudhury.com/weve-been-through-so-much-raw-emotion-our-whole-team-feels-we-need-some-counselling (accessed 2 October 2020).

172. Kaveree Bamzai, 'Aamir Khan: Mr. Blockbuster', *India Today*, 18 January 2010, 1.

173. Barry King, 'The Star and the Commodity: Notes towards a Performance Theory of Stardom', *Cultural Studies* 1, no. 2 (1987): 145–161, 149.

174. Madhava Prasad, 'Fan Bhakti and Subaltern Sovereignty: Enthusiasm as a Political Factor', *Economic and Political Weekly* 44, no. 29 (2009): 68–76.

175. Reliance, '"3 Idiots": A Vidhu Vinod Chopra Production, a Raj Kumar Hirani Film Starring Aamir Khan, Rewrites Indian Cinema Box Office History', http://www.rbe.co.in/news-big-pictures-67.html, 28 December 2009 (accessed 10 October 2014).

176. Ananth Krishnan, 'Success of 3 Idiots Breaks China's Bollywood Great Wall', *The Hindu*, 2 January 2012, https://www.thehindu.com/features/ cinema/Success-of-3-Idiots-breaks-Chinas-Bollywood-Great-Wall/ article13349901.ece (accessed 10 October 2020).

177. Esther Chin, *Migration, Media and Global–Local Spaces* (New York: Palgrave Macmillan, 2016).

178. Neepa Majumdar, 'Doubling, Stardom, and Melodrama in Indian Cinema: The Impossible Role of Nargis', *Post Script* 22, no. 3 (2003): 89–105.

179. Microuniverse, 'Awakening of National Gold Medal Consciousness and True Status of Indian Women', 12 January 2017, https://movie.douban. com/review/8289388 (accessed 2 April 2018).

180. Suan Cai Yu, 'I Would Like to Use All Noble Words to Tout Amir Khan, because He Deserves', 7 May 2017, https://movie.douban.com/ review/8523504 (accessed 1 February 2018).

CHAPTER 4

1. Teo Pau Lin, 'On the Rai-se', *Strait Times*, 28 January 2003, 1–3.

2. Alex Perry, 'The 2004 Time 100: Aishwarya Rai', *Time*, 26 April 2004, 1.

3. *Hindustan Times*, 'When Aishwarya Rai Turned Down Troy, Brad Pitt Expressed Regret: "I Think We Missed an Opportunity"', 15 July 2020, 1.

4. Sarah Pomeroy, *Goddesses, Whores, Wives, and Slaves: Women in Classical Antiquity* (New York: Schocken Books, 1975).

5. Colleen Ballerino Cohen, Wilk Richard, and Beverly Stoeltje, *Beauty Queens on the Global Stage: Gender, Contests, and Power* (New York: Routledge, 1996).

6. Stephen Kindel, 'Beauty You Can Take to the Bank', *Forbes*, 18 June 1984, 136–139.

7. Several articles about the contest from newspapers in 1952 note that there was a Miss India contest held and elaborately mention names of the organizers, such as Rama Rau, the president of the organizing committee, and co-sponsors James W. MacFarlane of Universal Pictures and F. E. Patanwala. The contestants and the contest winner, however, are always addressed in generic terms such as 'Indian beauty' or 'Indian beauties'. For more, see *Times of India*, 'Miss Universe 1953: Indian Beauty to Contest Title', 1 February 1952, 3. The first time these early beauty queens received an adulatory and much overdue acknowledgment was when Persis Khambatta, whom we will encounter a little later in this chapter, wrote the book *Prides of India* in 1997, narrating the history of the pageant in India and naming and claiming the first beauty queens. Her book notes that the first Miss India crowned in 1947 was Pramila. The next notable beauty queen was Nutan, who was crowned Miss Mussourie in the 1952 contest. Nutan was the daughter of a famous film actress, Shobhana Samarth, and went on to have a successful career in Bollywood.

8. R. R. Diwakar, 'International Film Festival: Delegates' Impressions', *Times of India*, 24 February 1952, 1.

9. Ibid.

10. Our Film Critic, 'The Last of Star Actresses', *Times of India*, 22 February 1991, 3.

11. Jyotika Virdi, 'The Sexed Body', in *The Cinematic Imagination: Indian Popular Films as Social History*, by Jyotika Virdi, 145–177 (New Brunswick, NJ: Rutgers University Press, 2003).

12. Ajay Gehlawat, 'The Construction of 1970s Femininity, or Why Zeenat Aman Sings the Same Song Twice', *South Asian Popular Culture* 10, no. 1 (2012): 51–62.

13. Radhika Parmeshwaran, 'Spectacles of Gender and Globalization: Mapping Miss World's Media Event Space in the News', *Communication Review* 7, no. 4 (2004): 371–406, 373.

14. This was because it was a rapidly globalizing medium whose neoliberal, capitalistic expansion was being supported by the government.

15. Radhika Parameswaran, 'Global Media Events in India: Contests over Beauty, Gender, and Nation', *Journalism and Communication Monographs* 3, no. 2 (2001): 51–105.

16. Madhu Jain, 'The Material Girls', *India Today*, 30 June 1996, 1–3.

17. Pierre Bourdieu, 'The Forms of Capital', in *Handbook of Theory and Research for the Sociology of Education*, ed. J. G. Richardson, 241–258 (New York: Greenwood Press, 1986).

18. *Times of India*, 'Ash You Like It', 19 July 2002, C3.

19. Denzil Gondinho, 'Aishwarya Rai, Chiselled Differently', *Times of India*, 23 November 1994, 9.

20. *India Today*, 'Aishwarya Rai Still Rides High on International Endorsements', 21 April 2009, https://www.indiatoday.in/movies/story/aishwarya-rai-still-rides-high-on-international-endorsements-45100-2009-04-21 (accessed 17 June 2021) (emphasis mine).

21. For more on this consumerist correlation, see Douglas B. Holt, 'Does Cultural Capital Structure American Consumption?' *Journal of Consumer Research* 25, no. 1 (1998): 1–25.

22. *Times of India*, 'Aishwarya Conveys Mandela's Message to PM', 20 December 1994, 15.

23. Susan Dewey, *Making Miss India Miss World: Constructing Gender, Power and the Nation in Post-Liberalization India* (Syracuse, NY: Syracuse University Press, 2008).

24. Afsana Ahmed, 'I Am Proud of Aishwarya', *Times of India*, 24 October 2004, A1

25. Celia Lury, 'Brand as Assemblage: Assembling Culture', *Journal of Cultural Economy* 2, nos. 1–2 (2009): 67–82.

26. Deepa Shah, 'The Hottest Dish in India', *Sunday Times*, 7 July 2002, 1.

27. Helene Ramackers, 'Longines History and Their Relationship with the Equestrian World', *Upscale Living Magazine*, 30 September 2019, https://www.upscalelivingmag.com/longines-history-and-their-relationship-with-the-equestrian-world/ (accessed 17 June 2021).

28. *India Today*, 'Aishwarya Rai Still Rides High on International Endorsements'.

29. Sarah Banet-Weiser, *The Most Beautiful Girl in the World: Beauty Pageants and National Identity* (Berkeley: University of California Press, 1999).

30. Monica G. Moreno Figueroa, 'Displaced Looks: The Lived Experience of Beauty and Racism', *Feminist Theory* 14, no. 2 (2013): 137–151.

31. Agence France Presse, 'Bollywood at Last Makes It to the Cannes Film Festival', 24 April 2002, 1.

32. Derek Elley, 'Bollywood Adds Spice to the Fest', *Variety*, 13–19 May 2002, 15.

33. Ranvir Nayar, 'Standing Ovation for "Devdas" at Cannes', *India Times*, 31 June 2002, 1–3.

34. Shah, 'The Hottest Dish in India'.

35. Ibid.

36. *Jeans* was produced by a separate company created by Amritraj, Amritraj Soloman Communications, which was under the aegis of Hyde Park Entertainment. See Michael W. Potts, '"Jeans": A Mega Hit in South Indian Theaters', *India West*, 1 May 1998, C1.

37. *Hindustan Times*, 'When Aishwarya Rai Turned Down Troy'.

38. Victor A. Gilsing, Myrium Cloodt, and Danielle Bertrand-Cloodt, 'What Makes You More Central? Antecedents of Changes in Betweenness—Centrality in Technology-Based Alliance Networks', *Technological Forecasting and Social Change* 111 (2016): 209–221.

39. *The Guardian*, 'Beckham's Chadha Nets Bollywood's Ash', 2 December 2002, 1.

40. Michelle Rocío Nasser de La Torre, 'Bellas Por Naturaleza: Mapping National Identity on US Colombian Beauty Queens', *Latino Studies* 11 (2013): 293–312, 294.

41. Oluwakemi M. Balogun, *Beauty Diplomacy: Embodying an Emerging Nation* (Redwood City, CA: Stanford University Press, 2020).

42. Mahendra Gaur, *Foreign Policy Annual 2006* (New Delhi: Kalpaz Publications, 2007), 354.

43. Oluwakemi M. Balogun and Kimberly Kay Hoang, 'Political Economy of Embodiment: Capitalizing on Globally Staged Bodies in Nigerian Beauty Pageants and Vietnamese Sex Work', *Sociological Perspectives* 61, no. 6 (2018): 953–972.

44. Oluwakemi M. Balogun, *Beauty Diplomacy: Embodying an Emerging Nation* (Redwood City, CA: Stanford University Press, 2020).

45. Nyay Bhushan, 'Look to Bollywood, U.S. Filmmakers Told', *Hollywood Reporter*, 9 September 2009, 31–32.

46. Christiane Brosius, 'The Gated Romance of India Shining: Visualizing Urban Lifestyle in Advertisement of Residential Housing Development', in *Popular Culture in a Globalised India*, ed. K. Moti Gokulsing and Wimal Dissanayake, 174–191 (New York: Routledge, 2008), 312.

47. Amelia Arsenault and Manuel Castells, 'The Structure and Dynamics of Global Multi-Media Business Networks', *International Journal of Communication* 2 (2008): 707–748.

48. Premila Nazareth Satyanand and Pramila Raghavendran, *Outward FDI from India and Its Policy Context*, (Columbia FDI Profiles) (New York: Vale Columbia Center on Sustainable Investment, Columbia Law School, 2010), 1–16.

49. Ibid., 4.

50. Ibid.

51. Peter Dicken, Philip F. Kelly, Kris Olds, and Henry Wai-Chung Yueng, 'Chains and Networks, Territories and Scales: Towards a Relational Framework for Analysing the Global Economy', *Global Networks* 1, no. 2 (2001): 89–112.

52. Binoy Prabhakar, 'Reliance Entertainment Still Bets in Hollywood While DreamWorks Struggle in Box Office', *Economic Times*, 20 November 2011, 1.

53. Nandini Lakshman, 'Why Reliance Is Buying US Cinemas', *Economic Times*, 16 April 2008, 1.

54. Purti Chaturvedi, personal interview with the author, 'Celebrity Consultant, CAA KWAN', 3 June 2016.

55. *Screen International*, 'CAA Form Joint Venture with Indian Talent Agency KWAN', 18 October 2012, 1.

56. Suresh Ramalingam Iyer, personal interview with the author, 'Celebrity in Bollywood', New Delhi, 1 June 2016.

57. Suhani Singh, 'Yes Mr. Superstar', *India Today*, 9 April 2013, 1.

58. KWAN bought out CAA's stake in their joint venture in 2014, and both companies now operate independently in India.

59. Purti Chaturvedi, personal interview with the author, 'Celebrity Consultant, CAA KWAN', 3 June 2016.

60. Nyay Bhushan, personal interview with the author, 'Priyanka Chopra in Hollywood', 29 April 2016.

61. Yola Robert, 'How Anjula Acharia Conquered Both Silicon Valley and Hollywood', *Forbes*, 9 February 2021, https://www.forbes.com/sites/yola robert1/2021/02/09/how-anjula-acharia-conquered-both-silicon-valley-and-hollywood/?sh=69e48cd6417e (accessed 12 November 2021).

62. Ibid.

63. Anahita Ghai, 'Anjula Acharia on Becoming an "Accidental Investor," Following Her Intuition and Working with Priyanka Chopra', *Harper's Bazaar*, 5 August 2021, https://www.harpersbazaararabia.com/culture/

people/anjula-acharia-on-becoming-an-accidental-investor-following-her
-intuition-and-working-with-priyanka-chopra (accessed 12 November 2021).

64. Cat Zakrzewski, 'Anjula Acharia Doubles as Investor and Hollywood Manager; The Former Entrepreneur Is Committed to Bringing Diversity to Both the Tech and Entertainment Industries', *Wall Street Journal*, 21 March 2017, 1–2.

65. Cision PR Newswire, 'Priyanka Chopra, Star of ABC's Quantico on Eros Now on Demand', 20 August 2015, https://www.prnewswire.com/ news-releases/priyanka-chopra-star-of-abcs-quantico-on-eros-now-on-demand-300131449.html (accessed 11 November 2016).

66. Megha Bahree, 'Anjula Acharia-Bath: The Angel Investor Propelling Priyanka Chopra's American Dream', *Mint*, 4 October 2015, 1.

67. Kabir Bedi, personal interview with the author, 'Global Forays of Indian Actors', 24 June 2016.

68. Purti Chaturvedi, personal interview with the author, 'Celebrity Consultant, CAA KWAN', 3 June 2016.

69. Sahaja, 'Pictures: Priyanka Chopra at Planes Premiere', FilmiBeat, 6 August 2013, https://www.filmibeat.com/bollywood/features/2013/priyanka-chopra -hollywood-animated-planes-premiere-los-angeles-116499.html (accessed 5 June 2023).

70. Prashant Singh, 'Want to See How the US and the World React to My Negative Role: Priyanka Chopra', *Hindustan Times*, 17 February 2017, https://www.hindustantimes.com/bollywood/want-to-see-how-the-us-and-the-world-reacts-to-my-negative-role-priyanka-chopra/story-EczAFGuSAIn75zIPBZwNYO.html (accessed 15 August 2019).

71. Priyanka Chopra, interview with Kelly Ripa and Jerry O'Connell, 'Quantico Star Priyanka Chopra', ABC, 30 September 2016.

72. See Jordanna Lippe, 'How "Quantico" Actress Priyanka Chopra Survives Her 20-Hour Commute', *Travel + Leisure*, 10 March 2017, http://www. travelandleisure.com/articles/bollywood-actress-priyanka-chopra (accessed 14 March 2017); Ali Booth, 'Priyanka Chopra Wears $5 Million Worth of Diamonds and More ICYMI Highlights from the 2017 Oscars Red Carpet', *US Weekly*, 3 March 2017, http://www.usmagazine.com/ entertainment/news/priyanka-chopra-wears-5-million-in-diamonds-more-icymi-highlights-w470264 (accessed 4 March 2017).

73. Patricia Garcia, 'Riding the Subway with Bollywood Superstar Priyanka Chopra', *Vogue*, 2 May 2017, http://www.vogue.com/article/priyanka--chopra-quantico-star (accessed 2 May 2017).

74. Kaitlin Frey, 'See Priyanka Chopra's 75-Foot Veil from Above as She Walks Down the Aisle toward a Teary Nick Jonas', *People*, 4 December 2018, https://people.com/style/see-priyanka-chopra-wedding-veil-walk-down-aisle (accessed 18 November 2021).

75. Marianna Cerini, 'Priyanka Chopra's Bold Fashion Has Made Her a Global Style Icon', CNN, 17 July 2020, https://www.cnn.com/style/article/priyanka-chopra-fashion-intl-hnk/index.html (accessed 17 November 2021).

76. See Ghai, 'Anjula Acharia on Becoming an "Accidental Investor"'.

77. Adrienne Gafney, 'How Anjula Acharia and Priyanka Chopra Are Redefining Tech', *Elle*, 21 February 2020, https://www.elle.com/culture/tech/a30897485/anjula-acharia-priyanka-chopra-tech (accessed 20 November 2021).

CHAPTER 5

1. Lachmi Deb Roy, 'Anil Kapoor on Thar: "It Is Liberating to Work for a Film an OTT"', *Firstpost*, 22 April 2022, https://www.firstpost.com/blogs/bollywood-blogs/anil-kapoor-on-thar-it-is-liberating-to-work-for-a-film-on-ott-10587251.html (accessed 11 May 2022).

2. It is important to note here that *Thar* featured Anil Kapoor's son, Harsh Vardhan Kapoor, as the main protagonist.

3. Swapnil Rai, 'May the Force Be with You: Narendra Modi and the Celebritization of Indian Politics', *Communication, Culture and Critique* 12, no. 3 (2019): 323–339.

4. Netflix India (@NetflixIndia), 'Saturday night got pretty Khantastic!', Twitter, 11 March 2017, https://twitter.com/netflixindia/status/840616731542507520 (accessed 19 December 2022).

5. Naman Ramachandran, 'Netflix Signs Content Deal with Shah Rukh Khan's Red Chillies', *Variety*, 15 December 2016, https://variety.com/2016/digital/asia/netflix-signs-content-deal-with-shah-rukh-khans-red-chillies-1201943116/ (accessed 10 January 2020).

6. Ibid.

7. Naman Ramachandran, 'Netflix, Shah Rukh Khan Partner on Indian Original "Bard of Blood"', *Variety*, 17 November 2017, 1.

8. Gitanjali Roy, 'Shah Rukh Khan and Netflix: Here Are Details of New Partnership', NDTV, 15 December 2016, https://www.ndtv.com/

entertainment/shah-rukh-khan-and-netflix-here-are-details-of-new-partnership-1638145 (accessed 16 May 2022).

9. Paul Duguid, 'Introduction: The Changing Organization of Industry', *Business History Review* 79, no. 3 (2005): 453–466.

10. *Knowledge at Wharton*, 'Network Synergy: A New Way to Value M&A', 22 May 2018, 1–5, https://knowledge.wharton.upenn.edu/podcast/knowledge-at-wharton-podcast/network-synergy-a-new-way-to-value-ma (accessed 31 May 2022).

11. In 2015, Chopra and her mother launched Purple Pebble Pictures, a film and television studio, to promote regional filmmakers. In 2018, she made her first big investment in Bumble, a dating app, following up with an investment in Holberton School for software engineering—a coding education start-up. In 2021, she invested in US-based rental marketplace Apartment List; and in Genies, a virtual avatar firm, along with Camila Cabello and Paris Hilton. She also opened a restaurant—Sona—in New York and released her own line of sustainable hair care products named Anomaly. At a start-up event in January, Chopra said she was looking to invest in start-ups that are a mix of beauty and tech, as well as education. For more, see Smita Tripathi, 'Priyanka Chopra: The Smart Investor', *Business Today*, 26 December 2021, https://www.businesstoday.in/specials/most-powerful-women in business/story/priyanka-chopra-the-smart-investor-315366-2021-12-13 (accessed 11 May 2022).

12. Devorah Lev-Tov, 'A First Look inside Priyanka Chopra Jonas's New Restaurant', *Vogue*, 24 March 2021, https://www.vogue.com/article/first-look-inside-sona-priyanka-chopra-jonas-new-restaurant (accessed 11 May 2022).

13. See Sneha Kalra, 'Priyanka Chopra Owns These 10 Ridiculously Expensive Luxury Items Which We Wish to Get Our Hands On', Pinkvilla, 27 February 2019, https://www.pinkvilla.com/fashion/celebrity-style/priyanka-chopra-owns-these-10-ridiculously-expensive-luxury-items-which-we-wish-get-our-hands-441527 (accessed 19 December 2022).

14. Elise Taylor, 'Priyanka Chopra Jonas Launches Sona Home, Her Ode to Indian Entertaining', *Vogue*, 22 June 2022, 1.

15. Martin Barker, 'Introduction', in *Contemporary Hollywood Stardom*, ed. Thomas Austin and Martin Barker, 1–24 (London: Arnold Publishers, 2003).

16. Geoff King, 'Stardom in the Willenium', in *Contemporary Hollywood Stardom*, ed. Thomas Austin and Martin Barker, 62–73 (London: Arnold Publishers, 2003).

17. Mustafa Emirbayer and Ann Mische, 'What Is Agency', *American Journal of Sociology* 103, no. 4 (1998): 962–1023.

18. Hans Joas, *The Creativity of Action* (Chicago: University of Chicago Press, 1996).

19. Namrata Joshi, 'Anushka Sharma: "I'm Drawn to Edgy, Clutter-Breaking Subjects"', *The Hindu*, 9 June 2020, 1.

20. Anthony Giddens. *The Constitution of Society* (Berkeley: University of California Press, 1984). See also Carl G. Herndl and Adela C. Licona, 'Shifting Agency: Agency, Kairos and Social Action', in *Communicative Practices in Workplaces and the Professions Cultural Perspectives on the Regulation of Discourse and Organizations*, ed. Charlotte Thralls and Mark Zachry, 133–153 (London: Taylor and Francis, 2017);

21. Lata Jha, 'Anushka Plans Women-Centric OTT Platform', *Mint*, 1 March 2022, https://www.livemint.com/industry/media/anushka-sharma-s-clean-slate-filmz-to-launch-women-focused-ott-platform-11646119807912.html (accessed 11 May 2022).

22. Michel Foucault, 'The Subject and Power', in *Michel Foucault: Beyond Structuralism and Hermenuetics*, ed. Paul Rabinow, Hubert Dreyfus, 208–228 (New York: Harvester Wheatsheaf, 1982).

23. Roland Bleiker, 'Discourse and Human Agency', *Contemporary Political Theory* 2 (2013): 25–47, 38.

24. Derrick Bell, 'Brown v. Board of Education and the Interest-Convergence Dilemma', *Harvard Law Review* 93, no. 3 (1980): 518–533.

25. Netflix, 'Red Chillies Entertainment & Eternal Sunshine Productions' "Darlings", Coming Soon to Netflix', 24 May 2022, https://about.netflix.com/en/news/red-chillies-entertainment-and-eternal-sunshine-productions-darlings-coming (accessed 30 May 20223).

26. *Firstpost*, 'Alia Bhatt Signs with WME, Hollywood Talent Agency Managing Oprah Winfrey, Gal Gadot, Emma Stone', 9 July 2021, https://www.firstpost.com/entertainment/alia-bhatt-signs-with-wme-hollywood-talent-agency-managing-oprah-winfrey-gal-gadot-emma-stone-9791261.html (accessed 11 May 2022).

27. For more, see Swapnil Rai, 'From Bombay Talkies to Khote Productions: Female Star Switching Power in Bollywood Production Culture', *Feminist Media Studies* 21, no. 7 (2020): 1–16. See the wedding photo at *Indian Express*, 'Alia Bhatt on How Life Changed after Wedding to Ranbir: "In Kapoor Family, You Eat Together, Do Aarti Together"', 6 July 2022, https://indianexpress.com/article/entertainment/web-series/alia-bhatt

-ranbir-kapoor-family-you-eat-together-do-aarti-together-8012256 (accessed 24 December 2022).

28. Raymond Williams, 'Dominant, Residual, Emergent', in *Marxism and Literature*, 121–127 (Oxford: Oxford University Press, 1977).

29. Kaveree Bamzai, 'How Dynasties Rule Bollywood', *Open*, 22 April 2022, https://openthemagazine.com/cover-stories/how-dynasties-rule-bollywood/ (accessed 26 May 2022).

30. Francisco Jr. Polidoro, Gautam Ahuja, and Will Mitchell, 'When the Social Structure Overshadows Competitive Incentives: The Effects of Network Embeddedness on Joint Venture Dissolution', *Academy of Management Journal* 54, no. 1 (2017): 203–223.

31. Karishma Upadhyay, 'Huma Goes to Hollywood', *The Hindu*, 19 May 2021, https://www.thehindu.com/entertainment/movies/huma-qureshi-about-working-in-la-chennai-and-mumbai-and-her-biggest-project-yet-zack-snyders-army-of-the-dead/article34595293.ece (accessed 20 July 2022).

32. Ananya Ghosh, 'The Many Facets of Ali Fazal', *Man's World India*, 20 February 2022, https://www.mansworldindia.com/currentedition/covers/the-many-facets-of-ali-fazal/ (accessed 20 July 2022).

33. Ibid.

34. PricewaterhouseCoopers (PwC), *Global Entertainment & Media Outlook 2022–2026: Industry Forecast* (New Delhi: PricewaterhouseCoopers, 2020).

35. Sarah Whitten, 'Reese Witherspoon on Why Now Was the Right Time to Sell Hello Sunshine', CNBC, 3 August 2021, https://www.cnbc.com/2021/08/03/reese-witherspoon-on-why-now-was-the-right-time-to-sell-hello-sunshine.html (accessed 11 May 2022).

36. Alison Brower, 'The Hollywood Reporter 100: The Most Powerful People in Entertainment 2019', *Hollywood Reporter*, 16 October 2019, https://www.hollywoodreporter.com/lists/thr-100-hollywood-reporters-powerful-people-entertainment-1246527 (accessed 11 May 2022).

37. Ibid.

38. See CricketNext, 'An Exclusive Interview with Brad Pitt and SRK', YouTube, 25 May 2017, https://www.youtube.com/watch?v=dYnKuPCsaxs (accessed 19 December 2022).

39. Ibid.

40. Benjamin Mullin and Miriam Gottfried, 'Reese Witherspoon's Hello Sunshine to Be Sold to Media Company Backed by Blackstone', *Wall Street Journal*, 2 August 2021, https://www.wsj.com/articles/reese-witherspoons

-hello-sunshine-to-be-sold-to-media-company-backed-by-blackstone
-11627914600 (accessed 11 May 2022).

41. L. D. Roy, 'Anil Kapoor on Thar'.

42. Ibid.

43. The director has since deleted his Twitter account, but the selfie was
retweeted by Bollywood actor Ranveer Singh. It can be accessed at Ranveer's
Cafe (@ranveercafe69), 'Selfie with the PM', Twitter, 10 January 2019,
https://twitter.com/ranveercafe69/status/1083337823522979841 (accessed
on 11 January 2019).

44. Ibid.

45. Ibid.

46. See Rai, 'May the Force Be with You'.

47. Ibid.

48. 'I Watched "Dangal" and Liked It: Chinese President Xi Jinping Tells
Prime Minister Modi', V6 News Telugu, Hyderabad, 10 June 2017;
'President Xi Told Me He Has Watched "Dangal", Says PM in Haryana
Rally', NDTV, New Delhi, 15 October 2019.

49. 'Guess Who Is Promoting His Film While Modi Is in China', *India Today*,
14 May 2015, https://www.indiatoday.in/world/asia/story/aamir-khan-china
-beijing-pk-narendra-modi-252944-2015-05-14 (accessed 15 May 2017).

50. Many scholars have written about it. For more, see Anustup Basu, *Hindutva
as Political Monotheism* (Durham, NC: Duke University Press, 2020).

51. Amongst the top three Khans, Aamir Khan was married to a Hindu, and
Salman Khan's mother was Hindu as well.

52. Microuniverse, 国家金牌意识的觉醒和真实的印度妇女地位 (The Awakening
of National Gold Medal Awareness and the Real Status of Indian Women)',
Douban, 12 January 2017, https://movie.douban.com/review/8289388
(accessed 1 January 2019).

53. Kardashev Makarov, Folder (1950–1960), 'To Com. Stepanov V.T.', Official
Letter, Ministry of Culture of the USSR, Moscow, 113. For more, see
Chapter 1.

INDEX